Cyberspace and Instability

Cyberspace and Instability

Edited by
Robert Chesney, James Shires and
Max Smeets

EDINBURGH
University Press

Edinburgh University Press is one of the leading university presses in the UK. We publish academic books and journals in our selected subject areas across the humanities and social sciences, combining cutting-edge scholarship with high editorial and production values to produce academic works of lasting importance. For more information visit our website: edinburghuniversitypress.com

We are committed to making research available to a wide audience and are pleased to be publishing an Open Access ebook edition of this title.

Edinburgh University Press Ltd
The Tun – Holyrood Road, 12(2f) Jackson's Entry, Edinburgh EH8 8PJ

This work was funded by a grant to the University of Texas at Austin from the William and Flora Hewlett Foundation.

Typeset in 10.5/13pt Bembo
by Cheshire Typesetting Ltd, Cuddington, Cheshire, and
printed and bound in Great Britain.

A CIP record for this book is available from the British Library

ISBN 978 1 3995 1249 7 (hardback)
ISBN 978 1 3995 1251 0 (webready PDF)
ISBN 978 1 3995 1252 7 (epub)

Contents

Notes on Contributors

Editors

Bobby Chesney is the Dean of Texas Law and holds the James A. Baker III Chair in the Rule of Law and World Affairs. He was previously the Associate Dean for Academic Affairs (2011–2022) and the Founding Director of the Robert S. Strauss Center for International Security and Law, a University-wide research unit bridging across disciplines to improve understanding of international security issues.

James Shires a Senior Research Fellow in Cyber Policy at the UK Royal Institute of International Affairs (Chatham House). He is a Fellow with The Hague Program for International Cyber Security and the Cyber Statecraft Initiative at the Atlantic Council. He is the author of *The Politics of Cybersecurity in the Middle East* (Hurst/Oxford University Press, 2021).

Max Smeets is a Senior Researcher at the Center for Security Studies (CSS), ETH Zurich. Max is Director of the European Cyber Conflict Research Initiative (ECCRI.eu) and Affiliate at the Center for International Security and Cooperation, Stanford University. He is the author of *No Shortcuts: Why States Struggle to Develop a Military Cyber-Force* (Hurst/Oxford University Press, 2022).

Contributors

Siena Anstis is a senior legal advisor at the Citizen Lab at the Munk School of Global Affairs & Public Policy, University of Toronto and a researcher in the areas of international law, human rights, technology, and migration.

Sophie Barnett is a litigation attorney in New York City. Previously, she was a research assistant at the Citizen Lab at the Munk School of Global Affairs & Public Policy, University of Toronto.

Ben Buchanan is an Assistant Teaching Professor at Georgetown University's School of Foreign Service, where he conducts research on the intersection of cybersecurity and statecraft.

Joe Burton is a Marie Curie Fellow (MSCA-IF) at Université libre de Bruxelles (ULB) completing a two-year European Commission-funded project on Strategic Cultures of Cyber Warfare (CYBERCULT).

Sharly Chan was a research assistant at the Citizen Lab at the Munk School of Global Affairs & Public Policy, University of Toronto.

Fiona S. Cunningham is Assistant Professor of Political Science at the University of Pennsylvania.

Ron Deibert is Professor of Political Science and Director of the Citizen Lab at the Munk School of Global Affairs & Public Policy, University of Toronto.

Mailyn Fidler is an Assistant Professor of Law at the University of Nebraska College of Law and an affiliate of the Berkman Klein Center for Internet & Society at Harvard University.

Emily O. Goldman is a cyber strategist and cyber persistence subject matter expert at US Cyber Command and the National Security Agency. From 2018 to 2019, she was cyber advisor to the director of policy planning at the US Department of State. From 2014 to 2018 she was Director of the US Cyber Command/National Security Agency Combined Action Group and led a team that wrote the 2018 U.S. Cyber Command Vision.

Jason Healey is a Senior Research Scholar at Columbia University's School for International and Public Affairs and formerly served as vice chair of the FS-ISAC and director for cyber and infrastructure policy at the White House.

Robert Jervis was the Adlai E. Stevenson Professor of International Affairs at Columbia University.

Jaclyn A. Kerr is a Senior Research Fellow for Defense and Technology Futures at the Institute for National Strategic Studies (INSS) at National Defense University (NDU).

Niamh Leonard is a law student at McGill University and was previously a legal extern at the Citizen Lab at the Munk School of Global Affairs & Public Policy, University of Toronto.

Densua Mumford is Assistant Professor of International Relations at the Faculty of Governance and Global Affairs, Leiden University.

Mark A. Raymond is the Wick Cary Associate Professor of International Security and the Director of the Cyber Governance and Policy Center at the University of Oklahoma.

Rebecca Slayton is an Associate Professor in the Science and Technology Studies Department and the Director of the Judith Reppy Institute for Peace and Conflict Studies, both at Cornell University.

Tim Stevens is Reader in Global Security and head of the Cyber Security Research Group, King's College London.

Preface

Whilst a wide range of actors have publicly identified cyber stability as a key policy goal, the meaning of stability in the context of cyber policy remains vague and contested: vague because most policymakers and experts do not define cyber stability when they use the concept; contested because they propose measures that rely – often implicitly – on divergent understandings of cyber stability.

This edited volume is a thorough investigation of instability within cyberspace and of cyberspace itself. Its purpose is to reconceptualize stability and instability for cyberspace, highlight their various dimensions, and thereby identify relevant policy measures.

We have asked seventeen influential scholars in the field to contribute to this edited volume – often jointly – offering different perspectives on the topic. Combined, this book critically examines both 'classic' notions associated with stability – for example, whether cyber operations can lead to unwanted escalation between great powers – as well as topics that have so far not been addressed in the existing cyber literature, such as the application of a decolonial lens to investigate Euro-American conceptualizations of stability in cyberspace.

We express our thanks to the authors, not only for their time and commitment to writing a chapter for this volume, but also for their willingness to engage with each other's work throughout the project and offer feedback on the organization of this volume. The COVID-19 pandemic unfortunately did not allow us to meet in person, but we organized three online workshops to discuss the findings of each chapter and share ideas and new paths for thinking about cyberspace and instability.

We are indebted to the Hewlett Foundation for funding this project and continuing to promote research in the field. Thanks to Doyle Hodges, *Texas National Security Review* devoted a special issue to cyber conflict and competition and included earlier versions of several chapters appearing in this edited volume. We are truly grateful for this collaboration.

It has been a pleasure to work with Ersev Ersoy, Joannah Duncan and the staff at Edinburgh University Press in preparing the book for publication.

An earlier version of Chapter 1 appeared in *Texas National Security Review* 3, no. 4 (Fall 2020), Special Issue on The Dynamics of Cyber Conflict and Competition as "The Escalation Inversion and Other Oddities of Situational Cyber Stability."

An earlier version of Chapter 2 appeared in *Texas National Security Review* 3, no. 4 (Fall 2020), Special Issue on The Dynamics of Cyber Conflict and Competition, as "Preparing the Cyber Battlefield: Assessing a Novel Escalation Risk in a Sino-American Crisis."

An earlier version of Chapter 5 appeared in *Texas National Security Review* 3, no. 4 (Fall 2020), Special Issue on The Dynamics of Cyber Conflict and Competition, as "From Reaction to Action: Adopting a Competitive Posture in Cyber Diplomacy."

An earlier version of Chapter 9 appeared in *Texas National Security Review* 4, no. 1 (Winter 2020/2021), Special Issue on The Dynamics of Cyber Conflict and Competition, as "What Is a Cyber Warrior? The Emergence of US Military Cyber Expertise, 1967–2018."

Introduction: Rethinking (In)stability in and of Cyberspace

Robert Chesney, James Shires, and Max Smeets

Many governments and intergovernmental organizations have declared stability to be a central goal of cyber policy. The European Council has called for an "open, stable, peaceful and secure cyberspace where human rights and fundamental freedoms and the rule of law fully apply."[1] NATO has recognized cyberspace as a new operational domain, in which it has pledged to maintain stability.[2] The United Kingdom has committed to "promote international security and stability in cyberspace,"[3] while the United States has repeatedly stressed the need to promote "greater predictability and stability in cyberspace."[4]

Stability is by no means an objective only promoted across the Atlantic. In the first drafting stage of the UN Open Ended Working Group (OEWG) on cyber security, China stressed that "the starting point and ultimate goal should be to ensure peace and stability in cyberspace."[5] Equally, India has repeatedly stated that it is committed to a "stable cyberspace environment."[6] The final report of the OEWG, released in March 2021, represents almost 100 states, as well as input from global civil society. It repeatedly emphasizes the triad of peace, security, and stability, as well as the longer formulation of an "open, secure, stable, accessible and peaceful [information and communications technologies] environment."[7]

Some countries have even promoted the establishment of international cyber initiatives specifically focused on stability. The Global Commission on the Stability of Cyberspace (GCSC) was established mainly through the initiative of the Dutch government, following the Global Conference on Cyberspace in The Hague in 2015. The GCSC aims to promote "mutual awareness and understanding among the various cyberspace communities working on issues related to international cybersecurity."[8] Its final report in 2019 recommended four principles of responsibility, restraint, requirements to act, and respect for human rights, to "ensure the stability of cyberspace."[9]

Stability is thus central to a cluster of terms used normatively in cyber policy to describe those qualities of cyberspace that must be preserved and protected against a wide variety of threats now, and expanded and improved in the future. This is hard to argue against: who wouldn't want cyberspace to be more stable?

Unfortunately – or perhaps intentionally, given the carefully negotiated nature of the quotations above – the meaning of stability in this context, along with its companions in the cluster, remains vague, ambiguous, and contested. Should stability be understood as a thin, technical term, describing the reliability and continuity of the complex layers of technologies that underpin cyberspace? Or, as the GCSC suggests, should it be understood in a "thicker," more substantive way, relating to the potential for war, conflict, and the preservation of individual rights and freedoms? Cyber norms efforts at the UN – and even several consensus reports of the UN Group of Governmental Experts – have highlighted the extent of disagreement between states about what stability includes, what are the most concerning threats to stability, and how to counter them.

Stability is thus a contested concept, with ongoing disputes about its proper use by different actors.[10] Choosing the referent object of stability – who or what is being stabilized – is part of this contest. In some instances, stability is about avoiding escalation between great powers. In other instances, it is about ensuring (authoritarian) regime survival. The stability of cyberspace is also frequently linked to protecting the "core" functionality of the internet or other critical functions of society. The widespread use of the concept of stability in relation to cyberspace obscures the fact that actors are often striving for different end-states, that cyber threats are not objectively given, and that actors mobilize politically in different ways.

Indeed, once we widen the scope of stability from a narrow focus on technical aspects of cyberspace, the normative value of stability as an uncontested good is less clear. Strategic, political, and economic stability (to take a few examples) have all been used historically to justify highly controversial actions, from colonial conquest to threats of nuclear weapons and modern armed interventions, and from repressive authoritarian practices to vastly unequal distribution of resources. In this way, the concept of stability can legitimize power imbalances, inequalities, violence, and injustice, meaning that seeking stability for some often increases instability for others. In other words, insofar as the status quo is problematic, whether from the perspective of those subject to reckless and disruptive cyber operations or those who reject the dominance of some states in internet governance, so is the concept of stability. We capture this problematic relationship between stability and instability – and their frequent coexistence – in a combined concept of (in)stability.

The purpose of this edited volume is to provide a thorough investigation of cyberspace and (in)stability. It seeks to reconceptualize (in)stability in relation to cyberspace, highlight its various dimensions, and, through this, identify relevant policy measures. It recognizes that the concept of stability as normatively desirable is baked deeply into cyber policy, and it balances this positive orientation toward stability with efforts to probe more critically at its consequences and assumptions. To this end, the volume is guided by a central research question: *How does the (in)stability of cyberspace interact with other kinds of (in)stability in international politics?*

This research question connects cyberspace and international politics in both directions, recognizing that the (in)stability of cyberspace has important consequences for broader strategic, political, economic, and even environmental (in)stability, while these wider (in)stabilities also shape the evolution and development of cyberspace as a complex socio-technical system. All the chapters in this book engage with this central research question, despite their wide range of topics and theoretical approaches. Moreover, while they all incorporate an analytically sophisticated approach to stability, there is, in our view, a productive tension between chapters that treat it more as an achievable goal and those that treat it as an object of critique and revision. This tension is central to the volume's design, and we underline it in this introduction through the concept of (in)stability.

The prominence of stability in cyber policy means that this is an important undertaking, on which thorough and insightful scholarship is urgently required. A quick glance at the news headlines any day underlines the importance of the stable functioning of cyberspace to the everyday lives of individuals around the world – especially during a global pandemic – as well as the myriad threats to and in cyberspace. Only by understanding (in)stability more deeply can we begin to achieve desired forms of (in)stability for cyberspace, and, perhaps more importantly, understand the means by which we wish to do so.

Thinking About Cyberspace and (In)Stability

Academia has hardly helped to conceptualize stability in relation to cyberspace. Only thirty journal articles were published in political science mentioning the concept "cyber stability" between 2005 and 2020, whilst related concepts were more often debated; "cyber resilience" was discussed in 166 articles, "cyber deterrence" in 220 articles, "cyber war" in 982 articles, and "cyber security" in over 5,000 articles.[11] This lack of direct focus on a core policy concept is surprising, but understandable. The other concepts above are all clearly related to stability, and so conceptualizations of stability draw on developments in these other areas. Before detailing the various contributions of this book, we first briefly outline how a richer concept of cyber (in)stability intersects with key aspects of both academic theories and cyber policy, such as resilience, deterrence, conflict, and security, as well as drawing on stability literature outside cyber concerns.

An obvious starting point for discussions of stability and cyberspace is the potential for cyber war or cyber conflict. While these terms have been much discussed – and criticized – in the last two decades, the potential of a cyber "attack" with effects similar to those of conventional arms could clearly impact the stability of the international system (otherwise known as "strategic stability").[12] Cyber capabilities could arguably trigger conflict between great powers, as well as enabling others (for example, smaller states or non-state actors) to enhance their capabilities and leverage. In this way, cyber operations increase risks of systemic instability, as well as potentially making it harder to resolve conflicts through the distorted effects of information operations. The cyber strategy literature predominantly addresses such effects on (in)stability in the international system through the lens of escalation. We devote the first section of the volume to these dynamics (detailed below).

However, systemic (in)stability and cyberspace do not only interact through the potential for cyber operations to have war-like effects. An extensive strand of literature in international relations (IR) has explored the structural stability of different systems, asking for example, whether a "balance" between two superpowers is more stable than a system dominated by a single hegemon.[13] In relation to cyberspace, we are clearly moving from the latter situation (where the internet and many digital technologies were developed, operated, and managed in the United States), to a multipolar cyberspace with several nodes of power: China representing an equal center of gravity to the United States, the European Union representing a node from a regulatory perspective, and India and many African states in terms of user numbers and information and communications technologies (ICT) skills. Thinking about systemic (in)stability and cyberspace requires us to first acknowledge such shifts, and then to parse their consequences for the technical operation – and in the extreme case, balkanization – of the internet, as well as their softer impacts on economic attractiveness, standards-setting, and norm development.

While systemic (in)stability is a clear first and expansive frame for our question, it is far from the only one. The current academic consensus is that cyber operations are primarily conducted below the threshold of armed conflict,[14] providing new means of covert action and intelligence gathering that collectively help states achieve strategic outcomes.[15] Although cyber operations in the "grey zone" can affect the stability of the system overall, they have more direct consequences for other kinds of stability, such as damaging the political stability of individual states through influence operations, or undermining economic stability through IP theft, fraud, or extortion. It is uncertain whether such cyber operations taking place below the threshold of armed attack can be adequately deterred (much has been written on the applicability of deterrence to this sphere),[16] or whether states should instead engage directly in "persistent" cyber activity, seeking to disrupt activity wherever the adversary maneuvers, reaching a form of stable but largely implicit "agreed competition."[17] What is clear is that here stability and instability are even further intertwined; the gains of one state are often the losses of another, and so such sub-system interactions can clearly benefit from analyses of (in)stability.

As with systemic (in)stability, there are also issues of (in)stability at a sub-system level that are not always related directly to cyber operations. For example, the impact of cyberspace on the political stability of states is another topic with an extensive literature, especially in relation to the role of social media networks in the 2011 Arab Spring protests and many others before and since.[18] For those participating in these protests, the ability to undermine the stability of decades-long authoritarian regimes through online connective action – and extensive offline confrontation – provided a rare opportunity to champion individual rights and freedoms. Conversely, the "digital authoritarian" reaction of such regimes, first improvising and later embedding extensive information controls to subdue and coerce their citizens into compliance, reveals the complex relationship between (in)stability and cyberspace at a national and regional level.[19] The proliferation of advanced targeted surveillance technologies, for example, maintains authoritarian control but violates individual rights and jeopardizes diplomatic relationships.

Finally, we must consider the relationship between cyberspace and (in)stability not just at the level of operations, incidents, and practices – state or non-state, system or sub-system – but also in terms of the structural foundations of how we perceive our world. Throughout history, particular worldviews – racist, sexist, imperial, colonial – have structured political interactions, and it is the (in)stability of these worldviews, their rise and fall, that has shaped the contemporary international system. Equally, stability itself is a signifier with gendered, racial, and colonial implications, which cannot be forgotten in its contemporary application. Cyberspace provides a unique platform for many fringe discourses, while also globalizing dominant ideals and practices through multimedia products with almost unfathomable reach to billions worldwide. At the most macro level, the stability of human life in an increasingly unstable climate, and the potential for digital technologies to both exacerbate and help ameliorate the climate emergency, underline the centrality of cyberspace for global (in)stability in the most literal sense. We hope that this volume starts a conversation that helps to address these vital issues.

Structure of the Book

The chapters of this book are ordered according to four themes, roughly in line with the unfolding discussion above: escalation, institutions, and infrastructures, with a final section on subaltern and decolonial perspectives on (in)stability in relation to cyberspace. Here, we provide a brief overview of each theme and summary of the chapters' contributions, as well as drawing out connections between them.

Part I Escalation

First, we examine cyberspace and (in)stability in terms of the risks of conducting cyber operations, especially around inadvertent escalation. Inadvertent escalation in the context of cyber operations has at least two different meanings. The first refers to the risk of cyber operations escalating into a major conventional conflict or war. The second refers to cyber espionage operations – or operational activity with defensive aims – ultimately leading to a more severe cyber response from an adversary. This topic has become particularly relevant as many states establish military cyber commands, and as the United States has shifted to a new military strategy of defending forward against adversaries in cyberspace, perceived as more "aggressive" by some observers.

Existing articles considering cyber operations and stability primarily assess states' ability to reduce the risk of inadvertent escalation through deterrence and norms-building measures. For example, Borghard and Lonergan explain how confidence-building measures can foster stability in cyberspace.[20] Geist assesses whether nuclear concepts and thinking on deterrence stability should be imported to the cyber domain, arguing that the United States should create a "strategy of technology", emphasizing "resilience, denial, and offensive capabilities."[21] Donnelly et al. argue that cyber stability can be achieved through a deterrence posture that includes clear communication of credible intention and capability.[22] Overall, the current academic literature largely conceives of cyber stability as a particular condition or state of affairs, whether narrowly as the absence of incentives to conduct (military) cyber operations and develop an offensive cyber capability, or more broadly as a peaceful and harmonious cyber environment for states to operate in and through.

In Chapter 1, Jason Healey and Robert Jervis introduce the concept of situational cyber stability, suggesting the key question is not "whether" cyber capabilities are escalatory per se, but rather how they are escalatory under certain geopolitical conditions. Their approach to stability is dynamic, rather than static. Healey and Jervis identify four key mechanisms: Pressure Release, Spark, Bring Out the Big Guns, and Escalation Inversion. They note that both optimists – arguing that cyber conflict is not escalatory – and pessimists – arguing that cyber conflict is escalatory – have each touched on parts of these mechanisms. This chapter integrates insights from both perspectives to better understand crisis stability in cyberspace across the range of geopolitical contexts from relative peace to impending war. The chapter also examines the role of surprise in cyber conflict and offers several policy recommendations to reduce the chances of crises escalating.

Healey and Jervis emphasize that certain features of cyber capabilities can create new pathways through which a great-power crisis could escalate into a larger conventional conflict. In Chapter 2, Ben Buchanan and Fiona Cunningham assess one particular pathway for interstate crisis escalation: the use of force in response to adversary hacking operations that are designed to enable high-end cyber attacks. Known as operational preparation of the environment, these kind of hacking operations lay the groundwork for future attacks but are difficult to distinguish from espionage. While some scholars argue that states might respond to the discovery of an intruder with the use of force, others have found little empirical evidence that cyber operations affect interstate conflict dynamics. To assess these competing claims, the authors go further than most in conducting a comparative examination of Chinese and US leadership views, organizational and operational practices for cyber conflict, and the bilateral cyber relationship, drawing on government and policy sources from both countries. Buchanan and Cunningham conclude that the risk of inadvertent escalation due to cyber capabilities in a future Sino-American crisis cannot be dismissed.

In Chapter 3, Jaclyn Kerr explains why the United States was surprised by Russian use of cyber-enabled information operations during the 2016 US presidential elections. She argues that the United States was poorly prepared to anticipate, defend against, or respond to these operations because of a long-developing security dilemma rooted in "domain concept misalignment" – that is, superficially overlapping but significantly different domain conceptualizations – resulting from a distinction in how democratic and non-democratic states conceptualize the scope and nature of the emerging digital and informational domain of military action. Kerr's findings reveal the importance of conceptual clarity and historical awareness in ensuring effective response and preventing escalation in the future.

Together, these three chapters address different aspects of escalation relating to cyber capabilities. They emphasize how strategic concepts affect the likelihood of escalation, whether in terms of specific doctrine on the risks of cyber operations (Buchanan and Cunningham), or broader ideas about the appropriate boundaries of the cyber domain overall (Kerr). They also highlight the contingency of escalation, teasing apart different mechanisms that lead to opposite outcomes (Healey and Jervis), addressing the consequences of the new US strategy, and exploring the complex relationship between internal bureaucratic divisions and international cyber strategy (Buchanan and Cunningham, Kerr). While these chapters largely focus on the dyadic dynamics of great power escalation, the next section investigates how institutions affect cyber (in)stability in more detail.

Part II Institutions

The accounts of systemic (in)stability above speak directly to long-standing realist traditions of IR thought. However, the more constructivist literature on cyber norms has an equally central relationship with the concept of stability.[23] There is little agreement over what a cyber norm should be (ranging from prescriptive norm lists to more diffuse ideas of tacit bargaining), let alone what norms are appropriate for cyberspace and how such norms can be implemented and enforced. For this reason, we approach this topic from the direction of institutions, noting that IR draws a firm connection between the two concepts, defining institutions as collections of principles, norms, rules, and decision-making procedures. The three chapters in this section examine institutions in both the IR and more vernacular senses: NATO, the US Department of State and the US Department of Defense. All three chapters ask how these institutions incorporate cyberspace into their pre-existing practices, how they adjust or reshape their norms and practices in response, and – crucially – how this re-orientation affects the possibility for cyber norms development more broadly. As Jon Lindsay has observed, cyberspace does not only have institutions, but in a much more fundamental sense cyberspace is itself an institution.[24]

We acknowledge that the choice of institutions in this section is highly skewed: namely, two US government organizations and a transatlantic military alliance dominated by the US. This in part reflects the scholarly networks and production process of the edited volume, with nearly all contributors and editors working in the US and Europe – sometimes as scholar/practitioners as well as academic "observers." It also reflects our access to and the availability of detailed information about institutional processes in these states, compared to other world regions.[25] Such US- and Euro-centricity is nonetheless an important limitation of this section. We seek to address this limitation in part later in the volume, especially in the section on subaltern and decolonial perspectives, but also recommend readers to see this section as an invitation to engage in wider comparative institutional analyses of (in)stability and cyberspace.

In Chapter 4, Joe Burton and Tim Stevens investigate the implications for strategic stability of NATO's operationalization of the cyber domain. Building upon an historical and theoretical understanding of alliances as stability mechanisms, they determine how NATO's evolving cyber posture – and associated discourses of stability – has been interpreted by its key adversaries, allies, and partners. The scholars thus not only analyze the classic elements of strategic interaction but also NATO's role as a normative actor in global cyber affairs. Overall, this chapter poses questions about how NATO's pursuit of political relevance and operational dominance in the cyber domain shapes and influences strategic stability. In an insightful comment highly pertinent to the devastating war in Ukraine that began toward the end of the writing of this volume, Burton and Stevens note that, for NATO, "Russian actions may have demonstrated [a] sort of stability paradox, wherein efforts to cause instability engender cohesion and collective responses." Such unintended consequences underline the complexity that alliance relationships bring to questions of (in)stability.

In Chapter 5, Emily Goldman examines the role of the US State Department in cyber diplomacy. Goldman begins by noting that American cyber diplomacy has improved but still leaves the United States vulnerable to continuous, state-sponsored cyber aggression that is having strategic effects, even though that aggression never rises to a "significant" level that would elicit an armed response. Goldman argues that the State Department can pivot – without risking armed conflict – from a "reaction-after-the-fact" posture to seizing the initiative from adversaries whose cyberspace campaigns erode US economic competitiveness, reduce military advantages, and weaken political cohesion. Goldman recommends that the US State Department re-examine assumptions about cyber conflict and norm emergence, adopt a competitive mindset, and prioritize efforts tailored for great-power competition. Ultimately, Goldman's conclusion that "restraint in the face of continuous aggression is destabilising because it emboldens aggressors" reveals another paradox of unintended consequences; this time, a reluctance to act diplomatically when faced with a rapidly shifting and institutionally divided policy landscape.

In Chapter 6, Rebecca Slayton observes that cyber competition is about more than technology – it is about the knowledge, skills, and capabilities of a relatively new kind of expert, the cyber warrior. However, the fundamental knowledge, skills, and capabilities needed to defend and attack computer networks are not new. They have been under continual development by computer scientists, in both classified and non-classified contexts, since the late 1960s. Consequently, the question this chapter explores is: how, when, and why did this expertise come to be institutionalized as a kind of warfighting, meriting the authority and resources reserved for a combatant command? Slayton argues that both the process by which military leaders came to appreciate the risks associated with vulnerable computer networks, and the dominant response to those risks, were shaped by military culture as much as they were shaped by technological imperatives. Slayton thus shows that that the role of cyber warriors in influencing the stability of the international order depends as much on how they are imbedded within their national (military) institutions, as their technical prowess.

Together, these chapters tackle the thorny question of how far institutional state or alliance objectives regarding stability contribute to the technical and normative stability of cyberspace more broadly. From Burton and Stevens' analysis of NATO's semi-successful efforts to advocate for improved cyber security defenses across and beyond its membership, to Goldman's dissection of the US State Department's sometimes uncomfortable commitment to norms of openness and interoperability, the relationship between institutions and their broader environment is neither simple nor straightforward. This comes to the fore clearly in Slayton's plea to consider the wider implications – and institutional prestige – of "defensive cyber operations, which stabilize technology for friendly operators." As Slayton argues, "if kinetic operations contribute to international instability, the cyber defenses that enable those operations enable that instability," thereby turning on their head standard assumptions of how offense and defense relate to stability. Such concerns lead us into the third section of the volume, which addresses global infrastructural issues more directly.

Part III Infrastructures

Cyberspace is dependent on multiple overlapping infrastructures, both in Edwards' definition of infrastructures as accumulated relational properties stretching across sectors, and in Starr and Ruhleder's observation that infrastructures are "intended not to be seen."[26] As Ensmenger notes, "technologies become infrastructure only after they are perfected to the point of being routine . . . we notice them only when they fail."[27] Despite – or, perhaps, due to – this near-invisibility, infrastructures are highly political. What does it mean to "perfect" a technology or a set of technologies? Whose routines do they enable and constrain? And how do they "fail"? These questions all speak to the (in)stability of the infrastructures that underpin cyberspace, and their implications for (in)stability of other kinds of infrastructures.

More specifically, an infrastructural lens connects (in)stability to its close cognate, the concept of resilience. It is widely accepted that cyber security, understood as the defense and protection of digital networks from intrusion and disruption, must be accompanied by cyber resilience in the form of post-incident detection and recovery, enabling targeted entities to return to normal functioning as quickly as possible. A stable infrastructure is a resilient infrastructure, possessing the ability to respond quickly to change, as well as the ability to manage unexpected events in a controlled manner. The two chapters in this section both address infrastructural aspects of (in)stability, highlighting how new technologies and the unexpected or problematic use of these technologies undermines the stability of various infrastructures supporting cyberspace. In the other direction of the relationship – examined throughout this volume – they address how cyberspace as an infrastructure raises questions of international governance more broadly.

In Chapter 7, Mark Raymond examines the rapid emergence and expansion of the Internet of Things (IoT), as it entangles the internet with an array of other issue areas. It thus generates potentially problematic interactions among the legacy internet governance regime, a host of other international regimes, and domestic governance arrangements in highly networked countries. The chapter argues that alongside the rapid diffusion of the internet, we are witnessing the metastasizing of the global cyber regime complex. As a result of this ongoing process, the viability of a variety of international regimes and domestic governance arrangements (and thus the stability of the international system more broadly) will increasingly depend on the efficacy and legitimacy of the global cyber regime complex. The chapter concludes by making the case for treating this regime complex as "critical governance infrastructure" in the international system. Just as electric grids, water systems, and financial systems are systemically important components of modern societies, the global cyber regime complex is rapidly acquiring a singular importance as a condition of possibility for the remainder of the present system of a rules-based global order and global governance; but one that is dangerously fragile. As Raymond astutely concludes, whatever our definition of (in)stability, "a world in which governance is less effective, less legitimate and more contested should be expected to be less stable."

In Chapter 8, Siena Anstis et al. advance a complementary argument by describing how the central characteristics of our evolving communications infrastructure (including devices, protocols, applications, and telecommunications networks) produce mounting insecurities for global civil society. Global civil society depends on a communications infrastructure that is constantly mutating, highly insecure, invasive by design, poorly regulated, and prone to abuse. This ecosystem was not developed with a single well-thought-out design plan, and security has largely been an afterthought. New applications have been thrown on top of legacy systems and then patched backwards haphazardly. In short, the dynamics of "surveillance capitalism, the products and services of the cyber warfare industry, and increasingly aggressive offensive cyber policies yield an insecure structure, contributing to an unstable environment for civil society." It is troubling that there is no single policy, technology, or application that will resolve this dysfunctional environment, and the authors argue that these conditions will almost certainly worsen as the "center of gravity" of cyberspace shifts to China, India, and the Global South.

Together, these two chapters examine the consequences for (in)stability of what Kerr, in this volume, calls the "arbitrary complexity of information systems." Raymond identifies the assemblage nature of cyberspace as a key source of instability, because "the complexity of the global cyber regime complex is itself likely to increase the odds of governance failures of various kinds" – with echoes of Kerr's analysis of competing institutional regimes earlier in the volume. Anstis et al. focus less on the arbitrariness of cyberspace governance, instead seeing unstable complexity as the result of deliberate actions. In doing so, they invert common statist notions of stability, arguing that "what state actors may consider to be beneficial for 'stability' can perversely end up being a threat to civil society." Consequently, for Anstis et al., "stability for civil society necessitates different norms altogether – affirming the ability to exercise human rights without reprisal." The fourth and final section of this volume carries this critique of stability further still.

Part IV Subaltern and Decolonial Perspectives

This section contains two chapters that are central to the project of this book. As is often the case for projects like this, several scholars who participated in the workshops in preparation for this volume were unable to contribute to the final output. However, one particular case stood out, when we asked a colleague to write a chapter on feminist approaches to cyberspace and (in)stability. After much discussion and thought, our colleague pulled out of the project because they could not see a fruitful line of argument between feminist

analyses of cyberspace – of which there are many – and the concept of (in)
stability. After initially seeking to argue against the instinctive valorization of
stability with which we opened this introduction, especially in a status quo
world where violence against women is frequent and, in many situations, normalized, our colleague rejected the concept altogether. This was an important
reminder that our choice of analytical frame always has downsides for someone. While we continue to believe that gendered investigations of (in)stability
are urgently required – and we invite scholars to contribute their thoughts –
we conclude the volume with two chapters that remind readers in other ways
to reflect on the assumptions behind their own conceptualization of stability
and cyberspace.

In Chapter 9, Mailyn Fidler surveys internet infrastructural developments
of the African Union and African states, which occupy a subaltern position
in the international system. Her starting point is that analyses of (in)stabil-
ity must focus as much on capacity as intent, because "even if relative peace
and strong desires exist between states, an imbalance in ability to respond can
exert a destabilising effect." The chapter challenges the dominant conception
that global integration brings stability through technical and regulatory openness, interoperability, and internationality. Instead, the case study analysis in
this chapter reveals that global integration can also bring instability through
dependence. As Fidler puts it, "For African countries, global integration can
bring instability through dependence, and attaining cyber stability can require,
at least initially, actions that the global community might view as destabilizing." Furthermore, Fidler argues that African states pursue stability through
control of laws and through selectivity in infrastructural investments, both of
which cut against typical expectations of subaltern states. In this way, Fidler's
chapter surfaces a tension between subaltern states' view of stability and the
human rights-focused civil society version advocated by Anstis et al. More
specifically, this tension stems from the co-option of human rights discourses
for state purposes: "just as Western countries might view an autocracy's views
about cyber-openness as a threat to their vision of stability, post-colonial states
might view a former coloniser's views of cyber-openness as a threat to theirs."

Finally, in Chapter 10, Densua Mumford applies a decolonial lens to argue
that any useful conceptualization of (in)stability in cyberspace will require a
critical and intersectional investigation of the Euro-American subject implied
in this project, especially what Mumford terms the "transnational techno-
elite." While Mumford underscores the downsides of pursuing state stability
explored in earlier chapters – noting that "when states try to establish stability
for themselves in cyberspace, various societal groups experience more instability" – this chapter takes this critique further. In particular, Mumford argues

that technical proposals designed to make it easier for users to change services or become less reliant on any single platform can usefully "undermine the stability of powerful platforms to the benefit of users." In some cases, the user benefit is precisely the introduction of instability; for example, "for LGBTQ youth, constructing an unstable online identity can be protective." In others, the presumptions of the transnational techno-elite act as "a destabilizing force in the social fabric of [marginalized] communities." Overall, Mumford shows that conceptualizations emerging from a Eurocentric perspective perpetuate coloniality by (de)stabilizing cyberspace in ways that are comfortingly familiar for dominant communities and further silence subaltern communities.

The analysis in this chapter raises some urgent critical questions, which we believe to be an appropriate note on which to conclude this introduction. Whose epistemologies are informing knowledge production and policymaking on (in)stability in cyberspace? On whose terms are such conceptualizations being made? Which knowledges are systematically privileged in these debates and which knowledges are systematically excluded or marginalized? The chapter recognizes that the nascent nature of debates about cyberspace creates an unprecedented opportunity to confront self-defeating practices of coloniality and to instead redefine traditional concepts such as (in)stability from within the epistemologies of subaltern communities across the Global South and North. That is, to be a concept that can be applied usefully to diverse lived experiences in cyberspace, (in)stability must itself incorporate diverse meanings.

Notes

1. European Council, "Declaration by the High Representative on Behalf of the European Union – Call to Promote and Conduct Responsible Behaviour in Cyberspace" (February 2020): https://www.consilium.euro pa.eu/en/press/press-releases/2020/02/21/declaration-by-the-high-rep resentative-on-behalf-of-the-european-union-call-to-promote-and-con duct-responsible-behaviour-in-cyberspace/
2. NATO, "Warsaw Summit Communiqué": https://ccdcoe.org/uploads /2018/11/NATO-160709-WarsawSummitCommunique.pdf
3. UK Foreign & Commonwealth Office, "Foreign Secretary welcomes first EU sanctions against malicious cyber actors" (July 30, 2020): https:// www.gov.uk/government/news/foreign-secretary-welcomes-first-eu-sa nctions-against-malicious-cyber-actors
4. The White House, "National Cyber Strategy of the United States of America" (September 2018): https://trumpwhitehouse.archives.gov/wp -content/uploads/2018/09/National-Cyber-Strategy.pdf

5. The White House, "China's Contribution to the Initial Pre-Draft of OEWG Report" (April 2020): https://front.un-arm.org/wp-content/up loads/2020/04/china-contribution-to-oewg-pre-draft-report-final.pdf

6. Elizabeth Roche, "UNSC: India says Cyber Tools are Used to Target Critical Infra," *Livemint* (June 29, 2021): https://www.livemint.com/ne ws/india/unsc-india-says-cyber-tools-are-used-to-target-critical-infra-11 624980216689.html

7. United States General Assembly, "Open-Ended Working Group on Developments in the Field of Information and Telecommunications in the Context of International Security: Final Substantive Report," Conference room Paper (2021, March 10).

8. Global Commission on the Stability of Cyberspace, "The Commission": https://cyberstability.org/about/

9. Global Commission on the Stability of Cyberspace, "Advancing Cyberstability: Final Report": https://cyberstability.org/report/#2-what -is-meant-by-the-stability-of-cyberspace

10. In this way, it mirrors similar developments in the concept of cyber secu- rity, which we capture elsewhere as "moral maneuvers." James Shires, *The Politics of Cybersecurity in the Middle East* (London: Hurst, 2021).

11. Over 5,000 articles were published discussing "cyber security" based on a search through JSTOR, a digital library of academic journals, books, and primary sources.

12. This could be deliberate or inadvertent, as is the case for cyber operations against nuclear command and control systems.

13. Arguing that an even distribution of power is more stable see: Hans Morgen- thau, *Politics among Nations*, (New York: Alfred Knopf, 1967); John Mear- scheimer, "Back to the Future," *International Security* 15, no. 1 (1990): 5–56; William C. Wohlforth, "The Stability of a Unipolar World," *International Security* 24, no. 1 (1999): 5–41. Arguing that preponderance is more stable see: Geoffrey Blainey, *Causes of War* (New York: Free Press, 1973).

14. Richard J. Harknett and Max Smeets, "Cyber Campaigns and Strategic Outcomes," *Journal of Strategic Studies* 45, no 4 (2020): https://doi.org/ 10.1080/01402390.2020.1732354

15. Joshua Rovner, "Cyber War as an Intelligence Contest," *War on the Rocks* (2019, September 16): https://warontherocks.com/2019/09/cyber-w ar-as-an-intelligence-contest/; Lennart Maschmeyer, "The Subversive Trilemma: Why Cyber Operations Fall Short of Expectations," *International Security* 46, no. 2 (2021): 51–90; Robert Chesney and Max Smeets (eds), *Deter, Disrupt, or Deceive? Assessing Cyber Conflict as an Intelligence Contest?* (Georgetown University Press: Forthcoming).

16. Lucas Kello, *The Virtual Weapon and International Order* (Yale: Yale University Press: 2017); also see: Uri Tor, "'Cumulative Deterrence' as a New Paradigm for Cyber Deterrence," *Journal of Strategic Studies* 40, no. 1–2 (2017): 92–117; Dorothy E. Denning, "Rethinking the Cyber Domain and Deterrence," *Joint Forces Quarterly* 77 (2015): 8–15; Joseph S. Nye, "Deterrence and Dissuasion in Cyberspace", *International Security* 43, no. 3 (Winter, 2016): 44–71.

17. Michael P. Fischerkeller and Richard J. Harknett, "What is Agreed Competition in Cyberspace?," *Lawfare*, February 19, 2019: https://www.lawfareblog.com/what-agreed-competition-cyberspace; James N. Miller and Neal A. Pollard, "Persistent Engagement, Agreed Competition and Deterrence in Cyberspace," *Lawfare*, April 30, 2019: https://www.lawfareblog.com/persistent-engagement-agreed-competition-and-deterrence-cyberspace.

18. Gadi Wolfsfeld, Elad Segev, and Tamir Sheafer, "Social Media and the Arab Spring: Politics Comes First," *The International Journal of Press/Politics* 18, no. 2 (2013): 115–137.

19. Shires, *The Politics of Cybersecurity in the Middle East.*

20. Erica D. Borghard and Shawn W. Lonergan, "Confidence Building Measures for the Cyber Domain," *Strategic Studies Quarterly* 12, no. 3 (2018): 10–49.

21. Edward Geist, "Deterrence Stability in the Cyber Age," *Strategic Studies Quarterly* 9, no. 4 (2015): 44–61.

22. Donnelly et al. define cyber stability as "absence of serious hostile cyber actions ... [between states], where the states have a sufficient common understanding of each other's capabilities and intentions so as to be inclined generally to avoid such actions, likely associated with a common belief that the costs of such conduct would outweigh the benefits"; D. A. Donnelly et al., "A Technical and Policy Toolkit for Cyber Deterrence and Stability," *Journal of Information Warfare* 18, no. 4 (2019): 53–69.

23. Martha Finnemore and Duncan B. Hollis, "Constructing Norms for Global Cybersecurity," *The American Journal of International Law* 110, no. 3 (2016): 425–480; Anders Henriksen, "The End of the Road for the UN GGE Process: The Future Regulation of Cyberspace," *Journal of Cybersecurity* 5, no. 1 (2019): 2.

24. Jon R. Lindsay, "Restrained by Design: The Political Economy of Cybersecurity," *Regulation and Governance* 19, no. 6 (2017): 493–514.

25. For comparison, see e.g. Shires, *The Politics of Cybersecurity in the Middle East.*

26. Susan Leigh Star and Karen Ruhleder, "Steps Toward an Ecology of Infrastructure: Design and Access for Large Information Spaces," *Information Systems Research* 7, no. 1 (1996): 111–134.
27. Nathan Ensmenger, "The Environmental History of Computing," *Technology and Culture* 59, no. 4 (2018): S7–S33, S14.

Part I
Escalation

1

The Escalation Inversion and Other Oddities of Situational Cyber Stability

Jason Healey and Robert Jervis

Are cyber capabilities escalatory? It is one of the most important and debated questions for policymakers and scholars of cyber conflict. The pessimists, in whose camp we normally reside, observe a two-decade trend of increasing cyber aggression acting like a ratchet, not a pendulum. Adversary groups aligned with states have caused physical destruction (starting with the US-Israeli Stuxnet attack on Iran); savaged private sector companies (Iran's attacks on US banks or the North Korean dismembering of Sony);[1] disrupted national healthcare systems (North Korea's WannaCry which disrupted the UK National Health Service),[2] electrical grids in wintertime (Russia's take-down of the Ukrainian grid),[3] and national elections (Russia again);[4] and recklessly created global havoc (Russia's NotPetya).[5] If "escalation" means a meaningful and potentially destabilizing upward spiral in the intensity of cyber hostilities, then cyber conflict may be "the most escalatory kind of conflict that humanity has ever come across."[6] States are getting closer to crossing the threshold of death and major destruction outside of wartime. How long until one state, through mistake, miscalculation, or maliciousness, crosses that line?

The optimists have equally compelling arguments, however – not least the contention that, so far, none of these admittedly worrying cyber attacks has ever warranted an armed attack with kinetic weapons in response.[7] How, they argue, can cyber conflict be escalatory when states have never responded to cyber attacks with traditional violence? Indeed, there is at least as much evidence for cyber capabilities reducing rather than causing or intensifying international crises – as when US President Donald Trump called off a deadly airstrike against Iran in June 2019 but allowed a non-lethal cyber strike as retaliation for attacks on oil tankers and the downing of a US drone.[8]

This chapter will examine this debate. Much of the dispute about the escalatory potential of cyber capabilities comes down to scope conditions. The question is not "whether" cyber capabilities are stabilizing or destabilizing. Rather, the issue is which outcome is more likely under certain geopolitical circumstances. Current literature often assumes the impact on stability to be situation-independent, which we find unlikely. The risks to stability can change, perhaps quite rapidly, depending on prevailing conditions between states. We analyze these conditions in a framework of "situational cyber stability" and see four main mechanisms: Pressure Release, Spark, Bring Out the Big Guns, and Escalation Inversion.

During periods of relative peace and stability – that is, since the end of Cold War in 1991 – several characteristics drive cyber capabilities to act as a pressure-release valve. Cyber capabilities provide stabilising, non-lethal options for decision-makers, less threatening than traditional weapons with kinetic effects. During periods of acute crisis, however, cyber capabilities have other, destabilizing characteristics. In these situations, there are greater opportunities for provocation, misperception, mistake, and miscalculation. Dangerous positive feedback loops can amplify cyber conflict so that it takes on a life of its own with diminishing room for strategic choice by policymakers. Table 1.1 summarizes our findings.

These findings are likely to have general applicability, applying to the relationship between the United States and its major cyber adversaries of Iran, North Korea, Russia, and China, and to relationships between rivals such as India and Pakistan.

The first section of this article defines key concepts: stability, escalation, and the new US cyber strategy of persistent engagement. We then examine the strong evidence supporting the argument that the use of cyber capabilities has generally not been destabilizing or escalatory (in the sense of leading to a larger, traditional conflict), and the theories as to why this is so. Next, we explore the circumstances under which this happy situation might change, with cyber capabilities inviting war. There are also sections on feedback loops in cyber conflict and the poorly understood role of surprise. We conclude with implications and recommendations for policymakers.

Concepts Old and New

Situational cyber stability links concepts which are rather old – including stability, escalation, and intensification – with concepts that are quite new, such as persistent engagement. It is worth explaining each concept in detail.

Table 1.1 Situational cyber stability

		Escalatory impact of cyber conflict in different geopolitical conditions		
Mechanism	Cross-domain relationship	During conditions of . . .	Then . . .	Because . . .	So, the overall impact is . . .
Pressure release	Cyber conflict *instead of* armed conflict	Relative peacetime (no major crisis) or both sides *strongly* want to limit conflict	Cyber capabilities generally not escalatory	They do not cause casualties and are temporary and covert, so states see them as less threatening	Stabilizing
Spark	Cyber conflict *begets* armed conflict	Tension in cyberspace between states	Cyber conflict can be the root cause of acute geopolitical crises	Cyber conflict is intensifying over increasingly existential issues and may break	Destabilizing
Bring Out the Big Guns	*Threat of armed conflict* begets cyber conflict	Frequent geopolitical crises	Temptation for less restraint and more aggressive cyber moves	States would be more risk-taking and less willing to accept cyber insults as mere "pressure release"	Destabilizing
Escalation inversion	Cyber conflict *precedes or accelerates* war	Major and acute geopolitical crisis	Cyber dynamics tempt early use in major crises when war may seem likely anyhow	Cyber capabilities are seen as best used in surprise attacks, with an asymmetric impact on infrastructure and military forces	Destabilizing

Stability

The technical definition of stability is *negative feedback* in the sense that moving a system in one direction calls up pressures or forces that move it back toward its original position This contrasts with *positive feedback*, in which movement in one direction leads to greater movement in that direction.[9]

In Cold War security literature, scholars distinguished between *arms-race* or *strategic stability* and *crisis stability*.[10] These concepts can be used quite successfully to analyze cyber conflict. Traditionally, arms-race stability meant that building a weapon or a force posture would lead to negative feedback encouraging the other side to build fewer or less dangerous weapons. This contrasts with a situation of positive feedback, in which more spending or building by one side would lead to more spending or building by the other side. The research here was highly debated, in part because data on Soviet spending were highly unreliable and arms procurement involved long time lags.

Crisis stability in a Cold War context meant that the moves that one side took in a crisis reduced the incentives for the other side to do something dangerous – in the extreme case, to start a war. The standard argument was that vulnerable weapons systems or force postures invited an attack, thus increasing crisis instability.

Escalation and Intensification

In the Cold War, scholars made the simple distinction between *vertical escalation* (increased intensity of violence) and *horizontal escalation* (geographic spread). The implication was that escalation brought one closer to all-out war. But, as with NATO's then-doctrine of "escalating to de-escalate," the reverse could also be the case.[11]

In cyber conflict, horizontal escalation has come to mean intensification within cyberspace itself and is generally considered less serious compared to vertical escalation out of cyberspace to the use of lethal, kinetic weapons. Martin Libicki defines escalation as "an increase in the intensity or scope of conflict that crosses threshold(s) considered significant by one or more of the participants." Intensity is both "number of troops committed to the fight" (measuring inputs, comparable to sending more infantry and Marines to Afghanistan) and cyber operations that have a more significant impact (measuring outputs or effects).[12] Libicki also adds a third element, determining if one incident was in response to another. We fully agree with the first two elements though, as we explore further below, we believe the third element may be unnecessary.

Persistent Engagement

Within the US military over the last two decades, the predominant image for what defined cyber success was rooted in Cold War traditions of deterrence: stability is achieved by having fearsome cyber capabilities and an understood willingness to use them if pressed. Since early 2018, thanks in large part to the work of several IR scholars, this has shifted to a different assessment: to achieve stability, the military must not only possess capabilities, but also routinely use them to counter adversaries.

The US Cyber Command vision in 2018 insisted on the need for fewer operational constraints. This would allow them to "defend forward," and "pursue attackers across networks and systems." With this agility, they can take the initiative to introduce "tactical friction . . . compelling [adversaries] to shift resources to defense and reduce attacks."[13] In addition, persistent engagement is expected to enable "tacit bargaining," as each side develops "more stable expectations of acceptable and unacceptable behavior," through repeated engagements.[14] Deterrence is expected to play a role as well, especially through cumulative frustration of adversary operations.[15]

Though persistent engagement is still in some sense an escalation − as it involves a more intense US response to cyber aggression − proponents argue it can "improve security and stability," because US adversaries will back off due to friction, tacit bargaining, and deterrence.[16] The argument that persistent engagement leads to stability requires the assumption that a more forward defense introduces negative feedback, to bring activity back toward historical (or agreed-to) levels. It is also possible, of course, that a more engaged forward defense might have the opposite effect − creating positive feedback where adversaries see the new, more active US position as a challenge to meet, rather than back away from.[17]

Many academics have cast doubt on whether cyber capabilities are effective means of coercion,[18] are effective on the battlefield,[19] or provide asymmetric and substantial advantage to attackers over defenders.[20] This chapter will argue that policymakers and militaries are generally acting as if cyber does give a substantial advantage against other states, before and during crises as well as on the battlefield.

Pressure Release: Cyber Capabilities Generally Not Escalatory During "Peacetime"

Cyber conflict has not escalated into more traditional kinetic conflict. In 2013, one of us looked back at the history of cyber conflict and wrote that "nations have not sought to cause massive damage . . . outside of larger geo-political conflicts" and "have stayed well under the threshold of conducting full-scale strategic cyber warfare and have thus created a de facto norm."[21] Newer research has significantly expanded such assessments.

During times of general peace and stability, or when all participants strongly want to limit their conflict, cyber capabilities have been dampening, providing negative feedback to geopolitical crises. States have not responded kinetically to cyber attacks from other states. Even the responses to the most provocative incidents – those which came closest to the level of an armed attack – have been non-kinetic and mild (or perhaps covert and not yet known). As summarized by Martin Libicki: "rarely do events in cyberspace – much less escalation in cyberspace – lead to serious responses."[22]

Perhaps the most comprehensive quantitative analysis on cyber incidents, by Brandon Valeriano, Ryan Maness, and Benjamin Jensen, found that "Rivals tend to respond only to lower-level incidents and the response tends to check the intrusion as opposed to seek escalation dominance . . . These incidents are usually 'tit-for-tat' type responses."[23]

Why do cyber capabilities act as a pressure release? Josh Rovner has compellingly argued that states see cyber competition largely as an intelligence contest which operates under different rules than a military one: "cyber operations may provide a non-kinetic option for leaders who feel pressure to act in a crisis, but who are wary of using force."[24] There are no clearer examples than the US-Iran conflict. President Donald Trump, wanting to punish Iran for attacks on oil tankers and downing a US drone in June 2019, canceled punitive US airstrikes out of fears of the casualties they would cause but allowed non-lethal cyber disruption of Iranian computer systems.[25] Likewise, according to anonymous US intelligence sources for *The New York Times*, "Iran's supreme leader has blocked any large, direct retaliation to the United States, at least for now, allowing only cyberactivity to flourish."[26]

Valeriano and Jensen argue that this is partly because cyber capabilities "offer great powers escalatory offramps [and] signaling mechanisms" and can "shape an adversary"s behavior without engaging military forces and risking escalation."[27] Michael Fischerkeller and Richard Harknett likewise describe the "cyber strategic competitive space short of armed conflict" where states "design operations to generate a range of damage . . . short of internationally agreed upon definitions of use of force and armed attack."[28] Adversaries have "tacitly agreed on lower and upper bounds" and accordingly "have mutual interests in avoiding escalation to violent conflict."[29]

Erica Borghard and Shawn Lonergan root their explanation less in the motivations of states than in the specific characteristics of cyber capabilities, which render them "imperfect tools of escalation." Capabilities may not be ready in time for a sudden crisis and have uncertain and often limited effects; their use creates important trade-offs (such as revealing specific, closable vulnerabilities); and there are few appropriate kinetic response options.[30]

Through survey data, Sarah Kreps and Jacquelyn Schneider found that "for the American public, cyberattacks are qualitatively different from those of similar magnitude from other domains," so that "Americans are far more reluctant to escalate in the cyber domain than for . . . conventional or nuclear attack" with the same impact.[31] This, they argued, reinforces a firebreak – a sharp discontinuity – between cyber and kinetic conflict.

Situational Cyber Stability: When Cyber Capabilities Can Be Destabilizing

To sum up the previous section: cyber conflict has not escalated and there are strong, theory-backed reasons why it provides negative feedback, as a pressure release defusing geopolitical crises. We agree with these conclusions, which explain why cyber conflict has not yet escalated and may not in future. However, we believe they hold only if the next few decades generally resemble the past few. This stability is situational, and we see three major, interrelated reasons why it may change, which we term Spark, Bring Out the Big Guns, and the Escalation Inversion. In short, cyber conflicts and competition are intensifying over increasing stakes and might inadvertently or intentionally spark a larger conflict; there is a higher likelihood of acute crises, far worse than the relatively bland geopolitical conditions of the past decades; and in times of acute crisis, the dynamics go through an inversion, encouraging rather than suppressing escalation.

Spark: Cyber Conflict can Cause Acute Geopolitical Crises

As cyberspace becomes increasingly existential for economies and societies, states compete more aggressively over the same cyber terrain and treasure. In such circumstances, cyber capabilities add positive feedback, intensifying conflict within cyberspace. Ben Buchanan has featured some of these dynamics in his book, *The Cybersecurity Dilemma*. If a "potential adversary bolsters its own security by increasing its methods of secrecy and ratcheting up intrusive collection of its own – or by shooting back at the collectors – the first state will often feel a need to respond" with "still more intrusive collection."[32] This situation is one which can easily notch upward but only, with great difficulty, be reversed. This section will summarize the relevant dynamics of cyber conflict, establish that conflict is escalating in cyberspace, and discuss how this dangerous mix of factors can spark war.

Escalation in cyberspace

Cyber conflict and competition are intensifying. A cyber incident might cross the threshold into armed conflict either through a sense of impunity or through miscalculation or mistake. Alternatively, the cyber attack might be brazen or reckless enough to demand a muscular response from the target state. Libicki's framework of cyber escalation requires three elements: an increase in intensity, the crossing of significant thresholds, and causal links between cyber incidents (that is, "one attack is in response to another").[33]

We believe the first two elements are important and it is not necessary to balance each incident with its tit-for-tat response. Cyber conflict can be escalatory even if there is not a direct retaliation ("you did A so we will do X") but rather a trend over time ("we caught you doing A and B, and suspect you of C . . . so we'll do X and Y and for good measure see no reason to further hold off on Z"). It is through this larger picture, the series of campaigns and capabilities, that the escalatory mechanics become obvious. Despite no provable chain of causation from A to Z, the series can show evidence of intensification and ignored thresholds, if the direction and magnitude of the vector are consistent over a long period of time. A full analysis of escalation requires its own paper, but as an initial analysis we have selected four points over forty years, each separated by a decade, in order to illustrate this trend.

First, in 1988, nations did not have major cyber organizations. Within the US Department of Defense, there were small groups planning and conducting offensive operations, but there was no dedicated civilian defensive team in the United States until the creation of the Computer Emergency Response Team, funded by the Defense Department, in November 1988. There were significant incidents, such as the Morris worm and a case known as the Cuckoo's Egg, in which German hackers who searched for information on US ballistic missile defense technologies then passed their finds along to the Soviet KGB. However shocking at the time, those incidents still had quite modest scope, duration, and intensity.[34]

Second, ten years later, in 1998, the first combat cyber unit, the 609th Information Warfare Squadron of the US Air Force, had already been in existence for three years, with ninety-three officers and enlisted persons.[35] The first major cyber bank heist had been in 1995 against Citibank, while the US military created the first cyber command in 1998 in response to the internal Eligible Receiver exercise and Solar Sunrise incident.[36] This command was staffed by about two dozen defenders (including one of the authors) and worked with the larger Computer Emergency Response Team and similar teams in the military services to defend against and trace the major Moonlight Maze espionage case to Russia.[37] Within two years, the command expanded and took on responsibilities to coordinate offensive operations, growing to 122 personnel with a US$26 million budget.[38]

Third, ten years after that, in 2008, Estonia suffered a debilitating cyber attack from Russia. Espionage against the United States from Russia became increasingly worrisome, including a case known as Buckshot Yankee, where Russian spies breached classified networks. Chinese theft of intellectual property would be known as the "greatest transfer of wealth in history" by 2012.[39] In direct response to these incidents, the Department of Defense combined their dedicated offensive and defensive task forces into a single US Cyber Command in 2010.[40] What had been a defensive-only command with twenty-five people in 1998 grew to cover both offense and defense with a staff of over 900 by 2011.[41]

Finally, in the decade leading up to 2018, the United States launched a sophisticated cyber assault on Iranian uranium enrichment facilities; Iran conducted sustained denial of service attacks on the US financial system; North Korea attacked Sony; and Russia disrupted the Ukrainian power grid in winter (twice) and the opening ceremony of the Olympics.[42] US Cyber Command grew to 6,200 personnel just in the operational element, the Cyber Mission Force.[43] Iran and China created their own cyber commands as did the Netherlands,[44] the United Kingdom,[45] France,[46] Singapore,[47] Vietnam,[48] Germany,[49] and others. If intensification is measured as worsening levels of violence, then cyber conflict has intensified across all periods. By 2018, the problems faced in 2008 seemed minor and the organizations small and limited, while the cyber incidents from 1998 and 1988 appeared positively trivial. Operations that had appeared risky twenty years before were now routine.

The intensification trend is also clear according to the measurement of Libicki's "number of troops committed to the fight." The Defense Department expanded the central cyber warfighting force from zero in 1988 to 25 in 1998, 900 in 2011, and at least 6,200 in 2018. The first commander of US Cyber Command noted in 2011 that its creation "garnered a great deal of attention from other militaries," which he hoped was not a sign of militariation but rather "a reflection of concern."[50] Nations must indeed be concerned, as there are now dozens of copycats. Jensen, Valeriano, and Maness, using more quantified methods, had similar findings to this qualitative assessment, tracking a strong growth of latent cyber power by Russia and China from 2001 through 2014.[51]

There is no obvious evidence pointing to a decrease or even a plateau in the intensity of cyber conflict, or that fewer thresholds are being passed now than ten, twenty, or thirty years ago. The direction and magnitude of the change over four decades has marched in only one direction: a relentless increase as nations build their organizations and employ them in more frequent and more dangerous incidents.

There are three potential criticisms of this assessment. First, few if any of these incidents can be proven to have been direct retaliation. The trend line is clear enough, however, and incidents have driven the creation of new organizations and more assertive strategies. Three generations of US cyber defense organizations were in direct response to incidents while General Paul Nakasone of US Cyber Command directly links his strategy of persistent engagement to the intransigence of others. Because adversaries have had "strategic impact" with their cyber operations, US Cyber Command evolved "from a response force to a persistence force."[52] Likewise, Stuxnet "generated [a] reaction" from Iran, according to the four-star general then leading US Air Force cyber capabilities, and as a result Iran would be "a force to be reckoned with" in cyberspace.[53]

Second, it is possible to argue that these attacks did not violate explicit norms or red lines. Yet, in a fast-moving area like cyber, it is reasonable for policymakers to only decide post facto that a transgression has occurred. The Iranian government did not, to our knowledge, specifically forbid cyber destruction of their uranium-enrichment infrastructure. Nor was the US electoral system, at the time of the Russian interference in 2016, specified as critical infrastructure and thus off-limits under stated US norms. Surely, it is not unreasonable to expect a US reaction nonetheless.

Third, it is possible that these trends may not indicate intensification as much as increased digital dependence or technological advancement. As the numbers of connected devices and networks skyrocketed over forty years, it would be no surprise if attacks and organizations scaled as well. We are not convinced by this argument, as the statements of participants in cyber incidents repeatedly and specifically denounce the intransigence and audacity of others, ratcheting up their response. Nor do we find the advancement of technology to be a satisfactory explanation. Adversaries took progressively more risks during the forty-year period under examination. Even technically similar attacks increased in intensity over time. The 2016 election interference was achieved through the hacking of emails – a kind of cyber incident that was neither rare nor advanced in 1998. Only the Russian audacity to release those emails to influence an election was novel. In 2008, both the Obama and McCain presidential campaigns suffered Chinese (and also possibly Russian) intrusions, but only as passive intelligence collection. The campaigns had apparently little concern that the stolen information would be doctored or released.[54] By 2018, conflict had intensified so that none could have such assurances.

A dangerous mix

Cyber conflict presents a situation that has no obvious parallels in military history. States covertly experiment with capabilities below the threshold of armed attack and implant them in adversary systems well before hostilities, creating an "environment in which multiple actors continue to test their adversaries' technical capabilities, political resolve, and thresholds," as the Director of National Intelligence testified in 2015.[55] Testing of capabilities and resolve will always increase the chances of miscalculation and mistakes.

The major cyber powers – and more than a few minor ones – behave greedily in cyberspace. Unhappy with the cyber status quo, they seek to seize as much "territory" (computers and servers in other countries; "grey space" in the US euphemism) and "high ground" (such as core internet routers) as they can.[56] Since no one else seems to be showing much restraint, it may seem a sucker bet to do so, especially with the growing sense that the advantage lies in seizing the initiative.

As US cyber operations are said to play "nice" and do not spread wildly or cause collateral damage,[57] many argue "the status quo is deteriorating into norms that by default are being set by adversaries."[58] Such conclusions, with the United States loudly asserting its victimhood, are based on a selective choice of evidence. It is easy when reading US official documents to forget that the United States was a predator long before it was prey.

US leaders have no problem recognizing that "autocratic governments . . . view today's open Internet as a lethal threat to their regimes." Yet they have more difficulty making connections between cause and effect or seeing the situation through the eyes of their rivals.[59] Adversaries perceive that the United States first broke the status quo (by dominating the early internet, pushing for a borderless cyberspace, and building a massive early lead in cyber espionage) and are hitting back, not acting first. To such states, calls to act "responsibly" may appear indistinguishable from acquiescence to a cyberspace inimical to their survival.

Adversaries also believe that the US does not play by its own rules. According to the US intelligence community, President Vladimir Putin of Russia was convinced that the release of embarrassing financial data from the Panama Papers was a US covert action. This was partly the cause for Putin's decision to interfere in the US elections, which in turn was met with disruptive attacks on the main Russian troll-farm by US cyber operators.[60] Chinese leaders may believe that US confidence building and transparency measures, such as discussing a new cyber strategy, are swaggering moves meant to cow Beijing.[61] Iran's cyber operations were almost entirely focused on dissidents until they were hit by the US-Israeli Stuxnet attack, after which Iran raced to build and use its own capabilities. After the revelations of Edward Snowden, European allies were astonished by the scope of US espionage and its lack of restraint.[62]

President Trump in 2018 reportedly approved the CIA to conduct significantly more operations under less oversight, including "cyberattacks on Iranian infrastructure" and "covert hack-and-dump actions aimed at both Iran and Russia."[63] Any Russian or Iranian attacks since then may have been reprisals, though this would be unknown to researchers, US citizens, and senior government officials and members of Congress without the need to know. There are few who know what punches a country is taking, which it is throwing, and the causal relationship between the two.

It is therefore misguided to base any cyber policy, theory, or strategy on statements that ignore the role US cyber operations have had in shaping the status quo. We do not argue there is any ethical equivalence between the cyber operations of the United States and other nations. Rather, there may be an escalatory equivalence when no one thinks anyone else is paying attention to complaints, redlines (tacit or explicit), or perceived norms.

In sum, cyber-induced crises which escalate into larger geopolitical crises are more likely in the coming years, fed by this intensification of operations, insensitivity to the perceptions of others and a fear of existential digital risks. States will increasingly feel angry, paranoid, trigger-happy, and vengeful, and they will turn to their militaries for salvation: a chaotic recipe, ripe for error, and potentially overwhelming any dampening effects of cyber capabilities. Cyberspace is no longer the preserve of researchers, e-commerce sites, and nerds. It is now existential to a growing number of states. Advanced states rely on connectivity, including the Internet of Things, not just for communication but control of the economy and industry. Cyber may be an intelligence contest, as Rovner and others contend – but if that is true, it is a contest taking place inside a $1.35 trillion digital economy (and that is just the contribution to the United States) and across insecure technologies that hold citizens' most intimate secrets.[64]

Bring Out the Big Guns: Acute Crises Invite More Aggressive Cyber Moves

Our second concern is that acute geopolitical crises – having little to do with cyber competition – will be more likely in coming years. Nationalism and populism are on the rise, while the mechanisms of global governance which have helped keep a lid on conflicts are steadily eroding. The intensity of acute crises, including the threat of great-power war, will create conditions well outside the scope of theories on the dampening effects of cyber capabilities.

As one of us has written with Jack Snyder:

> Cyber competition has developed during a period of relative peace and stability between major powers. Perhaps cyber competition has been below the threshold of armed attack simply because after the Cold War, post-1991, adversaries have been (relatively) restrained from armed attack in all its forms, not just cyber. The desire to avoid escalation, and cyber-as-pressure-release, may not be inherent to cyber competition but merely be an inherited characteristic from the global balance of power during the entire period under consideration. A decay of that geopolitical stability could light a match to significantly different and worsening cyber competition.[65]

In such a case, states may be unwilling to keep the tacit agreements of quieter times, limiting themselves to the relative restraint of an intelligence contest in cyberspace. If not all participants are strongly committed to limiting the conflict, then cyber will not be a reliable pressure release.

Harknett and Fischerkeller acknowledge the scope conditions of their own work, clarifying their prescriptions only apply to the "competitive space *short of* armed conflict" and not the "competitive space *of* armed conflict."[66] The barrier between the two may be quite thin, and the "grey zone" below the level or armed conflict may be narrower than policymakers, practitioners, and academics expect. A higher risk of crises also weakens the dampening effects cited by Borghard and Lonergan. States will use their stockpiled capabilities, accepting the higher risk of using uncertain capabilities and caring less about the trade-offs.[67] Adversaries on the receiving end of riskier, more dangerous attacks during a geopolitical crisis will feel less restraint in choosing harsh, even kinetic, responses.

Escalation Inversion: Dynamics Tempt Early Use in Acute Crises

The third concern of cyber situational stability is that the use (or fear) of cyber capabilities will escalate acute geopolitical crises. When major national interests are at stake, with the real threat of war, different dynamics of cyber conflict come into play. Indeed, for Erik Gartzke and Jon Lindsay, "The same strategic logic that leads us to view cyberwar as a limited political instrument in most situations also leads us to view it as incredibly destabilizing in rare situations."[68]

As crises intensify, the perceived advantage of going first will tempt many adversaries to conduct cyber attacks they might have withheld otherwise, overstressing the normal pressure-release mechanisms and encouraging rather than dampening escalation. Cyber capabilities may be to World War Three as mobilisation timelines were to World War One.

It is not terribly relevant whether cyber capabilities actually have such a strategic, surprise impact. Policymakers and elites seem to believe they can, as is made evident by the intensification discussed above, the reinforcing of critical infrastructure against cyber attacks, and the nearly thirty-year lifetime of the concept of a cyber Pearl Harbor – a sudden and major cyber attack that is carried out with no warning. If states launch a major cyber attack hoping for a surprise, strategic impact, taking such a shot and missing may lead to just as severe a backlash as succeeding, unless the successful defenders decide to shrug it off – unlikely in the middle of a major geopolitical crisis. If the cyber attack becomes publicly known, the policymakers may have no choice but to make a muscular response.

Because cyber capabilities are seen to favor the attacker or the actor taking the initiative, "incentives to strike first could turn crises into wars."[69] This effect is exacerbated if a nation simultaneously has ineffective defenses yet brags, as the Chairman of the US Joint Chiefs of Staff has done, of "incredible offensive capability" to "deter [adversaries] from conducting attacks."[70] As one of the authors has written elsewhere:

> Sixty years ago, during the Cold War, the preferred plan of Strategic Air Command (SAC) was to maximize striking potential by basing nuclear-armed bombers as close as possible to the Soviet Union. Albert Wohlstetter wrote in a RAND Corp. report that this invited a surprise attack: The bombers and tankers parked on those bases would be both existentially threatening to the Soviet Union and themselves vulnerable to a Soviet nuclear attack . . . The combination of a terrifying offense and weak defense would create perverse incentives for the Soviet leadership to launch a disarming strike as early as possible in any crisis . . . [S]ome adversaries will choose the surprise attack rather than waiting to face off with the deadliest gunfighter around. Indeed, the more the gunfighter improves on and boasts about his deadliness, the more he brandishes his pistols, the more incentive there is to get the drop on him, especially if a fight seems inevitable anyhow.[71]

A report on US-Russia crisis stability co-authored by Jim Miller, the former third-ranking Pentagon official, notes these larger dynamics of drawing first, before the other guy draws on you:

Cyberspace and outer space offer the attacker a very attractive combination: the potential for high impact on the other side's military, with the potential for limited, or even no, direct casualties . . . [T]here are likely to be strong incentives on each side to use these capabilities in large doses early in a major conflict to gain coercive and military advantage – and to attempt to prevent the other side from gaining such advantage. The incentive to use cyber weapons during a crisis or early in a conflict are therefore significant, due to the very nature of the weapons themselves. Combatants may worry that an adversary will take measures to reduce its cyber vulnerability, providing reason to strike early while the window to do so effectively appears open.[72]

Miller believes that "The incentives to start any military conflict with a significant attack in cyberspace and outer space," and to do so before an adversary, "are enormous." This effect is magnified if an adversary believes that strategic weapon systems (especially nuclear weapons or nuclear command and control) and space-based intelligence and detection systems may be vulnerable to a blinding or disarming cyber strike. Since the United States military may seem otherwise unbeatable, an adversary's "weakness may compel him to compensate with audacity in order to redress the balance."

In this situation, the sense that cyber is a pressure-release valve becomes positively dangerous. Optimism can be a self-denying prophecy. If decisionmakers believe that the system will be stable regardless of their actions, they will act uncaringly, in a way that ultimately destabilizes that system. If a little cyber is stabilizing, then a lot more cyber should be even better.

The findings of Kreps and Schneider, based on surveys of the American public, suggest a firebreak (a clear delineation, perhaps even associated with a taboo) between cyber and kinetic conflict. In their experiment, a cyber attack with a given impact (such as destruction of a power plant) was seen as less severe than a kinetic effect with the same impact. Americans were "considerably more restrained when it comes to aggressive retaliatory actions involving the use of force" to respond to cyber attacks. This finding may tell us less about firebreaks than about potshots. If the United States will not take a surprise cyber attack too seriously, even if it caused death and destruction, why not take such a shot? Rather than seeing this survey as soothing evidence, we fear it demonstrates worryingly destabilizing dynamics.

As it was for the Japanese in 1941, the question may become: if not now, when? And if not this way, how? The short shelf life of cyber capabilities may force use-or-lose choices once an adversary expects a conflict. If you have secret torpedoes which can be used in shallow harbors like Pearl Harbor, and conflict seems inevitable, why not use these weapons in a surprise attack before the adversary can counter your exquisite advantage?

Answering The Stability Question: Does Cyberspace Encourage Positive and Negative Feedback?

The accuracy of any analysis of cyber stability depends on whether cyberspace and cyber conflict are marked primarily by positive or negative feedback. Strategies and theories are often built on an implicit assumption of relative stability – that since it has been stable in the past it will continue to be so in the future.

If the overall system is marked by negative feedback, then it is like a nice, solid car, engineered for balance and tolerant of mistakes, such as those made by young and inexperienced drivers. If this holds for cyber conflict, the fluctuations caused by aggressive cyber moves by states, even during acute crises, will calm over time. The concerns of Spark, Bring Out the Big Guns, and the Escalation Inversion mechanisms will remain largely theoretical in the face of continued pressure release.

If the system is marked by positive feedback, though, then it is more like a clunky jalopy driven on icy roads. Relatively tiny inputs are all it can take to induce wild swings, which amplify unless actively and expertly countered by an alert driver. At some point, the driver is no longer in control, as the dynamics take on a life of their own with little role for steering input (or strategic choices). Cyber attacks, in this model, beget worse cyber attacks, eventually throwing the system out of whack, especially through Spark, but also Bring Out the Big Guns or an Escalation Inversion.

Our own preliminary conclusion is that cyber conflict induces positive feedback. In 1978, one of us wrote that security dilemmas of spiraling escalation between rivals would be "doubly dangerous," if it is hard to distinguish offense from defense and the offense has the overall advantage. Each side would see even defensive moves as escalatory and because defense was feckless, the "incentives to strike first could turn crises into wars."[73] In our view, cyber conflict is more than doubly dangerous, for the following reasons:

1. Offense and taking the initiative are seen to have the advantage – certainly in perception and perhaps in fact.
2. It is hard to distinguish offense from defense, but also from espionage, subversion, sabotage, or contingency preparation for some future attack.
3. There are such low barriers to entry that many states (and non-state groups)

are involved, producing a more complex situation than the dyadic US-Soviet confrontation of the Cold War.

4. Capabilities are not just kept in arsenal but used – covertly and with perceptions of impunity.

5. The complexity of cyberspace means even expert practitioners cannot understand it well, leading to a significant chance of cascading effects, while its novelty and otherness mean policymakers face greater uncertainty, expanding the role of miscalculation and mistake.[74]

Systems dominated by positive feedback "are characterized by a self-impelled 'switch' or discontinuity between two extreme states."[75] Cyber conflict may be relatively stable now only because the tipping point has not yet been reached. After that, there may be a new, harsher reality – where there are more predators than prey – from which it will be hard to return.

It is understandable for the US Department of Defense to pursue offense, which seems to have the advantage, as the best defense. But the cost of the new strategy of persistent engagement to suppress modest operations today may be the creation of even more aggressive and brazen adversaries tomorrow.

The Role of Surprise

Surprise is an important factor in our analysis of situational cyber stability and worth exploring in more depth. There are no references to surprise in the most-recent US Department of Defense Cyber Strategy, nor in earlier versions dating back to 2006.[76] Military cyber doctrine has been similarly silent, other than unhelpfully saying that surprise is "germane."[77] The term is also lacking from UK cyber strategies and key NATO cyber documents.[78]

Scholars, fortunately, have covered surprise in more depth. Emily Goldman, John Surdu, and Michael Weaver were among the first to suggest that "surprise probably plays a larger role in cyberspace than in any other domain."[79] Erik Gartzke and Jon Lindsay concluded that in cyber conflict one element of surprise, that of deception, is more central than in other kinds of warfare: "attackers who fail to be deceptive will find that the vulnerabilities on which they depend will readily be patched and access vectors will be closed."[80] Ben Buchanan, among others, focuses less on the likelihood of surprise than on its impact. States hide their operations and capability, so to reduce surprise adversaries must use intrusive cyber operations of their own. Such defensive espionage operations might be misread as (or, indeed, repurposed for) a future surprise attack.[81]

James J. Wirtz unpacked the problematic but perennial concept of a cyber Pearl Harbor, which conjures "up compelling images of a 'bolt from the blue' surprise attack in American political and strategic culture," which might induce "catastrophic paralysis rendering [the United States] unable to develop a military or politically effective response in wartime."[82] Goldman, Surdu, and Warner argue that:

> Conditions could entice an adversary to strike a similar, disabling blow against the United States in the hope of a quick victory that presents America with an undesirable strategic *fait accompli* with the possibility of removing the United States as an active opponent while inflicting minimal casualties or damage to US forces . . . The burden of escalation would then shift to US policymakers, who would have to choose war over political compromise.[83]

Here a surprise cyber attack is not meant to be debilitating, but a sharp jab to see if the adversary is actually serious about the geopolitical issue at stake. An attacker could also use a sudden cyber raid to "keep the victim reeling when his plans dictate he should be reacting"[84] or alternatively as a *coup de main*, where the attack is the main effort to settle the military question. Other states would of course have a reciprocal fear of such attacks from the United States.

Lawrence Freedman suspects this is overblown: "there is the question of what happens after the first blow. How would this turn into a lasting political gain?" Cyber troops only occupy virtual territory. Therefore "the victims would be expected to respond, even as they struggled to get the lights back on and systems working," even with a "classical military response."[85]

Across this literature, "surprise" is often quite a broad and ill-defined term. We find five related meanings – different ways that "surprise" applies to situational cyber stability. First, deception, concealment, and trickery are central to almost all cyber operations.[86] Second, cyber capabilities lend themselves to surprise because they can be unexpected or unforeseen as a new technological capability; an unexpected target; an unforeseen intensity, impact, or timing; unforeseen trends; and unexpected means. Third, cyber conflict is frequently marked by being sudden or fast.[87] Fourth, they are frequently audacious or daring.[88] Lastly, but most important for stability, cyber capabilities are likely to be used to attack early in a conflict, even as an opening strike.[89] This is, after all, central to the Cyber Pearl Harbor concept.

Any theory or strategy which limits itself to a subset of these meanings of surprise is likely to fall short. Deception is more relevant to tactical cyber operations than escalation and stability. The middle three (unexpected or unforeseen, sudden or fast, audacious or daring) combine their effects to increase the danger of a Spark, the first category of instability in which competition and conflict in cyberspace are the root causes of an acute geopolitical crisis. The last (early use in conflict) drives the escalation inversion, where cyber capabilities can accelerate the rush to war.

In most of the major cyber incidents to date, cyber defenders knew that such attacks were possible. After each, there have been experts who said, "Well, this shouldn't be a surprise. I've been saying for years it was bound to happen sometime." Indeed, Miller believes "a cyber surprise attack would be the least surprising of all the unsurprising 'surprise attacks.'"[90] As in almost all such attacks, "the striking thing . . . is that in retrospect one can never quite understand" how the surprise ended up being quite so surprising.[91] Pearl Harbor was presaged by Port Arthur in 1904 and Taranto in 1940 – in each instance, naval forces in port were caught off-guard by a sudden assault. Even defenders who can extrapolate from past trends are caught out by the specifics: the who, when, where, how, and how bad.

Surprise in cyberspace will be more destabilizing than in other domains, because the characteristics of cyber operations lend themselves to surprising uses across all five meanings of surprise. They rely on deception and trickery; enable the unexpected and unforeseen; are sudden and fast, audacious and daring; and especially useful early in a conflict. There are also significant first-use pressures, as they may make a security dilemma more dangerous. Because cyber capabilities are not easily observable, it is extremely difficult to assess an adversary's order of battle or relative strengths, or to detect the equivalent of tanks massing on the border. Any particular attack might have an asymmetric impact, keeping defenders on perpetual and exhaustive high alert.

There is also a nearly limitless realm of the possible. Cyber capabilities can bypass fielded military forces to affect a nearly limitless range of an adversary's society, economy, and psychology. The pace of innovation and dependence creates countless paths to attain technical surprise and the use of "existing weapons and forces in new and different ways."[92] Even more so than in other kinds of intelligence warning, "there are few limits on what can be imagined" so defenders have less chance of assessing "where a blow may strike."[93] Because everything is interconnected and deeply dependent, cyber capabilities offer an attacker more opportunities to shift the correlation of forces in their favor. Some experts assert that "[c]yber attack does not threaten crippling surprise or existential risk," as past attacks only disrupted computer components which can be replaced relatively quickly.[94] Yet this misses the scope of potential future cyber attacks. With the Internet of Things and cyber-physical systems, attacks now impact electrical grids, pipelines, and dams, objects made of concrete and steel. The potential impact of and opportunities for surprise attacks will soar in unappreciated ways.

There is lastly a high potential for mistake and miscalculation. The novel nature of cyber attacks means adversaries are likelier to misjudge how their operations will be perceived by the recipient. The attacker might believe their attack is within norms, justified because it is a tit-for-tat reprisal, or similar to past operations which were met with indifference. Cyber attacks are likely to flop (or worse, messily cascade) if not backed by meticulous intelligence, careful planning, and extensive testing – though these only reduce, rather than eliminate, the risks. Mistakes can take the adversary (and indeed, the attacker) by surprise, as happened to the North Koreans and Russians with WannaCry and NotPetya.[95]

During the Cuban Missile Crisis, US Navy commanders "kept down" Soviet submarines with depth charges, even at the height of the crisis, because that was the established, doctrinally correct procedure.[96] This nonchalant aggression, based on a standard operating procedure approved in more peaceful times, complicated US-Soviet signaling and courted thermonuclear disaster – if a submarine crew felt war had already started and use their nuclear-tipped torpedoes. Before the peak of the next Cuban Missile Crisis-style emergency, each state will be aggressively burrowing into each other's networks for advantage. Those cyber teams – often proxies or only loosely under a command hierarchy – will have even more operational leeway to punch and counterpunch than the Navy commanders of the 1960s. A large number of tactical commanders, often not under strict command and control, can unleash dangerous cyber capabilities and might be itching for a fight more than their seniors. Any mistake, by any side, might prompt an escalation, unexpected and unwanted, by the leadership of either side. The tempo of the situation can take on a life of its own, leaving less room for strategic choice.

Lessons for Stability

During relative peacetime, it is likely that cyber capabilities will continue to operate as a pressure release. However, at some point in the future, cyber capabilities will be the root cause of a major geopolitical crisis, through mechanisms of Spark, Bring Out the Big Guns, or the Escalation Inversion. States will engage in riskier behavior during crises, either because the stakes of the game remove their earlier inhibitions or because they will act to get their cyber strike in before the real shooting starts. From this analysis, we draw important lessons for stability across three areas.

New Models Required for Stability in Cyberspace

Stability and escalation in cyberspace work differently. To adapt to cyber situational stability, the existing language and models used by the national security community and international relations are insufficient and should be avoided, treated cautiously, or reconceptualized altogether.

Do not rely on "ladders of escalation"

Herman Kahn introduced "ladders of escalation": a hierarchical ranking of a set of actions and responses to understand the relationship of conventional and nuclear war.[97] The concept does not translate well to cyber conflict. Indeed, as Rebecca Hersman has written, the entire "new era of strategic competition" will be less predictable due to "intrusive digital information technologies, advanced dual-use military capabilities, and diffused global power structures" which will open "alternative and less predictable escalatory pathways."[98] Cyberspace underpins every aspect of modern society and economy. Cyber-escalation ladders will have such narrow bounds that a cunning adversary can find plenty of asymmetric vectors of aggression. There is not just one ladder, but many – if adversaries cannot escalate on one, they can jump horizontally to another.

Reduce one-sided knowledge

During the Cold War, Soviet military moves and capabilities were closely guarded secrets in the West, but relative government transparency and a free press ensured that the United States and NATO were open books in comparison. In cyber conflict, attacks from China, Russia, Iran, and North Korea are regularly splashed across the news, while those of the United States remain heavily classified.

Of the roughly 1.2 million people in the US government who hold at least a top-secret security clearance, probably only a few dozen people – in the National Security Council, Department of Defense, and Intelligence Community – know the totality of US operations against a particular adversary and its own operations against the United States.[99] When there is a leak about US capabilities and operations, US government personnel with clearances are forbidden to look, meaning they may actually know less about US operations than their adversaries or the informed public.[100]

American adversaries end up in a similar place but by a different path, as their governments typically have less strict controls over their cyber forces.[101] Their leadership may only have a dim sense of what the malfeasance is being done ostensibly on their nation's behalf, but likely still have their own national security experts and cyber defenders regaling them with tales of horror of what the United States is suspected of doing.

Accordingly, it is especially hard to develop a balanced, objective, or common understanding of the rights and wrongs, moves, and countermoves. Cause and effect become nearly impossible to distinguish. There are few recommendations here other than unilateral ones. The national security community must declassify and break down compartments to combat cognitive bias. The current situation –yelping about the adversary's punches but classifying one's own – is not tenable, leading to a biased view of cyber conflict that is poisonous in an open democracy. The US transparency over Operation Glowing Symphony, the cyber campaign against Islamic State, is an astounding case study in openness.[102] But more should be done with respect to operations directed against state adversaries who can shoot back, like Iran.

Missing Mechanisms for Stability that Must be Developed

The risks of accidental or inadvertent escalation in situational cyber stability require an emphasis on signaling, firebreaks, and off-ramps to deal specifically with cyber conflict. These must feature more prominently within policies, strategies, and projects.

Lack of effective signalling

It is particularly difficult in the cyber arena to signal resolve, intent, or displeasure, because there are few accepted rules and no clear escalation ladder.[103] There is little direct communication between major rivals. The mechanisms are either low-level and technical or high-level and political. While useful, neither is routine, timely, or useful for operational signaling.

China's leadership is still incensed over the US indictment of five army cyber officers and has banned military-to-military contacts.[104] While the US–Russian "cyber hotline" does connect the White House with the Kremlin, this is useful only for sending political messages, not for managing fast-moving crises. To punish Russia's invasion of Ukraine, the US Congress outlawed the more operationally relevant military-to-military contact.[105] The United States does maintain direct links between the Department of Homeland Security and its Chinese and Russian counterparts, but these are more useful for exchanging technical information between computer emergency response teams.[106]

Even in the best case, the US government may know the signal it is sending but cannot be sure of the signal being received. Feedback to avert and minimise crises will be delayed, unclear, and not relayed directly between the key participants until new hotlines are created or substituted with back-channel conversations by former policymakers and flag-level officers. These efforts must be lavishly funded – and will still be comparatively cheap – as a powerful negative-feedback hedge to a more aggressive persistent engagement.

Difficulty reaching global norms

International norms of behavior for cyber conflict will always be problematic: general principles have huge loopholes and can be ignored by states seeking advantages, while specific norms can usually be circumvented. Many destabilising, brazen, and reckless attacks have not violated the letter of US norms.[107] Neither the North Korean attack on Sony Motion Pictures in 2014 nor the Russian interference in US elections in 2016 technically violated the stated US norm proscribing attacks on "critical infrastructure." In other cases, it seems the United States wants norms for thee but not for me. For example, Chinese espionage into the Office of Personnel Management should have been unobjectionable per US statements. It was, in the words of a former head of CIA and NSA, "honorable espionage work." as the office was a "legitimate foreign intelligence target."[108] But yet the Obama administration decided to "retaliate."[109]

We believe there is little prospect for norms that are specific, binding, and global. Policymakers should instead push for a set of norms that attains at least two of these criteria, while collectively building toward a solution with all three. For example, the 2019 "Joint Statement on Advancing Responsible State Behavior in Cyberspace" brought together twenty-seven like-minded Western democracies to call out specific norms and "work together on a voluntary basis to hold states accountable when they act contrary to this framework [because] there must be consequences for bad behavior in cyberspace."[110]

Defense is likely the best defense

There is certainly a role for the new US concepts of persistent engagement and defending forward. When Russian cyber operatives disrupt the opening ceremony of the Olympic games[111] and North Koreans conduct cyber bank heists around the world, it seems disingenuous to badmouth US countermeasures as being escalatory. It is destabilizing, however, to elevate the operational concept of persistent engagement to a strategy, given the likelihood of destabilizing positive feedback.

A better option is for policymakers to reverse attacker advantage though "leverage." The New York Cyber Task Force analyzed five decades of "technology, operational, and policy innovations which most advantage the defender" and concluded a more defense-advantage cyberspace is possible with technical solutions that can scale across the entire internet (rather than just one enterprise at a time) and fresh investment in operational and process innovations.[112]

If cyberspace were more advantageous to the defender, many of the most destabilizing dynamics would lose force with higher barriers of entry leading to fewer capable adversaries and fewer serious attacks. Since fewer attacks might be catastrophic, the pressure for counter-offensive operations would be diminished with more room for agreement and norm building.

Measurement

This chapter has summarized much research on cyber stability and instability, escalation and de-escalation. Almost nothing of this research is based on significant measurement of what actions lead to what responses over time. Previous work co-authored by one of us with Neil Jenkins has proposed several frameworks to measure if persistent engagement is correlated with changes in adversary behavior:

> The advocates of persistent engagement and deterrence suggest it should have a substantial, perhaps unprecedented impact on adversary behavior. Anything other than a correspondingly strong reduction [in such behavior] suggests that the policy may not be working as intended. If the trend significantly worsens, it may be that a hypothesis that the new policy is inciting adversaries is a better fit to the curve.[113]

Such measurement need only be concerned with the direction and magnitude of the vector: is adversary behavior changing – or cyberspace becoming more stable or instable – and how fast? Categorizing and tracking this over time would be inexpensive and a worthy investment.

Hedge against Cyber Surprise

Military surprise in the initial phase of war usually succeeds, especially against the United States.[114] Our colleague Dick Betts wrote thirty-five years ago: "Some other problems may be more important [than preparing for surprise attack] but most of them are better understood."[115] Attention from academics, military professionals, intelligence officials, and policymakers to understand and counter the role of surprise cyber attack will have a low cost but high payoff.

The detection and attribution gaps

During the Cold War, both sides were wary of the danger of a surprise nuclear attack. It was stabilizing for each side to have capabilities to rapidly and reliably detect missile launches. The nuclear warfighters of the Strategic Air Command (and presumably their brethren in the Soviet Union) may not have liked the reduction of operational surprise, but the need for stability meant policymakers had an easy time overruling their concerns. Such "national technical means" were critical to stability and arms control and both nations agreed to have "open skies" to one another, allowed observation of major exercises, and reported major troop presence and movements in Europe. It was then and is still now stabilizing for each nation to possess a secure second-strike capability, as neither nation need worry quite as much about a debilitating first strike.

None of these stabilising factors applies to cyber conflict. The value of cyber operations, and the critical need for them to stay unobserved and covert, means steps to improve mutual visibility are impractical. Because the primary use of cyber capabilities today is espionage, mutually beneficial surveillance is impossible, leaving weaker powers feeling distinctly insecure. For example, one reason China may have difficulty agreeing to cyber norms is China's weak attribution capabilities vis-à-vis the perceived strength of the US government and commercial intelligence expertise.[116]

Here it is far from clear what practical recommendations to make. It is unthinkable that the United States might, in the name of stability, assist China to boost its attribution capabilities to better detect US cyber operations. Nor is it feasible for Russia and the United States develop virtual "open skies" to freely transit each other's networks.

Reduce the probability of surprise

The United States must act to reduce the probability of surprise. Increased intelligence and warning are useful but not game-changers unless the intelligence is particularly exquisite, such as persistent access to adversaries' networks. Such dominance is expensive, fleeting, and adds its own destabilizing pressure. More useful gains can be had by expanding defenders' imaginations and experience through exercises, experimentation, and curiosity about future forms of cyber conflict.[117]

US and allied militaries must recognize that an initial surprise attack is both likely to occur and likely to succeed. And since non-state actors "possess a greater range of capabilities than at any time in history," and cyber security and technology companies routinely and agilely respond to critical threats, those strategies and doctrines must include cooperative response to deal with surprise.[118] If the United States wants stability, and not merely superiority, then Russia and China (and, to a lesser degree, Iran and North Korea) should also have less fear of a surprise cyber attack.

Reduce the impact of surprise

The United States and its cyber adversaries work hard to avoid surprise attacks while simultaneously maximizing their own ability to carry out surprise attacks on foes. This is a solid policy in a stable environment but exceptionally risky in an unstable one. Perhaps the only way to meaningfully slice though this dilemma is through the "defense is the best defense" approach discussed above. The United States, the European Union, and China could cooperate to change the physics of the internet through new standards and engineering. This would stabilize the entire system, reducing the ability to surprise and the gains to be had. It would reduce their own offensive capabilities some but potentially drastically reduce those of criminal actors, Iran, North Korea, and third-tier adversary powers.

Secure cyber, space, and strategic systems

The most dangerous temptation is for a state to believe it can blind or disarm its rival's cyber capabilities, space systems, or nuclear weapons/command and control. States must spend resources to secure those systems most essential to great-power deterrence and strategic stability. The US Defense Science Board proposed a cyber-resilient "thin-line" of strategic forces to reduce the impact of surprise attack.[119] As Jim Miller shared with us, "cyber-resilience may be as important as dispersing bombers and deploying Polaris were in the early days of the Cold War."[120] Securing even a slice of space-based intelligence and warning systems reduces the temptation for a surprise attack. Space, strategic, and cyber forces do not need to be 100 percent resilient, just secure enough that an attacker could not have a realistic hope of a disarming attack.

Next Steps for Situational Cyber Stability

In the film comedy *Zoolander*, a group of not-too-bright male models have a gasoline fight at a filling station. Everyone watching is in on the joke: it is only a matter of time before one of these imbeciles, oblivious to the danger, lights a match. The punchline, a massive fireball, is a surprise to no one.

We hope this analogy to cyber conflict remains a silly one – there is no comparison to states playing a dangerous game, soaked in vulnerabilities, and complacent that no one will light up. But the dynamics of cyber conflict drive nearly all states to be greedy, expansionist powers. Every adversary is deeply vulnerable and obeying broadly the same imperatives – to collect intelligence, lay the groundwork for future attacks, and seize terrain in cyberspace to contest an adversary's operations – and assuming all others are maximally doing the same.[121] This competition is not carried out over physical territory but over network infrastructure and information, owned by the private sector and the lifeblood of modern economy and society. This drives positive feedback, possibly spiraling out of the willful control of the participants.[122]

If states are frustrated in their ability to achieve meaningful strategic gains, this may just fuel additional escalation in cyber capabilities. Each side will go back to their legislatures or paymasters, asking for a larger budget and looser rules, pointing to the other side's newly aggressive forward defense as proof of their intransigence. Since each side views the others as aggressive, there is "no reason to examine one's own policies," nor is there a "need to make special efforts to demonstrate willingness to reach reasonable settlements."[123] If concessions will not alter the other's actions, then restraint can seem a fool's choice – until everyone is soaking in gasoline.

Stability and restraint are both unlikely unless adversaries seek stability and act with restraint. This will be particularly hard now that the participants are engaged in relentless, persistent engagements. Conflict can lead to heightened emotions, unwillingness to compromise, and self-righteousness.[124] The United States believes, probably rightly, that it has showed restraint by eschewing large-scale disruptive operations or espionage for commercial gain, and it sets great store in how this restraint highlights US interests for a peaceful cyberspace. But these self-imposed limits have been overshadowed by near-limitless political-military espionage. American claims that its pervasive, persistent access on the global network is "just espionage" fall flat. Adversaries (and allies) could be forgiven for doubting US restraint, given their existential dependence on technology largely invented and created in a country seeking to bask in lasting cyber pre-eminence.

The technology community has been concerned about balkanization of the internet – what was once unified is now split by national borders like China's Great Firewall.[125] But cyberspace is also being balkanized in another sense, in that those involved are incapable of forgetting or forgiving insults they have suffered from others and blind to those they themselves have inflicted. Such long and selective memories are likely to be as destabilizing in the virtual world as in the real. For this and related reasons, "states' strategic responses should not be cyber operations," but rather sanctions, indictments, trade and immigration restrictions, or other levers of power.[126]

In terms of situational cyber awareness, the long-term goal might go beyond stability to order – order that players accept out of their own interest rather than through hegemonic pressure. For Russia and China to buy into such an order, it would need to include limits on cross-border flows of information and internet content. Such controls are hard to reconcile with traditional liberal democratic practice, though the transatlantic political pressure on companies like Facebook and Twitter to better police hate speech, terrorists, trolls, and foreign political meddling may make such a grand bargain more palatable in future.

If the United States wants a universal order, accepted by friends and rivals alike, it will have to make very serious compromises. If US decision-makers decide, either positively or through inaction, that they are unwilling to make such compromises, then for the duration of the digital age the United States will have to enforce its preferences through power. Many, and not just hawks, will accept this bargain gladly. But if cyberspace encourages positive feedback, it is unlikely to survive the conflict in anything like its form today. At the very least, the United States must acknowledge that adversaries see US actions and preferences as destabilizing – at least to their own domestic order. The aim for US policy should not only be combating adversaries but preventing destabilization itself. Stability should be the goal and not a side benefit expected from unending confrontation.

In many ways, cyber capabilities possess dynamics opposite to those of nuclear weapons.[127] By radically decreasing the cost of war, even to a state with significant relative disadvantages, cyber capabilities can drastically change world politics.

Notes

1. David E. Sanger and Nicole Perlroth, "U.S. Said to Find North Korea Ordered Cyberattack on Sony," *The New York Times*, December 17, 2014, World section: https://www.nytimes.com/2014/12/18/world /asia/us-links-north-korea-to-sony-hacking.html

2. Lily Hay Newman, "The Ransomware Meltdown Experts Warned About Is Here," *Wired*, May 12, 2017: https://www.wired.com/2017 /05/ransomware-meltdown-experts-warned/

3. Kelly Jackson Higgins, "Lessons From The Ukraine Electric Grid Hack," *Dark Reading*, March 18, 2016: https://www.darkreading.com/vulnerab ilities---threats/lessons-from-the-ukraine-electric-grid-hack/d/d-id/13 24743

4. Office of the Director of National Intelligence, "Background to 'Assessing Russian Activities and Intentions in Recent US Elections: The Analytic Process and Cyber Incident Attribution,'" January 2017: https://www .dni.gov/files/documents/ICA_2017_01.pdf

5. Ellen Nakashima, "Russian Military Was Behind 'NotPetya' Cyberattack in Ukraine, CIA Concludes," *The Washington Post*, January 12, 2018: https://www.washingtonpost.com/world/national-security/russian-mi

litary-was-behind-notpetya-cyberattack-in-ukraine-cia-concludes/2018
/01/12/048d8506-f7ca-11e7-b34a-b85626af34ef_story.html

6. Jason Healey, "Cyber Warfare in the 21st Century: Threats, Challenges, and Opportunities," § House Armed Services Committee (2017): https://docs.house.gov/meetings/AS/AS00/20170301/105607/HHRG-115-AS00-Bio-HealeyJ-20170301-U1.pdf

7. The main, publicly known case of a kinetic response to cyber attacks is the Israeli Defense Forces (IDF) attack on a Hamas hacking cell. Hamas is a non-state group and the IDF provided warning so that the building was empty when hit. See Lily Hay Newman, "What Israel's Strike on Hamas Hackers Means For Cyberwar," *Wired*, May 6, 2019: https://www.wired.com/story/israel-hamas-cyberattack-air-strike-cyberwar/

8. Julian E. Barnes and Thomas Gibbons-Neff, "U.S. Carried Out Cyberattacks on Iran," *The New York Times*, June 22, 2019, US section: https://www.nytimes.com/2019/06/22/us/politics/us-iran-cyber-attacks.html (accessed February 7, 2020).

9. Robert Jervis, *System Effects: Complexity in Political and Social Life* (Princeton, NJ: Princeton University Press, 1999).

10. Thomas C. Schelling, *Arms and Influence* (New Haven, CT: Yale University Press, 1966).

11. Robert McNamara, "Address by Secretary of Defense McNamara at the Ministerial Meeting of the North Atlantic Council," 1962.

12. Martin C. Libicki, "Correlations Between Cyberspace Attacks and Kinetic Attacks," in T. Jančárková, L. Lindström, I. Signoretti, and G. Visky Tolga (eds.), *Proceedings of 2020 12th International Conference on Cyber Conflict, "20/20 Vision: The Next Decade"* (2020), 15.

13. US Cyber Command, "Achieve and Maintain Cyberspace Superiority: Command Vision for US Cyber Command," March 2018: https://assets.documentcloud.org/documents/4419681/Command-Vision-for-USCYBERCOM-23-Mar-18.pdf

14. Michael P. Fischerkeller and Richard P. Harknett, "What Is Agreed Competition in Cyberspace?," *Lawfare*, February 19, 2019: https://www.lawfareblog.com/what-agreed-competition-cyberspace

15. Jason Healey, "The Implications of Persistent (and Permanent) Engagement in Cyberspace," *Journal of Cybersecurity* 5, no. 1 (2019): tyz008, https://doi.org/10.1093/cybsec/tyz008

16. US Cyber Command, "Achieve and Maintain Cyberspace Superiority: Command Vision for US Cyber Command."

17. Healey, "The Implications of Persistent (and Permanent) Engagement in Cyberspace."

18. Erica D. Borghard and Shawn W. Lonergan, "The Logic of Coercion in Cyberspace," *Security Studies* 26, no. 3 (July 3, 2017): 452–481, https://doi.org/10.1080/09636412.2017.1306396

19. Aaron F. Brantly, Nerea M. Cal, and Devlin P. Winkelstein, "Defending the Borderland: Ukrainian Military Experiences with IO, Cyber, and EW," 2017: https://vtechworks.lib.vt.edu/handle/10919/81979; Nadiya Kostyuk and Yuri M. Zhukov, "Invisible Digital Front: Can Cyber Attacks Shape Battlefield Events?," *Journal of Conflict Resolution* 63, no. 2 (2019): 317–347, https://doi.org/10.1177/0022002717737138

20. Rebecca Slayton, "What Is the Cyber Offense-Defense Balance? Conceptions, Causes, and Assessment," *International Security* 41, no. 3 (2017): 72–109, https://doi.org/10.1162/ISEC_a_00267; Jon R. Lindsay and Erik Gartzke, "Coercion through Cyberspace: The Stability-Instability Paradox Revisited," in *Coercion: The The Power to Hurt in International Politics*, ed. Kelly M. Greenhill and Peter Krause (New York: Oxford University Press, 2018).

21. Jason Healey, "A Fierce Domain: Conflict in Cyberspace, 1986 to 2012," Vienna, VA: Cyber Conflict Studies Association, 2013.

22. Libicki, "Correlations Between Cyberspace Attacks and Kinetic Attacks."

23. Brandon Valeriano, Benjamin Jensen, and Ryan Maness, *Cyber Strategy: The Evolving Character of Power and Coercion*, Oxford Scholarship Online (Oxford University Press, 2018), 76.

24. Josh Rovner, "Cyber War as an Intelligence Contest," *War on the Rocks*, September 16, 2019: https://warontherocks.com/2019/09/cyber-war-as-an-intelligence-contest/ (accessed February 5, 2020).

25. Barnes and Gibbons-Neff, "U.S. Carried Out Cyberattacks on Iran."

26. Julian Barnes, David Sanger, Ronen Bergman, and Lara Jakes, "As U.S. Increases Pressure, Iran Adheres to Toned-Down Approach," *The New York Times*, September 19, 2020: https://www.nytimes.com/2020/09/19/us/politics/us-iran-election.html

27. Benjamin Jensen and Brandon Valeriano, "What do We Know About Cyber Escalation? Observations from Simulations and Surveys," *Atlantic Council*, November 2019: https://www.atlanticcouncil.org/wp-content/uploads/2019/11/What_do_we_know_about_cyber_escalation_.pdf (accessed February 5, 2020).

28. Michael P. Fischerkeller and Richard J. Harknett, "Deterrence Is Not a Credible Strategy for Cyberspace," *Orbis* 61, no. 3 (2017): 381–393, https://doi.org/10.1016/j.orbis.2017.05.003

29. Fischerkeller and Harknett, "What Is Agreed Competition in Cyberspace?"

30. Erica D Borghard and Shawn W. Lonergan, "Cyber Operations as Imperfect Tools of Escalation," *Strategic Studies Quarterly* 13, no. 3 (2019): https://www.airuniversity.af.edu/Portals/10/SSQ/documents/Volume-13_Issue-3/Borghard.pdf (accessed February 5, 2020).

31. Sarah Kreps and Jacquelyn Schneider, "Escalation Firebreaks in the Cyber, Conventional, and Nuclear Domains: Moving beyond Effects-Based Logics," *Journal of Cybersecurity* 5, no. 1 (2019): https://doi.org/10.1093/cybsec/tyz007

32. Ben Buchanan, *The Cybersecurity Dilemma: Hacking, Trust and Fear between Nations* (Oxford University Press, 2017), 29: https://doi.org/10.1093/acprof:oso/9780190665012.001.0001

33. Libicki, "Correlations Between Cyberspace Attacks and Kinetic Attacks."

34. Healey, "A Fierce Domain: Conflict in Cyberspace, 1986 to 2012."

35. Sarah Payne White, "Subcultural Influence on Military Innovation: The Development of U.S. Military Cyber Doctrine," Dissertation, July 2019: https://dash.harvard.edu/bitstream/handle/1/42013038/WHITE-DISSERTATION-2019.pdf?sequence=1&isAllowed=y (accessed May 30, 2020).

36. Eligible Receiver was a major, no-notice cyber exercise run by the Joint Staff in the autumn of 1997 which alarmed the US military to the possibilities of a debilitating attack on the nation. Only a few months after that exercise, in February 1998, the US Air Force detected a string of intrusions possibly coming from Saddam Hussein's Iraq. See Healey, "A Fierce Domain: Conflict in Cyberspace, 1986 to 2012."

37. Moonlight Maze was a campaign of espionage against the US Department of Defense in the late 1990s and early 2000s, eventually traced back to Russia. The response, led by the FBI, was the first early test of the new military cyber commands. See Healey, "A Fierce Domain: Conflict in Cyberspace, 1986 to 2012."

38. US Strategic Command Public Affairs, "Joint Task Force – Computer Network Operations," press release, February 2003: http://www.iwar.org.uk/iwar/resources/JIOC/computer-network-operations.htm

39. Josh Rogin, "NSA Chief: Cybercrime Constitutes the 'Greatest Transfer of Wealth in History' – Foreign Policy," July 9, 2012: https://foreignpolicy.com/2012/07/09/nsa-chief-cybercrime-constitutes-the-greatest-transfer-of-wealth-in-history/

40. Healey, "A Fierce Domain: Conflict in Cyberspace, 1986 to 2012."

41. Keith B. Alexander, "Building a New Command in Cyberspace,"

Strategic Studies Quarterly 5, no. 2 (Summer 2011): 3–12, https://www.js tor.org/stable/26270554?seq=2#metadata_info_tab_contents

42. Iranian denial of service attacks: Nicole Perlroth and Quentin Hardy, "Bank Hacking Was the Work of Iranians, Officials Say," *The New York Times*, January 8, 2013, Technology section: https://www.nytimes.com /2013/01/09/technology/online-banking-attacks-were-work-of-iran -us-officials-say.html; North Korea Sony attack: Sanger and Perlroth, "U.S. Said to Find North Korea Ordered Cyberattack on Sony"; Kelly Jackson Higgins, "Lessons From The Ukraine Electric Grid Hack"; Olympic Ceremony hack: Andy Greenberg, "Inside Olympic Destroyer, the Most Deceptive Hack in History," *Wired*, October 17, 2019: https:// www.wired.com/story/untold-story-2018-olympics-destroyer-cyberat tack/

43. Mark Pomerleau, "Here's How DoD Organizes Its Cyber Warriors," *Fifth Domain*, September 13, 2018: https://www.fifthdomain.com/work force/career/2017/07/25/heres-how-dod-organizes-its-cyber-warriors/

44. Ministerie van Defensie, "Defence Cyber Command – Cyber Security – Defensie.Nl," onderwerp (Ministerie van Defensie, March 30, 2017): https://english.defensie.nl/topics/cyber-security/cyber-command

45. Cyber Security Intelligence, "The British Cyber Command," January 22, 2020: https://www.cybersecurityintelligence.com/blog/the-british -cyber-command-4748.html

46. Christina Mackenzie, "France's New Cyber Defense 'Conductor' Talks Retaliation, Protecting Industry," *Fifth Domain*, September 30, 2019: https://www.fifthdomain.com/international/2019/09/30/frances-new -cyber-defense-conductor-talks-retaliation-protecting-industry/

47. Prashanth Parameswaran, "What's Behind Singapore's New Integrated Military Cyber Command Objective?," *The Diplomat*, March 10, 2020: https://thediplomat.com/2020/03/whats-behind-singapores-new-integ rated-military-cyber-command-objective/

48. Prashanth Parameswaran, "What's Behind Vietnam's New Military Cyber Command?," *The Diplomat*, January 12, 2018: https://thediplo mat.com/2018/01/whats-behind-vietnams-new-military-cyber-com mand/

49. Ludwig Leinhos, "The German Cyber and Information Domain Service as a Key Part of National Security Policy," April 1, 2017: http://www .ethikundmilitaer.de/en/full-issues/20191-conflict-zone-cyberspace/le inhos-the-german-cyber-and-information-domain-service-as-a-key-part -of-national-security-policy/

50. Alexander, "Building a New Command in Cyberspace."

51. Valeriano et al., *Cyber Strategy: The Evolving Character of Power and Coercion*, 70.

52. Paul M. Nakasone, "A Cyber Force for Persistent Operations," *Joint Force Quarterly* 92, no. 22 (2019): https://ndupress.ndu.edu/Media/News/News-Article-View/Article/1736950/a-cyber-force-for-persistent-operations/

53. Andrea Shalal-Esa, "Iran Strengthened Cyber Capabilities after Stuxnet: U.S. General," *Reuters*, January 18, 2013: https://www.reuters.com/article/us-iran-usa-cyber-idUSBRE90G1C420130118

54. Michael Isikoff, "Chinese Hacked Obama, McCain Campaigns, Took Internal Documents, Officials Say," *NBC News.com*, June 10, 2013: http://www.nbcnews.com/id/52133016/t/chinese-hacked-obama-mccain-campaigns-took-internal-documents-officials-say/; Jeff Stein, "Exclusive: How Russian Hackers Attacked the 2008 Obama Campaign," *Newsweek*, May 12, 2017: https://www.newsweek.com/russia-hacking-trump-clinton-607956 (accessed June 7, 2020).

55. Director of National Intelligence James R. Clapper, "Worldwide Threat Assessment of the US Intelligence Community," § Senate Armed Services Committee (2015): https://www.armed-services.senate.gov/imo/media/doc/Clapper_02-26-15.pdf

56. Ben Buchanan cites Canadian documents which confirms they "acquire as many new [Operational Relay Boxes] as possible in as many non 5-Eyes countries as possible"; Buchanan, *The Cybersecurity Dilemma*, 48.

57. Zaid Shoorbajee, "Playing Nice? FireEye CEO Says U.S. Malware Is More Restrained than Adversaries," *CyberScoop*, June 1, 2018: https://www.cyberscoop.com/kevin-mandia-fireeye-u-s-malware-nice/

58. Richard Harknett, "United States Cyber Command's New Vision: What It Entails and Why It Matters," *Lawfare*, March 23, 2018: https://www.lawfareblog.com/united-states-cyber-commands-new-vision-what-it-entails-and-why-it-matters

59. Admiral Michael S. Rogers, "Statement of Admiral Michael S. Rogers Commander United States Cyber Command Before the Senate Armed Services Committee," § Senate Armed Services Committee (2015): https://fas.org/irp/congress/2015_hr/031915rogers.pdf (accessed May 11, 2020).

60. Office of the Director of National Intelligence, "Background to 'Assessing Russian Activities and Intentions in Recent US Elections'"; Ellen Nakashima, "U.S. Cyber Command Operation Disrupted Internet Access of Russian Troll Factory on Day of 2018 Midterms," *The Washington Post*, February 27, 2019: https://www.washingtonpost.com

/world/national-security/us-cyber-command-operation-disrupted-inter
net-access-of-russian-troll-factory-on-day-of-2018-midterms/2019
/02/26/1827fc9e-36d6-11e9-af5b-b51b7ff322e9_story.html (accessed
February 6, 2020).

61. Adam Segal, "What Briefing Chinese Officials On Cyber Really
Accomplishes," *Forbes*, April 7, 2014: https://www.forbes.com/sites
/adamsegal/2014/04/07/what-briefing-chinese-officials-on-cyber-real
ly-accomplishes/

62. Adam Segal, *The Hacked World Order: How Nations Fight, Trade, Maneuver,
and Manipulate in the Digital Age* (New York: PublicAffairs, 2017), 143–
151; off-the-record conversation at Munich with European heads of state
and members of parliament, and other policymakers, February 2014.

63. Zach Dorfman et al., "Secret Trump Order Gives CIA More Powers to
Launch Cyberattacks," *Yahoo News*, July 15, 2020: https://news.yahoo
.com/secret-trump-order-gives-cia-more-powers-to-launch-cyberattac
ks-090015219.html

64. US Bureau of Economic Analysis, "Digital Economy Accounted for 6.9
Percent of GDP in 2017," US Bureau of Economic Analysis, April 4,
2019: https://www.bea.gov/news/blog/2019-04-04/digital-economy
-accounted-69-percent-gdp-2017 (accessed February 7, 2020).

65. Draft paper, June 2020.

66. Fischerkeller and Harknett, "What Is Agreed Competition in
Cyberspace?"

67. Borghard and Lonergan, "Cyber Operations as Imperfect Tools of
Escalation."

68. Erik Gartzke and Jon Lindsay, "Thermonuclear Cyberwar," *Journal
of Cybersecurity* 3, no. 1 (2017): 37–48, https://academic.oup.com
/cybersecurity/article/3/1/37/2996537

69. Robert Jervis, "Cooperation under the Security Dilemma," *World Politics*
30, no. 2 (1978): 167–214, https://doi.org/10.2307/2009958

70. Mark Milley, "Gen Milley Chairman Confirmation Testimony,"
§ Senate Armed Services Committee (2019): https://www.c-span.org/vi
deo/?c4806722/user-clip-gen-milley-chairman-confirmation-testimony

71. Jason Healey, "Getting the Drop in Cyberspace," *Lawfare*, August 19,
2019: https://www.lawfareblog.com/getting-drop-cyberspace

72. James N. Miller Jr. and Richard Fontaine, "A New Era In U.S.-Russian
Strategic Stability," *Center for a New American Security*, September 2019:
48, https://www.cnas.org/publications/reports/a-new-era-in-u-s-russi
an-strategic-stability

73. Jervis, "Cooperation Under the Security Dilemma."

74. As Martin Libicki put it, "Normal human intuition about how things work in the physical world does not always translate". From Martin C. Libicki, *Crisis and Escalation in Cyberspace* (Santa Monica, CA: RAND, Project Air Force, 2012): https://www.rand.org/pubs/monographs/MG 1215.html

75. William Gosling, *Helmsmen and Heroes: Control Theory as a Key to Past and Future* (London: Weidenfeld and Nicolson, 1994).

76. Department of Defense, "The Department of Defense Cyber Strategy," 2015: https://archive.defense.gov/home/features/2015/0415_cyber-stra tegy/final_2015_dod_cyber_strategy_for_web.pdf; Office of the Chairman of the Joint Chiefs of Staff, "National Military Strategy for Cyberspace Operations (U)," *Homeland Security Digital Library*, November 30, 2006: https://www.hsdl.org/?abstract&did=

77. Joint Chiefs of Staff, "Joint Publication 3-12(R) Cyberspace Operations," February 5, 2013: https://www.hsdl.org/?view&did=758858

78. UK Ministry of Defence, "Cyber Primer (2nd Edition)" (July 2016): 100, https://assets.publishing.service.gov.uk/government/uploads/syst em/uploads/attachment_data/file/549291/20160720-Cyber_Primer_ed _2_secured.pdf; NATO, "NATO Cyber Defense," December 2017: https://www.nato.int/nato_static_fl2014/assets/pdf/pdf_2017_11/2017 1128_1711-factsheet-cyber-defence-en.pdf.

79. Emily O. Goldman, John Surdu, and Michael Warner, "The Cyber Pearl Harbor: The Attacker's Perspective," in *Cyber Analogies*, ed. Emily O. Goldman and John Arquilla (Monterey, California, Naval Postgraduate School, 2014), 29, https://apps.dtic.mil/dtic/tr/fulltext/u2/a601645.pdf

80. Erik Gartzke and Jon R. Lindsay, "Weaving Tangled Webs: Offense, Defense, and Deception in Cyberspace," *Security Studies* 24, no.2 (April 3, 2015): 316–348, https://doi.org/10.1080/09636412.2015.1038188, pp. 329, 326.

81. Buchanan, *The Cybersecurity Dilemma*, 123–130.

82. James J. Wirtz, "The Cyber Pearl Harbor," *Intelligence and National Security* 32, no. 6 (2017): 7, https://doi.org/10.1080/026 84527.2017.1294379

83. Goldman, Surdu, and Warner, "The Cyber Pearl Harbor," 26.

84. Richard K. Betts, *Surprise Attack: Lessons for Defense Planning* (Washington, DC: Brookings Institution), 5.

85. Lawrence Freedman, "Beyond Surprise Attack," *The US Army War College Quarterly* 47, no. 2 (Summer 2017): 12.

86. An attacker's infrastructure will be scattered around the world, in other jurisdictions, obscuring the ultimate "return address." It is relatively easy

to hide behind proxy groups and there is an entire class of attacks known as Trojan Horses.

87. Though planning a sophisticated campaign may take months or years, individual cyber operations occur at "network speed" or at or near the "speed of light." The 2003 SQL Slammer worm spread so quickly that only fifteen minutes after infecting its first computer, "huge sections of the Internet began to wink out of existence." Paul Boutin, "Slammed!", *Wired*, July 1, 2003: https://www.wired.com/2003/07/slammer/

88. The US government simply did not believe "the Russians would dare to leap the Atlantic and apply" their cyber techniques "to an election in the United States." David E. Sanger, *The Perfect Weapon: War, Sabotage, and Fear in the Cyber Age* (New York: Crown Publishing Group), xviii.

89. Israel apparently used cyber means to hide their strike aircraft from Syrian radars during Operation Orchard in 2007. The Department of Defense has reported that Chinese military writings "advocate targeting an adversary's C2 [command and control] and logistics networks to affect its ability to operate during the early stages of conflict". Fred M. Kaplan, *Dark Territory: The Secret History of Cyber War* (New York: Simon & Schuster, 2016), 160–161. Office of the Secretary of Defense, "Annual Report to Congress: Military and Security Developments Involving the People's Republic of China 2016," April 26, 2016: https://dod.defense.gov/Portals/1/Documents/pubs/2016%20China%20Military%20Power%20Report.pdf

90. James N. Miller, personal communication to the authors, May 29, 2020.

91. Ephraim Kam, *Surprise Attack: The Victim's Perspective* (Cambridge, MA: Harvard University Press, 2004).

92. Michael S. Goodman, "Applying the Historical Lessons of Surprise Attack to the Cyber Domain: The Example of the United Kingdom," in *Cyber Analogies*, ed. Emily O. Goldman and John Arquilla (Monterey, California, Naval Postgraduate School, 2014), 7, https://apps.dtic.mil/dtic/tr/fulltext/u2/a601645.pdf

93. Robert Jervis, *Why Intelligence Fails: Lessons from the Iranian Revolution and the Iraq War* (Ithaca, NY: Cornell University Press, 2010), 129.

94. James Andrew Lewis, *Rethinking Cybersecurity: Strategy, Mass Effect, and States* (Washington, DC: Center for Strategic & International Studies; Lanham, MD: Rowman & Littlefield, 2018): https://csis-prod.s3.amazonaws.com/s3fs-public/publication/180108_Lewis_ReconsideringCybersecurity_Web.pdf?ftGLYwJNUgSldpxN3g2K3g06kKVxicYq

95. Nakashima, "Russian Military Was Behind 'NotPetya' Cyberattack in Ukraine, CIA Concludes."

96. Graham Allison and Philip Zelikow, "Essence of Decision," *Foreign Policy*, no. 114 (1999): 121, pp. 234–237, https://doi.org/10.2307/114 9596

97. Nadiya Kostyuk, Scott Powell, and Matt Skach, "Determinants of the Cyber Escalation Ladder," *The Cyber Defense Review* 3, no. 1 (Spring 2018): 123–134.

98. Rebecca Hersman, "Wormhole Escalation in the New Nuclear Age," *Texas National Security Review* (Summer 2020): http://tnsr.org/2020/07 /wormhole-escalation-in-the-new-nuclear-age/ (accessed September 2, 2020).

99. National Counterintelligence and Security Center, Office of the Director of National Intelligence, "Fiscal Year 2017 Annual Report on Security Clearance Determinations," August 2018: https://www.dni .gov/files/NCSC/documents/features/20180827-security-clearance-de terminations.pdf

100. Ryan Gallagher, "U.S. Military Bans The Intercept," *The Intercept* (blog), August 20, 2014: https://theintercept.com/2014/08/20/u-s-military-ba ns-the-intercept/ (accessed May 11, 2020).

101. Iran and Russia, for example, extensively use proxies. See Tim Maurer, *Cyber Mercenaries: The State, Hackers, and Power* (Cambridge: Cambridge University Press, 2018).

102. Dina Temple-Raston, "How the U.S. Hacked ISIS," *National Public Radio*, September 26, 2019: https://www.npr.org/2019/09/26/763545 811/how-the-u-s-hacked-isis

103. See Ben Buchanan, *The Hacker and the State: Cyber Attacks and the New Normal of Geopolitics* (Cambridge, MA: Harvard University Press, 2020); especially Chapter 9, for more on the difficulties, using the Russian disruption of Ukrainian electrical grid as a case study.

104. From the author's experience in discussions with Chinese officials in track 1.5 discussions led by the Center for Strategy and International Security.

105. United States Congress, National Defense Authorization Act for Fiscal Year 2016, Section 1246, "Limitation on Military Cooperation Between the United States and the Russian Federation": https://www.govinfo .gov/content/pkg/PLAW-114publ92/html/PLAW-114publ92.htm

106. Sean Gallagher, "US, Russia to Install 'Cyber-Hotline' to Prevent Accidental Cyberwar," *Ars Technica*, June 18, 2013: https://arstechnica .com/information-technology/2013/06/us-russia-to-install-cyber-hotli ne-to-prevent-accidental-cyberwar/

107. Jason Healey and Tim Maurer, "What It'll Take to Forge Peace in

Cyberspace," *CSM Passcode*, March 20, 2017: https://www.csmonitor
.com/World/Passcode/Passcode-Voices/2017/0320/What-it-ll-take-to
-forge-peace-in-cyberspace

108. General Michael Hayden quoted by Julian Hattem, "Ex-CIA Head:
'Shame on Us' for Allowing Government Hack," *The Hill*, June 16,
2015: https://thehill.com/policy/national-security/245101-ex-cia-head
-shame-on-us-for-allowing-government-hack (accessed May 11, 2020).

109. David E. Sanger, "U.S. Decides to Retaliate Against China's Hacking,"
The New York Times, July 31, 2015, https://www.nytimes.com/2015
/08/01/world/asia/us-decides-to-retaliate-against-chinas-hacking.html

110. US Department of State, "Joint Statement on Advancing Responsible
State Behavior in Cyberspace," September 23, 2019: https://www.state
.gov/joint-statement-on-advancing-responsible-state-behavior-in-cyber
space/ (accessed May 6, 2020).

111. Russia attacks Olympic games: Greenberg, "Inside Olympic Destroyer,
the Most Deceptive Hack in History"; North Korean heists: Ben
Buchanan, "How North Korean Hackers Rob Banks Around the
World," February 28, 2020: https://www.wired.com/story/how-north
-korea-robs-banks-around-world/ (accessed May 11, 2020).

112. New York Cyber Task Force, "Building a Defensible Cyberspace,"
September 28, 2017: https://sipa.columbia.edu/ideas-lab/techpolicy/bu
ilding-defensible-cyberspace

113. Jason Healey and Neil Jenkins, "Rough-and-Ready: A Policy Framework
to Determine If Cyber Deterrence Is Working or Failing," in *2019 11th
International Conference on Cyber Conflict (CyCon)* (2019 11th International
Conference on Cyber Conflict, Tallinn, Estonia: IEEE, 2019): 1–20,
https://doi.org/10.23919/CYCON.2019.8756890

114. Betts, *Surprise Attack*, 4.

115. Betts, *Surprise Attack*, 3.

116. Scott Warren Harold, Martin C. Libicki, and Astrid Stuth Cevallos,
"Getting to Yes with China in Cyberspace," (Santa Monica, CA:
RAND, 2016): https://www.rand.org/content/dam/rand/pubs/resear
ch_reports/RR1300/RR1335/RAND_RR1335.pdf

117. Jason Healey, "What Might Be Predominant Form of Cyber Conflict?,"
in *2017 International Conference on Cyber Conflict (CyCon US)* (2017
International Conference on Cyber-Conflict, Washington, DC: IEEE,
2017): 36–44, https://doi.org/10.1109/CYCONUS.2017.8167511

118. On general non-state capabilities in national security, see Barry Pavel,
Peter Engelke, and Alex Ward, "Dynamic Stability: US Strategy for a
World in Transition," *Atlantic Council Strategy Papers* (March 2016): 17,

https://www.atlanticcouncil.org/wp-content/uploads/2015/04/2016
-DynamicStabilityStrategyPaper_E.pdf; for a cyber strategy built around
non-state entities and capabilities, see Jason Healey, "A Nonstate Strategy
for Saving Cyberspace," *Atlantic Council Strategy Papers*, 2017: http://
www.atlanticcouncil.org/images/publications/AC_StrategyPapers_No8
_Saving_Cyberspace_WEB.pdf

119. Department of Defense, Defense Science Board, "Task Force on Cyber
Deterrence" (February 2017): 44; Defense Science Board, "Task Force
Report: Resilient Military Systems and the Advanced Cyber Threat,"
January 2013: https://apps.dtic.mil/dtic/tr/fulltext/u2/1028516.pdf

120. James N. Miller, personal communication to the authors, May 29, 2020.

121. See especially Buchanan, *The Cybersecurity Dilemma*, 113–116, for more.

122. Robert Jervis, *Perception and Misperception in International Politics* (Princeton,
NJ: Princeton University Press), 64–65.

123. Jervis, *Perception and Misperception in International Politics*, 353.

124. For more on the role of emotions in cyber conflict, see Rose McDermott,
"Some Emotional Considerations in Cyber Conflict," *Journal of Cyber
Policy* 4, no. 3 (2019): https://doi.org/10.1080/23738871.2019.1701692

125. *The Economist*, "A Virtual Counter-Revolution," September 2, 2010:
https://www.economist.com/briefing/2010/09/02/a-virtual-counter
-revolution

126. Buchanan, *The Cybersecurity Dilemma*, 183.

127. Robert Jervis, *The Meaning of the Nuclear Revolution: Statecraft and the
Prospect of Armageddon* (Ithaca, NY: Cornell University Press, 1989); see
also Robert Jervis, "Author Response: Reflections on The Meaning of
the Nuclear Revolution, 30 Years Later," *Book Review Roundtable: The
Meaning of the Nuclear Revolution 30 Years Later* (Texas National Security
Review, 2020): http://tnsr.org/roundtable/book-review-roundtable-
the-meaning-of-the-nuclear-revolution-30-years-later/

2

Preparing the Cyber Battlefield: Assessing a Novel Escalation Risk in a Sino-American Crisis

Ben Buchanan and Fiona S. Cunningham

In the context of an increasingly competitive Sino-American relationship, US analysts are increasingly concerned about crisis instability, defined as the temptation for either country to use force rather than continue to bargain diplomatically during a crisis. Scholars and analysts focused on the US-China relationship have warned that cyber capabilities could add incentives for either the United States or China to use force in a crisis.[1] Despite these concerns, there is no consensus among cyber scholars that offensive cyber capabilities contribute to the risk of great-power political crises escalating into conflicts.[2]

As the previous chapter by Jason Healey and Robert Jervis has shown, certain features of cyber capabilities could create new pathways through which a great-power crisis could escalate into a conventional conflict.

This chapter examines one of these novel escalation pathways in the context of the Sino-American relationship: the difficulty of distinguishing between hacking for espionage and operational preparation of the environment (OPE), an essential precursor to most high-end cyber attacks. This OPE-espionage distinction problem creates pathways for inadvertent escalation, which occurs "when a combatant deliberately takes actions that it does not perceive to be escalatory but are interpreted that way by the enemy," during a crisis or conflict.[3] A state could correctly detect an adversary's OPE and, fearing an imminent cyber attack with severe consequences, choose to use force first, escalating the conflict with a cyber or even kinetic attack. But a state could also misperceive an adversary's efforts to collect intelligence via cyber means as OPE and pre-empt that attack with conventional or cyber attacks of its own.[4] A state discovering that its adversary has intruded into its nuclear command, control, and communications networks during a crisis presents a particularly concerning scenario.[5]

Despite these concerns, academic studies based on observational data, surveys, and simulations find little correlation between cyber attacks and escalation, either in peacetime or during conflicts.[6] Scholars have reasoned that most cyber attacks are simply not destructive enough to worsen crisis or conflict outcomes.[7] These limited effects, coupled with the bloodless, secret nature of cyber attacks, might instead open up new pathways for de-escalation and enhance crisis stability.[8] However, the external validity of existing empirical findings to military crises among great powers is limited because no such crisis has occurred in the past two decades and they are difficult to replicate in surveys, simulations, and wargames.[9]

To evaluate the diverging concerns of the US policy community and the ongoing scholarly debates on cyber escalation and crisis instability among great powers, this chapter examines the escalation risks created by OPE in a future crisis scenario involving the United States and China. Scholars have already identified several sources of crisis instability in the Sino-American relationship, including a systematic lack of attention among Chinese experts to inadvertent escalation risks in the nuclear, conventional, and space domains.[10] A Sino-American crisis scenario is a most likely case for theoretical claims that cyber capabilities create novel escalation risks. Both countries would be most likely to react to any independent effect of cyber technology on their incentives to use force, if such incentives exist, in a crisis. Indeed, scholars have already raised concerns that cyber capabilities could fuel Sino-American crisis instability, although they have not examined the OPE-espionage distinction problem in much detail.[11] To assess the escalation risks posed by this problem, we follow the methodological approach of scholars who have examined other sources of crisis instability in the Sino-American relationship. Specifically, we examine the two countries' leadership statements, threat perceptions, procedures for authorizing cyber operations, organizational structures, capabilities, and policies for evidence that they create, recognize, and seek to manage escalatory risks.

Our analysis suggests that inadvertent escalation risks associated with OPE would be present in a future Sino-American crisis scenario. Official US policy for offensive cyber operations recognizes the escalation risks associated with cyber espionage being mistaken for OPE, but recent changes to US cyber strategy may increase these risks. Meanwhile, Chinese writings recognize the difficulty of distinguishing between cyber attacks and OPE but appear to ignore the consequences for crisis instability. We also find that a lack of mutual understanding in the Sino-American cyber relationship adds to the likelihood of the two countries misperceiving each other's behavior.

Our empirical findings have two key limitations. First, our sources are scarce, imperfect, and some years old, especially on the Chinese side. We

follow best practices for using open sources to analyze Chinese military strategy, but caution is still needed when drawing conclusions from such sources.
Nevertheless, these sources still make a valuable contribution to existing policy
debates and scholarly research about cyber conflict, which rarely draws on
Chinese perspectives. Second, our empirical findings could support the claim
that cyber technology either does – or does not – add to crisis instability.
Leaders from both countries might choose to ignore the escalation risks posed
by the OPE-espionage distinction problem even if they are present. But neither country's relaxed approach to these risks is justified by a careful assessment
of the independent effect of cyber technology on an adversary's incentives to
use force in a crisis, which makes us hesitant to dismiss them.

This chapter begins with a brief explanation of OPE as a distinctive feature
of cyber attacks. The second section outlines the competing hypotheses about
cyber escalation in existing scholarly literature and the mechanisms that could
link detection of an intrusion in a crisis with the decision to use force. The
third, fourth, and fifth sections examine the evidence for these hypotheses in
US documents and statements, Chinese writings and organizational practices,
and the bilateral cyber relationship, respectively. The sixth section evaluates
the escalation risks.

Operational Preparation of the Environment

Performing OPE is essential to enabling significant cyber operations that could
have strategic effects on the target.[12] To develop a cyber capability with a
potent or customized effect on a target network, substantial reconnaissance
and preparation are required from within that targeted network. In 2010,
the Department of Defense defined "Cyber Operations in Preparation of the
Environment" as:

> Non-intelligence enabling functions within cyberspace conducted to plan
> and prepare for potential follow-up military operations. [Cyber-OPE]
> includes but is not limited to identifying data, system/network configu-
> rations, or physical structures . . . for the purpose of determining system
> vulnerabilities; and actions taken to assure future access and/or control of
> the system, network, or data during anticipated hostilities.[13]

While cyber OPE has analogues in other forms of military operations –
especially in the world of special operations and covert action – it differs from
operations that are more familiar to policymakers, such as conventional and
nuclear operations. Preparations to use cyber capabilities have different recon-

naissance requirements than most other operations.[14] Much of the development and preparation for a cyber operation requires access to or occurs within adversary networks. Moreover, the accesses and payloads that make offensive cyber operations possible are often specific to a particular network.[15]

Gaining and maintaining access to a target network is also generally difficult, resource intensive, and specific to the target network.[16] Overall, the effects of an attack, the ability to sustain those effects over time, and the ability of an attack to limit unintended consequences all depend on how well the attacker has prepared and understood the target network and the likely actions of the network's defenders once the attack commences.[17]

A few examples illustrate the importance of OPE to sophisticated offensive cyber operations. Stuxnet was enabled by months if not years of reconnaissance, while Iranian hackers spent months inside the computer networks of Sands Casino and Saudi Aramco before they attacked in 2012.[18] North Korean hackers did the same with their attacks on the computer networks of Sony Pictures.[19] Russian hackers prepared in a similar way for their NotPetya operation, which reportedly inflicted over $10 billion in damage.[20] Some attacks, most notably denial-of-service efforts, do not fit into this trend, but lack potency as a result.[21]

OPE is also difficult to distinguish from espionage once it is discovered by a target. In theory, there might be ways for a target to tell whether an intrusion is espionage or whether it facilitates an attack. But there are no foolproof solutions to this OPE-espionage distinction problem. For example, an uptick in communication between the attacker and malicious code implanted in the target system could signal its purpose, but an attack could occur without any of those signals. Those signals could also accompany routine intelligence collection.[22] Even if an attacker tries to use those signals to distinguish OPE from espionage, the target may not receive those signals or treat them as credible.[23] The nature of the target network may provide some hints – for example, critical infrastructure industrial control systems are more likely to be exploited for OPE than intelligence gathering – but this is not always the case.[24] Moreover, the exploitation of an adversary's networks for intelligence gathering could be repurposed for OPE without any tell-tale signs that the target might detect. For example, there is some evidence to suggest that the first blackout in Ukraine began with an espionage objective but later morphed into an attack operation.[25]

The Novel Escalation Risks of OPE

How and why could an intrusion discovered in the midst of a crisis between two great powers create incentives for the use of force? How and why might decision-makers choose to use force when faced with those incentives? Answers to these questions are key to understanding the potential for cyber operations to contribute to crisis instability – or stability.

We define a crisis as "a confrontation between two states involving a serious threat to vital national interests for both sides in which there is the expectation of a short time for resolution, and in which there is understood to be a sharply increased risk of war."[26] We define escalation as "an increase in the intensity or scope of conflict that crosses threshold(s) considered significant by one or more of the participants."[27] In a great-power crisis, escalation would involve the use of force, with either cyber or kinetic attacks.[28] We use the term "cyber escalation risks" to refer to an increased temptation to use force in a crisis due to the nature of cyber technology.

If decision-makers discover an intrusion into their key military or civilian networks during a crisis, most scholars agree that those decision-makers could not rule out the possibility that the intrusion enables OPE. The decision-makers' response to that discovery will depend on how they assess the seriousness of the threat posed by the intrusion and whether the state also has strategic or political incentives to use force. The interaction of these two factors suggests four possibilities: the *inadvertent escalation* and *deliberate escalation* hypotheses that expect the use of force, and the *bluster* and *countervailing* hypotheses that do not expect the use of force. We focus on the logic underpinning the inadvertent escalation hypothesis because it best represents the concerns in current US policy debates about the destabilizing effect of cyber technology in a future Sino-American crisis.

Intrusion Detection in a Crisis

The scenario in which OPE could trigger the use of force in a crisis would likely begin months if not years before the crisis. An adversary that wants the option to carry out offensive cyber operations in a future conflict against a state's important military or civilian networks would conduct OPE during peacetime. Once a crisis has begun it is almost certainly too late to complete this complex, time-consuming task.[29]

Once a political crisis began – for example, over an accidental collision between two rivals' military aircraft, the scenario that triggered the last Sino-American crisis in 2001 – decision-makers in both states would have to decide whether to back down, bargain diplomatically, or bargain with the use of force. During their deliberations, the target state's decision-makers might discover their adversary's intrusions into important computer networks, including those that might be OPE. Such discoveries are more likely in a crisis because states anticipate espionage and attacks in that context and will step up network defenses accordingly.[30] If target's decision-makers decide it is most prudent to treat the intrusion as OPE, and they believe that the intrusion poses a serious threat, the OPE-espionage distinction problem creates an incentive to use force rather than bargain diplomatically.

More generally, the OPE-espionage distinction problem complicates the task of the target's decision-makers charged with assessing the intent behind the intrusion. Motivations for the intrusion include OPE, monitoring the target's military operations, or gathering intelligence about its offensive cyber operations.[31] The specifics of the intrusion may provide some hints of intent but are unlikely to be definitive.[32] Testing of small-scale attacks or an uptick in communication between the intruder and code it has implanted in the target system could also signal that it is OPE.[33] The intruder would also have difficulty reassuring the target state of its intent if the intrusion is for intelligence purposes.[34] To preserve its operational security, the intruder would have incentives not to acknowledge which adversary networks it has exploited and for what purpose, lest the target use that information to remove the intruder.[35] Even if the intruder sought to reassure the target of its intent not to use the intrusion to enable an attack, it would have trouble credibly committing not to use the intrusion for OPE in the future.

The Inadvertent Escalation Pathway

The claim that cyber operations create incentives to use force in a crisis is a specific instance of a general claim that military operations and technology can cause misperceptions among adversaries with serious consequences for crisis stability and intra-war escalation.[36] One potential consequence of those misperceptions is inadvertent escalation. The canonical scenario of inadvertent escalation is a conventional war among nuclear powers in which one party conducts "large-scale conventional operations that produce patterns of damage or threat to the major elements of a state's nuclear force."[37] The target state interprets the attack as a deliberate attempt to degrade its nuclear force and responds by using nuclear weapons or accelerating preparations for their use.[38] Similarly, escalation to the use of cyber or kinetic force could occur in a crisis as an unintended consequence of the normal conduct of cyber espionage.

Misperceptions commonly associated with the security dilemma are one reason that inadvertent escalation could occur.[39] Specifically, the difficulty of distinguishing between an adversary's offensive and defensive military operations is sufficient to produce misperceptions about the intent of the attacking state within the target state.[40] The attacking state's conventional military operations could therefore make its adversary less secure in unintended ways,[41] which creates an incentive for the target state to use force sooner rather than later.[42] The target state need only calculate that its ability to achieve its conflict objectives will diminish in the future if it ignores the attacker's actions in the present.[43]

The OPE-espionage distinction problem could trigger the use of force if the target state's leaders make worst-case-scenario assessments of the attacker's intent and capability to damage an important information network. There are four mechanisms by which a state could make a worst-case-scenario assessment of the seriousness of the threat posed by an intrusion and decide to use force, whether a cyber or kinetic attack. First, a state that detects an adversary's OPE might use force to pre-empt a cyber attack that could put the state at a military disadvantage in a future conflict.[44] Second, the combination of the crisis environment and the OPE-espionage distinction problem could lead the state to attribute aggressive intentions to the adversary with regards to both the network intrusion and the overall crisis, incentivizing the use of force.[45] Third, the discovery of an intrusion that might be OPE could affect decision-makers' emotions in ways that make the use of force more likely.[46] Fourth, the uneven distribution of information about the nature of cyber operations in national security bureaucracies might make the use of force more likely when those bureaucracies discover intrusions in a crisis. Intrusions that some cyber specialists see as a routine part of cyber operations may alarm more senior generalists, especially in a crisis. Top decision-makers may not have sufficient knowledge or information to assess the risks posed by a cyber intrusion to their military capabilities.[47]

The Deliberate Escalation Pathway

States might assess that a cyber intrusion poses a serious but tolerable threat yet choose to use force in response because they have strategic and political incentives to escalate. Those strategic and political incentives usually involve gaining a military advantage, signaling resolve, or pre-empting an adversary's attempt to signal resolve by using force.[48] Scholars have questioned whether states make decisions to escalate because of the independent effects of technology alone. Based on historical case studies, Caitlin Talmadge argues that new technologies might not force decision-makers to take escalatory actions, but rather "seem likely to be an intervening variable." States seek out new technologies to enable them to increase the risk of escalation, or turn to them opportunistically in a conflict, rather than their hands being forced to escalate in a crisis because they did not anticipate the escalatory pressures created by their prior decisions to deploy certain military capabilities.[49] These actions involve deliberate escalation: "[when] a combatant deliberately increases the intensity or scope of an operation to gain an advantage or avoid defeat."[50]

The Bluster De-escalation Pathway

Decision-makers may decide not to use force if they discover an intrusion in a crisis – even if they are confident that the intruder has performed OPE – because they do not think the intrusion poses a serious threat. This "bluster" hypothesis suggests that cyber technology does not contribute to crisis instability and might even help to stabilize crises. It draws on existing empirical research which indicates that cyber attacks are perceived to be more bluster than bite. States and individuals tend not to retaliate in response to cyber attacks.[51] One explanation for this empirical finding is that decision-makers do not view cyber attacks as sufficiently damaging or destructive to warrant the use of force in response.[52] Applying these arguments to a crisis scenario in which an intrusion is discovered, decision-makers might calculate that the cost of the cyber attack is likely to be low and can be absorbed. This explanation suggests that states would not anticipate a military disadvantage from a cyber attack, contrary to the military disadvantage mechanism outlined above.

Decision-makers might even view cyber attacks as a signal that an adversary wants to avoid a conventional conflict. When the effects of cyber and kinetic attacks are held constant, Jacquelyn Schneider and Sarah Kreps found that US survey respondents were less likely to support retaliation for cyber attacks than kinetic attacks.[53] Decision-makers might therefore interpret the discovery of an intrusion as a signal of an adversary's intent to avoid crossing the threshold of conventional armed conflict,[54] rather than its hostile intent, contrary to the misperception mechanism outlined above.

The Countervailing De-escalation Hypothesis

Finally, decision-makers might view the intrusion as posing a serious threat but have countervailing political or strategic incentives not to respond with the use of force. Decision-makers could react to an intrusion in this de-escalatory manner if they want to defuse the crisis because, for example, the stakes of the crisis do not merit fighting a war, or if they lacked the conventional military power to achieve their political objectives if a conflict broke out. Decision-makers with multiple adversaries might also be wary of mis-attributing an intrusion carried out by one adversary to another if they cannot attribute the intrusion to its perpetrator with sufficient confidence in the time frame of the crisis.[55] Other countervailing incentives may also originate in domestic politics. The ambiguity of intent behind cyber intrusions could help more moderate decision-makers build a coalition for restraint in the crisis and counter pressure from decision-makers with more hawkish preferences.[56]

Evaluating Cyber Escalation Hypotheses

How might scholars determine which of these four hypotheses is most likely in a great-power crisis, when no crisis has occurred since China and the United States were both armed with military cyber capabilities? There is no perfect solution to this problem. To complement existing empirical studies, most of which capture US popular or elite views of cyber escalation, our approach focuses on capturing both US and Chinese elite views by examining their approach to cyber OPE, escalation, and military operations.

Our empirical analysis is guided by observable implications derived from the four hypotheses. The inadvertent escalation hypothesis would expect states to express concern about any intrusions into their networks and to recognize the OPE-espionage distinction problem. States might also recognize inadvertent escalation risks and take steps to manage cyber escalation risks in their procedures, authorities, and organizational structures for cyber operations. Inadvertent escalation is also more likely to occur when two states have a poor understanding of each other's cyber activities and lack crisis communications mechanisms to verify the nature of an intrusion. The bluster de-escalation hypothesis would expect states that possess good attribution capabilities, defend their networks against intrusions, and effectively repel intruders who do breach defenses to be more relaxed about discovering intrusions into their networks. Not only might they be less likely to experience worrying intrusions, but they might also be able to better assess the intent and the severity of the threat posed by an intrusion.

While it is difficult to describe the strategic and political incentives that could provide evidence to support the deliberate escalation or countervailing hypotheses in a future crisis, some *ex ante* features of a great-power relationship would shape those incentives. Deliberate escalation is more likely to occur when the state discovering the intrusion is conventionally stronger than its adversary, does not confront multiple nation-state adversaries in cyberspace, or has high political stakes in the crisis. The countervailing hypothesis is more likely to find support if the state discovering the intrusion is conventionally weaker than its adversary, faces multiple nation-state adversaries in cyberspace, or has low political stakes in the crisis. A scenario in which the conventional military balance is roughly equal and both states see the conflict as high stakes would be the most likely case for the inadvertent escalation hypothesis because it minimizes countervailing political and strategic incentives to de-escalate if a threatening cyber intrusion is discovered in a crisis. A US-China crisis scenario is more evenly matched than most cyber dyads, although it would still involve some asymmetries in stakes and the conventional military balance that could obfuscate the independent effect of cyber technology on the temptation to use force in a crisis.[57]

Escalation Risks in US Cyber Operations

US decision-makers recognize the inadvertent escalation risks posed by cyber operations, and OPE in particular, but they have taken steps to mitigate those risks. The Obama administration implemented organizational practices that carefully managed cyber operations that could produce escalation. The Trump administration relaxed those organizational practices after gaining confidence in operational practices. These practices provide evidence in favor of either the inadvertent escalation hypothesis or the bluster de-escalation hypothesis. As part of its more muscular approach, US Cyber Command has also concluded that most cyber intrusions could not produce serious enough effects to result in escalation. At first glance this judgment supports the bluster de-escalation hypothesis. But it could also support the countervailing de-escalation hypothesis. US adversaries might view its intrusions as very threatening but face disincentives to use force because of US conventional military preponderance.

Leadership Views of OPE

The public statements of leaders and government reactions to discoveries of intrusions into military networks indicate that the United States views intrusions as threatening, in part because they could be used either for OPE or intelligence gathering. After a Russian hack of Pentagon systems in 2015 that the United States was able to repel, then-Secretary of Defense Ash Carter summarized the American position aptly when he said, "[It] can't be good for anybody to be inside of our networks – whatever their motivation."[58] Similarly, Gen. Paul Nakasone, the head of the National Security Agency (NSA) and US Cyber Command, and his adviser Michael Sulmeyer explained that the United States turned to a more aggressive policy "to prevent toeholds from turning into beachheads so that a single compromise will not threaten the military's ability to accomplish its mission."[59]

While the details of most US responses to foreign hacking efforts are not public, two historical cases demonstrate that policymakers worried about the implications of minor intrusions. In a 1998 hack known as Solar Sunrise, intruders penetrated the US military's logistics and communications networks. The Joint Staff general in charge of information operations, John Campbell, worried that the breach would permit significant attacks, especially at a time of heightened tensions with Iraq. "If you take one part of that machine, and disable it," he said, "you['ve] got a real problem trying to make a deployment take place."[60] Campbell's comments reflect an assessment that the intrusion could have placed the United States at a military disadvantage in a conflict. The discovery did not take place during a major crisis and therefore lacked the time pressure element that would create incentives to use force. Nevertheless, an investigation concluded the breach was the work of three teenagers and their 20-year-old mentor after various parts of the US government had already spun up to prepare for a response.

A second incident, Moonlight Maze, occurred in 1998 and 1999 and involved Russian penetration of unclassified American networks. The US government hacked back into Russian computers to gain more intelligence.[61] One of the White House's top national security officials, Richard Clarke, labeled the activities "cyberwar reconnaissance."[62] Then-Deputy Secretary of Defense John Hamre indicated that the United States was "in the middle of a cyber war" to the Intelligence Committees of Congress during a classified briefing.[63]

OPE in Cyber Operations

US operators and decision-makers have recognized the need for OPE to conduct sophisticated cyber operations since at least 2010. The vice chairman of the Joint Chiefs of Staff issued a memo in 2010 mandating the use of the term "Cyber Operations in Preparation of the Environment," which referred to those cyber operations that serve "as an enabling function for another military operation."[64] From the earliest days of the US Cyber Command, secret documents – now declassified – indicated that conducting OPE was one of its core tasks.[65]

Planners at the highest levels of the US government eventually recognized the importance of OPE. During the Obama administration, the most significant high-level document governing America's offensive cyber capability was *Presidential Policy Directive 20* (PPD-20). The president signed the classified document in secret in the fall of 2012. The White House released a fact sheet that made no mention of offensive cyber capabilities,[66] but the full classified document, leaked in 2013 by Edward Snowden, reveals a strategy that directly considers offensive action and contrasts it with other forms of cyber operations. The strategy lays out a clear typology of cyber activity. This includes "cyber collection," which refers to intelligence-gathering activities for purposes other than offensive preparation. It also includes "non-intrusive defensive counter-measures," meaning steps taken within one's own network, such as deploying antivirus and other basic security measures. The document also introduces the concept of "Defensive Cyber Effects Operations," defined as efforts that have an effect on an adversary's computer systems – presumably, hacking or other interference – but only for the purposes of defense. PPD-20 provides high-level procedures for managing this kind of aggressive defensive action.[67]

Most significantly, though, the classified version of PPD-20 defines offensive action in some detail. It introduces the concept of "Offensive Cyber Effects Operations" (OCEO), which are distinct from cyber collection, non-intrusive defensive countermeasures, or defensive cyber effects operations. Instead, these efforts are designed to cause effects in adversary networks.[68] The document extols the unique virtues of these kinds of offensive cyber operations, which "can offer unique and unconventional capabilities to advance U.S. national objectives around the world with little or no warning to the adversary or target and with potential effects ranging from subtle to severely damaging."[69]

PPD-20 acknowledges the need for OPE to realize these offensive options. It indicates that "the development and sustainment of [offensive cyber] capabilities, however, may require considerable time and effort if access and tools for a specific target do not already exist."[70] PPD-20 directs the US government to begin this operational preparation. The relevant agencies "shall identify potential targets of national importance where OCEO can offer a favorable balance of effectiveness and risk as compared with other instruments of national power, [and] establish and maintain OCEO capabilities integrated as appropriate with other U.S. offensive capabilities."[71] With his signature, President Barack Obama authorized the preparatory activity.

Procedures for Managing Escalation Risks

PPD-20 reveals US policymakers' cognisance of the risks that arise from actually using offensive cyber capabilities. As a result, the document highlights a process to carefully manage offensive actions that might do serious harm or invite escalation. It emphasizes inter-agency coordination, balancing defense and national security interests with diplomatic and economic ones. Most notably, the process requires the highest level of executive branch oversight – presidential approval – for any cyber operation that is "reasonably likely to result in significant consequences."[72] This term is broadly defined: "Loss of life, significant responsive actions against the United States, significant damage to property, serious adverse U.S. foreign policy consequences, or serious economic impact on the United States."[73] It is likely that cyber operations that do not meet that threshold could otherwise be approved by the agency carrying out the operation without such high-level inter-agency vetting.

Crucially, PPD-20 does not limit these restrictions to cyber attacks but emphasizes that they apply to all cyber operations. In short, President Obama wanted direct oversight of any operation that might meet the threshold of significant consequences – regardless of whether that operation involved collecting intelligence, defending American computers, preparing an offensive capability, or launching an attack. The directive suggests that the Obama administration was concerned, at least in theory, about the risks of cyber escalation even as it appreciated the operational necessity to prepare offensive capabilities in advance.

The Trump administration adopted a more relaxed set of organizational procedures for managing cyber escalation risks. Upon unveiling its new national cyber strategy in 2018, the Trump White House criticized the preceding administration for what it saw as its overly cautious posture and promised to be more aggressive in its engagements with adversaries. Then-National Security Adviser John Bolton said, "Our hands are not tied as they were in the Obama administration." Nor was the need for more aggressive action just a partisan view. In his confirmation hearing, the incoming NSA director and commander of US Cyber Command Gen. Paul Nakasone warned that the United States had to do more because American adversaries "don't fear us."[74]

These views were translated into policy by President Donald Trump's signature on "National Security Presidential Memorandum 13." The goal of the memorandum, which remains classified, is to provide military commanders with greater flexibility to integrate cyber operations into their overall approach to warfighting and deterrence.[75] By delegating this authority to the Pentagon, the Trump administration attempted to foster a faster and more aggressive process, one that would generate more operational effects more quickly. But this approach also rebalanced the trade-off between operational agility and whole-of-government coordination to manage cyber escalation risks in favor of the former. According to the general on the Joint Staff responsible for cyber operations, this change sharply contrasted with the Obama administration's approach, which was "an interagency process that went through the National Security Council . . . to deputies' committee to principals' committee and [where], in effect, anyone could stop the process along the way." Nor, he argued, was the distinction just semantics or bureaucratic minutia, but one that "makes all the difference in the world in terms of the speed at which you can move."[76]

It is unclear whether current US policy, set by the Trump memorandum, frees commanders to both prepare for and launch cyber capabilities. But there are hints that the memo and complementary legislative changes implemented by Congress provide a freer hand in developing the malicious code and gaining access to target networks required to provide commanders with offensive options. For example, in a media interview, the former deputy commander of U.S. Cyber Command, Lt. Gen. Vincent Stewart, indicated that changes to congressional legislation "freed us up to do some of the things, the operational preparation of the environment, that we were limited from doing outside of the counterterrorism mission and now can do much more broadly against all of our peers and competitors."[77] In addition, a *New York Times* story from June 2019 describes more aggressive American preparatory measures against the Russian power grid.[78]

Overall, the Trump administration was much less worried about the escalation risk associated with cyber operations than the Obama administration. The Biden administration appears to have largely continued this approach since taking office in 2021. Michael Daniel, the former coordinator for cyber security in the Obama White House, observed that the Trump administration was "willing to take more risks than previous administrations."[79] While the Trump administration's approach was untested in a crisis with a near-peer competitor, it was informed by the US experience with cyber conflict over the past decade as well as the increasing risk tolerance of US decision-makers. To justify its new posture, US Cyber Command has argued that "adversaries continuously operate against us below the threshold of armed conflict," in what it described as a "new normal."[80] Moreover, the command argued that US efforts to counter this adversarial activity will not lead to retaliation in or outside of cyberspace that would cross that threshold.

These claims have been fiercely debated in the academic literature, with critics of the so-called persistent engagement approach arguing that the new strategy could produce escalation. For example, some contend that the thresholds for armed conflict are not as clear as US Cyber Command has suggested. Others argue that persistent engagement creates too many red lines for adversaries and is therefore not a realistic means for shaping behavior.[81] Nakasone and Sulmeyer responded to these concerns with reassurance that:

> Cyber Command takes these concerns seriously, and reducing this risk is a critical part of the planning process. We are confident that this more proactive approach enables Cyber Command to conduct operations that impose costs while responsibly managing escalation.[82]

Capabilities for Managing Escalation Risks

In the past decade, the United States has developed some of the world's most sophisticated cyber capabilities to better defend its networks, attribute intrusions, and expel intruders in peacetime. To better defend networks, the United States has invested in major systems, such as EINSTEIN 3, that aim to thwart intrusions. To improve rapid attribution of intrusions and increase situational awareness, the United States established various cross-agency working groups and bulked up teams within the NSA and US Cyber Command. To the extent that these capabilities are effective, they might mitigate cyber escalation risks by reducing the likelihood that intruders will successfully break into US networks and alarm policymakers who have to decide on how to respond within the compressed time period of a crisis. However, the compromise of SolarWinds network management system in 2021, which enabled Russian government operators to intrude into numerous US government systems for months without detection, suggests that defense and attribution capabilities are imperfect and do not eliminate the possibility of the United States discovering an intrusion during a crisis.

Escalation Risks in Chinese Cyber Operations

There is little evidence to indicate that China has scrutinized the inadvertent escalation risks posed by OPE as carefully as the United States, although Chinese sources bearing on this question are older, scarcer, and less authoritative than those for the United States.[83] This lack of attention could be evidence of the bluster de-escalation hypothesis, as it might reflect a judgment that cyber intrusions pose a manageable threat to China's leaders. But this lack of concern should be interpreted in the context of a relative lack of concern about inadvertent escalation risks posed by nuclear, space, and conventional military operations among Chinese experts. As such, we favor the interpretation of China's inattention to inadvertent cyber escalation risks as support for the inadvertent escalation hypothesis. Inattention to the inadvertent escalation risks associated with OPE could help to realize such risks in a crisis for three reasons. First, China is more likely to misperceive US cyber intrusions. Second, it is more likely to overlook the ways that its own cyber intrusions could be misperceived. Third, China is much less likely to take steps to mitigate these risks. Available sources provide little insight into whether the People's Liberation Army (PLA) has put in place organizational or operational practices to manage inadvertent cyber escalation.

Leadership Views of OPE

Chinese policymakers' fears about foreign hackers have grown in tandem with the expansion of the Chinese government's and military's dependence on computer networks. In a major speech on national cyber security policy in 2016, Communist Party General Secretary Xi Jinping stated that, "Cyber security has a strong covert character; a technological vulnerability or security risk can stay hidden for a number of years without being discovered." As a result, "we do not know who came in, whether it was an enemy or a friend, or what they did." Xi implied that while this enemy or friend's intrusion could remain "latent" inside a network for a long time, it could be "activated whenever (*yidan jiu fazuo le*)."[84]

The Chinese government has not publicly acknowledged any specific incidents in which it discovered that foreign state actors had exploited its government or military networks. China's closest analogue to the Solar Sunrise and Moonlight Maze incidents was Edward Snowden's revelations regarding US government surveillance of Chinese computer networks. Snowden's revelations are often cited by the country's cyber security scholars as evidence of China's vulnerability and the inadequacy of its network defenses, which failed to prevent or detect US government intrusions. Chinese experts claim that the NSA also targeted the country's military networks.[85] A Chinese cyber security firm reported that the CIA had spied on Chinese state–owned enterprises but did not identify any government networks penetrated.[86] There is no detailed evidence about how the Chinese government responded to any of these incidents, nor did they occur in the context of a major crisis.

Chinese writings examining US cyber operations can provide insights into how Chinese experts view these operations in the absence of open discussions about these topics in China. Chinese experts affiliated with the PLA note that OPE is one of the cyber missions outlined in US doctrinal publications but do not mention the crisis escalation risks that could result from the OPE-espionage distinction problem.[87] While the Trump administration's more muscular approach to cyber operations raised concerns among Chinese authors for its emphasis on pre-emption and potential to spark arms race instability, those experts are less focused on crisis instability than US scholars.[88] There are some recent exceptions. For example, former PLA officer Lyu Jinghua writes that

> it is worthwhile to explore whether the tension in cyberspace can be de-escalated or whether the chances of the breakout of crisis can be lowered if there could be a basic consensus among countries that cyber activities

conducted or supported by countries during peacetime are a contest of intelligence rather than conflicts or preparation of conflicts.[89]

It remains unclear whether Chinese decision-makers share the views of experts who worry about the escalation risks of OPE and whether those concerns have led to practices to mitigate those risks.

OPE in Cyber Operations

Like US officials, PLA strategists also distinguish between cyber surveillance, offense and defense, and deterrence as the main styles of cyber struggle.[90] PLA texts do not use the term "operational preparation of the environment" when describing PLA operations, but they do recognize that effective offensive cyber operations require extensive advance preparation. A 2015 book authored by experts from the PLA Army Engineering University, 54th Institute, and other PLA organizations acknowledges that significant advance preparations are needed to ensure that cyber operations can be used to diminish an adversary's combat power. While many methods of attack are available, "a cyber attack capable of producing significant effects is a cyber attack for which ample preparations have already been made at an earlier time . . . it is not a decision that one makes as the situation requires."[91]

PLA writings indicate that China places a similar degree of emphasis on OPE as the United States. The 2015 book characterizes OPE as more demanding than network exploitation for espionage:

> It is necessary to carry out careful and meticulous reconnaissance and scanning of the target, in order to obtain even more detailed, specific information about it. As such, we must carry out deeper reconnaissance and scanning of the target, [and] the extent of secrecy and concealment [of those tasks] far exceeds the extent of carrying out [those] tasks for computer network exploitation.[92]

But reconnaissance and scanning are only the first steps in preparations for an attack. The authors emphasize the importance of obfuscation throughout the various procedures required to prepare for offensive cyber operations: selecting and employing a method of gaining access to the target network, moving laterally through it, gaining privileges, and maintaining access.[93] An intrusion can serve multiple purposes: "attack actions occur after the intrusion of computer networks, escalating privileges and exfiltrating all required data."[94]

PLA writings recognize that holding targets at risk for the purpose of deterrence also requires OPE. An article outlining principles of cyber deterrence authored by an unnamed Academy of Military Science expert in 2016 indicated that successful cyber deterrence, which included carrying out coercive and retaliatory attacks, required "complete and meticulous preparation in peacetime." Those preparations included "long-term, sustained network reconnaissance" to become familiar with an adversary's network situation, map the structure of its networks, and discover hardware and software vulnerabilities. Vulnerabilities could be used to leave backdoors, set up "springboards," and install logic bombs and Trojan horses "to retain points of penetration to launch future cyber attacks."[95]

PLA texts recognize the OPE-espionage distinction problem. The 2013 *Science of Military Strategy* published by the Academy of Military Science acknowledges that, "from a technological perspective, the principles of the task (*gongzuo yuanli*) of cyber surveillance and cyber attacks are essentially identical." The book explains: "cyber surveillance means and methods are often also the means and methods of cyber attacks." Furthermore, it highlights that cyber espionage can easily be turned into an attack: "According to the aspirations and intentions of the actor, it is possible to just press a key or initiate a sequence of commands, and the conversion between cyber surveillance and cyber attack is immediately completed." The authors conclude that the relationship between cyber espionage and combat cannot be severed.[96]

In addition, OPE can erode the distinction between peacetime and conflict in cyberspace. The 2017 *Science of Military Strategy* published by the National Defense University indicates that, "compared to traditional domains, the boundary between war and peace in the cyber domain is fuzzier." The book describes the lack of clear boundaries as follows: "cyber and electronic domain warfare already exists in peacetime; when war is imminent (*linzhan*) it becomes more intense; [and] often sustained confrontation directly merges into actual war."[97] These views are repeated in a revised edition of the book published in 2020.[98] Two PLA authors affiliated with the former General Staff Research Institute argue that one reason for the blurred boundary between war and peace in cyberspace is that "'backdoors' and 'exploits' are pre-placed in an enemy's network systems early; it is very difficult to determine from which moment war begins."[99] This view contrasts with US Cyber Command's views of a clearer threshold of armed conflict in cyberspace.

As in the United States, PLA texts indicate that China intends to conduct offensive cyber operations. OPE will therefore likely be necessary to target the high-value military and civilian critical infrastructure networks that could contribute to crisis instability. A 2013 Academy of Military Science textbook describes "'soft' paralysis of the information network nodes of adversary warfare systems" that the PLA could implement alongside kinetic attacks and psychological operations in a future joint information operations campaign. The book indicates that the PLA would need to "completely analyze the structure and relationship of interconnections and restrictions among the adversary's systems for command and control, intelligence and warning, and firepower attack (*huoli daji*), and their support and sustainment," to select the appropriate means for offensive cyber attacks. Those means include offensive cyber operations that would require OPE: "systems intrusion, computer virus attacks, attacks to cut off servers, and network deception attacks." The book indicates that PLA attacks would not be limited to military networks, but could also "infiltrate, attack, and paralyze the adversary's important civilian networks (*minyong wangluo xitong*)."[100] The PLA has moderated its expectations of the ease and effectiveness of such attacks as it has learned more about offensive cyber operations over time.[101] But has by no means taken them off the table, as demonstrated by its ongoing exploitation of Taiwanese critical infrastructure, and Indian critical infrastructure networks during the conflict along the Sino-Indian border in 2020.[102]

Procedures for Managing Escalation Risk

PLA texts do not discuss the danger of the OPE–espionage distinction problem and the risk of escalation if an intrusion is discovered in a crisis. It is unclear whether Chinese decision-makers have implemented procedures for managing inadvertent escalation risks posed by its cyber operations. Past PLA writings do not indicate that managing those risks was a priority in organizational procedures for cyber operations. This inattention to inadvertent cyber escalation risks specifically is surprising given that China has paid increasing attention to three other types of escalation risks: deliberate cyber attacks that could result in an adversary overreaction, unauthorized and accidental cyber attacks perpetrated by the PLA, and the potential for North Korean cyber attacks to be mis-attributed to China and draw it into a conflict with one of Pyongyang's enemies.

The 2013 *Science of Military Strategy* indicates that "every country in the world is conducting cyber reconnaissance activities of differing degrees, but the possibility of this triggering a bilateral crisis, or a war starting because of this reason, is not high."[103] The authors do not reconcile this observation with their observation that cyber surveillance and attack are indistinguishable. Similarly, the Academy of Military Science expert writing in 2016 warned of escalation risks from cyber operations that are too weak or too strong in their effects on an adversary. The expert called for unified control over all aspects of cyber operations but did not recognize the possibility that espionage could be misperceived as OPE and prompt an adversary to use force.[104]

Chinese researchers writing for academic and policy audiences vary in their assessments of whether cyber operations in general contribute to crisis instability, but they also do not pay specific attention to the OPE inadvertent escalation pathway. Associate Professor Liu Yangyue at the National University of Defense Technology is generally sanguine about the effects of cyber operations on strategic stability. He dismisses the argument in Western literature that a state could escalate in response to an initial cyber attack to stop an adversary from conducting further attacks.[105] Drawing on the same observational data used in Western cyber security scholarship, he argues that "when they face cyber attacks (believed to come from their enemies), states do not inevitably make worst-case calculations in their style of behavior, or let this guide their policies for responding."[106] Similarly, Li Bin and Zhao Tong report that:

> Some Chinese experts have challenged the popular view that cyber technology will negatively affect crisis stability, because they believe this conclusion is based completely on logical deduction, instead of empirical evidence. These experts have noted that states are usually very cautious about launching military retaliations to cyber attacks, and it is very rare for cyber attacks to lead to escalation.[107]

Nevertheless, Liu does express concern about the escalation risks posed by the difficulty of attribution. Citing the example of the Solar Sunrise intrusion discovered prior to US airstrikes against Iraq in 1998, he argues that if third-party espionage or OPE "is coincidentally discovered during a military mission, or the attacker uses more sophisticated means to conceal their identity, then this kind of attack could become a fuse for an unintended crisis."[108]

Other Chinese scholars are less sanguine about the escalation risks in cyberspace. But they tend to focus on the use-or-lose incentives to carry out cyber attacks early in a crisis or conflict, rather than inadvertent escalation due to the discovery of an intrusion.[109] PRC experts have also expressed concern about the US concept of "cross-domain deterrence," which they interpret as threats to use conventional military operations (or even nuclear threats) to retaliate for cyber attacks.[110] The Carnegie Endowment for International Peace's Ariel Levite and former PLA Col. Lyu Jinghua wrote in *China Military Science* that in a Sino-American conflict scenario, "one of the earliest and most destabilising venues for conflict would be cyberspace, thanks to the potential military utility of early employment of cyber assets." Levite and Lyu acknowledge that "cyber actions in these scenarios also hold serious escalatory potential, complicating the challenges of keeping conflicts below the level of outright military confrontation." They acknowledge the OPE inadvertent escalation risk, but only briefly: "intelligence operations to monitor these networks might be misinterpreted as attacks on them, or at least attack preparations."[111]

It is unclear whether PLA planning for offensive cyber operations accounts for the escalation risks associated with OPE and, if so, how those risks are managed. The PLA promulgated a new generation of doctrine in November 2020, the first update to its official doctrine since 1999.[112] Unfortunately, no information about their content was available at the time of writing. Up until at least 2015, official PLA doctrine for offensive cyber operations was likely covered by doctrine for information operations, which combined electronic, cyber, and kinetic attacks.[113] PLA texts published before 2015 hinted that, in the future, the PLA might have operational doctrine for stand-alone cyber operations as well as joint information operations involving cyber attacks.[114]

The PLA established the Strategic Support Force (SSF) in 2015–2016, during one of the most significant set of reforms in its history. The SSF consolidated most existing PLA cyber offense, defense, and espionage units from separate parts of its former General Staff Department and services into a Network Systems Department within the Strategic Support Force. Before the reforms, the PLA General Staff Department's Third Department was believed to be the primary organization for cyber espionage within the PLA, while the Fourth Department was believed to have primary responsibility for offensive cyber operations.[115] The consolidation of the former Third and Fourth departments into one organization is likely to enable the PLA to better integrate cyber operations for espionage and attack.[116]

These new organizational arrangements for military cyber operations should in theory improve the ability of top leaders to recognize and manage the crisis escalation risks associated with OPE. One of the key effects, if not drivers, of the consolidation of Chinese military cyber forces into the SSF is to enable top military leaders to exercise stricter oversight over PLA cyber operations to prevent accidental and unauthorized cyber attacks.[117] Indeed, PLA writings published around the time the SSF was created emphasize the principle of "unified command" (tongyi zhihui) of cyber offense, defense, espionage, and control, and both PLA and non-PLA cyber capabilities.[118] Details of how this principle of unified command is implemented in practice are scarce. Moreover, the ability of the new command structure to manage escalation risks in practice might have taken a back seat to other force building priorities. For example, the PLA's efforts to guard against unauthorized and accidental use of cyber operations is in tension with its efforts to recruit the best cyber talent from outside of the PLA. The SSF's use of contractors may revive many of the problems with oversight of cyber operations that China's leaders encountered prior to the 2015–2016 reforms.[119]

The nature and extent of leadership oversight of PLA cyber operations are difficult to determine. It is possible that China has established a formal institutional structure for inter-agency vetting of military plans and operations that crosses civilian and military lines. Drawing on a PLA publication about cyber operations published in 2017, John Chen, Joe McReynolds, and Kieran Green observe that "peacetime planning and guidance of cyberspace operations . . . at the strategic level rest in the hands of such national network security leadership organizations as the [Communist Party] Cybersecurity and Informatization Commission, while planning and guidance during wartime are the responsibility of the [PLA] CMC Joint Operations Command Center."[120] In other words, a civilian Party body takes the lead in peacetime and the PLA's Central Military Commission takes the lead in wartime. It remains unclear how this dual command structure functions in practice. Most importantly, it remains unclear whether and, if so, to what degree managing inadvertent escalation risks resulting from OPE is a priority for the military and civilian leaders with oversight over PLA cyber operations.

Capabilities for Managing Cyber Risk

China is developing cyber situational awareness capabilities, including attribution capabilities. But they likely lag behind the United States in its development of capabilities that could disambiguate between attackers and mitigate inadvertent escalation risks. An official white paper outlining China's international cyberspace strategy published in 2017 indicated that:

> [China] will expedite the development of a [military] cyber force and enhance capabilities in terms of situational awareness, cyber defense, supporting state activities and participating in international cooperation, to prevent major cyber crisis, safeguard cyberspace security, and maintain national security and social stability.[121]

It is difficult to assess the extent of improvement in China's attribution and defense capabilities since adopting these priorities in 2015. The Chinese government's procedures for defending its networks are unclear and it has not publicly attributed cyber attacks to another state. Nevertheless, in 2018 Xi Jinping acknowledged the deterrent effect of China's improved capability to detect intruders.[122] Some Chinese cyber security firms have begun to publicly attribute intrusions to known groups of hackers using industry identifiers.[123] They have also called for greater efforts to prevent OPE within critical infrastructure networks. For example, the Chinese company Antiy argued that China needed to "make progress in weakening the ability of an adversary to 'prepare the battlefield' in our industrial control [systems] and infrastructure to achieve [serious] consequences."[124]

Misperception in the Sino-American Cyber Relationship

Do the United States and China have a shared understanding of the nature of cyber conflict, the role of OPE, and the potential for crisis instability because of the OPE-espionage distinction problem? Comparing US and Chinese approaches to cyber conflict reveals some similarities, as well as differences that could hamper future bilateral efforts to manage cyber escalation risks. Both countries recognize that OPE is necessary for sophisticated offensive cyber operations yet is indistinguishable from intrusions for the purpose of espionage, defense, or data theft. Both countries view the presence of nation-state hackers in their networks as threatening. But the two countries do not appear to share an understanding of the inadvertent escalation risks posed by the OPE-espionage distinction problem or the clarity of the threshold of an armed attack in cyberspace.

The comparison also reveals asymmetries in the relative maturity of cyber doctrine and capabilities in both countries. These asymmetries might explain the lack of attention to inadvertent escalation risks in China's approach to cyber conflict. China's doctrine, procedures, and authorities for conducting cyber operations appear to have been overhauled by the 2015–2016 PLA reforms and took some years afterwards to crystallize into their current form. As a result, the PLA has less experience integrating espionage, offensive, and defensive cyber operations and incorporating civilian oversight into its cyber operations than the United States. The PLA operational regulations promulgated in late 2020 might have included more guidance on OPE and managing its escalation risks that is not reflected in the sources examined here. Meanwhile, US cyber capabilities and strategy are relatively more mature. US organizations demonstrate growing confidence in attribution capabilities, the clarity of escalation thresholds, and US ability to control escalation from OPE or low-level cyber attacks. These factors have led to a doctrine for cyber operations that gives the military a freer hand.

Neither China nor the United States appears to be overly concerned about its espionage activities being misperceived as OPE during a crisis, albeit for different reasons. On the one hand, China appears to be inattentive to the specific escalation risks posed by OPE. On the other hand, the United States appears to be aware of the specific escalation risks associated with OPE but is confident that they can be mitigated. This suggests that both states might approach a crisis confident that their intrusions will not be discovered, misperceived, or lead to the use of force. The PLA's attention to the escalation risks associated with OPE might increase as Chinese cyber doctrine and capabilities further develop. But increased awareness is by no means a given. Chinese experts and writings on crisis management and nuclear strategy – areas where PLA doctrine and capabilities are more mature – have also tended to downplay drivers of inadvertent escalation.

Of course, the lack of concern about the escalation risks associated with OPE could reflect a shared lack of concern that cyber attacks could cause much harm in a crisis, supporting the bluster de-escalation hypothesis. OPE may simply be accepted practice between these two countries.[125] They might expect that some of their key networks will be disabled by their adversaries' offensive cyber operations during future conflicts. They might prepare to fight without those networks instead of pre-empting cyber attacks that could disable them. We are cautious, however, about interpreting the evidence as confirmation of the bluster hypothesis. Evidence that China both acknowledges and shares US confidence that inadvertent cyber escalation risks can be managed – which we did not find – would have reduced the need for caution in interpreting the evidence in favor of the bluster de-escalation hypothesis.

Initiatives to Mitigate Misperceptions

In the absence of a shared understanding of cyber conflict, two initiatives could reduce the risk of inadvertent cyber escalation via the misperception pathway in a future Sino-American crisis: dialogue to ensure that both parties understand each other's approach to cyber operations, and a crisis communication mechanism specific to cyber operations. Dialogue and crisis communication could reduce the likelihood of either side misperceiving the other's cyber intrusion as OPE, or as confirmation of the other's hostile intentions, because of differences in their understandings of cyber conflict and operations.[126] Unfortunately, China and the United States do not currently have an official military cyber dialogue that could bridge some of the gaps in their understandings of military cyber operations before a crisis emerges, despite establishing official dialogues to enable cooperation in non-military areas of the cyber relationship in 2015. Nor do China and the United States currently have a mechanism in place for crisis communications dedicated to cyber matters. By contrast, the United States has a three-tier cyber communications protocol in place with Russia that involves a direct line between the White House and the Kremlin.[127]

Conclusion

Could military cyber capabilities contribute to the outbreak of conflict in a future crisis involving the United States and China? Although our empirical analysis is unable to provide a definitive answer to this question, it provides enough evidence to suggest that inadvertent escalation could occur if one state discovered the other's cyber intrusions in a crisis. Over the past decade or so, the United States has made unilateral attempts to limit the risks of inadvertent escalation occurring, first with strict organizational procedures governing all cyber operations and later with more robust operational procedures to defend its networks. There is little evidence that China has taken similar steps to unilaterally mitigate inadvertent escalation risks from cyber operations. The bilateral cyber relationship also lacks the shared understandings of these risks, and mechanisms for dialogue in peacetime or communications in crises, that could improve crisis stability.

Even a small probability of inadvertent escalation could have extremely serious consequences, given how destructive a Sino-American conflict could be and the variety of other escalation risks present in the relationship. Our empirical analysis could also support the claim that cyber capabilities do not pose a serious enough threat for decision-makers to use force – whether cyber or kinetic – to pre-empt or retaliate. However, in the absence of stronger evidence to support this bluster hypothesis, we do not dismiss the risk that the OPE-espionage distinction problem could add to crisis instability given the stakes at hand.

This chapter suggests that further research is needed to establish whether US confidence that cyber operations do not add to crisis stability is well founded. US adversaries' reluctance to escalate in response to cyber attacks or intrusions might reflect their countervailing strategic and political disincentives to escalate, rather than the stabilizing nature of cyber operations.[128] Brandon Valeriano, Benjamin M. Jensen, and Ryan C. Maness find that the United States has been successful in using cyberspace to coerce adversaries.[129] Scholars have pointed out that cyber operations are likely to have their greatest effects on international relations when combined with superior conventional military power.[130] The possibility that US conventional military power might mask the destabilizing effects of cyber operations suggests that the United States should be cautious as Chinese conventional military capabilities improve. If a Sino-American crisis had occurred during the past decade, Beijing would have faced strong countervailing pressures not to use force in response to a cyber intrusion, even if it judged that intrusion to pose a serious threat. Going forward, even if the PRC views an intrusion as a serious but manageable threat, its growing conventional capabilities and tense relationship with Washington could create an excuse for deliberate PRC escalation. And if the intrusion were intolerable, political and strategic disincentives could not be counted on to restrain China's leaders from using force.

Notes

1. Kurt M. Campbell and Ali Wyne, "The Growing Risk of Inadvertent Escalation Between Washington and Beijing," *Lawfare*, August 16, 2020: https://www.lawfareblog.com/growing-risk-inadvertent-escalation-between-washington-and-beijing; Avery Goldstein, "US-China Rivalry in the Twenty-First Century: Deja vu and Cold War II," *China International Strategy Review* 2, no. 1 (2020): 48–62.

2. For key contributions to that debate, see, Martin Libicki, *Crisis and Escalation in Cyberspace* (Santa Monica, CA: RAND Corporation, 2012); Sarah Kreps and Jacquelyn Schneider, "Escalation Firebreaks in the Cyber, Conventional, and Nuclear Domains: Moving beyond Effects-Based Logics," *Journal of Cybersecurity* 5, no. 1 (2019): 8–9, https://doi.org/10.1093/cybsec/tyz007; Brandon Valeriano and Ryan Maness, *Cyber War Versus Cyber Realities: Cyber Conflict in the International System* (New York: Oxford University Press, 2015); Jon R. Lindsay, "Stuxnet and the Limits of Cyber Warfare," *Security Studies* 22, no. 3 (2013): 365–404, https://doi.org/10.1080/09636412.2013.816122; Erik Gartzke, "The Myth of Cyberwar: Bringing War in Cyberspace Back Down to Earth," *International Security* 38, no. 2 (Fall 2013): 41–73, https://doi.org/10.1162/ISEC_a_00136; Erica D. Borghard and Shawn W. Lonergan, "The Logic of Coercion in Cyberspace," *Security Studies* 26, no. 3 (July 3, 2017): 476–478, https://doi.org/10.1080/09636412.2017.1306396; Joseph S. Nye Jr., "Deterrence and Dissuasion in Cyberspace," *International Security* 41, no. 3 (Winter 2016): 44–71, https://doi.org/10.1162/ISEC_a_00266; Erik Gartzke and Jon R. Lindsay, "Coercion Through Cyberspace: The Stability-Instability Paradox Revisited," in *Coercion: The Power to Hurt in International Politics*, ed. Kelly M. Greenhill and Peter Krause (New York: Oxford University Press, 2018), 179–203.

3. Forrest E. Morgan, Karl P. Mueller, Evan S. Medeiros, Kevin L. Pollpeter, and Roger Cliff, *Dangerous Thresholds: Managing Escalation in the 21st Century* (Santa Monica, CA: RAND Corporation, 2008), xiii.

4. See for example, Libicki, *Crisis and Escalation in Cyberspace*; Herbert Lin, "Escalation Dynamics and Conflict Termination in Cyberspace," *Strategic Studies Quarterly* 6, no. 3 (Fall 2012): 46–70, https://www.jstor.org/stable/26267261.

5. See for example, James M. Acton, "Cyber Warfare & Inadvertent Escalation," *Daedalus* 149, no. 2 (Spring 2020): 133–149, https://doi.org/10.1162/daed_a_01794; Erik Gartzke and Jon R. Lindsay, "The Cyber Commitment Problem and the Destabilization of Nuclear Deterrence," in *Bytes, Bombs, and Spies: The Strategic Dimensions of Offensive Cyber Operations*, ed. Herbert Lin and Amy Zegart (Washington, DC: Brookings Institution Press, 2019), 195–234.

6. Valeriano and Maness, *Cyber War Versus Cyber Realities*, chapter 5; Nadiya Kostyuk and Yuri M. Zhukov, "Invisible Digital Front: Can Cyber Attacks Shape Battlefield Events?," *Journal of Conflict Resolution* 63, no. 2 (2017): 317–347, https://doi.org/10.1177%2F0022002717737138; Jacquelyn G. Schneider, "The Information Revolution and International Stability: A Multi-Article Exploration of Computing, Cyber, and Incentives for Conflict" (Ph.D. dissertation, George Washington University, 2017), 119; Kreps and Schneider, "Escalation Firebreaks in the Cyber, Conventional, and Nuclear Domains."

7. Gartzke, "The Myth of Cyberwar"; Borghard and Lonergan, "The Logic of Coercion in Cyberspace"; Erica D. Borghard and Shawn W. Lonergan, "Cyber Operations as Imperfect Tools of Escalation," *Strategic Studies Quarterly* 13, no. 3 (2019): 122–145, https://www.jstor.org/stable/26760131; Brandon Valeriano, Benjamin M. Jensen, and Ryan C. Maness, *Cyber Strategy: The Evolving Character of Power and Coercion* (New York: Oxford University Press, 2018).

8. Valeriano, Jensen, and Maness, *Cyber Strategy*; Joshua Rovner, "Cyber War as an Intelligence Contest," *War on the Rocks*, September 16, 2019: https://warontherocks.com/2019/09/cyber-war-as-an-intelligence-contest/; Austin Carson, *Secret Wars: Covert Conflict in International Politics* (Princeton, NJ: Princeton University Press, 2018), 295–297.

9. For a useful discussion of the external validity of surveys and the ecological validity of wargames, see, Kreps and Schneider, "Escalation Firebreaks in the Cyber, Conventional, and Nuclear Domains," 9; Schneider, "The Information Revolution and International Stability," 122–130; Erik Lin-Greenberg, Reid B. C. Pauly, and Jacquelyn G. Schneider, "Wargaming for International Relations Research," *European Journal of International Relations* (2021): https://doi.org/10.1177/13540661211064090

10. See James M. Acton, "Escalation Through Entanglement: How the

Vulnerability of Command-and-Control Systems Raises the Risks of an Inadvertent Nuclear War," *International Security* 43, no. 1 (Summer 2018): 89–92, https://doi.org/10.1162/isec_a_00320; Thomas J. Christensen, "The Meaning of the Nuclear Evolution: China's Strategic Modernization and US-China Security Relations," *Journal of Strategic Studies* 35, no. 4 (2012): 482–484, https://doi.org/10.1080/01402390 .2012.714710; Fiona S. Cunningham and M. Taylor Fravel, "Assuring Assured Retaliation: China's Nuclear Strategy and U.S.-China Strategic Stability," *International Security* 40, no. 2 (Fall 2015): 7–50, https://doi .org/10.1162/ISEC_a_00215; Fiona S. Cunningham and M. Taylor Fravel, "Dangerous Confidence? Chinese Views of Nuclear Escalation," *International Security* 44, no. 2 (2019): 61–109, https://doi.org/10.11 62/isec_a_00359; Goldstein, "First Things First: The Pressing Danger of Crisis Instability in U.S.-China Relations," *International Security* 37, no. 4 (2013), 79–82; Alastair Iain Johnston, "The Evolution of Interstate Security Crisis-Management Theory and Practice in China," *Naval War College Review* 69, no. 1 (Winter 2016): 28–71, https://di gital-commons.usnwc.edu/cgi/viewcontent.cgi?article=1118&contex t=nwc-review; Joshua Rovner, "Two Kinds of Catastrophe: Nuclear Escalation and Protracted War in Asia," *Journal of Strategic Studies* 40, no. 5 (2017): 696–730, https://doi.org/10.1080/01402390.2017.12 93532; Caitlin Talmadge, "Would China Go Nuclear? Assessing the Risk of Chinese Nuclear Escalation in a Conventional War with the United States," *International Security* 41, no. 4 (Spring 2017): 50–92, https://doi.org/10.1162/ISEC_a_00274; Zhao Tong and Li Bin, "The Underappreciated Risks of Entanglement: A Chinese Perspective," in *Entanglement: Russian and Chinese Perspectives on Non-Nuclear Weapons and Nuclear Risks*, ed. James M. Acton (Washington, DC: Carnegie Endowment for International Peace, 2017), 59–63.

11. David C. Gompert and Martin Libicki, "Cyber Warfare and Sino-American Crisis Instability," *Survival* 56, no. 4 (2014): 7–22, https:// doi.org/10.1080/00396338.2014.941543; Ariel (Eli) Levite and Lyu Jinghua, "Chinese-American Relations in Cyberspace: Toward Collaboration or Confrontation?," *China Military Science*, January 24, 2019: https://carnegieendowment.org/2019/01/24/chinese-american -relations-in-cyberspace-toward-collaboration-or-confrontation-pub -78213; Adam Segal, "U.S. Offensive Cyber Operations in a China--U.S. Military Confrontation," in *Bytes, Bombs, and Spies: The Strategic Dimensions of Offensive Cyber Operations*, ed. Herbert Lin and Amy

Zegart (Washington, DC: Brookings Institution Press, 2019), 319–341; Acton, "Escalation Through Entanglement"; Zhao and Li, "The Underappreciated Risks of Entanglement," 320.

12. Thomas Rid and Peter McBurney, "Cyber-Weapons," *RUSI Journal* 157, no. 1 (2012): 6–13, https://doi.org/10.1080/03071847.2012.66435 4; Lin, "Escalation Dynamics and Conflict Termination in Cyberspace," 50–51.

13. Vice Chairman of the Joint Chiefs of Staff, Department of Defense, "Memorandum: Subject: Joint Terminology for Cyberspace Operations," 2010: 7, from "The United States and Cyberspace: Military Organization, Policies, and Activities," Document 10, *National Security Archive*, January 20, 2016: https://nsarchive.gwu.edu/briefing-book/cyber-vault/2016 -01-20/united-states-cyberspace-military-organization-policies-activities

14. See, for example, Austin Long, "A Cyber SIOP?," in *Bytes, Bombs, and Spies: The Strategic Dimensions of Offensive Cyber Operations*, ed. Herbert Lin and Amy Zegart (Washington, DC: Brookings Institution Press, 2019), 116–122.

15. Long, "A Cyber SIOP?," 121.

16. Borghard and Lonergan, "Cyber Operations as Imperfect Tools of Escalation," 126.

17. Lin, "Escalation Dynamics and Conflict Termination in Cyberspace," 50–51.

18. Ben Elgin and Michael Riley, "Now at the Sands Casino: An Iranian Hacker in Every Server," *Bloomberg*, December 11, 2014: https:// www.bloomberg.com/news/articles/2014-12-11/iranian-hackers-hit -sheldon-adelsons-sands-casino-in-las-vegas; Chris Kubecka, "How to Implement IT Security after a Cyber Meltdown," YouTube, December 29, 2015: https://www.youtube.com/watch?v=WyMobr_TDSI

19. Department of Justice, "United States of America v. Park Jin Hyok," June 8, 2018: 45–53, from "Cyber Brief: DOJ's Park Jin Hyok Criminal Complaint and North Korean Cyber Operations," *National Security Archive*, September 6, 2018: https://nsarchive.gwu.edu/news/cyber-vault/2018-09-06/cyber-brief-dojs-park-jin-hyok-criminal-complaint-north-korean-cyber-operations

20. Andy Greenberg, "The Untold Story of NotPetya, the Most Devastating Cyberattack in History," *Wired*, August 22, 2018: https://www.wired .com/story/notpetya-cyberattack-ukraine-russia-code-crashed-the-world/

21. Department of Justice, "United States of America v. Ahmad Fathi, Hamid Firoozi, Amin Shokohi, Sadegh Ahmadzadegan, Omid Ghaffarinia, Sina

Keissar, and Nader Saedi," March 24, 2016: https://www.justice.gov/opa/file/834996/download

22. Martin C. Libicki, "Drawing Inferences from Cyber Espionage," *CyCon X: Maximizing Effects*, 10th International Conference on Cyber Conflict, NATO Cooperative Cyber Defence Centre of Excellence, Tallinn, 2018, 4–6: https://ccdcoe.org/uploads/2018/10/Art-06-Drawing-Inferences-from-Cyber-Espionage.pdf

23. Libicki, "Drawing Inferences from Cyber Espionage," 4–6.

24. Buchanan, *The Cybersecurity Dilemma*, chapters 3 and 8.

25. Kim Zetter, "Inside the Cunning, Unprecedented Hack of Ukraine's Power Grid," *Wired*, March 3, 2016: https://www.wired.com/2016/03/inside-cunning-unprecedented-hack-ukraines-power-grid/

26. Goldstein, "First Things First," 51.

27. Morgan et al., *Dangerous Thresholds*, xi.

28. The use of force in cyberspace is distinguished from other cyber acts by the level of harm and qualitative features such as its severity, immediacy and directness of effects, invasiveness, military character, and state involvement. See Michael N. Schmitt (ed.), *Tallinn Manual 2.0 on the International Law Applicable Cyber Operations*, 2nd edition (New York: Cambridge University Press, 2017), 333–337.

29. The time required to prepare a network for offensive cyber operations may vary according to the vulnerability of the target. See Long, "A Cyber SIOP?," 120–121; Borghard and Lonergan, "Cyber Operations as Imperfect Tools of Escalation," 125–131.

30. Lin, "Escalation Dynamics and Conflict Termination in Cyberspace."

31. Buchanan, *The Cybersecurity Dilemma*, chapters 3 and 8.

32. For example, the target could use forensics to determine whether the intrusion took place during or just before the crisis, which could signal that an intruder intends to use it to influence the crisis. The ease with which the intrusion is discovered could also signal that the intruder intended to use it immediately and chose not to take the time to develop a stealthier presence.

33. Libicki, "Drawing Inferences from Cyber Espionage," 4–6.

34. Ben Buchanan, *The Hacker and the State: Cyber Attacks and the New Normal of Geopolitics* (Cambridge, MA: Harvard University Press, 2020); Jacquelyn G. Schneider, "Deterrence In and Through Cyberspace," in *Cross-Domain Deterrence: Strategy in an Era of Complexity*, ed. Erik Gartzke and Jon R. Lindsay (New York: Oxford University Press, 2019), 116–118; Valeriano, Jensen, and Maness, *Cyber Strategy*.

35. For discussion of this principle and how information aids defense, see

Buchanan, *The Cybersecurity Dilemma*, chapter 3. See also, Erik Gartzke and Jon R. Lindsay, "Politics by Many Other Means: The Comparative Strategic Advantages of Operational Domains," *Journal of Strategic Studies* (2020): 23–24, https://doi.org/10.1080/01402390.2020.1768372. For a skeptical view that offensive cyber capabilities would be lost if signaled to an adversary, see Herb Lin, "U.S. Cyber Infiltration of the Russian Electric Grid: Implications for Deterrence," *Lawfare*, June 18, 2019: https://www.lawfareblog.com/us-cyber-infiltration-russian-electric-grid-implications-deterrence

36. Robert Jervis, "Cooperation Under the Security Dilemma," *World Politics* 30, no. 2 (January 1978): 199–214, https://www.jstor.org/stable/2009958; Caitlin Talmadge, "Emerging Technology and Intra-War Escalation Risks: Evidence from the Cold War, Implications for Today," *Journal of Strategic Studies* 42, no. 6 (2019): 864–887, https://doi.org/10.1080/01402390.2019.1631811

37. Barry R. Posen, *Inadvertent Escalation: Conventional War and Nuclear Risks* (Ithaca, NY: Cornell University Press, 1991), 3.

38. The victim state could, however, also ignore the attack. Posen, *Inadvertent Escalation*, 3–4.

39. Other factors include organizational repertoires and the fog of war. See Posen, *Inadvertent Escalation*, 14–29.

40. Jervis, "Cooperation Under the Security Dilemma," 186–187. The offense-defense balance does not need to favor the offense for inadvertent escalation to occur, although it can intensify the victim state's incentives to use force.

41. Posen, *Inadvertent Escalation*, 1–3.

42. This calculation is distinct from, but could be enhanced by, a first-mover advantage. Offense-defense theorists disagree on whether first-mover advantages should be included in the offense-defense balance. See Jervis, "Cooperation Under the Security Dilemma," 189; Charles L. Glaser and Chaim Kaufmann, "What Is the Offense-Defense Balance and How Can We Measure It?," *International Security* 22, no. 4 (1998): 71–72, https://doi.org/10.1162/isec.22.4.44; Rebecca Slayton, "What is the Cyber Offense-Defense Balance? Conceptions, Causes, and Assessment," *International Security* 41, no. 3 (2017): 72–109, https://doi.org/10.1162/ISEC_a_00267

43. This could involve a state facing pressure to either "use or lose" its weapons or signal resolve in case its adversary's conflict objectives expand in future. See Jervis, "Cooperation Under the Security Dilemma," 189; Thomas C. Schelling, *Arms and Influence* (New Haven, CT: Yale

University Press, 1966), chapter 6; Talmadge, "Would China Go Nuclear?," 57.

44. Posen, *Inadvertent Escalation*, 2.

45. 46 Rose McDermott, "Some Emotional Considerations in Cyber Conflict," *Journal of Cyber Policy* 4, no. 3 (2019): 316, https://doi.org/10.1080/23738871.2019.1701692

47. Scholars have suggested that similar organizational dynamics might occur within an attacking state in inadvertent escalation scenarios because the military often does not involve civilians in operational planning and/or inform them about ongoing operations in a timely manner. See Posen, *Inadvertent Escalation*, 16–19.

48. Goldstein, "First Things First," 75–77.

49. Talmadge, "Emerging Technology and Intra-War Escalation Risks," 890, 868–869.

50. Morgan et al., *Dangerous Thresholds*, xii.

51. See, for example, Kreps and Schneider, "Escalation Firebreaks in the Cyber, Conventional, and Nuclear Domains"; Schneider, "The Information Revolution and International Stability"; Benjamin Jensen and Brandon Valeriano, "What Do We Know About Cyber Escalation? Observations From Simulations and Surveys," *Atlantic Council*, November 2019; Valeriano and Maness, *Cyber War Versus Cyber Realities*.

52. Valeriano, Jensen, and Maness, *Cyber Strategy*; Borghard and Lonergan, "Cyber Operations as Imperfect Tools of Escalation," 131–133; Borghard and Lonergan, "The Logic of Coercion in Cyberspace," 466–471; Gartzke, "The Myth of Cyberwar"; Lindsay, "Stuxnet and the Limits of Cyber Warfare"; Gartzke and Lindsay, "Politics by Many Other Means," 21–24.

53. Kreps and Schneider, "Escalation Firebreaks in the Cyber, Conventional, and Nuclear Domains."

54. Carson, *Secret Wars*, 296.

55. Thomas Rid and Ben Buchanan, "Attributing Cyber Attacks," *Journal of Strategic Studies* 38, no. 1–2 (2015): 32, https://doi.org/10.1080/01402390.2014.977382

56. Carson, *Secret Wars*, 296.

57. Eric Heginbotham et al., *The U.S.-China Military Scorecard: Forces, Geography, and the Evolving Balance of Power, 1996–2017* (Santa Monica, CA: RAND Corporation, 2015); M. Taylor Fravel, "China's 'World Class Military' Ambitions: Origins and Implications," *The Washington Quarterly* 43, no. 1 (2020): 85–99; National Defense Strategy Commission, "Providing for the Common Defense: The Assessments

and Recommendations of the National Defense Strategy Commission" (Washington, DC: United States Institute of Peace, November 2018): https://www.usip.org/publications/2018/11/providing-common-de fense

58. Shane Smith, "Cyberspies, Nukes, and the New Cold War: Shane Smith Interviews Ashton Carter (Part 1)," *Vice*, May 15, 2015: 2:13, https://www.vice.com/en/article/xw3b4n/cyberspies-nukes-and-the-new-co ld-war-shane-smith-interviews-ashton-carter-part-1

59. Paul M. Nakasone and Michael Sulmeyer, "How to Compete in Cyberspace," *Foreign Affairs*, August 25, 2020: https://www.foreignaffai rs.com/articles/united-states/2020-08-25/cybersecurity

60. Thomas Rid, *Rise of the Machines: A Cybernetic History* (New York: W. W. Norton & Company, 2016), 315.

61. Rid, *Rise of the Machines*, 327.

62. Ibid., 336.

63. *Newsweek*, "We're in the Middle of a Cyberwar," September 19, 1999: https://www.newsweek.com/were-middle-cyerwar-166196. See also Rid, *Rise of the Machines*, 338.

64. Vice Chairman of the Joint Chiefs of Staff, "Memorandum: Subject: Joint Terminology for Cyberspace Operations," 2010, 7: http://www.nsci-va.org/CyberReferenceLib/2010-11-Joint%20 Terminology%20for%20Cyberspace%20Operations.pdf. This memo updated a vaguer 2005 instruction that referred to the need to shape the digital environment to aid operations. See Chairman of the Joint Chiefs of Staff, "The National Military Strategy for Cyberspace Operations (U)," November 30, 2006: 2, https://www.hsdl.org/?abstract&did=35693

65. US Strategic Command, "CYBERCOM Announcement Message," May 21, 2010: 2, from "The United States and Cyberspace: Military Organization, Policies, and Activities," *National Security Archive*, January 20, 2016: https://nsarchive.gwu.edu/briefing-book/cyber-vault/2016 -01-20/united-states-cyberspace-military-organization-policies-activities

66. The White House, "Fact Sheet on Presidential Policy Directive 20," Federation of American Scientists, 2012: https://fas.org/irp/offdocs/ppd /ppd-20-fs.pdf

67. Barack Obama, "Presidential Policy Directive/PPD-20, Subject: U.S. Cyber Operations Policy," October 16, 2012: 2–3, from *National Security Archive*: https://nsarchive2.gwu.edu/dc.html?doc=2725521-Document -2-9

68. Ibid., 2–3.

69. Ibid., 9.

70. Ibid.
71. Ibid.
72. Ibid.
73. Ibid., 3.
74. David E. Sanger, "Trump Loosens Secretive Restraints on Ordering Cyberattacks," *The New York Times*, September 20, 2018: https://www.nytimes.com/2018/09/20/us/politics/trump-cyberattacks-orders.html
75. Mark Pomerleau, "New Cyber Authority Could Make 'All the Difference in the World'," *Fifth Domain*, September 17, 2018: https://www.fifthdomain.com/dod/cybercom/2018/09/17/new-cyber-authority-could-make-all-the-difference-in-the-world/
76. Pomerleau, "New Cyber Authority Could Make 'All the Difference in the World'"; Sydney Freedberg, "Trump Eases Cyber Ops, but Safeguards Remain: Joint Staff," *Breaking Defense*, September 17, 2018: https://breakingdefense.com/2018/09/trump-eases-cyber-ops-but-safeguards-remain-joint-staff/
77. Mark Pomerleau, "Is Cyber Command Really Being More 'Aggressive' in Cyberspace?," *Fifth Domain*, April 25, 2019, quoted in Jason Healey, "The Implications of Persistent (and Permanent) Engagement in Cyberspace," *Journal of Cybersecurity* 5, no. 1 (2019): 3, https://doi.org/10.1093/cybsec/tyz008
78. David E. Sanger and Nicole Perlroth, "U.S. Escalates Online Attacks on Russia's Power Grid," *The New York Times*, June 15, 2019: https://www.nytimes.com/2019/06/15/us/politics/trump-cyber-russia-grid.html
79. Nakashima, "White House Authorizes 'Offensive Cyber Operations' to Deter Foreign Adversaries," *Washington Post*, September 20, 2018: https://www.washingtonpost.com/world/national-security/trump-authorizes-offensive-cyber-operations-to-deter-foreign-adversaries-bolton-says/2018/09/20/b5880578-bd0b-11e8-b7d2-0773aa1e33da_story.html
80. US Cyber Command, *Achieve and Maintain Cyberspace Superiority: Command Vision for US Cyber Command*, March 2018: 3, https://assets.documentcloud.org/documents/4419681/Command-Vision-for-USCYBERCOM-23-Mar-18.pdf
81. For arguments in support of persistent engagement, see Michael P. Fischerkeller and Richard J. Harknett, "Persistent Engagement, Agreed Competition, Cyberspace Interaction Dynamics, and Escalation" (Washington, DC: Institute for Defense Analyses, May 2018); Michael P. Fischerkeller and Richard J. Harknett, "What Is Agreed Competition in Cyberspace?," *Lawfare*, February 19, 2019: https://www.lawfareblog.com

/what-agreed-competition-cyberspace. For critiques, see Healey, "The Implications of Persistent (and Permanent) Engagement in Cyberspace"; Max Smeets, "There Are Too Many Red Lines in Cyberspace," *Lawfare*, March 20, 2019: https://www.lawfareblog.com/there-are-too-many -red-lines-cyberspace; Jason Healey and Robert Jervis, "The Escalation Inversion and Other Oddities of Situational Cyber Stability," *Texas National Security Review* 3, no. 4 (Fall 2020): 30–53, http://dx.doi.org /10.26153/tsw/10962. See also Aaron Brantly (ed.), *The Cyber Deterrence Problem* (New York: Rowman & Littlefield, 2020).

82. Nakasone and Sulmeyer, "How to Compete in Cyberspace."

83. The Chinese government does not officially acknowledge that the PLA has an offensive cyber operations capability. But China's offensive cyber capabilities are acknowledged in the teaching, research, and strategy publications of influential PLA organizations such as the Academy of Military Science and National Defense University. The PLA's official newspaper and cyber security publications associated with civilian government agencies also discuss offensive cyber capabilities.

84. Xi Jinping, *Zai wangluo anquan he xinxihua gongzuo zuotanhui shang de jiangzuo [Speech at the Cybersecurity and Informatization Work Symposium]* (Beijing: Renmin chubanshe, 2016), 17.

85. Lyu Jinghua, *Meiguo wangluo kongjianzhan sixiang yanjiu [A Study of US Thought on Cyber Warfare]* (Beijing: Junshi kexueyuan chubanshe, 2014), 241.

86. "The CIA Hacking Group (APT-C-39) Conducts Cyber-Espionage Operation on China's Critical Industries for 11 Years," Qihoo 360 Threat Intelligence Center, March 2, 2020: https://blogs.360.cn/post /APT-C-39_CIA_EN.html

87. Cai Jun, He Jun, and Yu Xiaohong, "Meijun wangluo kongjian zuozhan lilun [Theories of US Cyberspace Operations]," *Zhongguo junshi kexue [China Military Science]* 1 (2018): 151.

88. See, for example, Lu Chuanying, "Forging Stability in Cyberspace," *Survival* 62, no. 2 (2020): 128, https://doi.org/10.1080/00396338.2020 .1739959; Tan Yushan, "Toushi: Telangpu Zhengfu wangluo anquan mian mianguan [Perspective: A Comprehensive Survey of Cybersecurity under the Trump Administration]," *Zhongguo xinxi anquan [China Information Security]* 7 (2018): 89, http://www.cnki.com.cn/Article/CJ FDTotal-CINS201807035.htm; Lyu Jinghua, "Daguo hezuo yinling wangluo kongjian guoji zhixu cong chongtu zouxiang wending [Great Power Cooperation Showing the Way in the Cyberspace International Order From Conflict Towards Stability]," *Zhongguo xinxi anquan [China*

Information Security] 11 (2018): 34, http://www.cnki.com.cn/Article /CJFDTotal-CINS201811017.htm. See also Lyu Jinghua, "A Chinese Perspective on the Pentagon's Cyber Strategy: From 'Active Cyber Defense' to 'Defending Forward'," *Lawfare*, October 18, 2018: https:// www.lawfareblog.com/chinese-perspective-pentagons-cyber-strategy-a ctive-cyber-defense-defending-forward; Ariel Levite et al., *China-U.S. Cyber-Nuclear C3 Stability* (Washington, DC: Carnegie Endowment for International Peace, April 2021). It remains unclear whether China might emulate the US approach of defending forward outside of its networks.

89. Lyu Jinghua, "A Chinese Perspective on the New Intelligence Framework to Understand National Competition in Cyberspace," in *Deter, Disrupt or Deceive? Assessing Cyber Conflict as an Intelligence Contest*, ed. Robert Chesney and Max Smeets (forthcoming, Georgetown University Press).

90. Shou Xiaosong (ed.), *Zhanlue xue [The Science of Military Strategy]* (Beijing: Junshi kexueyuan chubanshe, 2013), 192–194; Xiao Tianliang (ed.), *Zhanlue xue [The Science of Military Strategy]*, revised edition (Beijing: Guofang daxue chubanshe, 2017), 150–152; Ye Zheng (ed.), *Xinxi zuozhan xue jiaocheng [Study Guide to Information Warfare]* (Junshi kexueyuan chubanshe, 2013), 167–168, 177–178, 207–208.

91. Li Zhaorui (ed.), *Wangluo zhan jichu yu fazhan qushi [Cyber War Foundations and Development Trends]* (Beijing: Jiefangjun chubanshe, 2015), 71. The 54th Institute was subordinated to the Strategic Support Force in 2016. See Elsa B. Kania and John K. Costello, "The Strategic Support Force and the Future of Chinese Information Operations," *The Cyber Defense Review* 3 (Spring 2018): 111, https://cyberdefensereview.army.mil /CDR-Content/Articles/Article-View/Article/1589125/the-strategic-support-force-and-the-future-of-chinese-information-operations/

92. Ibid., 72.

93. Ibid., 72–76.

94. Ibid., 75.

95. "Junshi Kexue Yuan zhuanjia jiemi wangluo kongjian weishe [Academy of Military Sciences Expert Reveals Cyberspace Deterrence]," China Military Online, January 6, 2016: http://military.people.com.cn/n1/20 16/0106/c1011-28020408.html

96. Shou, *Zhanlue xue*, 192.

97. Xiao, *Zhanlue xue*, 148, 229. See also Li, *Wangluo zhan Jichu yu fazhan qushi*, 71.

98. Xiao, *Zhanlue Xue*, 150, 237.

99. Yu Saisai and Du Yucong, "Wangluo zhan dui xiandai zhanzheng fa tixi de yingxiang," *Waiguo junshi xueshu [Foreign Military Arts]* 5 (2015): 71.

100. Zhou Xinsheng (ed.), *Junzhong zhanlue jiaocheng [Study Guide to Military Service Strategy]* (Beijing: Junshi kexue yuan chubanshe, 2013), 126.

101. Lyu, "A Chinese Perspective on the New Intelligence Framework to Understand National Competition in Cyberspace."

102. Ting-yu Lin, "PLA Cyber Operations: A New Type of Cross-Border Attack," in *The PLA Beyond Borders: Chinese Military Operations in Regional and Global Context*, ed. Joel Wuthnow et al. (Washington, DC: National Defense University Press, 2021), 302–303; Inksit Group, "China-Linked Group RedEcho Targets the Indian Power Sector Amid Heightened Border Tensions" (Recorded Future, February 28, 2021).

103. Shou, *Zhanlue xue*, 192.

104. "Junshi Kexue Yuan zhuanjia jiemi wangluo kongjian weishe."

105. Liu Yangyue, "Wangluo kongjian guoji Chongtu yu zhanlue wendingxing [International Crises in Cyberspace and Strategic Stability]," *Waijiao pinglun [Foreign Affairs Review]* 4 (2016): 112–115, http://www.cnki.com .cn/Article/CJFDTOTAL-WJXY201604005.htm

106. Liu, "Wangluo kongjian guoji Chongtu yu zhanlue wendingxing," 118; Liu uses the same large-N and qualitative data as Western cyber security scholarship to draw his conclusions.

107. Zhao and Li, "The Underappreciated Risks of Entanglement," 62–63.

108. Liu, "Wangluo kongjian guoji chongtu yu zhanlue wendingxing," 125.

109. See for example, Lu, "Forging Stability in Cyberspace."

110. Xiao Tiefeng, "Wangluo Weishe Yu He Weishe: Qubie Yu Jiejian [Cyber Deterrence and Nuclear Deterrence: Differences and Lessons]," *Waiguo Junshi Xueshu*, no. 4 (2013): 1–5.

111. Levite and Lyu, "Chinese-American Relations in Cyberspace."

112. "China's Guidelines on Joint Operations Aim for Future Warfare: Defense Spokesperson," *China Military Online*, November 27, 2020: http://english.scio.gov.cn/pressroom/2020-11/27/content_76954237 .htm

113. Xue Xinglin, *Zhanyi lilun xuexi zhinan [Campaign Theory Study Guide]* (Beijing: Guofang daxue chubanshe, 2001), 53; Ye, *Xinxi zuozhan xue jiaocheng*.

114. Ren Jian (ed.), *Zuozhan Tiaoling Gailun [An Introduction to Operations Regulations]* (Beijing: Junshi Kexue Yuan Chubanshe, 2016), 93.

115. Mark A. Stokes, "The Chinese People's Liberation Army and Computer Network Operations Infrastructure," in *China and Cybersecurity: Espionage, Strategy, and Politics in the Digital Domain*, ed. Jon R. Lindsay, Tai Ming Cheung, and Derek S. Reveron (New York: Oxford University Press, 2015), 163–187.

116. John Costello and Joe McReynolds, *China's Strategic Support Force: A Force for a New Era* (Washington, DC: Institute for National Strategic Studies, National Defense University, September 2018), 23–25: https://inss.ndu .edu/Portals/68/Documents/stratperspective/china/china-perspectives _13.pdf; Elsa B. Kania and John Costello, "Seizing the Commanding Heights: The PLA Strategic Support Force in Chinese Military Power," *Journal of Strategic Studies* 44, no. 2 (2020): 27–29.

117. Fiona S. Cunningham, "China's Search for Coercive Leverage in the Information Age," working paper; Kania and Costello, "Seizing the Commanding Heights," 14.

118. "Junshi Kexueyuan zhuanjia jiemi wangluo kongjian weishe"; Xiao Tianliang (ed.), *Zhanlue xue [The Science of Military Strategy]* (Beijing: Guofang daxue chubanshe, 2017), 388–389.

119. John Chen, Joe McReynolds, and Kieran Green, "The PLA Strategic Support Force: A 'Joint' Force for Information Operations," in *The PLA Beyond Borders: Chinese Military Operations in Regional and Global Context*, ed. Joel Wuthnow et al. (Washington, DC: National Defense University Press, 2021), 160–163. For a description of those oversight problems, see Cunningham, "China's Search for Coercive Leverage in the Information Age."

120. John Chen, Joe McReynolds, and Kieran Green, "The PLA Strategic Support Force: A 'Joint' Force for Information Operations," 156.

121. "Full Text: International Strategy of Cooperation on Cyberspace," *Xinhua News Agency*, March 1, 2017: http://news.xinhuanet.com/eng lish/china/2017-03/01/c_136094371_2.htm

122. Zhonggong Zhongyang Dangshi he Wenxian Yanjiuyuan (ed.), *Xi Jinping Guanyu Wangluo Qiangguo Lunshu Zhaibian [Extracts from Xi Jinping's Expositions on a Cyber Superpower]* (Beijing: Zhongyang Wenxian Chubanshe, 2021), 99.

123. "The CIA Hacking Group (APT-C-39) Conducts Cyber-Espionage Operation on China's Critical Industries for 11 Years."

124. Antian Shiyan Shi [Antiy Labs], "Wukelan Tingdian Shijian Qishilu [Revelations from the Ukrainian Power Outage Incident]," *Zhongguo Xinxi Anquan [China Information Security]* 4 (2016): 51, http://www.cnki .com.cn/Article/CJFDTotal-CINS201604021.htm

125. Rovner, "Cyber War as an Intelligence Contest."

126. Christopher P. Twomey, *The Military Lens: Doctrinal Difference and Deterrence Failure* (Ithaca, NY: Cornell University Press, 2010).

127. Of course, in a crisis situation, leaders from both countries would have access to a general defense hotline established in 2008. Lindsay Beck,

"China and U.S. Sign Accord on Defense Hotline," *Reuters*, February 29, 2008: https://www.reuters.com/article/us-china-us-defence-idUSP EK7130320080229

128. Richard J. Harknett and Michael P. Fischerkeller, "Through Persistent Engagement, the U.S. Can Influence 'Agreed Competition'," *Lawfare*, April 15, 2019: https://www.lawfareblog.com/through-persistent-enga gement-us-can-influence-agreed-competition

129. Valeriano, Jensen, and Maness, *Cyber Strategy: The Evolving Character of Power and Coercion.*

130. See, for example, Gartzke, "The Myth of Cyberwar."

3

Concept Misalignment and Cyberspace Instability: Lessons from Cyber-Enabled Disinformation

Jaclyn A. Kerr[1]

Today there is general awareness that the 2016 demonstration of novel offensive information operation techniques by Russia hit the United States as a surprise – one which the US was poorly prepared to anticipate, defend against, or respond to. And this was despite the fact that, by all public accounts, the US was one of the most advanced countries in the world at the time in its cyber domain capabilities. This shock led to immediate and understandable hand-wringing over apparent cyber domain strategic failure, prompting significant new strategy development efforts and ongoing debates in the US and with US allies. What is somewhat less obvious is whether the correct lessons have been learned from the nature of the surprise itself and what it says about threat perception, domain conceptualization, and emulation dynamics in the evolution of the cyber domain, and the repercussions for potential future stability. Put differently: beyond considering the immediate strategic solution to address this new challenge, what universe of challenges is it an instance of and what broader lessons must be learned to avert equivalent future cases of surprise and inadvertent escalation? Clear understanding here is essential both for correctly addressing the challenge at hand and for avoiding future cycles of escalation.

This chapter argues that this instance of surprise escalation was the result of a long-developing security dilemma rooted in "domain concept misalignment" – i.e. superficially overlapping but significantly different domain conceptualizations – resulting from the distinction in how democratic and non-democratic states approached conceptualizing the scope and nature of the emerging digital and informational domain of military action. While domain concepts and strategy have now begun to adjust to the new perceived threat of cyber-enabled information operations,[2] the chapter argues that this specific sort of escalatory spiral, fueled by domain concept misalignment and "diagonal escalation" – i.e. within-domain for one actor, but outside for the other – is an endemic challenge of the cyber domain. All strategies aim, on some level, to influence the behavior of adversaries and shape the long-term development of systemic behavioral norms. But strategies – involving whatever overall mix of threat-based deterrence, defense and denial, or norm promotion – can only explicitly seek to mitigate threatening behaviors they have awareness of and can anticipate. Surprise attacks are therefore unlikely to be effectively prevented by any strategy if they lie well outside the bounds of aggression forms that the current domain concepts and strategy conceive of and aim to address.

Without heightened efforts at mutual awareness and broad consideration of alternative conceptual frameworks, cycles of surprise and escalation will be recurrent in cyberspace, not only making development of desirable norms difficult and the cyber domain unstable, but even destabilizing the concepts on which it is premised. To manage these underlying conditions and reduce instability, cyberspace strategy development processes must thoughtfully integrate mechanisms to foster greater awareness of domestic politics and threat perspectives of other states, and processes of cross-silo and cross-technology issue engagement across the interagency. In addition, it is critical to avoid bureaucratic and conceptual stove-piping based on prior stages of technology development, maintaining a fluid and evolving understanding of the nature of cyberspace and the constantly changing social, economic, and political interdependencies it makes salient.

The remainder of the chapter is divided into two sections. The first section addresses the question of how it was possible for the global leader in the development of cyber domain capabilities to be caught off guard by Russia's 2016 operations – especially given that the use of such tactics by Russia was not entirely novel at the time and that Russia and other states had for nearly two decades expressed concerns in international forums about the potential destabilizing influence and national security threat stemming from transnational flows of information. In examining the relationship between domain concept development and threat perception in cyberspace, the section traces how democratic and non-democratic states came to understand the military and strategic possibilities of and threats from the emerging domain differently, allowing for significant concept misalignment and the possibility of surprise action by the technically weaker party. Examining the reactions of the US and its democratic allies to the newly perceived threat and the potential consequences of these reactions, the section points to the importance of renewed conceptual clarity and historical awareness in order to enable a coherent and effective response while also learning the correct lessons to prevent future instances of surprise and escalation.

The second section takes a step back from the immediate case of cyber-enabled information operations to address the broader problem this case indicates in the ongoing development of concepts, strategy, and norms to limit instability in cyberspace. Examining the breadth and complexity of cyberspace and the surrounding regime complex, the section argues that the most salient threat perceptions often vary between states, leading to the emergence of distinct understandings of cyberspace's security threats and potential military uses. The resulting domain concept misalignment poses a recurrent risk to stability in cyberspace. Considering how this dynamic should impact our approach to strategic thinking in cyberspace, the section highlights the risks associated with overly reactive responses to new threats once they have led to surprise escalation. While strategic adaptation to address newly demonstrated threats will often be reactive, seeking to fix newly apparent vulnerabilities and emulate an adversary's successful strategic approach, the section argues, such "domain concept stretching" and "strategic emulation" responses are not always optimal as they can occur iteratively without deliberate reflection on the trade-offs entailed. Shifts in domain concepts may lead to an over-securitization of new issue areas, impinging on prior existing governance arrangements. Not all strategic innovations can be equally effectively adopted by all states, with efforts to emulate potentially chafing against existing institutional or cultural constraints, possibly strengthening the strategic position of the adversary. Where possible, longer-horizon processes should therefore be prioritized in cyberspace strategy development, with a focus on norm-building and strategic foresight to avert future instances of concept misalignment-fueled surprise and escalation. In responding to known instances of concept misalignment, the repercussions of emulation should be considered and weighed against those of alternative asymmetric or hardening-based defensive approaches.

The chapter concludes with a call for fostering greater cross-silo engagement across areas of expertise and across the inter-agency, and for building mechanisms of strategic foresight into future cyberspace strategy development processes. In the long term, these steps will improve security while retaining as much as possible of the value associated with cyberspace's global digital interdependence.

Cyber-Enabled Disinformation and The New Threat Perception in the West

In the aftermath of 2016, in US national security policy circles, it became common to hear Russia's surprise initial usage of cyber-enabled information operations described as having demonstrated a unique and sophisticated strategic approach to the cyber domain, showing that Russia was out-thinking the US on understanding the domain's basic attributes and strategic possibilities. The translation of a 2013 speech by the Chief of the General Staff of the Russian Armed Forces, General Valery Gerasimov, was widely read and often held up as an example of new military "doctrine" that Russia had been developing for years before using this approach in its surprise attack on the West.[3] The failure of US cyber defense strategy to prevent this Russian aggression was held up as proof of the inadequacy of the prior strategic approach to the cyber domain. How else to explain the US being owned in a domain that it had helped pioneer and in which it was thought to hold such superior capabilities that a common term of cyber strategy parlance, "NOBUS," referred bluntly to the existence of certain domain capabilities that were achievable by "nobody but us"?

What many of these initial reactions failed to note was that the quoted Gerasimov speech and many other Russian strategic writings from that time were framed explicitly in terms of reaction to perceived US aggression and an effort to understand and respond to what was thought to be existing US strategy.[4] Whether focused on perceived US support for independent civil society and media since the 1990s, "Orangist forces" behind colored revolution events in Russia's backyard through the 2000s, or the Arab Spring and Russia's own White Ribbon Protest Movement in 2011–2012, Russian strategic commentary often focused on a perceived intentional threat to its regime's survival, and perceived superior strategy involving manipulation of information and the exploitation of psychological and social forces within society – an approach from which to learn and a threat to prepare against. It seems fairly clear in retrospect that US cyber strategists were not fully aware of this Russian perception of threat and aggression (or did not take it seriously). No intentional military threat of this nature had been mounted. What is more, the supposed threat vector fell so far outside the conceived of role of the cyber domain that a 2015 Defense Science Board report explicitly calling on the defense community to prepare better against surprise cyber attacks failed to mention any notion of cyber-enabled informational or psychological operations at all, focusing exclusively on critical infrastructure and cyber-to-kinetic threats.[5]

"Cyber security" Versus "Information Security"

By 2016, the use of cyberspace as a domain for military and intelligence operations had been developing for decades – and was perceived to be of increasing strategic importance to the US and allies, as well as adversaries. But the degree of shock and consternation resulting from the initial revelation of Russian election interference and disinformation campaigns suggested a strategic blind spot had developed in the Western approach. One significant reason for this lack of strategic foresight had to do *not* with a lack of capability in the cyberspace domain as the US had defined it, and instead with a lack of adequate awareness or understanding of the distinct way in which non-democratic regimes saw national security threats from cyberspace differently and how that motivated alternative forms of defensive and offensive capability development, and the potential for escalation.

Both democratic and non-democratic states had long been aware of pronounced benefits and security risks resulting from the growth of cyberspace. But they differed in the positive visions they embraced and sought to promote, and in the threat perceptions around which they crafted security concepts and military capabilities. These differences were particularly pronounced in relation to the content layer of the internet and the transnational flows of ideas and information it permitted. In the decades of the internet's expansive growth following the end of the Cold War, democracies largely followed a dual approach which separated considerations of the new highly technical military domain from that of the global communications network. So while the US accepted and promoted a globalist vision of "internet freedom," it simultaneously embraced a more narrowly and technically understood "cyberspace domain" of national security interest and military conflict. This approach contrasted with the alternative vision of cyberspace pursued and promoted by Russia, China, and other non-democratic states, concerned with notions of "internet sovereignty" and domestic "information security."

The United States' internet freedom agenda is best captured in the January 2010 Newseum speech by then-Secretary of State Hillary Clinton.[6] The speech laid out an agenda for a strengthened US diplomatic stance regarding the global protection of "internet freedom." Describing this freedom as a twenty-first-century human right akin to freedoms of expression, association, media, religion, and other basic rights globally acknowledged during the twentieth century, Clinton emphasized the technology's role in permitting new forms of civic engagement, political speech, economic modernization and opportunity, and information sharing, but also highlighted the risks it now faced as authoritarian regimes sought to censor, surveil, and control the internet's content and use within their territories. Stressing the US's support for an uncensored universal internet that allowed everyone everywhere access to the same content and safe use of internet-based technologies, Clinton used her address to name and shame authoritarian regimes for erecting a new "information curtain" and promised US support for the creation and distribution of tools permitting censorship circumvention by internet users under repressive governments. She called on states to work together so that "we can create norms of behavior among states and encourage respect for the global networked commons."

While the US was also concerned about national security in cyberspace, its focus was predominantly on a relatively narrow understanding of cyber security and cyber conflict in which aggression was conceptualized particularly in terms of destructive or kinetic effects – from sabotage of equipment to mass-casualty-inducing destruction of critical infrastructure. Cyberspace was first recognized as a "'domain' of conflict" by the US military in 2004 in the *National Military Strategy*.[7] By this point, threat perceptions around technical cyber attacks on computing systems and critical infrastructure as a risk to national security had been building for decades. As computer networks had expanded through the 1970s and 1980s, early significant security incidents had shaped this concern. By the 1990s, the idea of a paralyzing and devastating bolt-from-the-blue "cyber Pearl Harbor" was a much-repeated threat narrative. This threat perception would be a guiding force in the development of US cyber doctrine, policy, strategy, and military institutions. The first US cyber operational unit was created within the Defense Information Systems Agency in 1998, undergoing rapid growth and a series of changes in organizational structure, mission, and location, before forming the United States Cyber Command (USCYBERCOM) in 2010.[8] The Department of Defense's (DoD) first *Strategy for Operating in Cyberspace* was issued in 2011,[9] and the Pentagon issued its first joint doctrine specifically dedicated to "cyberspace operations" in 2013.[10] Through the course of these developments, numerous potential ways to conceptualize threats pertaining to digital networks and information were explored and considered, but the emphasis remained ultimately technical in nature, with limited focus on the holistic role of information or its impact on public opinion and discourse.

Ultimately, the internet freedom agenda's endorsement of the ideal of a global uncensored internet implicitly relied upon a conceptual delineation between the issues pertaining to national security in cyberspace and those relating to freedom of expression. For democracies, this norm promotion effort was not seen as contradicting national security imperatives relating to the new domain. But it was a direct challenge to the efforts by Russia and other non-democratic and hybrid regime states during this same period to promote norms that ensured their own national security in cyberspace as they understood it. From the beginning, these governments' threat perceptions were focused on information flows and internet content, not just on technical cyber attacks.[11] They worried about the impact on domestic political stability and control. They were quick to see new instances of protest mobilization through the prism of regime change and foreign intervention.[12] The concept of "information security" captured this distinct threat perception as it was understood to relate to national security. Russia adopted its first "Information Security Doctrine" in September of 2000, during the first year of Vladimir Putin's presidency.[13] The doctrine laid out a foundation for considering media or information flows as potential threats to political stability and national security, and for seeing the large-scale intentional manipulation of information as a possible form of interstate aggression. The doctrine used some language similar to US military doctrinal documents, suggesting that it was viewed at least partly as a response to US strategy at the time.[14]

Russia and like-minded states also strategically and energetically pursued norms and security relationships that would limit the legitimate use of information aggression by other states. In 1998, Russia submitted to the UN General Assembly its first of many draft resolutions on "Developments in the field of information and telecommunications in the context of international security," which pointed to concern about the potential impact of information warfare on international peace and stability.[15] In 2011 and 2015, Russia and China led blocks of countries in submitting drafts of an "International Code of Conduct for Information Security" to the United Nations General Assembly.[16] Russian efforts through regional organizations, including the Collective Security Treaty Organization (CSTO) and the Shanghai Cooperation Organization (SCO), also sought to promote cooperation around defending "information security," often explicitly referencing the threat of Arab Spring-type events. In May of 2015, Russia and China also adopted an "Information Security Non-Aggression Pact."[17] The United States and its democratic allies objected to Russia's norm-building efforts around "information" as opposed to "cyber" non-aggression, arguing that, by including the content layer of the internet, media, and other information flows as potential vehicles of aggression, these efforts aimed to legitimize domestic policies of internet and media censorship where regimes felt threatened by the free flow of information.

In the wake of Russia's 2016 election interference campaign, the point has frequently been made that authoritarian states have an asymmetric advantage in the use of disinformation because these states constrain their own domestic information environments, providing them some shield from a similar form of aggression. But this inadequately captures the role that perceptions of an escalating threat to regime survival played in disinformation capability development, through these states' iterative efforts to build domestic resilience against destabilizing information flows.[18] The difference in cyberspace threat perceptions between democratic and non-democratic states ultimately played an important role in the development of each sides' defensive and offensive capabilities and military strategy. With an apparent perception of playing catch-up and being on the defensive, a critical component of Russia's strategy and capability development in cyberspace through the 2000s and 2010s consisted in finding ways to defend against perceived internet-mediated threats to national security in the form of domestic instability. This led to experimentation with the development of new capabilities for control *and manipulation* of the domestic information environment. Some of these capabilities also had significant offensive applicability.[19]

Western Reactions and Strategic Adaptation

As they have sought to address the newly perceived threat posed by deliberate manipulation of online discourse, the US and other democracies have attempted a variety of solutions. Reaction to cyber-enabled information operations was one impetus for changes in US cyber domain strategy after the 2016 interference, for example. The US's "2018 DOD Cyber Strategy" published in the wake of the 2016 election explicitly indicated Russia's use of these operations to influence public opinion and affect electoral processes as one challenge the new strategy aimed to address in cyberspace.[20] One of the first publicized demonstrations of USCYBERCOM's new strategic approach described in its 2018 "Command Vision" was its interference with the Saint Petersburg-based troll farm, the Internet Research Agency (IRA), on election day in November 2018.[21] It went largely un-noted at the time that one of the major threat vectors which the new strategy was crafted to address was a form of aggression that would not have even been acknowledged as falling within the "cyberspace domain" only a few years earlier.

Reactions to the newfound democratic vulnerability did not stop with alterations to existing military security strategies, however. With the threat's crossover into new areas of digital governance that had once been thought of strictly in terms of the digital public sphere and internet freedom agenda, there has been considerable pressure on other parts of government and society to contribute to the solution. Policymakers have considered or adopted new regulations aimed at reducing the foothold of foreign online disinformation campaigns. Diplomatic engagements have sought to name and shame perpetrators and collaborate with allies to punish state sponsors of foreign "malign influence," promote preferrable behavior, and foster mutual protection. In response to negative publicity, government pressure, and growing awareness of the problem, private sector internet platforms have also taken a panoply of "self-regulatory" steps to address the problems through changes to platform policies or algorithms. Educators, civil society, and academic groups, public-private partnerships, and collaborations across stakeholders have also all played roles in researching and seeking solutions to the problem.

While these efforts to address the new threat have constituted important and valuable strategic adaptations, many of the potential solutions explored also come with their own risks and complications. Too much focus on platform-level solutions effected through changes to algorithms or terms of service, for example, might result in various forms of over-removal, algorithmic bias, and reduction in online freedom of expression. Too much emphasis on national-level regulatory fixes might threaten core democratic principles of free expression, put a heavy burden on innovation through increasing the toll of intermediary liability, and lead to a reduction of the internet's trans-national and globalist character with increased fragmentation along national lines. Too much attention to the role of diplomacy for confidence building, signaling, and norm promotion or negotiation might become an appeasement-laced exercise in futility, having little impact on the behavior of adversaries, restraining defensive options, and sowing false confidence in unenforceable aspirational norms. Too much reliance on military operational persistence and constant competition in relation to the online discourse space might lead to an over-militarization of the public sphere, prove escalatory, and fail to result in desirable normative outcomes, with ever more state and non-state actors entering the cyber-enabled information competition, and even democracies potentially adopting similar tactics of information aggression despite the nox-iousness of such practices to core democratic values.

Each of these approaches, architected and undertaken by highly skilled elites – expert technicians, lawyers, diplomats, and military strategists – also suffers from a problem of democracy deficit. While this might be a common complication pertaining to matters critical to national security, it can be a reason for alarm when those matters happen to also be as crucial to democracy as questions of how to govern public discourse.

These democratic reactions to cyber-enabled information operations demonstrate some of the challenges and risks associated with addressing a newly perceived threat in cyberspace that emerges suddenly after a long period of concept misalignment. The reactive posture of responding to a suddenly evident and imminent threat has meant that core conceptual questions and normatively fraught value trade-offs resulting from the tension between dem-ocratic and non-democratic approaches to cyberspace have often not been at the forefront of discussion. An inadequate understanding of the key role played by concept misalignment in Russia's surprise escalation has been detrimental to the coherence and effectiveness of the overall response effort.

To achieve greater long-term cyberspace stability will require understand-ing the potential for recurrent concept misalignment and less reactive strategic mitigations.

The Recurrent Conceptual Challenge to Cyberspace Stability

The interaction between the US and Russia concerning the role of transnational flows of information in relation to national security has played out as a slow-moving security dilemma-fueled escalatory spiral over the last two-plus decades. It is a spiral, to the extent that the Russian strategic community perceived itself as responding to US strategy, capabilities, and aggression, and that then, years later, the US strategic community similarly considered its situation as one of responding to unprovoked aggression, superior capabilities, and strategic innovation. This is not just a matter of the 2016 aggression or immediate prior provocations. It is also visible in various democracy promotion, norm advocacy, and naming and shaming activities, and diplomatic exchanges over years prior, as well as in the various information resiliency-building adaptations by authoritarian states, and the early applications of cyber-enabled information manipulation capabilities in smaller arenas. But this is also a unique sort of security dilemma, insofar as it demonstrates the escalatory risk posed by concept misalignment of a sort to which the cyber domain is particularly predisposed.

Domain concept development is always intimately intertwined with threat perception. Given the complexity and novelty of cyberspace, the interconnection with numerous and varying systems cutting across all sectors of the economy and society, most of which are civilian systems and fall well outside the conventional scope of war-making, the understanding of the scope and nature of the cyber domain for military competition conducted in and through cyberspace has tended to be particularly shaped by existing perceptions of threats. These can fail to align in significant ways between actors. There is no reason to assume that the case examined here relating to differences in threat perceptions between democratic and non-democratic regimes is *sui generis*. It is much more likely that such concept misalignment-based security dilemmas will be frequent given the nature of cyberspace.

Domain Concepts and Cyberspace Complexity

What makes repeated concept misalignment possible and even likely in cyberspace? The answer hinges on correctly understanding the multidimensionality of the areas of social, political, and economic life which are affected by cyberspace and could, as a result, potentially one day be subject to dynamics of competitive manipulation. And this itself, of course, is a shifting and expanding terrain.

On one level, we are discussing here the possibility for misalignment in understanding of the military cyberspace "domain" or "operational space" and how this might be conceived and operationalized. For example, even in the United States there was significant early debate as to whether the growth of the global internet warranted the definition of a new operational domain and, if so, how it should be defined. But even this debate about "domains" was culturally specific, rooted in US military strategic and organizational culture. The idea of domains tends to already encourage a certain conceptual approach – breaking up the realm of possible environments for military action into a covering set of non-overlapping "spaces" in which such action can potentially occur. It brings a physical and materialist focus, stovepipes attention to types of domain-specific operations and missions.[22] But it doesn't necessarily answer the question "what are all the imaginable and strategically significant things that one adversary could do to another utilizing this new medium?" or the follow-on question "imaginable by whom?"

Of equal significance to the discussion at hand, then, are the distinct threat perceptions that emerge pertaining to cyberspace, which in turn shape the military strategic, organizational, and capability developments of rival actors. This is as much about emphasis and what is not mentioned as it is about absolute potential scope of the logical extension of a given domain concept definition. This is because the domain itself is actualized in terms of real organizational infrastructure, human capital investment, and boots on the ground (or code in the network) capabilities. While a definition might be (even deliberately) vague and broad in scope, leaving ample room for further development and evolution, the actual organization of capabilities and manpower says more, more precisely, about the real expectations of utility and limits of imagination at a given moment. Given the entanglement of cyberspace with so many different aspects of political, social, and economic life across different societies, the potential for different perceived threats and opportunities concerning effects on these systems is likely to be somewhat boundless. Insofar as states define their own postures in cyberspace in relation to the threats of which they are most keenly aware, these perceptions might relate to any area in which they perceive risks to their country's stability and regime survival, whether those are actual physical or overtly military threats, or potential challenges to core social, economic, or political systems.

As the internet and digital technologies become ever more embedded in all areas of life and society, this cross-cutting digital substrate has become the ultimate "complex system" – a system of a type so vast and complicated that no one individual can know and understand all parts and their interconnections. Rather, individual specialists in all the areas of expertise and endeavor now interconnected with this substrate must learn and concern themselves with those areas of digital technology and interconnectivity that pertain to their specific work. Each of these different areas of endeavor has distinct characteristics, as does its form of dependence on and interconnectivity with cyberspace. Some of these sub-systems certainly constitute the sorts of complex, tightly-coupled systems, with potential for catastrophic cascading effects of failure that have been discussed in the context of "normal accident theory"[23] – a characterization that is likely appropriate, for example, for precisely the types of critical infrastructure that first aroused "cyber Pearl Harbor" fears within the United States. But here we must ask ourselves, what *other* types of catastrophic threats to national security might different countries fear the most, and how might these be subject to strategic effects involving cyberspace? The possibilities are vast.

Key to these considerations is an understanding of the breadth of societal systems which could be potentially implicated. As opposed to technical or socio-technical layers, of which a finite number can be easily enumerated, one must here account for the wide variety of governance issues that in some way now involve the internet and digital technologies. These can be anything from the governance of the internet's core infrastructure and global interconnectivity to far-flung policy areas in disparate communities on topics ranging from policing and law enforcement to public health, and from media and public communications to transportation systems or property rights. Each issue area has its own surrounding systems of laws, norms, rules, institutions, and interested actors, at various jurisdictional levels from local and national to global. Some of these constitute long-standing governance regimes on mutually unrelated issues. But with the growing embeddedness of digital technologies and networks, each is now cross-cut by and entangled with mechanisms of cyberspace governance.

The governance of cyberspace has developed as a complex ecosystem of interrelated actors, forums, issues, and technologies. This emerging complexity is what led Laura Denardis to observe about the global internet (which is a critical subset but by no means the entirety of cyberspace) that "Internet governance is not a monolithic system with keys that can be handed over to one group or another . . . Thus a question such as 'who should control the Internet . . .' makes no sense whatsoever. The appropriate question involves determining what is the most effective form of governance in each specific context."[24] In a similar vein, Joseph Nye has discussed the "cyber regime complex" pointing to the breadth that already existed in the dimensionality of cyberspace and its global and national levels of governance.[25] Nye's work builds on the understanding from international relations theory that, while normative "regimes" are broadly understood in international relations theory to mean sets of "principles, norms, rules and procedures that govern issue areas in international affairs,"[26] a "regime complex" represents "a collective of partially overlapping and nonhierarchical regimes."[27] As Nye explained, "[a] regime has a degree of hierarchical coherence among norms. A regime complex is a loosely coupled set of regimes. On a spectrum of formal institutionalization, a regime complex is intermediate between a single legal instrument at one end and fragmented arrangements at the other."[28] The cyber regime complex has only gotten more complicated with time, as noted by Mark Raymond (Chapter 7, this volume) in examining how the expansion of the Internet of Things (IoT) pushes the regime complex into more areas of overlap and tension with other areas of global and national governance.

This growing overlap between old normative regimes and governance structures and new digital technologies is critical to explaining the universe of potential new dimensions for concept misalignment and surprise. The key insight is that, while the global expansion of interconnected digital technologies has entangled many other issue areas, the governance of this technological substrate does not replace existing governance institutions and norms around those issues; it rather creates areas of loose interdependency and linkage across otherwise heterogeneous governance regimes. A number of areas which ostensibly could fit under a broad understanding of internet governance or the cyber regime complex tend to be dealt with by different parts of government, different intergovernmental organizations, as well as having distinct ecosystems of surrounding outside non-governmental organizations, private sector actors, and other stakeholders involved in their functioning and governance. Despite growing theoretical and practical connections between these various issue areas, they can persist as distinct fields, surrounded by different policy and epistemic communities, separate areas of expertise, different interested stakeholders, different governance processes and institutions, different degrees of norm agreement and compliance across actors – and indeed only limited interconnectivity between these siloes. Even as stark conceptual distinctions between some issue areas might come to seem a little less clear as a result of growing interdependence, bureaucratic and departmental divisions between previously completely separate areas of governance, policy, and strategy exert significant institutional path dependence. These fixed divisions also have ripple effects, shaping surrounding fields of policy, advocacy, and academic expertise outside of government.

This conceptual and structural path dependence is important to explaining why concept misalignment-based strategic surprise can occur – and in particular why it can occur even in cases where some forms of early warning clearly existed. As we have seen with the weaponization of online discourse manipulation, for example, there were ample earlier indicators of Russian focus on information, both as threat and tool. Yet knowledge of this claimed threat perception, the related norm promotion efforts in regional and international forums, and the capability development and use in the regional theater some-how failed to deeply inform US cyber defensive strategy and planning with regard to anticipated adversary cyber strategy and offensive capability uses. One contributing factor was clearly the division between the functional and substantive areas of focus and expertise in the different government organizations involved in the cyberspace *defense strategy* and *norm promotion* processes respectively. As a result of dynamics resulting partly from these bureaucratic divisions, the question was never sufficiently considered, "what if they take this stuff seriously? what are the *security* implications of that for us, and is there anything there we need to be preparing against?"

Concept misalignment is as much organizational as it is cognitive. Concepts play a key role in shaping organizational and functional processes driving strategic foresight and decision-making. When concept misalignment makes surprise more likely to occur, this is not just about a rigid lack of awareness or inability to see the potential threats that are animating an adversary. This plays a role among some actors certainly, but it does not have to be close to universal. Equally or more important is the impact of foundational concepts on the organizational structures and divisions between different silos of relevant expertise, capabilities, decision-making authorities, and responsibility.

Leading up to 2016, the relative disconnect in the US between the internet freedom agenda norm-building efforts and cyber domain strategy development appears to have played an instrumental role in facilitating the lack of strategic foresight. The divisions between fields and governance structures surrounding "cyber security" versus those surrounding "internet freedom" or "internet governance" were still quite stark at the time, with the development of the military cyberspace domain handled by distinct government entities from those most familiar with and responsible for diplomacy surrounding multistakeholder governance of the global internet, promotion or contestation of norms around internet freedom, or even overseeing areas pertaining to domestic online internet content governance issues.

This conceptual organization reflected in government was also reproduced by divisions in aligned policy and research communities. Major research universities at the time supported separate research centers or initiatives focused on distinct topics of cyber security, on the one hand, and some mix of internet governance and internet freedom related topics, on the other. Philanthropic funding lines, non-governmental organizations, private sector activity, and think tank policy research programs also supported this conceptual reification. This heavily siloed research environment gave little incentives for looking at cross-cutting topics like how the adaptive domestic control approaches being experimented with in hybrid and authoritarian regimes could have consequences for international cyber conflict and domain stability (for example).

Such path dependencies and siloed divisions are common in relation to the large and expanding number of issue areas now cross-cut by digital technologies, networks, data, and adjacent policy concerns. The multiplicity of these distinct issues and governance arenas in turn allows for many potential dimensions of emergent political, economic, social, or security effects. These new interdependencies created by cyberspace all have potential for vulnerability and for weaponizability.

Given the vast potential for wide differences in the conceptual understanding of cyberspace among actors at any given time as well as the ongoing changes in cyberspace technologies and the cyber regime complex, it remains likely that misalignments of the sort discussed here will occur repeatedly, introducing a distinctive form of recurrent threat to cyberspace stability.

Concept Misalignment, Security Dilemmas, and Surprise

Concept misalignment exacerbates security dilemmas, creating a distinctive type of surprise escalation risk. It is common in *security dilemma* situations for actors to miscalculate and not correctly assess how their own strategic behavior is perceived by others. Security dilemmas emerge when two or more parties each respond to perceived threats to their security, but where each actor's respective efforts to improve their own security intensify the perceived imperilment of others, leading ultimately to outcomes undesired by any party. When domain concepts fail to align, this adds an additional possible extremity of misperception on the part of one or more parties involved: the so-called attacker might have acted in ways it sees as outside the scope of any military domain. As such, it might not even know that its behavior is perceived as strategically relevant at all, even while the self-understood victim perceives it as a first strike requiring retaliation.

Given that the behaviors in question are considered as falling far outside the scope of military action by the country undertaking them, this could even lead to situations where behaviors considered as military aggression by one state were not even undertaken with military consultation in another. In some situations, the behaviors in question might even involve an aggregate of nongovernmental organizations, private citizens, businesses, media outlets, contractors, criminal networks, and any number of other actors based out of or in some way affiliated with the country in question but not under direct governmental control.

A critical aspect of this type of concept misalignment-based security dilemma is that it is particularly prone to generating instances of strategically significant *surprise*. The surprise can be twofold in nature: an actor that is completely unaware that its own behavior has been perceived as of military or strategic significance will naturally be surprised by a *sudden*[29] act of aggression, even while the aggressor views its action as a necessary retaliatory response. Likewise, to the extent that the response is conducted as some form of tit-for-tat in-kind reprisal, given that such action previously fell outside the bounds of the now-victim's domain concept, the *form* of the aggression itself is likely to be regarded as surprising – potentially in an additionally emotional and inflammatory manner insofar as it transgresses perceived prior boundaries of war-making and in some new way targets civilian society.

These types of surprises have a risk of being particularly escalatory, prompting emotional and reactive responses. Since states experiencing such instances of surprise are likely to interpret the aggression to which they were subject as more extreme and incendiary than understood by the perpetrator, this has the potential to fuel precisely the types of *positive feedback loop cycles of escalation* that have been discussed as a danger of cyber domain strategic interactions by Jason Healey and Robert Jervis (Chapter 1, this volume). The targeted state, looking to defend itself by any effective means from what is perceived as an unprompted and novel form of aggression, may look to "hit back" even as the aggressor sees itself also as behaving defensively.

Such concept misalignment-fueled surprise events and responses have the potential to prompt dramatic and rapid changes in understanding of the scope of a domain itself, with one party abruptly *stretching their domain concept* to incorporate the new area of threat and capability they have seen demonstrated. Even small shifts in domain concepts are significant, as these are embodied within national security and military institutions and are the subject of specialized training, capability development, authorities, and strategy. Since the cyber domain exists within a broader conceptual field around the global internet, digital technologies, and cyberspace – a field itself dense with actors and interests and with cross-cutting interactions across many areas of society – shifts in this domain concept carry potentially significant repercussions beyond the strategic military interaction.

This necessarily then raises the question whether concept stretching and strategic emulation or some other (less reactive) approach is the appropriate response to cases of surprise of the sort here discussed. What is more, how can the *recurrent* potential for concept misalignment in cyberspace be addressed to limit *future* instability?

Reactive Responses and Strategic Implications

As we have seen in the post-2016 Western strategic reconsiderations about the role of internet content in the cyberspace domain following the demonstrated threat of cyber-enabled information operations, one potential reaction to the demonstration of a novel threat emerging from a rival domain conceptualization is to adjust one's own domain concept accordingly. But such a reactive approach is not without significant risks. What is more, if the set of potential new dimensions to emulate in this way is large and possibly non-finite over time, stretching into many areas of society, this puts the question of domain concept realignment in a new light. This is not a situation where just one expansion of the domain concept will solve the problem for the foreseeable future.

Given the potential for emergent crises and instability associated with incidents of concept misalignment, it is important to understand that the known case of misalignment under discussion in this chapter (captured roughly as "'cyber security' versus 'information security'") is unlikely to have been unique, but rather that further instances of such misalignment events should be expected in continuing strategic competition between state adversaries in and through cyberspace. This observation, in turn, raises additional questions as to the appropriate strategic approach to concept misalignment – both in terms of how to adjust in given instances, and in terms of mitigating future potential flashpoints for misalignment-fueled instability and escalation.

Conscious strategic adaptation to address new threats that emerge from incidents of strategic surprise rooted in concept misalignment tends to focus on fixing presumed flaws in the prior strategic logic rather than explicitly clarifying the conceptual misalignment issues. In some cases, this may indeed be an important part of the adaptation process necessary for confronting new threats. But it is unlikely to be sufficient to remedy the underlying insecurity that created the potential for such bolt-from-the-blue surprises, as it only partially correctly diagnoses the source of this vulnerability. What is more, by failing to correctly apprehend the cyber domain concept's situatedness within a broader arena of cyberspace issues and their governance or the role of concept misalignment in leading to surprise, the strategic adaptation process often unconsciously embraces an iterative shift in its own domain concept and operational and strategic vision that I call here "domain concept stretching" and "strategic emulation." This means that, in cases of concept misalignment-based surprise, following demonstration of a new threat involving unique offensive capabilities and a distinct strategic approach, the victim of the surprise aggression will often stretch their own domain understanding to better match the adversary's concept and seek to emulate some aspects of the adversary's operational and strategic approach.[30]

In the absence of sustained clear strategic consideration of alternatives, this reactive conceptual and strategic realignment is likely to be the most common response to instances of concept misalignment-fueled surprise and the demonstration of a new potential dimension of cyberspace conflict. But such responses are not always optimal and, in some cases, can have undesired consequences. These responses – focused on whichever new dimension appears salient in the moment – do little to identify or reduce the risk of future cycles of concept misalignment-fueled security dilemma and instability (involving additional dimensions). Reactive responses likewise carry significant potential negative externalities, due to the situatedness of the cyberspace domain – and any new strategic dimension thereof – within the broader cyber regime complex with its entanglement with other governance issues and arenas. If domain concept stretching and strategic emulation are entered into unconsciously, the consequent risks and trade-offs are not a primary early locus of attention and are unlikely to be weighed in a deliberate decision process. Difficult to resolve tensions and tests of societally crucial norms and values might already be established by the time frictions with existing frameworks and structures around the new dimension become apparent.

There might be sound strategic reasons to *not* want to securitize or militarize some dimensions. One reason could be simple lack of manpower. It is better to focus on the most significant current threats than to spread national military capability developments too thin – even across areas with demonstrated threat potential. Beyond this though, another important reason is likely to be that not all shifts are equally advantageous (or easy to accomplish). This is because not all states are equally equipped to adopt the same innovations in military capability development – whether those be more strategic and conceptual or technological. There are a number of factors that influence this difference in ability to adopt particular innovations, including differences in national wealth, technological capability, industrial capacity, organizational capabilities, strategic intellectual capabilities, organizational culture, and societal values and normative constraints.[31] Such barriers to adoption efficacy will likely be most pronounced in cases of significant domain concept misalignment. Concepts can be both value-laden[32] and organizationally embodied, with stark differences in domain conceptualization creating several obstacles to reactive emulation. We see the important role that domestic cultural and normative constraints can play in restricting adoption in commentary over the last several years concerning Western approaches to cyber-enabled information operations.[33]

Conceptual misalignment, in other words, if deep enough, can make it difficult to adopt innovations emerging from the misaligned alternative conceptualization. This is likely particularly true when the domain is situated within a cross-cutting governance regime, entangled with other areas of society with existing governance structures, rules, and values, where a change in the relation between the domain and these other areas is likely to lead to areas of prolonged legal and governance friction domestically and internationally, and where they also are likely to create norm-based reputational concerns particular to democracies invested in the international rules-based order.

Reactive emulation, without a clear evaluation of the above questions of efficacy and trade-offs, risks further undermining stabilizing norms without increasing security. Not only is there the possibility that we might not be very capable at emulating certain new dimensions of military competition in cyberspace; it also is likely that attempting to copy some such domain concept extensions will actually better serve the interests of our adversaries. In cases where a new dimension of cyberspace strategic competition would otherwise be seen by many actors as violating democratic values or important international norms, for example, attempting to emulate the new approach would help legitimize the first mover's behavior, thus reducing reputational costs of perceived norm violation and potentially prompting a wave of further diffusion of the new approach as other states update their cost-benefit priors and follow suit. Given that some such innovations in cyber domain conceptualization and strategy may be already systematically more challenging for the US and its democratic allies to adopt for the above reasons, such a mistaken strategic response could serve to both undercut existing international norms and systematically disadvantage like-minded countries.

Despite the potential negative repercussions of reactive responses, some slippage into concept stretching and strategic emulation is a likely consequence of concept-misalignment-fueled strategic surprise. To mitigate the worst effects of such conceptual drift, in known cases of concept misalignment that have led to surprise threat demonstrations, distinct effort needs to be made in the responsive strategy development process to clarify the nature of the underlying conceptual misalignment and the potential risks or negative externalities associated with the particular realignment. Both governmental and non-governmental non-military expert communities involved with related governance arenas should be consulted on this. With careful consideration of systemic effects and long-term behavioral outcome goals, non-emulatory alternative strategic adaptations should be considered – particularly those involving asymmetric approaches and a focus on defensive hardening and denial as opposed to tit-for-tat offensive emulation. All governmental (and, where possible, non-governmental) adaptations to address the new threat should be clearly tracked and coordinated across actors with an eye to avoiding unnecessary levels of securitization or other suboptimal overall (whole of government/ whole of society) response profiles.

Recognizing the repeated and destabilizing nature of concept misalignment-fueled surprise and reaction dynamics, it also is critical to find better strategic solutions to avert *future* instances of surprise and thus limit the dynamics of reactive securitization affecting other areas of society and governance connected to the cyber regime complex. An overarching approach to avert surprise and increase stability must, on some level, take account of the whole of cyberspace and the surrounding cyber regime complex. Considering the whole realm of possibility of what *could* be securitized through new dimensions of cyberspace aggression, such an approach must work strategically to prevent that eventuality in areas where disadvantageous to democracies and the liberal international order. It must also involve broad situational awareness of the strategic environment and the full panoply of available foreign policy tools for shaping that environment.

This requires a coherent, coordinated, whole-of-government approach, building greater mutual awareness across separate but interrelated stovepipes and policy arenas. In the US, processes fostering smoother and more integrated strategic cooperation on cyber (and related digital) topics across the inter-agency will be crucial. Though such efforts have been made in the past, they have not fully displaced a functional bifurcation in which, for example, "cybernorm development projects" are a subject of diplomatic engagement, "cyberspace domain strategy" is a product of military strategic thought, and the two processes subsist in separate bureaucratic and epistemic siloes. Rather, these and other tools of state power projection need to be part of an explicitly integrated and coherent strategic approach with the end objectives in cyberspace of both maintaining national security in the immediate term and shaping the normative regime environment in ways to provide for that security through longer-term stability. Any cyber domain strategy undertaken will influence norms[34] of expected behavior *ex post*, both by involving shifts in our own behavior and by using various tools to attempt to influence and alter the behavior of others. The normative goals of this influence should be considered explicitly. Likewise, while focusing on desired norm "content" and aspirational end goals with regard to behavior and stability in cyberspace is critical – and diplomatic engagement a vital piece of their pursuit – further strategic attention should be paid to process, tactics, and the use of a variety of forums, institutions, and tools of power projection to shape behavioral outcomes.[35]

Efforts to build greater long-term stability in cyberspace cannot stop at seeking to deter or defend against active adversary cyber aggression or build norms in areas already fraught with confrontation. There must also be a robust simultaneous effort to bolster strategic foresight to identify and address emergent security dilemmas rooted in concept misalignment before they lead to conflict. Central to this undertaking is fostering more awareness at a national strategic level of the emerging threat perspectives of other states as these pertain to cyberspace. This will, among other things, require substantially greater insight into the domestic governance processes, regime type, and political, economic, and cultural tensions within other societies.

The interdependencies created by cyberspace insuperably tie *domestic* stability and security with its *international* counterparts. As we've seen with hybrid regimes and authoritarian adaptation in relation to globalization and the internet, stability is closely related to the balance of legitimacy and coercion in the relation between a state's government and society. To understand what is vital to regime stability, look to what is critical to its claims of legitimacy and public support on the one hand, and its coercive capacity on the other. How might new entanglements of the cyber regime complex be seen as undercutting old bases of legitimacy or control or upsetting other vital societal arrangements?

Operationally, the strategic integration of these insights is no small task. Due to long-standing disciplinary and bureaucratic divisions, the domestic politics, economics, culture, and social order of other societies is often not a subject of significant attention in discussion of international strategic competition, let alone in the definition of defense strategy priorities. In the policy and research communities around cyberspace strategy, this is often no different, with issues of domestic digital politics of other countries, digital authoritarianism, or cyberspace-related violations of human rights often sequestered to their own siloes or thinly represented within a globally focused policy discourse.

Fostering greater integration of these areas of expertise into cyberspace strategy development processes is smart, however, even from the perspective of defense and national security. The issues coming to the attention of rights defenders and scholars of authoritarianism, for example, are often indicative of core national security concerns and threat assessments within authoritarian regimes at the time (e.g. the rights abuses are often undertaken in reaction to presumed internal threats to regime control, stability, and survival). As such, these issues can serve as an early warning for how regimes are understanding threats in and through cyberspace and how they might therefore be defining their own concepts of the military domain and relevant defensive and offensive capabilities. Greater integration of this expertise into strategic planning therefore can help to prevent strategic surprise by focusing our national security attention on areas where our adversaries are also looking but which otherwise might have fallen off our radars.

Conclusion: Addressing Concept Misalignment While Building Stability

This chapter has examined the case of the emergence of cyber-enabled disinformation and its implications for the future stability of cyberspace. Unlike previous scholarship, I have argued that this sudden expansion of military cyberspace domain thinking to encompass a new dimension of conflict was not a necessarily unique occurrence. Instead, it was indicative of a broader problem in the way we approach the development of concepts, strategy, and norms to limit instability in cyberspace. In taking a step back from the specific challenge of cyber-enabled information operations, the chapter suggested that the abrupt emergence of this surprising strategic innovation was a case of a more general phenomenon – a novel threat emerging suddenly as a result of domain concept misalignment, a condition which is an endemic challenge in the cyber domain and, without specific precautionary interventions, is likely to also yield future instances of surprise and escalatory spiral.

Today, the cyber regime complex continues to change and adapt with the development of new interconnected technologies and surrounding sociotechnical systems. We see rapid technological growth as well as ongoing competition surrounding the Internet of Things and next-generation network infrastructures, cryptocurrency markets and digital stock trading, blockchain applications, digital supply chains, and emerging digital technologies from AI to quantum computing or additive manufacturing. These additional levels of complexity suggest the potential near-term emergence of new areas of friction around developing interdependencies and regime complex entanglements, all with the capacity to alter threat perceptions, domain concepts, and engender new dynamics of instability. Yet these issues are still often dealt with piecemeal and by different parts of government with inadequate bridging mechanisms for understanding their combined effects or how they might be perceived by other states. At the same time, there is also a lack of connective tissue between the national security policy community and those with rich expertise on domestic politics and culture that could shed important light on the threat perspectives of other countries. Given the interconnectedness of cyberspace with so many different dimensions of societal political, economic, and cultural life, this insight is critical for preventing repeated cycles of concept misalignment-fueled security dilemmas and escalatory domain-enlarging strategic surprise.

To ensure greater long-term stability and security in cyberspace, next efforts at strategy development must start from an understanding of the breadth and multidimensionality of cyberspace and the entangled issues involving all areas of social, political, and economic life. They must account for the fact that these issues continue to shift and change as does the underlying technology. These processes have the potential to create emergent tensions and frictions with existing regimes, institutions, and entrenched interests, potentially unsettling existing mechanisms of stability and drawing awareness to new risks and threats that might be distinctive to or perceived differently by particular governments and societies. Insofar as new areas of this cyber governance arena are perceived as potentially posing security threats to a country's vital interests, they are likely eventually to be integrated into national security concepts and military strategy for cyberspace, effectively adding new dimensions to cyber domain concepts. The numerous possible dimensions of domain expansion put together with the wide potential variation in national threat perspectives make it likely that domain concepts will not always align. This creates a condition of instability that is likely to be characterized by repeated cycles of divergent threat perceptions, concept misalignment, security dilemma, and strategic surprise.

To mitigate the impact of these underlying conditions and reduce instability, cyberspace strategy development processes must thoughtfully incorporate awareness of these dynamics.

First, this means integrating several mechanisms to foster strategic foresight. Greater awareness of domestic politics and threat perspectives of other states must be built into the strategy development process, including through both the observations of diplomatic engagement and expert attention to domestic politics. Particular attention should be given to cyber-related human rights violation issues, as these might serve as flags of domestic stability and security concerns deep enough that regimes are willing to risk potential legitimacy costs associated with overt high-intensity coercion. Equally important, in support of cyber strategy and norm building efforts, processes of cross-silo and cross-technology issue engagement should be built within departments and across the inter-agency. These should integrate key insights and expertise of specialists on different aspects of the cyber regime complex and build ongoing mechanisms for tracking new potentially strategically salient areas of entanglement and friction as technologies and surrounding governance arrangements change.

Second, the strategy development processes around both norm shaping and the cyberspace domain need to be tightly integrated, incorporating the complementary strategic effects that can be achieved through combined use of different tools of foreign policy and international influence, including both diplomatic and military. Shaping the normative environment around cyberspace to reduce instability should be treated as a critical objective of cyberspace strategy. Where possible, this should be achieved in a way which protects existing areas of generativity and positive sum interaction mediated by digital technologies.

Past efforts here can be a guide as well as a cautionary note. The dual approach to cyberspace issues recounted in this chapter – with its seemingly disconnected conceptualizations of the "global internet" versus the military "cyberspace domain" – was a powerful early paradigm for making sense of an explosive new technological phenomenon which in many ways transgressed traditional categories of understanding in global politics. But this approach also had serious faults. The Internet Freedom Agenda was, at its core, a norm entrepreneurship campaign focused primarily on the content layer of the internet and the online realization of democratic principles of freedom of expression and association. It was largely conceptually and institutionally unmoored from what was going on in DoD with regard to Cyber Domain strategy and capabilities development. These two efforts – to shape norms in cyberspace, and the development of cyberspace strategy – need to occur together, because, ultimately, their fates are tied. This will require complex trade-offs to balance values around issues of national security, economic growth, and democracy, but that effort is worth it to better protect the values and institutions of greatest importance.

Finally, in undertaking this renewed effort to build a coherent conceptualization of the democratic normative agenda and defense strategy in cyberspace, it is important that the US and allies not lose sight completely of the value of the early internet's globalist interdependent vision. It is easy today to focus on the many risks associated with interdependence – its weaponization and the vulnerabilities it opens us to. This is especially true in reflexive responses after a new dimension of digital interdependence has been weaponized in a surprising way against us. As we've seen, the natural reaction will often incline toward a rapid securitization and conceptual and strategic emulation, even if this runs into friction with existing norms and institutions. But the risks of interdependence must not be viewed in isolation. They must be weighed against those of its absence. Neither is a panacea, and accommodations must be made in some instances for security, but it still remains likely that global technological interdependence provides a better protection against unrestrained aggression. In many arenas it also better serves the interests of democracy.

Addressing the immediate challenge of cyber-enabled information operations discussed in this chapter will necessarily be a first test for this strategic approach.

Notes

1. The views expressed in this chapter are those of the author and do not reflect the official policy or position of the National Defense University, the Department of Defense, or the US Government.

2. The terms "cyber-enabled information operations" and "cyber-enabled disinformation campaigns" are used interchangeably in this chapter to refer to the new form of cyber aggression demonstrated by Russia in 2016. For more detailed explanation, see Herbert Lin and Jaclyn Kerr, "On Cyber-Enabled Information Warfare and Information Operations," in *Oxford Handbook of Cyber Security*, ed. Paul Cornish (Oxford: Oxford University Press, 2021), 251–272.

3. For the English translation of Gerasimov's January 2013 speech, see Valery Gerasimov, "The Value of Science is in the Foresight: New Challenges Demand Rethinking the Forms and Methods of Carrying out Combat Operations," *Military Review* (January–February 2016): 23–29.

4. Dmitry Adamsky, "Cross-Domain Coercion: The Current Russian Art of Strategy," Institut Français des Relations Internationales, Paris, France, November 2015; Keir Giles, *Handbook of Russian Information Warfare* (Rome: NATO Defense College, 2016).

5. Defense Science Board, *DSB Summer Study Report on Strategic Surprise* (2015).

6. Hillary Rodham Clinton, "Internet Freedom: The Prepared Text of U.S. of Secretary of State Hillary Rodham Clinton's Speech, Delivered at the Newseum in Washington, D.C.," *Foreign Policy*, January 21, 2010.

7. Chairman of the Joint Chiefs of Staff (CJCS), "National Military Strategy of the United States of America 2004: A Strategy for Today; A Vision for Tomorrow," Department of Defense, 2004; Michael Warner, "Notes on Military Doctrine for Cyberspace Operations in the United States, 1992–2014," *Cyber Defense Review*, August 27, 2015; US Cyber Command, "U.S. Cyber Command History": https://www.cybercom.mil/About/History/ (accessed September 6, 2021); Department of Defense, *Quadrennial Roles and Missions Review Report*, January, 2009.

8. Jason Healey, "A Fierce Domain: Conflict in Cyberspace 1986 to 2012" (Vienna, VA: Cyber Conflict Studies Association, 2013).

9. Department of Defense, *Department of Defense Strategy for Operating in Cyberspace*, July 2011.

10. Joint Chiefs of Staff, "Joint Publication 3-12(R), Cyberspace Operations," February 5, 2013; Warner, "Notes on Military Doctrine for Cyberspace Operations in the United States, 1992–2014."

11. Jaclyn A. Kerr, *Authoritarian Management of (Cyber-) Society: Internet Regulation and the New Political Protest Movements* (Washington, DC: Georgetown University, 2016); Maria Repnikova, "Media Openings and Political Transitions: Glasnost versus *Yulun Jiandu*," *Problems of Post-Communism*. 64, no. 3–4 (2017): 141–151; Adam Segal, "Chinese Cyber Diplomacy in a New Era of Uncertainty," *Aegis Paper Series*, no. 1703 (2017).

12. Kerr, *Authoritarian Management of (Cyber-) Society*; Giles, *Handbook of Russian Information Warfare*.

13. See Russian Federation, "Information Security Doctrine Of The Russian Federation," United Nations International Telecommunications Union (ITU) Archive, September 9, 2000; Kerr, *Authoritarian Management of (Cyber-) Society*; Russian Federation, "Doctrine Of Information Security Of The Russian Federation," December 5, 2016.

14. Keir Giles, "Chapter 5. 'Information Troops' – A Russian Cyber Command?" in *2011 3rd International Conference on Cyber Conflict*, ed. Katharina Ziolkowski, Christian Czosseck and Rain Ottis (Tallin, Estonia: CCDCOE Publications, 2011), 45–60: https://ccdcoe.org/uploads/2018/10/InformationTroopsARussianCyberCommand-Giles.pdf

15. This led to the establishment of the first UN Group of Governmental Experts (GGE) on the Developments in the Field of Information and Telecommunications in the Context of International Security in 2004.

16. Permanent Representatives of China, the Russian Federation, Tajikistan and Uzbekistan, "Developments in the Field of Information and Telecommunications in the Context of International Security (UN A/66/359)," United Nations General Assembly, 66th session, September 14, 2011; Permanent Representatives of China, Kazakhstan, Kyrgyzstan, the Russian Federation, Tajikistan and Uzbekistan, "Developments in the Field of Information and Telecommunications in the Context of International Security (UN A/69/723)," United Nations General Assembly, 69th session, January 13, 2015.

17. Jaclyn Kerr, "Information, Security, and Authoritarian Stability: Internet Policy Diffusion and Coordination in the Former Soviet Region," *International Journal of Communication* 12 (2018): 3814–3834.

18. See Adamsky, "Cross-Domain Coercion"; Giles, *Handbook of Russian Information Warfare*.

19. Jaclyn A. Kerr, "The Russian Model of Digital Control and Its Significance," in *Artificial Intelligence, China, Russia, and the Global Order: Technological, Political, Global, and Creative Perspectives*, ed. Nicholas Wright (Montgomery, AL: Air University Press, 2019), 62–74.

20. Department of Defense, *Department of Defense Cyber Strategy 2018: Summary* (September, 2018), 1.
21. US Cyber Command, "Achieve and Maintain Cyberspace Superiority: Command Vision for US Cyber Command," March 23, 2018.
22. Glenn Alexander Crowther, "The Cyber Domain," *The Cyber Defense Review* 2, no. 3 (Fall 2017): 63–72; Erik Heftye, "Multi-Domain Confusion: All Domains Are Not Equal," *Real Clear Defense*, May 26, 2017; Frank Hoffman and Michael Davies, "Joint Force 2020 and the Human Domain: Time for a New Conceptual Framework?" *Small Wars Journal*, June 10, 2013; US Air Force, "USAF Doctrine Update on Domains and Organizing for Joint Operations," Curtis LeMay Center, Air University, 2013.
23. Charles Perrow, *Normal Accidents: Living with High-Risk Technologies* (New York: Basic Books, 1984).
24. Laura DeNardis, *The Global War for Internet Governance* (New Haven, CT: Yale University Press, 2014), 226.
25. Joseph S. Nye, "The Regime Complex for Managing Global Cyber Activities," *Global Commission on Internet Governance Paper Series* (Center for International Governance Innovation, May 20, 2014).
26. Stephen D. Krasner, "Structural Causes and Regime Consequences: Regimes as Intervening Variables," in *International Regimes*, ed. Stephen D. Krasner (Ithaca, NY: Cornell University Press, 1983), 1–21; Nye, "The Regime Complex for Managing Global Cyber Activities."
27. Kal Raustiala and David G. Victor, "The Regime Complex for Plant Genetic Resources," *International Organization* 58, no. 2 (April, 2004): 277–309; Mark Raymond, Chapter 7, this volume.
28. Joseph S. Nye, 'The Regime Complex for Managing Global Cyber Activities', *Global Commission on Internet Governance Paper Series*, Center for International Governance Innovation, May 20, 2014: https://www.ci gionline.org/publications/regime-complex-managing-global-cyber-activi ties
29. From this actor's perspective, the aggression is not only sudden but also *unprovoked*.
30. Giovanni Sartori, "Concept Misformation in Comparative Politics," *The American Political Science Review* 64, no. 4 (December, 1970): 1033–1053.
31. Michael C. Horowitz, *The Diffusion of Military Power: Causes and Consequences for International Politics* (Princeton, NJ: Princeton University Press, 2010); Thomas G. Mahnken, *Technology and the American Way of War Since 1945* (New York: Columbia University Press, 2010); Dmitry Adamsky, *The Culture of Military Innovation: The Impact of Cultural Factors on*

the Revolution in Military Affairs in Russia, the US, and Israel (Stanford, CA: Stanford University Press, 2010); Thomas Maddux and Diane Labrosse (eds.), "Roundtable 3-10 on *The Diffusion of Military Power: Causes and Consequences for International Relations,*" *H-Diplo/ISSF Roundtable III,* no. 10 (February 29, 2012).

32. Charles Taylor, "Neutrality in Political Science," *Philosophy, Politics and Society* 3 (1967): 25–75.

33. Herbert Lin, "Doctrinal Confusion and Cultural Dysfunction in DoD," *The Cyber Defense Review,* Special Edition: Information Operations/ Information Warfare, 5, no. 2 (Summer 2020): 89–108; Jessica Brandt, "How Democracies Can Win an Information Contest Without Undercutting Their Values," Carnegie Endowment, August 2, 2021, https://carneg-ieendowment.org/2021/08/02/how-democracies-can-win-informa-tion-contest-without-undercutting-their-values-pub-85058.

34. Norms are "expectations of proper behavior by actors with a given iden-tity." See Peter Katzenstein, *The Culture of National Security: Norms and Identity in World Politics* (New York: Columbia University Press, 1996).

35. Martha Finnemore and Duncan B. Hollis, "Constructing Norms for Global Cybersecurity," *The American Journal of International Law,* 110, no. 3 (July 2016): 425–479.

Part II
Institutions

4

System, Alliance, Domain: A Three-Frame Analysis of NATO's Contribution to Cyber Stability

Joe Burton and Tim Stevens

The "stability-instability paradox" suggests that when there is a balance of power between states in the nuclear realm (stability), low-intensity conflict in the international system is likely to increase (instability).[1] In the modern era, such low-intensity conflict often takes place in cyberspace, with cyber operations quickly becoming a replacement or substitute for the use of military force and a way for states to achieve their strategic objectives without costly and escalatory military confrontations. This may help explain why there are lower levels of concern about great-power war in the twenty-first century, and constant tensions between great powers over emerging technologies and constant conflict in non–conventional domains of conflict. The stability-instability paradox concept has salience for alliances too. NATO, for example, provides the main mechanism for a balance of both nuclear and conventional forces, both within the European context and globally, but it is also now dealing with instability emanating from cyberspace, and from offensive cyber operations launched by its geopolitical adversaries. While NATO must now contribute to great-power stability within the international system, it is also involved increasingly in low-intensity conflicts at the periphery of its core historical role. What role does NATO play in contributing to international stability in the modern era? How does it contribute to international stability and intra-alliance stability now, in the context of a more complex and globalized security environment characterized by new security challenges? Does NATO have a role to play in cyber stability, and how can we conceptualize that in a modern, multinational alliance framework?

This chapter sets out to explore these key questions. In doing so we seek to build an analysis of NATO's contribution to "cyber stability" across three principal areas. First, we outline how NATO's political-military machinery and capabilities have contributed over the last two decades to enhancing cyber stability in the international system (*system stability*). Salient dynamics include: NATO's designation of Article 5 of the North Atlantic Treaty (the "collective defence" clause) as applicable under certain conditions to adversarial cyber attacks; its role in crafting a cyber deterrence posture for the alliance, focused especially on Russian cyber operations; and its role in preventing escalation of cyber conflicts, whether in the cyber domain exclusively or regarding kinetic armed conflicts in which NATO has been involved operationally. Second, we examine NATO's contribution to cyber stability internally through intra-alliance processes and functions (*intra-alliance stability*). NATO is a forum in which intra-alliance disputes have been addressed, including concerns about 5G vulnerabilities and how to reconcile allies' divergent doctrines, particularly around the development and use of offensive cyber operations. It has also facilitated the sharing of cyber threat intelligence, promoted allied capacity building, and assisted in crisis resolution, such as events in Estonia in 2007.

NATO's third contribution to cyber stability has been with respect to the domain of cyberspace itself (*domain stability*). This includes NATO's contributions to the promotion and setting of international norms of state behavior in cyberspace and its designation and operationalization of cyberspace as a domain of operations, a process stemming from the Wales Summit of 2014.

As well as conceptualizing NATO's role in cyber stability across these three areas, and mapping their interrelationships, we provide a critical analysis of the effects and impacts of NATO's contributions to cyber stability. Our principal argument is that while NATO has made many positive contributions across these three functions, the alliance has performed less well in other areas, including taking actions that have not fostered cyber stability. At times, cyber stability has simply been unattainable for NATO as an organization. In this respect, the designation of cyberspace as a domain has contributed to the ongoing securitization of cyberspace, with potentially deleterious effects on stability. In addition, the actions of some allies have eroded trust within the alliance, including suboptimal information sharing – such as knowledge of the exploit upon which the WannaCry ransomware was based – and the use of espionage capabilities against other allies. Despite an agreement at the recent NATO summit in Brussels to establish minimum standards for national resilience in the NATO area,[2] the alliance has limited control over critical infrastructures in the transatlantic region and does not own the digital infrastructure on which its operations and digital security depend. It also has no formal legal or enforcement powers, limiting its capacity to contribute to domain stability.

This chapter is organized in four parts, beginning with a historical overview of NATO and stability. In the second section, we provide a discussion of alliances as stability mechanisms, highlighting both academic debates and how NATO policymakers have framed NATO's role in providing international stability. We find a lack of differentiation and awareness of the types of stability NATO provides, both in cyber security and in its wider role in international affairs; we contend therefore that alliance theory needs a reboot in its application to cyber stability. The third section presents the three pillars of our approach to cyber stability, highlighting in turn system stability, intra-alliance stability, and domain stability as the core of NATO's contributions. The last concluding section analyzes NATO's performance across these three areas, highlighting implications for future NATO policy, as well as opportunities for further research.

NATO's Historical Role in Stability

NATO has always been in the stability business. Its role in this field extends from its founding in 1949, when protecting the allied zones of Berlin from possible Red Army aggression helped stabilize Western Europe. As NATO's international role developed, the US commitment to Europe's defense had cascading effects in Europe, allowing allies to further their post-war economic recovery and shift from national defense to collective security, and provided assurances to new NATO members still experiencing domestic instability, including resisting communist forces within their own countries.[3] During the Cold War, NATO helped develop a deterrence posture that supported a bipolar division of power in Europe, which, according to many scholars, imparted stability and predictability to European affairs.[4] The alliance incrementally built an institutional structure within Europe, encouraging cooperation and trust to emerge within the alliance itself. NATO contributed to stability within the international system but also stabilized relationships within and between its members. The US commitment to Europe was resolute, based on containing the Soviet threat – including its attempts at foreign coercion and espionage – and it helped cultivate mutual understanding and expectation within the transatlantic area that engendered effective collective decision-making and action. This allowed the alliance to deal with (and recover from) the many contentious issues it has faced, including crises stretching from Suez in 1956 to the fallout over the Iraq war in 2003 and beyond.[5]

Despite NATO fulfilling an important stabilizing role internally, when NATO leaders discuss stability today it is usually in the context of issues and challenges arising outside Europe. After the Cold War, "stability" and the more active noun, "stabilization," have most often described the aim and practice of NATO missions and operations in the former Yugoslavia, including SFOR, the NATO-led stabilization force in Kosovo, and in Afghanistan from

2003 onwards. The alliance's role in international stability has shifted from the more structural bipolar contribution to stability during the Cold War to the challenges of weak and failed states and the security implications of their disintegration. Historically, instability for NATO is something that is integrally linked to its neighboring states and its near abroad.[6] Its post-Cold War enlargement, which saw the alliance grow from sixteen to thirty members, was also framed in the context of stability. Alliance leaders and NATO scholars debated whether extending alliance borders closer to Russia would undermine the fragile post-Cold War peace. Or would it contribute to the stability of new members (and the broad Euro-Atlantic region) by facilitating their integration into the security architecture of Western Europe, enhancing civilian control over their militaries, and promote the "denationalization" of defense and security policy?[7] More recently, NATO leaders have referred to an "arc of instability" on NATO's southern flank, characterized by weak states, threats from terrorist groups and people smugglers, and the challenges associated with increased migration caused by wars and conflicts in Yemen, Libya, and elsewhere.[8] Instability is often presented as emerging from non-NATO states and rippling back into the NATO zone.[9]

Since 2016, not least because of Russian cyber operations against US electoral processes, there has been increased reference to the connection between cyber and hybrid operations and political instability within the NATO membership and with NATO partners, including Ukraine.[10] Hack-and-leak operations and the manipulation of social media have been linked to instability, and the Putin government has seen the utility of cyber operations in destabilizing the Western alliance.[11] This includes driving NATO members apart, creating mistrust within NATO countries – especially between publics and their elected representatives – and through manipulating elections in support of candidates who advocate nationalist or populist policy positions disruptive to established patterns of international cooperation.[12] The new challenges presented by 5G have also been framed in the context of stability, with disagreements emerging among NATO members about how to deal with Chinese 5G suppliers, coupled with an apparent lack of multinational policy coherence.[13] Additionally, the continued decoupling of Western telecommunications provision and Chinese companies could pose long-term threats to the stability of the internet itself, including its potential bifurcation or fragmentation.[14]

The degree of political stability within NATO, therefore, has historically been affected by purposive interventions but also by changes in the technological environment, including the nature of cyberspace and the technology deployed within it. At the strategic level, analysts have linked cyber operations to wider instability between NATO and its adversaries, including potential instability within the nuclear deterrence paradigm.[15] Constant cyber conflict has contributed to an overall deterioration in the stability of the rules-based order and worsening relations between its most powerful actors. Omitted from these debates is the question of NATO's own agency in stability. In other words, instability is more often framed as something that happens to NATO. The alliance's role in positively or proactively creating, shaping, or sustaining stability is less explored. What then do we know about alliances as active contributors to and agents of stability, or as stability mechanisms in their own right? Can we adapt these ideas to explain NATO's roles in cyber stability?

Three pillars of cyber stability

Alliances as Stability Mechanisms

Primarily, alliances contribute to balances of power in the international system (system stability) that discourage revisionist or aggressive states from undertaking offensive military action. The principal mechanism for promoting balances of power is capability aggregation: alliances pool resources. Small or weak states benefit from access to the military might of stronger and larger allies and by political assurances that the latter will use those capabilities in their defense. Balances of power provide stability because they create and extend deterrence. Minor powers are less vulnerable because larger cohesive political units create greater risks and costs for potential aggressors. In Walt's seminal account, alliances help to balance threats, especially when those threats are from states that are geographically proximate and that have both aggressive intentions and capabilities.[16] Alliances are therefore more than just military agreements but serve as critical tools in international politics.[17]

Stabilizing alliances are founded on strong leadership, which can be maintained most readily by the more powerful states in an alliance.[18] Alliances will be less stable when such leadership is not present. This has salience for NATO, as a principal explanation for NATO's durability has been the constant leadership of the United States.[19] Until the Trump administration challenged such consistency, this commitment had been constant and unwavering, as successive US administrations acknowledged the overall importance of NATO to US security interests.[20] Stability is also often linked to bipolar systems led by two strong states.[21] Clusters of aligned states provide a foundation for international interaction, guard against instability occurring in peripheries, provide incentives to maintain a balance of forces on either side, and allow crises to be managed with caution and moderation.[22] This classic model of alliance stability is foundational to how the US has constructed its alliance relationships in Europe and in Asia.[23]

Much also depends on factors internal to alliances (intra-alliance stability). Intra-alliance dynamics – the ways allies relate to and interact with one another – are as important as external dynamics, such as the formation of balances of power or the overarching influence of globalization. By this logic, the internal politics of alliances are analytically distinct from what happens outside of them. NATO's formation, for example, was intended to deter the Soviet Union (an external goal), but it was also the mechanism that kept the US engaged in European security after the Second World War and helped to bring (West, and then East) Germany back into the Western security architecture (internal goals). As NATO Secretary General Lord Ismay famously put it, NATO's role was "to keep the Americans in, the Soviets out, and the Germans down."[24]

In some analyses, intra-alliance dynamics make alliances more prone to instability than other organisational units, including nation-states.[25] Instability risks are driven by various factors, including that alliances cross multiple territories as well as cultural and national boundaries, are structurally more fragile structures than other political entities, are susceptible to intra-alliance crises and conflicts (including entrapment – where alliance members are drawn into conflicts involving other members),[26] and are prone to higher levels of relational risks than other forms of political organization. NATO's proclivity to crises, for example, is extensive – these crises are driven by differences between NATO members, including diverging threat perceptions.[27] Conversely, highly institutionalized alliances, especially those of extended longevity like NATO, can help overcome internal instability and contribute to alliance durability.[28] Levels of trust increase over time, whilst alliances provide channels for small states to influence larger alliance partners. Loyalty to the alliance itself can develop, which in some cases supersedes what is conventionally understood as a state's national interest.[29] Fear of abandonment by larger alliance powers also drives accommodation and compromise.[30]

Alliances can function as security communities, which create norms – broadly defined here as expectations of behavior – and socialize new members to the values of international and regional organizations, thereby contributing to intra-alliance stability.[31] Security communities coalesce around common international objectives and can create solidarity, a sense of common identity and loyalty which transcends sovereign concerns over policies adopted by other alliance members. The war in Afghanistan was one example of states valuing their commitment to each other and to a common cause, and the NATO-led International Security Assistance Force (ISAF) helped to distribute risk within the alliance and provide a degree of international legitimacy for a controversial military operation. Afghanistan operations were framed as necessary for stability and therefore supported by a broad coalition of states, as opposed to a unilateral action by a unipolar power.[32] The political and social dynamics created by alliances could thus be effective lenses through which to view NATO's role in cyber stability. While NATO takes measures and adopts policies that contribute to system stability, its actions might also encourage intra-alliance dynamics that affect stability within and between its members, especially in dealing with sometimes controversial cyber security issues.

The aspect of NATO's role in international stability that is less easy to conceptualize is the alliance's contribution to the stability of cyberspace itself (domain stability). There is practically no academic work that directly addresses this issue – indeed, the foundations of alliance theory were developed predominantly during and immediately after the Cold War and did not account for, or indeed foresee, the emergence of a global network of computer systems. However, analyzing NATO's role in managing other domains is a potential route forward. In the maritime domain, for example, NATO has acted to project stability, such as counter-piracy operations off East Africa (Operation Ocean Shield), and the Active Endeavour and Sea Guardian operations in the Mediterranean, intended to counter terrorism, provide maritime situational awareness, and stop people smuggling and illicit trade.[33] NATO has contributed to stability in the space domain too, with its members playing an integral political role in the management of space-based missile defense systems.[34] Yet, as we describe below, the cyber domain is sufficiently different from other domains that we cannot simply transpose models of stability from one to the other.

There are also tensions here between how domains are managed in an alliance framework. NATO's European members' reluctance to utilize space for warfighting, for example, contrasts sharply with the Trump administration's plans for a military Space Force and the development of offensive capabilities for the denial of adversaries' space-based systems in the event of conflict.[35] This signals that NATO can potentially play a role across these different dimensions – in intra-alliance management of technological change, to the normative environment in respect of how a domain is used, and by reconciling the interests of its members through the development of alliance doctrine. It also suggests that managing domains subject to novel forms of technological competition will be difficult and contentious. While NATO has no regulatory, legal, or economic tools at its disposal (unlike the EU, for example), its impact in cyberspace as a domain could, at least theoretically, be achieved through its political role in international affairs, including establishing patterns of cooperation and through the promotion of international norms. In this respect, domain stability involves the recognition, management, and nurturing of cyberspace stability for all, not just for NATO mission assurance or for the benefit of the alliance and its partners. This leads to important questions. Can NATO actions provide stability in the cyber domain? Or, do NATO attempts to project power and capability in the cyber domain destabilize instead?

In the following section, we examine evidence for NATO's impact and effectiveness in contributing to stability in each of these three areas – system, intra-alliance, and domain. This tripartite approach should not be understood as a taxonomy but as frames that overlap in concept and in practice, as discussed in our subsequent analysis of their interrelationships. We argue that this framework provides more nuanced understanding of the main components of how alliances contribute to stability and builds on previous treatments of "cyber stability" outlined in the introduction to this volume. In so doing, we seek to extend a multidimensional analysis of NATO's role in cyber stability, which is weakly articulated in the existing literature.

Three pillars of cyber stability

System Stability

NATO is the world's premier military alliance and inevitably influences the overall stability of the international system. It creates deterrence against revisionist powers and extends it to minor ones, balancing threats through a variety of means. Concurrently, it is in constant competition with other powers and alliances that can affect system stability negatively. This is equally the case in respect of its cyber activities, which have the potential to contribute to or detract from overall stability. Efforts to improve the stability of cyberspace overall (domain stability; see below) are part of this dynamic, although NATO's identification of cyberspace as an operational domain has its own implications. For instance, whilst overlooking their own cyber activities, China and Russia are keen to call out Western "militarization" of cyberspace as a net contributor to global cyber instability.[36] At the same time, in common with individual states, it has proven difficult to deter adversarial cyber operations, which continue to afflict its members and NATO itself. This is despite highly developed national cyber and non-cyber capabilities and their aggregation under the NATO umbrella. As a result, NATO allies are beginning to push back against hostile state cyber activity using multiple levers of individual and collective power and influence.[37]

One of these levers is an offensive cyber capability that hypothetically might be used to deter hostile cyber actions and, when deterrence fails or operational exigencies demand, to punish an adversary through computer network operations that deny, degrade, disrupt, or destroy their digital assets and dependencies.[38]

NATO has been engaged in defensive cyber operations and network-enabled warfighting since at least the Balkan wars of the 1990s. The subsequent elevation of "cyber defence" in NATO's security agenda has tended to avoid public discussion of allied use of offensive cyber capabilities, although it is hinted at in NATO policy of the last decade. It is only with the 2016 recognition of cyberspace as an operational domain and the 2017 announcement of a new Cyber Operations Centre (CyOC), that offensive cyber has been fully integrated into NATO planning and operations.[39] NATO will integrate allies' offensive cyber capabilities via the Sovereign Cyber Effects Provided Voluntarily by Allies (SCEPVA) arrangement.[40] CyOC will not be fully operational until 2023 and the details of its mission are not yet well known, least of all whether it heralds a shift toward a more "offensive" NATO cyber posture generally.[41] While noting in 2014 that NATO avowal of offensive cyber capabilities "would be greeted with vitriol and alarm in Moscow," James Lewis also proposed that the destabilizing effects of a move like CyOC would be minimal.[42] Given the background deterioration in relations between NATO and Russia, it is difficult to test this proposition, but it does seem as if NATO's adversaries see greater problems in individual allies' strategic cyber postures than with NATO's per se. Specifically, this means that the US and UK and, to a lesser extent, France, Germany and the Netherlands, each of which has renewed publicly their willingness to develop and deploy offensive cyber capabilities. The pooling of resources via SCEPVA – and the unity of purpose created by adoption of the Cyber Defence Pledge – may in time alter the balance of power in favor of NATO, but it is too early to determine the precise systemic effects involved.

NATO is not a norms-organization, but its actions are framed explicitly with respect to international norms pertaining to the pursuit of international peace, security, stability, and adherence to international law. It therefore follows existing normative pathways set out by other organizations, like the United Nations (UN) and the Organization for Security and Co-operation in Europe (OSCE).[43] NATO internalizes voluntary norms of state behavior developed in these fora, while upholding them in practice. These include those calling explicitly for states "to increase stability and security in the global [information and communications technologies] environment."[44] NATO has committed to such stabilizing measures, including the rule of law, the principle of restraint, enhanced cyber resilience, and practices of mutual assistance and cooperation.[45] There arises, therefore, a problem for NATO's normative obligations when the principal allied power, the United States, speaks openly of developing a new norm for cyber conflict, one of "agreed competition." Two of the intellectual architects of this position articulate the need to set a new "norm" through practice, one in which competition is bounded by inactivity at one end and cyber operations equivalent to armed attacks at the other.[46] They argue that understanding the environment as one of constant competition and engaging directly with this situation, rather than wishing it away, is likely to generate responsible behaviors sooner than waiting for top-down norms negotiated by diplomats.[47] As adversaries learn the bounds of acceptable behavior this will encourage stability in what Healey has termed "persistent engagement stability theory."[48]

It is too soon to know whether the US posture will bring stability, but the possibilities for systemic instability are many, particularly if other states – including adversaries – adopt similar postures that in time turn out to be less stabilizing than currently promoted.[49] It is not yet apparent how or if the NATO cyber posture in respect of offensive cyber operations will be influenced by the revised US strategy.[50] Will its broader cyber defense mission necessarily involve "out-of-network" operations in non-permissive environments that channel the emerging US-led norm of persistent engagement? If this is the case, it is possible that NATO operations may contribute to greater system instability, thereby undercutting its long-standing constitutional and normative commitments. Negotiating this situation without generating destabilizing system effects will be a challenge for the allies in the medium to long term.

Intra-Alliance Stability

How does intra-alliance stability affect cyber policy within the alliance and its role in international cyber affairs, and how do cyber threats emanating from an unstable domain affect the stability of NATO? This section analyzes some of the key internal cyber security dynamics within and between NATO members, including: the impact of the Trump administration on alliance cyber security policy and strategy; how NATO members have responded to the challenge of new technologies, such as 5G, including the lack of political convergence surrounding them; internal NATO challenges presented by a more offensive US cyber posture; and how capacity building across the alliance has alleviated free-rider concerns.

NATO's stability was tested by the Trump administration's abrasive approach to alliance politics, which affected the norms (expectations of behavior), trust, and loyalty that existed within the alliance. This supports one of the core theoretical predictions of the alliance literature: without strong leadership, alliances will be weak and fractured. Alliance stability during President Trump's tenure was affected directly by cyber security issues. Concerns about threat perception and common attribution were the most serious issues, including internal contestation around the attribution of cyber operations against the US and other NATO members. When President Trump questioned US intelligence services' assessment of the Russian threat in a 2018 press conference with President Putin, this pointed to fractured NATO leadership and the potential intra-alliance friction arising from internally divergent cyber threat perceptions and political instability within the US itself.[51] However, this should not be overstated, as NATO has historically united against the Russian threat. Russian cyber operations against NATO members and partners, including against Estonia in 2007 and Ukraine since 2014, have been met with concerted responses and driven efforts to enhance cyber security standards, doctrine, and capability within the alliance.

These disagreements were serious, but they did not threaten the alliance itself nor impact the overall coherence of US cyber strategy.[52] As history suggests, NATO has tended to recover from serious disputes, including after Suez, during Reagan's second term, and George W. Bush's second term after the Iraq invasion. Joe Biden's presidency may foster similar "self-healing" effects.[53] Moreover, Russian attempts to destabilize NATO states through cyber means have historically had the opposite effect and galvanized the NATO membership. Russian actions may have demonstrated another sort of stability paradox, wherein efforts to cause instability engender cohesion and collective responses.

Another issue of intra-alliance concern is the rollout of 5G technologies. This has occasioned US political pressure on allies and its criticism of European states for giving Chinese providers a role in their digital networks. Although not solely a "cyber" issue, allies disagree about the risks posed by Chinese 5G technologies. Germany, for example, will allow Huawei to operate in its domestic market; German telecoms companies are already embedding Huawei technology in their networks. As Thomas has argued, this has implications for NATO: "With Germany seeking to shore up and encourage America's recommitment to the organisation, the decisive indecisiveness it has adopted on Huawei is a step backwards in re-engaging with Washington."[54] The 5G dispute exemplifies the need to build collective security within the alliance as well as collective defense against external threats, by taking domestic actions that do not adversely affect other allies. There is also the sense that European NATO members risk becoming entrapped in broader disputes between the US and Beijing over digital markets and trade issues. This sense feeds debates about European strategic autonomy and digital sovereignty on the one hand and calls for a new digital alliance between the US and European powers on the other.[55] 5G debates have thus been contentious, pushing the alliance out of a stable equilibrium, and exemplifying how domain instability (discussed below) relating to emergent technologies can affect intra-alliance stability.

A more serious intra-alliance dispute could be emerging over the US strategy of persistent engagement and defend forward, the US Department of Defense and US Cyber Command strategies unveiled in 2018.[56] While this policy has been driven by wider systemic competition between the US and its main cyber adversaries (Russia, China), it has also affected NATO internally. Some have called for NATO to follow suit and adopt a similarly robust approach, including the use of offensive cyber capabilities to disrupt and deter adversaries in non-permissive environments.[57] There has been a sense of unease among NATO membership on this point. In 2016, before the revisions to its cyber posture, the US conducted an anti-ISIS operation in German networks without consulting German authorities, prompting concerns over breaches of German sovereignty.[58]

As Healey has argued, the new policy may require a redefinition of sovereignty for the digital age, which allows adversaries to be tracked by US authorities as they cross digital borders; any blame for sovereignty breaches would lie with the hackers rather than with those pursuing them.[59] Smeets has further identified negative effects of the policy, including: a "loss of allied trust," with implications for alliance stability; and potential disruption of allied intelligence operations and capabilities, especially if US operations burn capabilities or impact other agencies' abilities to collect intelligence on intruders in their networks.[60] To ensure that such operations do not create unnecessary frictions and affect alliance stability, Smeets highlights the potential need for an intra-alliance memorandum of understanding to deconflict military cyber operations.[61] Kehler et al. similarly identify the need for alliance rules of engagement (ROE) that recognize "the potential of cyber operations to occur and create effects in multiple international political jurisdictions."[62] The development of such mechanisms would be further evidence of NATO finding an institutional resolution of cyber issues affecting alliance stability.

Another important facet of intra-alliance stability is capacity building within and between its members. This includes: training, skills development and cyber education programmes; cyber exercises like Locked Shields, Crossed Swords, Trident Juncture, and Cyber Coalition; and common strategy and doctrine development through a variety of NATO and NATO-affiliated bodies,[63] including the NATO summits, which act as a fulcrum for alliance policy, and various funding initiatives and conferences that have promoted collaboration. It is difficult to quantify the effects of these programmes and institutions, but they appear to promote alliance stability in several ways. First, alliances can be unstable if states do not contribute sufficiently to the security of other members. In "free-riding" behaviors, small alliance partners benefit from larger states' security provision without contributing anything meaningful to alliance security itself. The NATO Cyber Defence Pledge (2016), for example, is a cross-alliance commitment to cyber security that alleviates intra-alliance tensions over contribution asymmetries. Although there is no information in the public domain relating to the impact of the Pledge, building institutional capacity to respond to security issues is a way of distributing the work of the alliance and thereby helping to enhance alliance cohesion, both of which are important elements of stability. Second, various institutional mechanisms underpin NATO's political role in providing intra-alliance stability on cyber issues by brokering and resolving disputes between members and encouraging consensus to emerge on difficult issues. However, as we argue in the following section, capacity building, especially NATO training and exercises, in addition to fostering intra-alliance stability, may affect the domain stability of cyberspace itself.

Domain Stability

It has long been argued that cyberspace is less stable than other domains. The list of reasons is familiar: its offense-dominance and escalation propensity; the likelihood of unintended consequences; its potential to "level the playing field" for weaker actors, and so on.[64] However, it is apparent that cyberspace as a socio-technical environment[65] is remarkably stable most of the time, albeit this is no reason for complacency, nor for ignoring the efforts expended in making it so. The role of NATO in advancing the domain stability of cyberspace is rarely explored but is not coterminous with its 2016 affirmation of cyberspace as an operational domain.[66] Indeed, NATO's operationalization of cyberspace and its linking to its core task of deterrence implies a commitment to offensive capabilities that could destabilize the alliance, the domain, and the international system.[67]

One frame through which cyberspace is often viewed is as a "global commons." This has gained traction in recent years and is consistent with the stated positions of major NATO countries like the US and the UK. Mueller argues that the global commons of cyberspace is a "virtual space for interaction" arising from the shared deployment of global protocols and standards, themselves "global public goods" on account of their unrestricted availability to all.[68] As the latter precede and enable cyberspace itself, any sovereign claims to "national" fractions of this environment are post hoc and lack legitimacy. Furthermore, amongst the global public goods enabled by the global commons, we may number security and stability in general, cyber or otherwise.[69] International organizations like NATO have the potential to assist in the provision of global public goods on account of their predictability, longevity – which can ameliorate leadership problems – and ability to sanction non-compliance with norms and standards.[70]

Cyberspace exists only through the concerted ongoing activities of diverse agents: NATO is but one actor in a transnational multistakeholder community. Domain stability therefore requires NATO to look beyond its membership and contribute to cooperative frameworks that focus on cyber security, standards, and operational resilience.[71] These enhance "the security and stability of the overall ecosystem," rather than serving narrow self-interest and parochial security concerns.[72] NATO has historically had little reach into key communities like industry and civil society and was therefore poorly positioned to develop "standards and operational approaches" to cyber domain stability in-house.[73] However, NATO can claim some success in engaging with non-alliance parties on technical interoperability and standardization, including through its NATO Standardization Office, which helps bolster alliance identity and cohesion also.[74] This presents opportunities for NATO, although most of these activities have been with respect to military materiel, rather than the diverse challenges of sustaining stability in the global cyber commons. For instance, NATO would need to demonstrate its relevance in an environment dominated by private and civilian concerns that ordinarily outweigh the influence and competences of a military organization.[75]

Tighter EU-NATO cyber security cooperation is one expression of NATO's need to find intermediaries to help shape research agendas, training requirements, and information exchange.[76] This has yet to translate formally beyond a single technical arrangement for information sharing between NCIRC and the EU's Computer Emergency Response Team (EU-CERT), but the new *EU Cybersecurity Strategy* commits to furthering cyber defense interoperability, cooperative diplomatic responses to cyber incidents, and to shared understandings of the threat landscape.[77] NATO can add value in all these aspects, even as the EU and NATO each looks to establish distinct roles for themselves in cyber defense and security. In turn, NATO can help meet its stated resilience ambitions in the Cyber Defence Pledge (2016) by learning from the EU's long-term political and operational focus on cyber resilience.[78] Cyber resilience and other forms of regulation and governance help to generate community "trust and stability of expectations,"[79] thereby encouraging cooperative behaviors and reducing escalation risks. In addition, EU and NATO memberships overlap to such an extent that closer EU-NATO working makes fiscal as well as practical sense.

As EU-NATO statements recognize, a key factor in furthering domain stability is the sharing of cyber threat intelligence (CTI). NATO has partially addressed this internally through its intelligence structures and, since 2013, its Malware Information Sharing Platform (MISP).[80] MISP has delivered enhanced CTI to allies, national computer emergency response teams (CERTs), and industry partners but is hampered by a narrow focus on technical information at the expense of wider-aperture intelligence and by mismatches between partners' expectations and cultures.[81] A virtuous circle with benefits for domain and alliance stability therefore consists in understanding community requirements better, with a view to enhancing existing CTI frameworks and trust networks. There may also be value in reinvigorating under-used capabilities like NATO's cyber Rapid Reaction Teams. NATO may not be an overt international norm-setter, but what it says and does influences attitudes and behaviors. It can therefore play a role in promoting and socializing norms around CTI, cyber resilience, technical assistance, confidence-building measures, and public-private cyber security cooperation, all of which contribute to domain stability and to system stability.

Conclusion

Our analysis has established a three-frame approach to NATO's role in cyber stability, but there are complex connections and interdependencies between system, alliance, and domain stability. This is not surprising in a globalized world, in which both internal and external security issues contribute to the security environment. Globalized transnational threats, including but not limited to cyber attacks, cross borders with ease, and increasingly diverse assemblages of security actors influence stability. More precisely, NATO contributions to domain and system stability appear to be affected by, or are contingent upon, the degree of intra-alliance stability. NATO's ability to act externally and have meaningful agency in the cyber domain is compromised by contentious alliance relationships. Intra-alliance stability therefore precedes and is a contributing variable to domain and system stability. One example of this would be NATO's ability to promote or otherwise contribute to international cyber norms. It is unlikely to be able to do so effectively if it is out of equilibrium, or if NATO is experiencing serious internal disagreements on cyber policy.

Conversely, wider instability in international affairs, including cyber threats and/or domain instability, has influenced NATO's internal stability. In some cases, this has been a positive influence and has galvanized the alliance. In others, it has been destabilizing and has presented challenges to the alliance to achieve coherence, common threat perceptions, and collective action. Alliance stability can be affected by the development and deployment of new cyber technologies. While Russia and China clearly have strategic interests in using technology to disrupt NATO and the EU, integrating 5G, Internet of Things, quantum and artificial intelligence into alliance operations presents significant practical and doctrinal challenges, especially as the supply chains for these technologies are global and prone to interruption and subversion. Technological change may have a fracturing effect, leading to calls for digital sovereignty, contributing to polarization within and between societies, and being reflected in the challenges NATO has experienced relating to information, intelligence, and data sharing. However, NATO recognizes that a more coherent and forward-looking approach to these issues is needed. Instability in the cyber domain is thus a catalyst for further alliance adaptation.

Beyond the policy realm, the theoretical literature on alliance theory would benefit from a reboot. Clearly there are concepts that can help us understand the impact of new technologies, but existing approaches need to be revised, reframed, and built upon. This suggests that new thinking is needed on how alliance change, adaption, and evolution are affected by new technologies. These are issues that have been covered elsewhere only in respect of the systemic effects of nuclear technologies, and the alliance concept has been insufficiently conceptualized from the standpoint of emerging technologies. The effects of technological change on alliances are thus an area ripe for further analysis and theorizing. In this context, our three-frame analysis could be generalizable to other alliances. The US hub-and-spokes system in Asia or the Axis of Resistance alliance between Iran, Syria, and Hezbollah, for example, could be analyzed in this context of system, intra-alliance, and domain dynamics. We recognize that NATO is in many ways the *sui generis* military alliance, but it is also the case study on which broader alliance theory has been built and tested.

NATO is currently reviewing its doctrine as part of the NATO 2030 process, which may result in a new Strategic Concept, the alliance's main guiding document. The recommendations provided by the group of experts appointed by the NATO Secretary General as part of this process mention the challenge of providing stability in the North Atlantic area. They highlight that political coherence on new security challenges is a prerequisite for NATO to be a "source of stability for an unstable world."[82] The report also states that NATO's response to cyber issues will be part of that mission and perhaps most importantly that NATO's role in "projecting stability" will need to be taken forward in the context of its other roles and functions, such as defense capacity building.[83] It follows that there is further scope to think about the implications of cyber stability for other areas of alliance policy. How does cyber stability relate to NATO operations? Can NATO contribute to cyber stability through its defense planning processes, or through its industry partnerships? How should cyber stability contribute to stability in other domains, and vice versa?

If stability is a key goal for NATO, then it will be necessary to work with other actors to achieve this goal. Here, NATO's political role will continue to be important. Further developing relations and cooperation on cyber security with the EU, for example, will be essential, and NATO's work with its partners in this area – including in the Asia Pacific (Partners Across the Globe), the Gulf region (Istanbul Cooperation Initiative), and with other international organizations, such as the UN and OSCE – could also contribute to both domain and system stability in cyberspace. NATO is no stranger to diplomacy, but it will need to find new ways of working with a wider group of partners than has traditionally been the case. This may raise difficult questions about the proper role of a military organization in international affairs, a situation ripe for exploitation by actors hostile by default to NATO. It has been suggested that friendly efforts should be directed toward an "uneasy stability in cyberspace."[84] If NATO efforts to increase domain stability threaten system stability, managing this unease will be a critical challenge.

This is a challenge also to researchers. NATO is being tested in novel fashion by diverse adversaries, with concomitant effects on alliance cohesion, identity, and agency. Our preliminary analysis proposes that we can better understand the notion of cyber stability in the alliance context by teasing out its dynamics in three distinct but interpenetrating registers: alliance, domain, system. It also suggests that further work is required on the theory of alliances under conditions of technological change and on the interplay of system, alliance, and domain stability in socio-technical contexts like cyber security. NATO cyber challenges and opportunities can be analyzed through these framing devices and this chapter serves only as a provocation to further effort in this respect.

Notes

1. Glenn Snyder, "The Balance of Power and the Balance of Terror," in *The Balance of Power*, ed. Paul Seabury (San Francisco, CA: Chandler, 1969), 185–201; See also, Robert Jervis, "Why Nuclear Superiority Doesn't Matter," *Political Science Quarterly* 94, no. 4 (1979): 619.

2. Nato, "Resilience and Article 3," June 11, 2021: https://www.nato.int/cps/en/natohq/topics_132722.htm

3. Lawrence A. Kaplan, "The United States and the Origins of NATO 1946–1949," *The Review of Politics* 3, no. 2 (1969): 215.

4. For example, Kenneth Waltz, "The Stability of a Bipolar World," *Daedalus* 93, no. 3 (1964): 881–909.

5. Wallace J. Theis, *Why NATO Endures* (Cambridge: Cambridge University Press, 2009).

6. Rubén Díaz-Plaja, "Projecting Stability: An Agenda for Action," March

13, 2018: https://www.nato.int/docu/review/articles/2018/03/13/pro jecting-stability-an-agenda-for-action/index.html

7. James B. Steinberg and Philip H. Gordon, "NATO Enlargement: Moving Forward; Expanding the Alliance and Completing Europe's Integration," *The Brookings Institution Policy Brief* 90, November (2001): https://www .brookings.edu/research/nato-enlargement-moving-forward-expanding-t he-alliance-and-completing-europes-integration/

8. NATO, "Current Security Challenges and the Role Of NATO and the European Union. Speech Delivered by the Chairman of the NATO Military Committee, General Petr Pavel, at The European Parliament," October 20, 2015: https://www.nato.int/cps/en/natohq/opinions_1241 28.htm?selectedLocale=en

9. NATO, "London Declaration Issued by the Heads of State and Government Participating in the Meeting of the North Atlantic Council in London," December 3, 2009: https://www.nato.int/cps/en/natohq/official_texts _171584.htm; NATO, "Enlargement," May 5, 2020: https://www.nato .int/cps/en/natolive/topics_49212.htm; NATO, "NATO 2030: United for a New Era," November 25, 2020: https://www.nato.int/nato_static _fl2014/assets/pdf/2020/12/pdf/201201-Reflection-Group-Final-Repo rt-Uni.pdf

10. Stephen Blank, "Cyber War and Information War À La Russe," in *Understanding Cyber Conflict: 14 Analogies*, ed. George Perkovich and Ariel E. Levite (Washington, DC: Georgetown University Press, 2017), 81–98.

11. James Shires, "The Simulation of Scandal: Hack-And-Leak Operations, the Gulf States, and US Politics," *Texas National Security Review* 3, no. 4 (2019): 10–28; Ofer Fridman, *Russian Hybrid Warfare: Resurgence and Politicisation* (London: Hurst and Company, 2018); Scott Jasper, *Russian Cyber Operations: Coding the Boundaries of Conflict* (Washington, DC: Georgetown University Press, 2020).

12. Michael Imerson, "Russia's Efforts to 'Destabilise Western Democracy' Increase Cyber Insecurity," *Financial Times*, May 25, 2017: https://www .ft.com/content/93f6a15c-2424-11e7-a34a-538b4cb30025

13. Lindsay Gorman, "5G is Where China and the West Finally Diverge," *The Atlantic*, January 5, 2020: https://www.theatlantic.com/ideas/archive /2020/01/5g-where-china-and-west-finally-diverge/604309/

14. Samantha Hoffmann, Dominique Lazanski, and Emily Taylor, "Standardising the Splinternet: How China's Technical Standards Could Fragment the Internet," *Journal of Cyber Policy* 5, no. 2 (2020): 239–264; M. L. Mueller, *Will the Internet Fragment? Sovereignty, Globalization and Cyberspace* (Cambridge: Polity, 2017).

15. Andrew Futter, *Hacking the Bomb: Cyber Threats and Nuclear Weapons* (Washington, DC: Georgetown University Press, 2018); Paul Bracken, "The Cyber Threat to Nuclear Stability," *Orbis* 60, no. 2 (2016): 188–203.

16. Stephen M. Walt, *The Origins of Alliances* (Ithaca, NY and London: Cornell University Press, 1987).

17. James D. Morrow, "Alliances and Asymmetry: An Alternative to the Capability Aggregation Model of Alliances," *American Journal of Political Science* 35, no. 4 (1991): 904–933.

18. Waltz, "The Stability of a Bipolar World."

19. Joe Burton, *NATO's Durability in a Post-Cold War World* (New York: State University of New York Press, 2018).

20. Magnus Petersson, "The Strategic Importance of the Transatlantic Link," in *Military Strategy in the Twenty-First Century: The Challenge for NATO*, ed. Janne Haaland Matláry and Robert Johnson (London: Hurst and Company, 2020), 27–42.

21. There is disagreement on this issue, with some arguing multipolar systems can be more stable under some circumstances. See Karl W. Deutsch and David J. Singer, "Multipolar Power Systems and International Stability," *World Politics* 16, no. 3 (1964): 390–406.

22. Waltz, "The Stability of a Bipolar World," 321–323.

23. Glenn Snyder, "Alliances, Balance, and Stability," *International Organization* 45, no. 1 (1991): 121–142.

24. Victor David Hanson, "Lord Ismay, NATO, and the Old-New World Order," *National Review*, July 5, 2017: https://www.nationalreview.com/2017/07/nato-russians-out-americans-germans-down-updated-reversed/

25. Xu Jiang, Yuan Li, and Shanxing Gao, "The Stability of Strategic Alliances: Characteristics, Factors and Stages," *Journal of International Management* 14, no. 2 (2008): 173–189.

26. The US, for example, was reluctant to becoming entrapped in the French and British dispute with Egypt over the Suez Canal (Suez Crisis, 1956), and many NATO members resisted being drawn into the Iraq War in 2003.

27. Theis, *Why NATO Endures*; O. Wright, "The Trans-Atlantic Alliance: Strength Through Crisis," *SAIS Review* 5, no. 1 (1985): 201–210; Jeffrey Anderson, G. John Ikenberry, and Thomas Risse-Kappen, *The End of the West? Crisis and Change in the Atlantic Order* (Ithaca, NY: Cornell University Press, 2008).

28. Celeste Wallander, "Institutional Assets and Adaptability: NATO After the Cold War," *International Organization* 54, no. 4 (2000): 705–735; Alexandra Gheciu, (2005) "Security Institutions as Agents of Socialization? NATO

and the 'New Europe',", *International Organization* 59, no. 4 (2005): 973–1012; Frank Schimmelfennig, "NATO Enlargement: A Constructivist Explanation," *Security Studies* 8, no. 2–3 (1998): 198–234.

29. Helene Sjursen, "On the Identity of NATO," *International Affairs* 80, no. 4 (2004): 687–703.

30. Glenn Snyder, "The Security Dilemma in Alliance Politics," *World Politics* 36, no. 4 (1984): 461–495; Glenn Snyder, *Alliance Politics* (Ithaca, NY and London: Cornell University Press 1997); Michael C. Williams and Iver B. Neumann, "From Alliance to Security Community: NATO, Russia, and the Power of Identity," *Millennium* 29, no. 2 (2000): 357–387.

31. Emmanuel Adler and Michael Barnett, *Security Communities* (Cambridge: Cambridge University Press, 1998); Emmanuel Adler, "The Spread of Security Communities: Communities of Practice, Self-Restraint, and NATO's Post-Cold War Transformation," *European Journal of International Relations* 14, no. 2 (2008): 195–230.

32. David P. Auerswald and Stephen Saideman, *NATO in Afghanistan: Fighting Together, Fighting Alone* (Princeton, NJ and Oxford: Princeton University Press, 2014).

33. NATO, "NATO's Maritime Activities," June 2, 2020: https://www.nato .int/cps/en/natohq/topics_70759.htm

34. Alexandra Stickings, "Space as an Operational Domain: What Next for NATO?," *RUSI Newsbrief* 40, no. 9 (2020): https://rusi.org/sites/default /files/stickings_web_0.pdf

35. Ibid.

36. Lu Chuanying, "Forging Stability in Cyberspace," *Survival* 62, no. 2 (2020): 125–136; P. Meyer, "Norms of Responsible State Behaviour in Cyberspace," in *The Ethics of Cybersecurity*, ed. Markus Christen, Bert Gordijn, and Michele Loi (Cham: Springer, 2020), 347–360.

37. HM Government, "Foreign Secretary: Russia Must Face Cost for Malign Activity," March 24, 2020: https://www.gov.uk/government /news/foreign-secretary-russia-must-face-cost-for-malign-activity; Helen Warrell, "Solarwinds and Microsoft Hacks Spark Debate Over Western Retaliation," *Financial Times*, March 21, 2021: https://www.ft.com/con tent/0548b0fb-4dce-4b9e-ab4b-4fac2f5ec111

38. NATO, "Allied Joint Doctrine for Cyberspace Operations," AJP-3.20, Ed. 1, Version A (January 2020): https://www.gov.uk/government/pub lications/allied-joint-doctrine-for-cyberspace-operations-ajp-320

39. Robin Emmott, "NATO Cyber Command to Be Fully Operational in 2023," *Reuters*, October 16, 2018: https://www.reuters.com/article/us -nato-cyber-idUSKCN1MQ1Z9

40. Wiesław Goździewicz (2019), "Cyber Effects Provided Voluntarily By Allies (SCEPVA)," *Cyber Defense Magazine*, November 11, 2019: https://www.cyberdefensemagazine.com/sovereign-cyber/

41. Daniel Moore and Max Smeets, "Why We Are Unconvinced NATO's Cyber Policy Is More Aggressive, and That's a Good Thing," *Council on Foreign Relations*, January 30, 2018: https://www.cfr.org/blog/why-we-are-unconvinced-natos-cyber-policy-more-aggressive-and-thats-good-thing

42. James A. Lewis, "The Role of Offensive Cyber Operations in NATO's Collective Defence," *Tallinn Paper* 8 (2015): 6, https://www.ccdcoe.org/uploads/2018/10/TP_08_2015_0.pdf

43. Neil Robinson and Chelsey Slack, "Co-Operation: A Key To NATO's Cyberspace Endeavour," *European Foreign Affairs Review* 24, no. 2 (2019): 153–166, 164–165.

44. UN General Assembly, "Group of Governmental Experts on Developments in the Field of Information and Telecommunications in the Context of International Security, Note by the Secretary-General," July 22, 2015: https://www.un.org/ga/search/view_doc.asp?symbol=A/70/174

45. Steven Hill and Nadia Marsan, "International Law in Cyberspace: Leveraging NATO's Multilateralism, Adaptation, and Commitment to Cooperative Security," in *Governing Cyberspace: Behavior, Power, and Diplomacy*, ed. Dennis Broeders and Bibi van den Berg (Lanham, MD: Rowman & Littlefield, 2020), 173–185.

46. Michael P. Fischerkeller and Richard J. Harknett, "Persistent Engagement, Agreed Competition, Cyberspace Interaction Dynamics, and Escalation" (Washington, DC: Institute for Defense Analyses, May 2018).

47. Michael P. Fischerkeller and Richard J. Harknett, "Deterrence is Not a Credible Strategy for Cyberspace," *Orbis* 61, no. 3 (2017): 381–393.

48. Jason Healey, "The Implications of Persistent (and Permanent) Engagement in Cyberspace," *Journal of Cybersecurity* 5, no. 1 (2019): 5.

49. Brandon Valeriano and Benjamin Jensen, "The Myth of the Cyber Offense: The Case for Cyber Restraint," *Cato Institute Policy Analysis* 862 (2019): https://www.cato.org/policy-analysis/myth-cyber-offense-case-restraint; Smeets, "US Cyber Strategy."

50. Max Smeets, "NATO Allies Need to Come to Terms With Offensive Cyber Operations," *Lawfare*, October 14, 2019: https://www.lawfareblog.com/nato-allies-need-come-terms-offensive-cyber-operations

51. "Trump Sides With Russia Against FBI at Helsinki Summit," *BBC News*, July 16, 2018: https://www.bbc.co.uk/news/world-europe-44852812

52. Joe Devanny, "'Madman Theory' or 'Persistent Engagement'? The

Coherence of US Cyber Strategy Under Trump," *Journal of Applied Security Research* (2021), DOI: 10.1080/19361610.2021.1872359.

53. Thies, *Why NATO Endures*; Brian Sayers, "The North Atlantic Treaty Organization: A Study in Institutional Resilience," *Georgetown Journal of International Affairs* 12, no. 2 (2011): 48–55.

54. Beryl Thomas, "What Germany's New Cyber Security Law Means for Huawei, Europe, and NATO," *European Council on Foreign Relations*, February 5, 2021: https://ecfr.eu/article/what-germanys-new-cyber-security-law-means-for-huawei-europe-and-nato/

55. Tom Wheeler, "Time for a US-EU Digital Alliance," *Brookings*, January 21, 2021: https://www.brookings.edu/research/time-for-a-us-eu-digital-alliance/

56. Jacquelyn G. Schneider, "Persistent Engagement: Foundation, Evolution and Evaluation of a Strategy," *Lawfare*, May 10, 2019: https://www.lawfareblog.com/persistent-engagement-foundation-evolution-and-evaluation-strategy

57. Franklin D. Kramer, Lauren Speranza, and Conor Rodihan, "NATO Needs Continuous Responses in Cyberspace," *New Atlanticist*, December 9, 2020: https://www.atlanticcouncil.org/blogs/new-atlanticist/nato-needs-continuous-responses-in-cyberspace/

58. Ellen Nakashima, "US Military Operation to Attack IS Last Year Sparked Heated Debate Over Alerting Allies," *The Washington Post*, May 9, 2017.

59. Healey, "The Implications of Persistent (and Permanent) Engagement in Cyberspace," 6.

60. Max Smeets, "US Cyber Strategy of Persistent Engagement and Defend Forward: Implications for the Alliance and Intelligence Collection," *Intelligence & National Security* 35, no. 3 (2020): 444–453.

61. Ibid.

62. C. Robert Kehler, Herb Lin, and Michael Sulmeyer "Rules of Engagement for Cyberspace Operations: A View From the USA," *Journal of Cybersecurity* 3, no. 1 (2017): 73.

63. These include the North Atlantic Council, NATO Cooperative Cyber Defence Centre of Excellence (CCD COE), Cyber Defence Management Board (CDMB), NATO Communications and Information Agency (NCIA), Allied Command Transformation (ACT), NATO Industry Cyber Partnership (NICP), NATO Computer Incident Response Capability (NCIRC), and NATO's partnerships with a range of countries.

64. For example, Joseph S. Nye Jr., "Nuclear Lessons for Cyber Security," *Strategic Studies Quarterly* 5, no. 4 (2011): 18–38.

65. Jon R. Lindsay, "Restrained by Design: The Political Economy of

Cybersecurity," *Digital Policy, Regulation and Governance* 19, no. 6 (2017): 493.

66. NATO, "Warsaw Summit Communiqué," July 9, 2016: https://www.na to.int/cps/en/natohq/official_texts_133169.htm

67. Lewis, "The Role of Offensive Cyber Operations in NATO's Collective Defence"; Jeppe T. Jacobsen, "Cyber Offense in NATO: Challenges and Opportunities," *International Affairs*, 97, no. 3 (2021), DOI: 10.1093/ia/ iiab010.

68. Milton L. Mueller, "Against Sovereignty in Cyberspace," *International Studies Review* 22, no. 4 (2020): 790.

69. Sandra R. Leavitt, "Problems in Collective Action," in *Conflict and Cooperation in the Global Commons: A Comprehensive Approach for International Security*, ed. Scott Jasper (Washington, DC: Georgetown University Press, 2012), 25.

70. Leavitt, "Problems in Collective Action," 33.

71. Robinson and Slack, "Co-Operation."

72. Mueller, "Against Sovereignty," 796.

73. Franklin D. Kramer, "Achieving International Cyber Stability," *Georgetown Journal of International Affairs*, (International Engagement on Cyber 2012: Establishing Norms and Improving Security 2012, 2012), 134.

74. Jan Angstrom and Peter Haldén, "The Poverty Of Power In Military Power: How Collective Power Could Benefit Strategic Studies," *Defense & Security Analysis* 35, no. 2 (2019): 170–189.

75. Melissa E. Hathaway, "Toward a Closer Digital Alliance," *SAIS Review of International Affairs* 36, no. 2 (2016): 60.

76. NATO, "NATO and the European Union Enhance Cyber Defence Cooperation," February 10, 2016: https://www.nato.int/cps/en/natohq /news_127836.htm

77. European Commission, "The EU's Cybersecurity Strategy for the Digital Decade," *European Commission*, December 16, 2020: https://ec.europa.eu /digital-single-market/en/news/eus-cybersecurity-strategy-digital-decade

78. George Christou, *Cybersecurity in the European Union: Resilience and Adaptability in Governance Policy* (Basingstoke: Palgrave Macmillan, 2016).

79. Myriam Dunn Cavelty and Florian J. Egloff, "The Politics of Cybersecurity: Balancing Different Roles of the State," *St. Antony's International Review* 15, no. 1 (2019): 41.

80. NATO, "Sharing Malware Information to Defeat Cyber Attacks," November 29, 2013: https://www.nato.int/cps/en/natolive/news_1054 85.htm

81. Michael Daniel and Joshua Kenway, "Repairing The Foundation: How

Cyber Threat Information Sharing Can Live Up To Its Promise And Implications For NATO," in *Cyber Threats and NATO 2030: Horizon Scanning and Analysis*, ed. Amy Ertan, Kathryn Floyd, Piret Pernik, and Tim Stevens (Tallinn, Estonia: NATO CCD COE Publications, 2020), 178–193; Chon Abraham and Sally Daultrey, "Considerations For NATO In Reconciling Barriers To Shared Cyber Threat Intelligence: A Study Of Japan, The UK And The US," in Ertan et al., *Cyber Threats and NATO 2030*, 194–214.

82. NATO, "NATO 2030: United for a New Era," 10.

83. Ibid.: 34.

84. James A. Lewis, "Toward a More Coercive Cyber Strategy: Remarks to US Cyber Command Legal Conference," March 4, 2021: https://www.cs is.org/analysis/toward-more-coercive-cyber-strategy

5

From Reaction to Action: Revamping Diplomacy for Strategic Cyber Competition

Emily O. Goldman

Most state-sponsored malicious cyber activity takes the form of campaigns conducted outside of armed conflict. These are producing meaningful strategic gains for the major state sponsors of those activities – China and Russia. These gains have come through intellectual property theft that degrades economic competitiveness, as well as theft of research and development. Malign cyber activity includes supply-chain manipulation to undercut US and allied national security and military capabilities. State actors regularly conduct campaigns of disinformation and information manipulation to weaken domestic political cohesion and undermine confidence in democratic institutions.

The United States and its democratic allies have ceded the initiative in strategic cyber competition. The 2017 US "National Security Strategy" coined the phrase "competitive diplomacy" with appeals to "upgrade our diplomatic capabilities to compete in the current environment and to embrace a competitive mindset."[1] Nowhere is this more necessary than in cyber diplomacy, which engages the state sponsors of malicious cyber campaigns while simultaneously working with allies and partners in resisting such threats.

This chapter describes how current cyber diplomatic priorities, approaches, and conceptual frameworks need to change for the United States and its partners to reset the dynamics of strategic cyber competition. It recommends new diplomatic initiatives, engagement priorities, operational partnerships, and a shift in mindset to help thwart adversary cyber campaigns. These changes can close gaps that allow adversaries to set de facto cyber norms.

The argument unfolds in five sections. The first explains the context of strategic cyber competition and its relationship to cyber stability. The second summarizes the current state of cyber diplomacy as practiced by the US and its diplomatic partners. The third and fourth explain the need to revise long-standing approaches to norm construction and deterrence. The last section offers recommendations that – if adopted – would increase US ability to regain the initiative in strategic cyber competition and contribute to cyber stability.

Strategic Cyber Competition and Cyber Stability

There is consensus across the US government that great-power competitors are making strategic gains in and through cyberspace with persistent, targeted campaigns that never rise to the level of a catastrophic or even significant cyber attack. Strategic gains are being accrued outside the traditional route of war, cumulatively over time in and through cyberspace at unprecedented speed and scale. Adversaries deliberately act below internationally accepted thresholds without physically crossing territorial borders, thus minimizing risk to themselves while reaping the cumulative benefits of their cyber behavior.[2]

Cyberspace has become a major battleground for great-power competition because of the nature of the operating environment. Cyberspace is globally interconnected, distinguished by constant (rather than imminent, potential, or episodic) contact, influenced by difficulty of attribution, characterized by contested borders and informal thresholds that are limited in adherence, and lacks sanctuary and operational pause. Moreover, an abundance of vulnerabilities in cyberspace offers endless opportunities for states to exploit. For all these reasons, cyberspace offers new ways to erode national power and thereby shift the relative balance of interstate power.

There is an ideological dimension further fueling this competition, one that pits free societies against authoritarian regimes that view an open cyberspace and information freedom as existential threats to their power.[3] Illiberal regimes are working to shape the digital ecosystem in line with authoritarian values and influencing mandates and agendas in standards bodies and international organizations to support information control.[4] They promote, and at times advance, "cyber sovereignty" as an organizing principle of governance in cyberspace.[5] Cyber sovereignty asserts that states have the right to censor and regulate the internet to prevent exposing their citizens to ideas and opinions deemed harmful by the regime. It calls for states to govern the internet instead of the current multistakeholder model that also includes businesses, civil society, research institutions, and non-governmental organizations in dialogue, decision-making, and implementation of solutions. The subordination of cyberspace to the interests of the state reflects that authoritarian governments value regime security over individual liberty.

China is developing and exporting technologies and networks that erode civil society, privacy, and human rights.[6] Russia successfully advocated for the establishment of the Open-Ended Working Group in the United Nations, an alternative norms-creating forum that threatens to dilute progress made under the UN Group of Governmental Experts (GGE) process.[7] In spite of the Budapest Convention on Cybercrime, Russia secured UN support for a cyber crime resolution that may make it easier to repress political dissent.[8] In concert with these diplomatic achievements, authoritarian regimes continually exploit open networks and platforms to destabilize democratic societies from within, illicitly acquire intellectual property and personally identifiable information, and disrupt critical infrastructure.[9]

Clearly, states retain significant diverging interests and normative preferences for the future of cyberspace. Renewed great-power competition with ideological adversaries need not alter the liberal vision for cyberspace (an open, interoperable, secure, reliable, market-driven domain that reflects democratic values and protects privacy). However, it does require an empirically based view of the cyberspace strategic environment as one characterized by strategic competition and contested principles and norms, which has evolved away from the vision of international liberal markets buttressed by an open, worldwide internet.[10]

By adopting a competitive mindset, cyber diplomacy can be more responsive to the international environment and contribute to cyber stability. This chapter defines cyber stability as a condition within the cyber strategic environment in which states are not incentivized to pursue armed-attack-equivalent cyber operations or conventional/nuclear armed attack.[11]

Cyber diplomats can contribute to cyber stability by "maturing the competition space" in the following ways. They can help define what constitutes an operation or campaign of armed-attack equivalence; address cumulative gains, not just significant consequences; encourage clarity on how international law applies to cyberspace; accelerate consensus on what is and is not acceptable below the use-of-force threshold; and mobilize coalitions to collectively push back on adversary aggression in and through cyberspace.

Arriving at an international agreement on what constitutes an operation of armed-attack equivalence would set an explicit threshold, the breaching of which represents a violation of international law and legitimizes a response in self-defense that could include kinetic capabilities. Thus, an agreement and clarity on the consequence of its breaching could contribute to cyber stability by serving as a deterrent to such operations.

Diplomatic efforts can contribute further to stability by focusing more on the cumulative nature of gains in cyberspace.[12] Any single action, hack, or incident alone might not be strategically consequential, but cumulatively gains can rise to that level. Thus, efforts to prevent "significant" incidents or catastrophic attacks must be coupled with an approach designed for campaigns comprised of activities whose individual effects never rise to the level of a significant incident, and therefore rarely elicit a timely response, but which can cumulatively threaten core interests and values.

Diplomatic efforts should also encourage states to define how international law, particularly the UN Charter and customary international law derived from the charter, applies in the cyber context. Uncertainty poses numerous challenges to stability and so clarity in states' positions could certainly contribute to cyber stability.

Accelerating consensus on what is and what is not acceptable below the use-of-force threshold would further contribute to the maturation of the cyber competition space short of armed-attack equivalence. Cyberspace is a new competitive space where agreement over the substantive character of acceptable and unacceptable behaviors is immature. Competition, in time, can become mutually limited such that restraint above the armed-attack threshold occurs alongside routinization below that threshold in non-violent actions that do not threaten states' core interests and values.

Finally, mobilizing coalitions to push back on adversary aggression can contribute to cyber stability. We have yet to see escalation out of cyber competition into armed conflict, and states have demonstrated the ability to preclude and disrupt cyber aggression without escalating to armed conflict. Restraint in the face of continuous aggression is destabilizing because it emboldens aggressors. Thus, explicit bargaining in international fora should be reinforced by tacit bargaining with non-like-minded states that builds and reinforces mutual understandings of what is and is not acceptable competition.

The Current State of Cyber Diplomacy

Cyber diplomacy is the use of diplomatic tools to resolve issues arising in cyberspace.[13] The US approach to cyber diplomacy promotes a vision of an open, interoperable, reliable, and secure information and communications technology infrastructure and governance structures to support international trade and commerce, strengthen international peace and security, and foster free expression and innovation.[14] Cyber diplomacy as practiced by the United States also seeks to build strategic bilateral and multilateral partnerships, expand capacity-building activities for foreign partners and enhance international cooperation.[15] Key lines of effort include building consensus among like-minded states on norms of responsible state behavior in cyberspace;[16] encouraging international participation in a deterrence framework that involves collective attribution and swift imposition of consequences on those who violate those norms;[17] exposing and countering foreign disinformation and propaganda efforts;[18] promoting access to markets and leadership in digital technologies;[19] building cyber security capacity of allies and foreign partners; and ensuring that 5G technology deployed around the world is secure and reliable.[20]

The US State Department has never produced a cyber strategy. The closest approximation may be the Obama administration's 2011 *International Strategy for Cyberspace*, an initiative spearheaded by Christopher Painter who became the State Department's top cyber diplomat.[21] Current lines of effort being pursued by US diplomats still closely align to the 2011 strategy, even though the world has dramatically changed since that time.

The 2011 strategy ties global stability to the establishment of norms by like-minded states. Toward this end, the strategy calls on the United States to (1) engage in urgent dialogue to build consensus around principles of responsible behavior in cyberspace; (2) build international understanding around cyberspace norms, beginning with like-minded countries in bilateral dialogues; (3) carry this agenda into international organizations; (4) deter malicious actors from violating these norms; and (5) facilitate cyber security capacity building.[22] The United States has steadily pursued these goals, even as authoritarian regimes strive to reshape the digital environment and rewrite international norms and standards.[23]

International diplomats have had some success in reaching agreement on principles of responsible state behavior in cyberspace.[24] The 2013 and 2015 meetings of the United Nations' cyber-specific GGE reached a consensus on the applicability of international law in cyberspace, but established only voluntary, non-binding norms – which was their stated objective.[25] The 2017 UN GGE failed to deliver a consensus report.[26] The 2021 consensus report elaborated on the voluntary norms agreed to in 2015.[27]

This decades-long cyber norms-building project – determining how existing binding norms apply in cyberspace and using non-binding norms to set expectations of behavior that could eventually be codified – has been a top-down process, based on the belief that diplomatic consensus on normative taboos can shape state behavior. Agreements on the non-proliferation of nuclear weapons and on the non-use of chemical weapons are cited as evidence of this approach.[28] Yet these conventions were possible because the technologies were well developed, and their effects understood. By contrast, the risks and ramifications of cyber capabilities are not yet widely recognized. Norms can be powerful tools, but as Stefan Soesanto and Fosca D'Incau demonstrate, "their creation is contingent upon a history of transnational interaction, moral interpretation, and legal internalisation. Only through this tedious multi-pronged process is there any hope for national interests to be reframed and national identities to be reconstructed."[29] In other words, international norms are constructed from the bottom up.

Strategic cyber competition – continuous campaigns outside of armed conflict that cumulatively produce strategic gains – demands new initiatives, planning assumptions, and thinking. Adapting diplomacy to strategic cyber competition requires dislodging some of the assumptions guiding current diplomatic approaches in bilateral and multilateral fora – specifically those associated with how norms are constructed and the applicability of a strategy of deterrence to competition in cyberspace.

Constructing Norms

An imperfect analogy has distorted the US approach to norm development, one rooted in America's post-Second World War success in fashioning a global political-economic structure of rules reinforced with institutions. At the time, the United States produced 60 percent of the world's gross economic product, held a monopoly on nuclear weapons, and had accrued a reservoir of trust in the eyes of most of the international community. America's dominance over the distribution of political-economic benefits meant that Washington could provide those benefits to states that adopted American-inspired norms. Conversely, the United States could deny such advantages to states that rejected those norms. This temporary apex of American influence enabled the United States to reform the world's financial and trading systems, taking key steps at the Bretton Woods conference in 1944. The United States was in a unique position to credibly establish norms for a critical mass of states.[30]

Such is not the case today. While American institutions and corporations retain significant influence over the technical aspects of computing, networking, and telecommunications, US dominance in cyberspace ebbed and was lost by the late 1990s and early 2000s. Unsurprisingly, the US government has not been able to shape and enforce norms of behavior in cyberspace. For example, in September 2016, while President Obama was telling reporters at the G20 Summit that the US goal is to "start instituting some norms so that everybody's acting responsibly,"[31] Russia was flouting norms of responsible behavior by mounting a multipronged cyber campaign to influence the American presidential election.

American diplomats have worked actively as norm entrepreneurs. They have attempted to call attention to problematic cyber behavior; set the agenda in international venues that possess the requisite membership, mandate, and legitimacy; advocated candidate norms; persuaded and pressured (through naming, blaming, and shaming) other states to embrace these norms; and built coalitions of like-minded norm addressees to lead by example.[32] These efforts have yielded some positive results. The year 2013 was a high-water mark with both Russia and China agreeing that "international law, and in particular, the United Nations Charter, applies in cyberspace."[33] From the US perspective, agreement on the UN Charter implied acceptance of the Geneva Conventions and the applicability of the laws of armed conflict to cyberspace. However, progress stalled shortly thereafter. Chinese officials emphasized the UN GGEs' embrace of state authority over cyber issues. The 2015 GGE made incremental progress by recommending eleven voluntary, non-binding norms, rules, or principles of responsible behavior of states for consideration.[34] The 2017 GGE failed to reach consensus and advance how international law applies in cyberspace.

In terms of advancing the norms dialogue, the 2021 consensus report adds commentary on the meaning and means of complying with the eleven voluntary, non-binding norms agreed upon in the 2015 report.[35] It also acknowledges that international humanitarian law applies to cyber operations during armed conflict but reaches no agreement on how it applies. Thus, it marks the same moment in 2015 where all states agreed that the UN Charter applies, but none agreed on how it applies. Several years later we still have no agreement on how, and states continue to experiment with different ways to use cyber to achieve strategic gains. Also, the debate over whether sovereignty is a primary rule of international law, or only a principle that itself has no binding effect, remains unsettled.

Research has shown that certain states are critical to norm adoption – particularly those states without which the achievement of the substantive norm goal is compromised, either because they possess the capabilities or engage in the behavior the norm is intended to regulate, or because they possess moral stature in the view of most members of the community.[36] China and Russia qualify as critical states because of their cyberspace capabilities and willingness to use them. States opposed to a particular norm may be motivated to adhere to it because they identify as a member of an international society and thus will behave in a manner conducive to cementing their status within that society.[37] China, in particular, wants to be accepted as a member of international society but as a norm maker, not a norm taker: it does not wish to yield to the self-interested standards of liberal states.[38] China is currently acting on the belief that it can shape norms to serve its specific interests. The approach of the US and its like-minded partners to building cyber norms must adapt to the realities that no hegemon exists to impose norms and that what is and is not currently acceptable varies greatly depending on national perspectives, even among liberal democratic states.

An alternative approach to building norms is to model good behavior. Convergence of norms will occur over time as other actors see that more beneficial outcomes flow from modeled good behavior than from bad behavior. This approach presents several challenges. First, behavior that might be categorized as unacceptable still produces benefits that outweigh costs. Second, adversaries cite various allegations of American bad behavior in cyberspace – global surveillance and the Stuxnet hack of the Iranian nuclear program are two examples – in labeling the United States a hypocritical standard-bearer for norms. Third, as both state and non-state actors continue to advance their interests through behaviors that others might consider unacceptable, modeling can easily be misunderstood as tacit acceptance.[39]

A third approach is reaction to a massively disruptive or destructive event that galvanizes global attention. This is how norms against genocide were set after the Holocaust. This approach presents obvious challenges. Relying on disaster to set norms is not an acceptable strategy. Nor does it seem likely that cyber capabilities will generate the level of abhorrence that characterizes attitudes toward nerve agents, for example, and which have led to self-imposed proscriptions on their use.[40]

A fourth approach is for convergence of expectations to organically evolve through interaction. Common law demonstrates how norms emerge through practice and mature through political and legal discourse. The process of norm convergence for cyberspace has been troubling, however. For the last ten years, the world has witnessed the emergence of de facto norms, defined by massive theft of intellectual property, expanding control of internet content, attacks on data confidentiality and availability, violations of privacy, and interference in democratic debates and processes. These activities have become normalized because liberal states did not push back on them persistently and early on.[41] This has encouraged more experimentation and envelope-pushing short of armed conflict. Conversely, if the United States and its allies and partners actively contest such practices, it could help to counteract this trend and encourage a form of normalization more suited to liberal interests.

These pathways can be mutually reinforcing. The first two approaches have largely succeeded with US allies and partners, but important differences with major competitors remain. In the opening decades of the twenty-first century, no state is sufficiently powerful to dictate the rules of the road. The third approach – waiting for a disaster – is politically and morally problematic. The fourth approach of "normalization" holds more promise for engaging with Moscow and Beijing. Norms are constructed through "normal" practice and then become codified in international agreements. By persistently engaging and contesting cyberspace aggression, the US and its allies can draw parameters around what is acceptable, nuisance, unacceptable, and intolerable. The international community should not abandon UN First Committee processes on responsible state behavior in cyberspace, or other avenues for socialization such as international institutions or cyber capacity-building programs. But to be more effective, explicit bargaining must be reinforced by tacit bargaining through maneuver with non–like-minded states in the strategic space below armed conflict.[42] Diplomats have an important role to play in this process.[43] They possess the skills to mobilize coalitions – of governments, industry, academia, and citizenry, at home and abroad – for competition with ideological foes.

Scoping Deterrence

Another major thrust in the cyber diplomacy of the US and its diplomatic partners is an international cyber deterrence initiative.[44] The 2018 *US National Cyber Strategy* asserts that, "the imposition of consequences will be more impactful and send a stronger message if it is carried out in concert with a broader coalition of like-minded states." Therefore, "the United States will launch an international Cyber Deterrence Initiative to build such a coalition ... The United States will work with like-minded states to coordinate and support each other's responses to significant malicious cyber incidents."[45] The cyber deterrence initiative is a US government-wide, State Department-led initiative with other US government agencies that proposes options for use in response to a significant cyber incident. Allies are encouraged to develop options as well. However, the preponderance of cyberspace aggression falls outside the initiative's purview.

The Cyber Deterrence Initiative strives for collective attribution and responses when norms are violated. It concentrates on responding to significant cyber incidents, which aligns with deterrence strategy's focus on reaction and episodic contact. Yet the empirical reality in cyberspace is that adversaries are continuously operating against the United States and its allies and partners below the threshold of armed attack. Strategic significance in cyberspace is not the result of any single event, but stems from the cumulative effect of a campaign comprising many individually less-consequential operations and activities carried out toward a coherent strategic end. Moreover, significant cyber incidents are not "bolts from the blue." Rather, the ability to cause unacceptable harm or engage in otherwise destructive, disruptive, or destabilizing activities are the result of advanced persistent campaigns.

A strategy based on response after the fact to significant incidents is not flexible enough to address most malicious cyber activity. Response per se does not deter; only responses that outweigh benefits can change the perceptions and behavior of an ideologically motivated actor. Sanctions, indictments, expulsions, designations, and naming and shaming can all in principle constrain an adversary's freedom of maneuver by exposing bad behavior, but they are not likely to impose sufficient costs to deter (prevent from acting) or compel (stop acting). Relying on redlines and responding to incidents after the fact have not stemmed malicious cyberspace activity, and there is no reason to believe such measures will suddenly dissuade authoritarian sponsors of cyber misbehavior. More of the same will not produce different results. A strategy of deterrence has conspicuously failed to prevent cyberspace aggression where it is most prevalent – outside of armed conflict – yet the deterrence frame, rather than the realities of strategic cyber competition, continues to guide key elements of cyber diplomacy practiced by the US and its partners.[46]

An alternative approach was introduced in 2018 by the US Department of Defense. Measures to ensure deterrence of significant cyber incidents (that is, cyber "armed-attack" equivalent operations) would be pursued in tandem with steady, sustained activities that persistently push back against adversary cyberspace campaigns below the level of armed conflict.[47] The Department of Defense adopted the strategy of defend forward and the operational approach of persistent engagement.[48] Both depart from the 2011 *International Strategy for Cyberspace* reliance on "credible response options" to dissuade and deter – reactive approaches based on threats of prospective action and episodic response after a declared threshold has been crossed.[49]

This pivot to a proactive approach acknowledges that cyberspace is an active operational space. Its dynamic terrain, regenerating capabilities, low entry costs, anonymity, pervasive vulnerabilities, and prospect of cumulative gains rewards continuous action, initiative-seeking, and sustained exploitation. Therefore, relying on threats to impose consequences after the fact cedes initiative and lets others set norms by default.[50] The pivot also addresses the challenge presented by persistent campaigns, which produce cumulative gains for adversaries while also permitting them to cause unacceptable harm.

Diplomatic and military efforts to counter malicious cyberspace behavior must be mutually reinforcing. Diplomacy can strengthen collective efforts to degrade, disrupt, and contest malicious cyberspace activities and campaigns below the level of armed conflict by leveraging diplomatic channels to increase routine and agile collaboration with partners and allies. The goal would be to proactively constrain adversaries' strategic options and frustrate and thwart cyberspace aggression before it harms the United States, its allies, and partners.

The military's adoption of persistent engagement below the level of armed conflict, to complement deterrence of armed-attack equivalent effects, can in turn bolster diplomatic efforts. Closer synergy between promoting norms of responsible state behavior in international venues and conducting persistent cyberspace operations that expose and contest behavior inconsistent with such norms has the best chance of producing a convergence of expectations on acceptable behavior.

Cyber Diplomacy for Great-Power Competition: Seizing and Sustaining Initiative

Russia and China's aggressive information, political, and economic warfare campaigns have highlighted the risks to the US, its allies, and partners and the need to focus diplomatic efforts on building coalitions for continuous pressure against adversary cyberspace campaigns outside of armed conflict.[51] Such joint efforts will normalize collaborative cyberspace operations for mutual defense, reinforcing principles of responsible state behavior with actions that contest and preclude violations of those principles. In other words, the US and its allies must seize the initiative in cyberspace. This will require national and allied dialogues to define boundaries of acceptable behavior below the level of armed conflict as a precursor to constructing consensus with competitors, and mobilization of international coalitions to reinforce those boundaries. Diplomatic discourse must be accompanied by persistently engaging and defending forward in cyberspace below the level of armed conflict − a necessary ingredient for constructing norms through interaction. With these goals in mind, the following recommendations are offered as a roadmap for implementing competitive cyber diplomacy.

Enable Collective Efforts to Defend Forward

A framework of responsible state behavior in cyberspace, one that ensures there are consequences for irresponsible behavior, must be pursued in tandem with an active approach to stem ongoing adversarial cyberspace campaigns outside of armed conflict and mitigation of threats before they reach the US and allied and partner networks. It is time for cyber diplomats to join in these efforts.

The United States needs to operate continuously alongside allies and partners. Leadership from the State Department can increase the speed, agility, and scale of defend forward activities and operations by working through diplomatic channels to set the conditions for the United States to operate by, with, and through foreign partners and their networks to expose, contest, and defend against adversary cyber aggression. Sustained diplomacy can help institutionalize these operational partnerships and make defending forward more anticipatory and effective. Institutionalized cooperation, including the conduct of joint and coalition operations and the development of agreed-upon legal and policy frameworks, is essential to prevail in long-term strategic competition.

Diplomats can proactively set the conditions for consensual foreign partner-enabled discovery operations ("hunt forward" operations) through bilateral engagements.[52] Then the United States, working side by side with partners, can gain insight into adversary tactics, techniques, and procedures, which in turn enables more effective collective network defense, improves anticipatory resilience, and thwarts cyberspace aggression before it reaches friendly networks.

Mobilize Coalitions

The US State Department has a history of coalition building, most recently with the Global Coalition to Defeat ISIS formed in 2014. It is uniquely equipped to mobilize partners to sustain pressure on adversary cyberspace behavior and cyber-enabled campaigns. A three-tiered coalition could increase information sharing, agile collaboration, and operational agility against persistent adversary cyberspace campaigns.

At the core of this coalition would be states that possess the capability and capacity to conduct full-spectrum cyberspace operations and work with diplomatic, law enforcement, and industry partners. A second tier would comprise less-capable or less-committed states that core states operate with (and through) to counter and contest aggression below the level of armed conflict. The United States has extensive experience negotiating basing and transit rights in sovereign territory along the Soviet perimeter during the Cold War. It should negotiate the cyber analogue of basing and transit rights to set the conditions for swift and persistent action. The transit issue is likely to be less controversial for allies and partners than for remote cyber operations on infrastructure within another state's territory, which is addressed below (Recommendation 4).

A third tier would comprise public and private actors across the broadest practicable set of countries in a resilience consortium to leverage collective market power, secure the internet and counterbalance the illiberal vision of information control promoted by Russia and China.[53] This is especially urgent as countries shift from 3G and 4G to 5G communications networks. By offering attractive financial terms, authoritarian governments can dominate the telecommunications industry in developing countries and control digital tools that increase censorship, repression, and surveillance. It is imperative that public and private actors assist the broader coalition in combating such trends.

Several pillars for a resilience consortium already exist. Cyber security capacity building received a boost when the US State Department and USAID launched the Digital Connectivity and Cybersecurity Partnership in July 2018, with a focus on the Indo-Pacific region.[54] In July 2019, USAID launched a development framework called Countering Malign Kremlin Influence. The framework was designed to build the economic and democratic resilience of countries targeted by Russia. Cyber security is considered high priority.[55] The launch of the US Development Finance Corporation in October 2019 can attract private capital flows into contested markets to stem the spread of surveillance networks.[56] In November 2019, the United States, Australia, and Japan announced the Blue Dot Network to promote high-quality and trusted standards for global infrastructure development as an alternative to the predatory lending and debt-trap diplomacy of China's Belt and Road Initiative.[57] Re-prioritizing emerging market economies for affordable and reliable internet access and infrastructure can shore up internet freedom, ensure economic prosperity for the United States and its partners, and secure the outer ring of telecommunications networks as a first line of cyber defense.

Another initiative launched by the Trump administration, the Clean Network program, envisioned a comprehensive effort by a coalition of like-minded countries and companies to secure their critical telecommunications, cloud, data analytics, mobile apps, Internet of Things, and 5G technologies from malign actors. The coalition would rely on trusted vendors who are not subject to unjust or extra-judicial control by authoritarian governments.[58] Proposed lines of effort aimed to ensure telecommunication carriers, mobile app stores, apps, cloud-based systems, and undersea cables would all be rooted in digital trust standards.[59] More than thirty countries and territories are Clean Countries, and many of the world's biggest telecommunications companies are Clean Telcos.[60] These efforts have laid the foundation for a broader coalition that can be mobilized to implement competitive cyber strategies.

Accelerate Consensus on What Constitutes a Cyber Armed-attack Equivalent and on Conventions Below the Use of Force

What constitutes acceptable cyber behavior outside armed conflict? While there is a normative prohibition against crossing the threshold of armed conflict and while states appear to tacitly agree on many types of behavior that cross that threshold, the unilateral ingenuity displayed in developing novel approaches to achieving strategic gains invites the potential for miscalculations

on and around this threshold. As a first step, arriving at an international agreement on what constitutes a cyber-armed-attack equivalent operation would set
an explicit threshold and could serve as a deterrent. Yet so long as the strategic
competitive space outside of armed conflict is maturing, rules will be malleable
and mutual understandings of acceptable and unacceptable behavior will be
limited.[61]

The US and its partners need to reach consensus on the preferred boundaries of acceptable behavior outside of armed conflict and promote them in
international fora. Discussions should proceed in tandem with consultations
with the private sector. Agreed-upon conventions can then be reinforced by
the actions of all US departments and agencies. Working bilaterally, multilat-
erally, and through international institutions, the United States and its partners
can influence and message what behaviors they consider unacceptable. This
can help reduce the ambiguity that adversaries exploit, enhance the ability to
build coalitions against adversary campaigns, and secure commitments from
like-minded countries to impose consequences on those whose actions are
counter to the principles.

However, the United States and its partners must first decide what each
believes are the boundaries of acceptable and unacceptable behavior. This
requires each to detail how national interests manifest in cyberspace and the
security postures needed to defend those interests.[62] The issue is where there is
convergence, not just with like-minded states, but with adversaries. Examples
that come to mind are the integrity of the global financial infrastructure;
nuclear command, control, and communications; and disinformation that dis-
rupts public health efforts – an issue which is of special relevance considering
the current global health crisis.[63]

Shape International Discourse on Cyber Operations and Sovereignty

One of the greatest concerns for US allies and partners are operations that
generate cyber effects outside US military networks. These operations are
designed to disrupt the ability of an adversary to conduct malicious cyber
operations against the United States, its allies, and partners.[64] There is no
US declaratory policy on the sovereignty implications of cyber operations.
Specifically, the United States has not declared its position on whether remote
cyber operations that generate effects on infrastructure within another state's
territory require that state's consent. There is a divide among states on this
issue, and on whether such acts require international legal justification.[65] There
is also divergence in state views on how international law applies to states'
conduct of cyber operations below the threshold of a use of force and outside

the context of armed conflict.[66] On one end of the spectrum is the United Kingdom, which has publicly declared that remote cyber operations below the non-intervention threshold are not prohibited by international law and do not require consent.[67] On the other end of the spectrum, the Netherlands agrees with the 2017 *Tallinn Manual 2.0 on the International Law Applicable to Cyber Operations* that such operations violate state sovereignty and require consent.[68]

The United Kingdom and the Netherlands have officially declared their respective positions and they have polar opposite views on this core question. Estonia, Australia, and the United States have officially articulated their positions on the applicability of international law to cyber operations yet have not weighed in on this particular issue. Gary Corn considers this range of positions "*prima facie* evidence of the unsettled nature of the question."[69] The most explicit official US statement comes from the Department of Defense general counsel:

> For cyber operations that would not constitute a prohibited intervention or use-of-force, the Department believes there is not sufficiently widespread and consistent State practice resulting from a sense of legal obligation to conclude that customary international law generally prohibits such non-consensual cyber operations in another State's territory. This proposition is recognised in the Department's adoption of the "defend forward" strategy: "We will defend forward to disrupt or halt malicious cyber activity at its source, including activity that falls below the level of armed conflict." The Department's commitment to defend forward including to counter foreign cyber activity targeting the United States – comports with our obligations under international law and our commitment to the rules-based international order.[70]

This is an area where the State Department should be leading internationally if the United States hopes to persuade others to adopt its preferred norms, particularly as allies wrestle with legal ambiguities surrounding cyber operations.[71]

Adopt a Competitive Mindset

Cyberspace is a contested domain where two distinct models are competing to shape the infrastructure, standards, conventions, and norms of the global information environment – a liberal model of information freedom and an authoritarian model of information control. There are two distinct approaches to this strategic cyber competition: China and Russia rely on continuous action to exploit cyberspace for strategic advantage; the US and its partners rely on imposing consequences after the fact – react and respond. Given that cyberspace is an environment of continuous activity, these disparate approaches have produced an imbalance of initiative in China's and Russia's favor, and cumulative losses for the US and its partners.

Adversarial competition is not new. During the Cold War, nuclear deterrence pushed competition between the superpowers below the threshold of conventional US-Soviet armed conflict. Today, however, below-the-threshold actions are being employed to strategic effect rather than merely in peripheral conflicts. They are helping position authoritarian states to compete more effectively and to define the rules and norms of a new international order.

Meeting this challenge requires the US and its partners to adopt a "competitive mindset." This means being proactive and anticipatory; continuously seeking and actively sustaining initiative; and working across traditional bureaucratic lines and stovepipes to address multifaceted cyber problems which cross jurisdictional and territorial boundaries, and which engage multiple authorities, actors, and organizations. It means transcending inter-bureaucratic differences so that all tools of national power are leveraged toward a coherent strategic objective – a secure, stable cyberspace based on principles of information freedom.

Adopting a competitive mindset also means recognizing that cyberspace operations have become a standard tool of diplomacy and competition; adversaries are executing continuous campaigns of non-violent operations in day-to-day competition; and these persistent campaigns are a prerequisite to engaging in destructive, disruptive, or destabilizing activities that may cause unacceptable harm. What works to deter catastrophic cyber attacks will not dissuade adversaries from routinely operating in and through cyberspace for strategic gain. Rather than relying on response after the fact, we need coordinated and sustained energy and resources across the US government, and with allies and partners, all focused on strategic cyber competition.

Conclusion

Cyberspace is replete with vulnerabilities that adversaries can exploit for strategic gain without ever crossing a threshold that calls for self-defense under international law. Cyberspace aggression (and our approach to thwarting it) is continuous across space and time. It cannot be confined to "areas of hostility." There is no operational pause. This does not mean being everywhere all the time; it does mean that the struggle to retain the initiative in cyberspace is enduring and relying on episodic responses after the fact has failed to make cyberspace more secure and stable.

Up until now, the potential roles for diplomats in strategic cyber competition have been under-utilized. Instead of continuing to focus primarily on deterrence and defining redlines for response after the fact, cyber diplomacy should mobilize partners to preclude and contest adversary cyber misbehavior before it breaches US, allied, and partner networks. Forging coalitions of partners for agile collaboration and continuous pressure against authoritarian adversaries also has the best chance of producing a convergence of expectations on acceptable behavior through tacit bargaining with non–like-minded states. Then liberal democracies will be in a position to define a framework of responsible state behavior and collectively enforce consequences for irresponsible acts.

Notes

1. The White House, "National Security Strategy of the United States of America," December 2017: 33, https://www.whitehouse.gov/wp-con tent/uploads/2017/12/NSS-Final-12-18-2017-0905.pdf

2. Michael J. Fischerkeller, Emily O. Goldman, and Richard J. Harknett, *Cyber Persistence: Redefining National Security in Cyberspace* (New York: Oxford University Press, 2022); Richard Harknett and Max Smeets, "Cyber Campaigns and Strategic Outcomes," *Journal of Strategic Studies* 45, no. 4 (2020): https://doi.org/10.1080/01402390.2020.1732354

3. Michael Warner, "Invisible Battlegrounds: On Force and Revolutions, Military and Otherwise," in *The Palgrave Handbook of Security, Risk and Intelligence*, ed. Robert Dover, Huw Dylan, and Michael Goodman (London: Palgrave Macmillan, 2017), 254.

4. James A. Lewis, "Cyber Solarium and the Sunset of Security," *Center for Strategic & International Studies*, March 13, 2020: https://www.csis.org/ana lysis/cyber-solarium-and-sunset-cybersecurity; US-China Economic and Security Review Commission, "A 'China Model?' Beijing's Promotion of Alternative Global Norms and Standards," March 13, 2020: https:// www.uscc.gov/hearings/postponed-china-model-beijings-promotion-al ternative-global-norms-and-standards

5. Niels Schia, Niels Nagelhus, and Lars Gjesvik, "China's Cyber Sovereignty," *Norwegian Institute for International Affairs (NUPI)*, January 1, 2017: www.jstor.org/stable/resrep07952; Niels Nagelhaus and Lars Gjesvik, "The Chinese Cyber Sovereignty Concept (Part 1)," *The Asia Dialogue*, September 7, 2018: https://theasiadialogue.com/2018/09/07 /the-chinese-cyber-sovereignty-concept-part-1/

6. "China Exports AI Surveillance Tech to Over 60 Countries: Report," *Nikkei Asian Review*, December 16, 2019: https://asia.nikkei.com/Busi

ness/China-tech/China-exports-AI-surveillance-tech-to-over-60-count
ries-report; Steven Feldstein, "The Global Expansion of AI Surveillance,"
Carnegie Endowment for International Peace, September 17, 2019: https://
carnegieendowment.org/2019/09/17/global-expansion-of-ai-surveillan
ce-pub-79847

7. Samuele de Tomas Colatin, "A Surprising Turn of Events: UN Creates
Two Working Groups on Cyberspace," *NATO Cooperative Cyber Defence
Centre of Excellence*: https://ccdcoe.org/incyder-articles/a-surprising-tu
rn-of-events-un-creates-two-working-groups-on-cyberspace/; Shannon
Vavra, "World Powers Are Pushing to Build Their Own Brand of Cyber
Norms," *CyberScoop*, September 23, 2019: https://www.cyberscoop.com
/un-cyber-norms-general-assembly-2019/

8. UN General Assembly, "Countering the Use of Information and
Communications Technologies for Criminal Purposes," November 2,
2018: https://undocs.org/A/C.3/73/L.9/Rev.1

9. Andy Greenberg, "The Untold Story of NotPetya, the Most Devastating
Cyberattack in History," *Wired*, August 22, 2018: https://www.wired.com
/story/notpetya-cyberattack-ukraine-russia-code-crashed-the-world/;
The White House, "Press Briefing on the Attribution of the WannaCry
Malware Attack to North Korea," December 19, 2017: https://www.
whitehouse.gov/briefings-statements/press-briefing-on-the-attribution-
of-the-wannacry-malware-attack-to-north-korea-121917/

10. Chris C. Demchak and Peter Dombrowski, "Rise of a Cybered
Westphalian Age," *Strategic Studies Quarterly* 5, no. 1 (Spring 2011): 32–61,
https://www.jstor.org/stable/26270509

11. Michael P. Fischerkeller, Emily O. Goldman, and Richard J. Harknett
(eds.), *Cyber Persistence: Redefining National Security in Cyberspace* (Oxford
University Press, 2022).

12. NATO has recently said that cumulative attacks may constitute an armed
attack: https://www.defenseone.com/ideas/2021/06/when-does-cyber-
attack-demand-retaliation-nato-broadens-its-view/175028/

13. Shaun Riordan, "Cyber Diplomacy v. Digital Diplomacy: A Terminological
Distinction," *University of Southern California, Center on Public Diplomacy*,
May 12, 2016: https://www.uscpublicdiplomacy.org/blog/cyber-diplo
macy-vs-digital-diplomacy-terminological-distinction

14. US Department of State, International Security Advisory Board, "Report
on a Framework for International Cyber Stability," July 2, 2014: https://
2009-2017.state.gov/documents/organization/229235.pdf

15. Chris Painter, "Diplomacy in Cyberspace," *The Foreign Service Journal*,
June 2018: https://www.afsa.org/diplomacy-cyberspace

16. This mission falls to State's Office of the Coordinator for Cyber Issues. See Painter, "Diplomacy in Cyberspace."

17. This mission falls to State's Office of the Coordinator for Cyber Issues.

18. This mission falls to the Global Engagement Center, which is distinct from the Office of the Coordinator for Cyber Issues with its focus on technical cyber incidents. Statement of Lea Gabrielle, Special Envoy & Coordinator for the Global Engagement Center, US Department of State (Before the Senate Foreign Relations Subcommittee on State Department and USAID Management, International Operations, and Bilateral International Development): "Executing the Global Engagement Center's Mission," March 5, 2020: https://www.foreign.senate.gov/imo/media/doc/0305 20_Gabrielle_Testimony.pdf

19. This mission falls to the Bureau of Economic and Business Affairs, which is lead for the 5G campaign.

20. US Department of State, "Senior State Department Official on State Department 2019 Successes on Cybersecurity and 5G Issues," January 9, 2020: https://www.state.gov/senior-state-department-official-on-state-de partment-2019-successes-on-cybersecurity-and-5g-issues/

21. *International Strategy for Cyberspace: Prosperity, Security, and Openness in a Networked World*, May 2011: https://obamawhitehouse.archives.gov/sites /default/files/rss_viewer/international_strategy_for_cyberspace.pdf. The State Department raised the profile of cyber issues in US foreign policy with Christopher Painter's appointment in 2011 as the department's cyber coordinator and his establishment of the Office of the Coordinator for Cyber Issues.

22. *International Strategy for Cyberspace*, 11–15.

23. Adam Segal, "China's Alternative Cyber Governance Regime," *Council on Foreign Relations*, March 13, 2020: https://www.uscc.gov/sites/default /files/testimonies/March%2013%20Hearing_Panel%203_Adam%20Segal %20CFR.pdf

24. "G7 Declaration on Responsible States Behavior In Cyberspace," April 11, 2017: https://www.mofa.go.jp/files/000246367.pdf

25. UN General Assembly, "Group of Governmental Experts on Developments in the Field of Information and Telecommunications in the Context of International Security, Note by the Secretary-General," June 24, 2013: https://www.un.org/ga/search/view_doc.asp?symbol=A/68/98; UN General Assembly, "Group of Governmental Experts on Developments in the Field of Information and Telecommunications in the Context of International Security, Note by the Secretary-General," July 22, 2015: https://www.un.org/ga/search/view_doc.asp?symbol=A/70/174

26. US Department of State, "Explanation of Position at the Conclusion of the 2016–2017 UN Group of Governmental Experts (GGE) on Developments in the Field of Information and Telecommunications in the Context of International Security," June 23, 2017: https://www.state.gov/expla nation-of-position-at-the-conclusion-of-the-2016-2017-un-group-of -governmental-experts-gge-on-developments-in-the-field-of-informati on-and-telecommunications-in-the-context-of-international-sec/; Adam Segal, "The Development of Cyber Norms at the United Nations Ends in Deadlock, Now What?," *Council on Foreign Relations*, June 19, 2017: https://www.cfr.org/blog/development-cyber-norms-united-nations-en ds-deadlock-now-what; Elaine Korzak, "UN GGE on Cybersecurity: The End of an Era?," *The Diplomat*, July 31, 2017: https://thediplomat .com/2017/07/un-gge-on-cybersecurity-have-china-and-russia-just-ma de-cyberspace-less-safe/

27. Nakashima, Ellen and Joseph Marks, "Russia, U.S. and Other Countries Reach New Agreement Against cyber Hacking Even as Attacks Continue," *The Washington Post*, June 12, 2021: https://www.washingtonpost.com /national-security/russia-us-un-cyber-norms/2021/06/12/9b608cd4-86 6b-11eb-bfdf-4d36dab83a6d_story.html

28. Richard Price and Nina Tannenwald, "Norms and Deterrence: The Nuclear and Chemical Weapons Taboos," in *The Culture of National Security: Norms and Identity in World Politics*, ed. Peter J. Katzenstein (New York: Columbia University Press, 2009), 114–152.

29. Stefan Soesanto and Fosca D'Incau, "The UN GGE is Dead: Time to Fall Forward," *Council on Foreign Relations*, August 15, 2017: https://www.ec fr.eu/article/commentary_time_to_fall_forward_on_cyber_governance; Cedric Sabbah, "Pressing Pause: A New Approach for International Cybersecurity Norm Development," 2018: https://ccdcoe.org/uploads /2018/10/Art-14-Pressing-Pause.-A-New-Approach-for-International -Cybersecurity-Norm-Development.pdf

30. Finnemore and Sikkink define a critical mass as one-third of the total states in the system. Martha Finnemore and Kathryn Sikkink, "International Norm Dynamics and Political Change," *International Organization* 52, no. 4 (Autumn 1998): 901, https:// www.jstor.org/stable/2601361

31. The White House, Office of the Press Secretary, "Press Conference by President Obama after G20 Summit," September 5, 2016: https://obam awhitehouse.archives.gov/the-press-office/2016/09/05/press-conference -president-obama-after-g20-summit

32. Elvira Rosert, "Norm Emergence as Agenda Diffusion: Failure and Success in the Regulation of Cluster Munitions," *European Journal of International*

Relations 25, no. 4 (2019): 1103–1131, https://doi.org/10.1177%2F13540
66119842644

33. UN General Assembly, "Group of Governmental Experts," 2013.
34. UN General Assembly, "Group of Governmental Experts," 2015.
35. "Report of the Group of Governmental Experts on Advancing Responsible State Behavior in Cyberspace in the Context of International Security," May 28, 2021: https://front.un-arm.org/wp-content/uploads/2021/06/final-report-2019-2021-gge-1-advance-copy.pdf
36. Finnemore and Sikkink, "International Norm Dynamics," 901.
37. Finnemore and Sikkink, "International Norm Dynamics," 902.
38. Ian Clark, "International Society and China: The Power of Norms and the Norms of Power," *The Chinese Journal of International Politics* 7, no. 3 (Autumn 2014): 315–340, https://doi.org/10.1093/cjip/pot014
39. I am indebted to Richard Harknett for these insights.
40. Scott N. Romaniuk and Francis Grice, "Norm Evolution Theory and World Politics," *E-International Relations*, November 15, 2018: https://www.e-ir.info/2018/11/15/norm-evolution-theory-and-world-politics/
41. Martin C. Libicki, "Norms and Normalization," *The Cyber Defense Review* (Spring 2020): 41–52, https://cyberdefensereview.army.mil/Portals/6/CDR%20V5N1%20-%2004_Libicki_WEB.pdf
42. Michael P. Fischerkeller and Richard J. Harknett, "Persistent Engagement and Tacit Bargaining: A Path Toward Constructing Norms in Cyberspace," *Lawfare*, November 9, 2018: https://www.lawfareblog.com/persistent-engagement-and-tacit-bargaining-path-toward-constructing-norms-cyberspace
43. Laura Bate et al., "Defending Forward by Defending Norms," *Lawfare*, March 11, 2020: https://www.lawfareblog.com/defending-forward-defending-norms
44. Theresa Hitchens, "US Urges 'Like-Minded Countries' to Collaborate on Cyber Deterrence," *Breaking Defense*, April 24, 2019: https://breakingdefense.com/2019/04/us-urging-likeminded-countries-to-collaborate-on-cyber-deterrence/
45. The White House, "National Cyber Strategy of the United States of America," September 2018: 21, https://www.whitehouse.gov/wp-content/uploads/2018/09/National-Cyber-Strategy.pdf
46. It also pervades the Cyberspace Solarium Commission, as James Lewis cogently explains; see Lewis, "Cyber Solarium and the Sunset of Security." A focus on "attacks of significant consequence" by Cyberspace Solarium Commission staff reveal that they have not internalized core tenets of cyber competition. See Laura Bate et al., "Defending Forward by Defending Norms."

47. Richard J. Harknett and Michael P. Fischerkeller, "Deterrence is Not a Credible Strategy for Cyberspace," *Orbis* 61, no. 3 (Summer 2017): 381–339, https://doi.org/10.1016/j.orbis.2017.05.003

48. "Defend forward" and "persistent engagement" are new terms that were introduced into the Defense Department lexicon in 2018. Both terms first appear in the US Cyber Command Vision released in March 2018. Defend forward next appears in the *Department of Defense Cyber Strategy* released in September 2018. See US Cyber Command, "Achieve and Maintain Cyberspace Superiority: Command Vision for US Cyber Command," March 2018: https://www.cybercom.mil/Portals/56/Documents/USCYBERCOM%20Vision%20April%202018.pdf?ver=2018-06-14-152556-010

49. Defend forward and persistent engagement do not reject a deterrence strategy entirely. The United States is deterring cyber aggression that causes death and destruction. Defend forward and persistent engagement were adopted to address continuous cyberspace campaigns and operations in the strategic competition space below the level of armed conflict.

50. Harknett and Fischerkeller, "Deterrence is Not a Credible Strategy for Cyberspace."

51. China, Russia, and Iran are currently executing widescale disinformation and influence operations around coronavirus. See, US Department of State, "'Briefing on Disinformation and Propaganda Related to COVID-19,' Lea Gabrielle, Special Envoy and Coordinator of The Global Engagement Center," March 27, 2020: https://www.state.gov/briefing-with-special-envoy-lea-gabrielle-global-engagement-center-on-disinformation-and-propaganda-related-to-covid-19/; see also Julian E. Barnes, Matthew Rosenberg, and Edward Wong, "As Virus Spreads, China and Russia See Openings for Disinformation," *The New York Times*, March 28, 2020: https://www.nytimes.com/2020/03/28/us/politics/china-russia-coronavirus-disinformation.html; Sarah Jacobs Gamberini and Amanda Moodie, "The Virus of Disinformation: Echoes of Past Bioweapons Accusations in Today's Covid-19 Conspiracy Theories," *War on the Rocks*, April 6, 2020: https://warontherocks.com/2020/04/the-virus-of-disinformation-echoes-of-past-bioweapons-accusations-in-todays-covid-19-conspiracy-theories/

52. "Hunt forward" operations deploy defensive cyber teams around the world at the invitation of allies and partners to look for adversaries' malicious cyber activity.

53. Chris C. Demchak, "Three Futures for a Post-Western Cybered World," *Military Cyber Affairs* 3, no. 1 (2018): https://scholarcommons.usf.edu/cgi/viewcontent.cgi?article=1044&context=mca

54. USAID, "Advancing Digital Connectivity in the Indo-Pacific Region": https://www.usaid.gov/sites/default/files/documents/1861/USAID_DC CP_Fact_Sheet_080719f.pdf

55. USAID, "USAID Administrator Mark Green's Remarks on Countering Malign Kremlin Influence," July 5, 2019: https://www.usaid.gov/news-information/press-releases/jul-5-2019-adminis trator-mark-greens-remarks-countering-malign-kremlin-influence; USAID, "Remarks by Assistant Administrator Brock Bierman at the German Marshall Fund: USAID's Countering Malign Kremlin Influence Development Framework," October 1, 2019: https://www.usaid.gov/news-information/speeches/remarks-assistant-adminis trator-brock-bierman-german-marshall-fund-usaids

56. Daniel F. Runde, "America's Global Infrastructure Opportunity: Three Recommendations to the New U.S. Development Finance Corporation," *Center for Strategic & International Studies*, April 11, 2019: https://www.csis.org/analysis/americas-global-infrastructure-opportunity-three-recommendations-new-us-development-finance

57. US Department of State, "Blue Dot Network": https://www.state.gov/blue-dot-network/

58. US Department of State, "The Clean Network": https://www.state.gov/5g-clean-network/

59. US Department of State, "Announcing the Expansion of the Clean Network to Safeguard America's Assets," August 5, 2020: https://www.state.gov/announcing-the-expansion-of-the-clean-network-to-safeguard-americas-assets/

60. US Department of State, "The Tide is Turning Toward Trusted 5G Vendors," June 24, 2020: https://www.state.gov/the-tide-is-turning-to ward-trusted-5g-vendors/

61. Catherine Lotrionte, "Reconsidering the Consequences for State-Sponsored Hostile Cyber Operations Under International Law," *Cyber Defense Review* 3, no. 2 (Summer 2018): 73–114, https://cyberdefenserev iew.army.mil/Portals/6/Documents/CDR%20Journal%20Articles/CDR _V3N2_ReconsideringConsequences_LOTRIONTE.pdf?ver=2018-09 -05-084840-807

62. For an approach to how the US can identify how its national interests manifest in cyberspace, see Jan-Philipp Brauchle et al., "Cyber Mapping the Financial System," *Carnegie Endowment for International Peace*, April 7, 2020: https://carnegieendowment.org/2020/04/07/cyber-mapping-financial-system-pub-81414

63. Gary Corn, "Coronavirus Disinformation and the Need for States to

Shore Up International Law," *Lawfare*, April 2, 2020: https://www.law
fareblog.com/coronavirus-disinformation-and-need-states-shore-interna
tional-law

64. US Cyber Command, "Achieve and Maintain Cyberspace Superiority";
    Max Smeets, "Cyber Command's Strategy Risks Friction With Allies,"
    Lawfare, May 28, 2019: https://www.lawfareblog.com/cyber-commands
    -strategy-risks-friction-allies

65. Jack Goldsmith (ed.), *The United States' Defend Forward Cyber Strategy:
    A Comprehensive Legal Assessment* (New York: Oxford University Press,
    2022).

66. Michael Schmitt, "The Netherlands Releases a Tour de Force on
    International Law in Cyberspace: Analysis," *Just Security*, October 14, 2019:
    https://www.justsecurity.org/66562/the-netherlands-releases-a-tour-de
    -force-on-international-law-in-cyberspace-analysis/; Michael N. Schmitt,
    "Taming the Lawless Void: Tracking the Evolution of International Law
    Rules for Cyberspace," *Texas National Security Review* 3, no. 3 (Summer
    2020): https://tnsr.org/2020/07/taming-the-lawless-void-tracking-the-
    evolution-of-international-law-rules-for-cyberspace/

67. Jeremy Wright, "Speech: Cyber and International Law in the 21st
    Century," United Kingdom Attorney General, May 23, 2018: https://
    www.gov.uk/government/speeches/cyber-and-international-law-in-the
    -21st-century

68. The Netherlands, Ministry of Foreign Affairs, "Letter of 5 July 2019 from
    the Netherlands Minister of Foreign Affairs to the President of the House
    of Representatives on the International Legal Order in Cyberspace,"
    2019:   https://www.government.nl/ministries/ministry-of-foreign-
    affairs/documents/parliamentary-documents/2019/09/26/letter-to-the-
    parliament-on-the-international-legal-order-in-cyberspace

69. Gary Corn, "Punching on the Edges of the Grey Zone: Iranian Cyber
    Threats and State Cyber Responses," *Just Security*, February 11, 2020:
    https://www.justsecurity.org/68622/punching-on-the-edges-of-the-
    grey-zone-iranian-cyber-threats-and-state-cyber-responses/

70. Hon. Paul C. Ney, Jr., "DOD General Counsel Remarks at U.S. Cyber
    Command Legal Conference," March 2, 2020: https://www.defense.gov
    /Newsroom/Speeches/Speech/Article/2099378/dod-general-counsel-re
    marks-at-us-cyber-command-legal-conference/

71. Matthias Schulze, "German Military Cyber Operations are in a Legal Gray
    Zone," *Lawfare*, April 8, 2020: https://www.lawfareblog.com/german-mi
    litary-cyber-operations-are-legal-gray-zone

6

(De)Stabilizing Cyber Warriors: The Emergence of US Military Cyber Expertise, 1967–2018

Rebecca Slayton

The race for cyber warriors is on. The United States has led the way, establishing its first joint force for computer network defense in the late 1990s, then gradually expanding and elevating it to become US Cyber Command, the 10th unified combatant command, in 2018. Competitors around the world, including China, Russia, and Iran, have responded by training, equipping, and deploying their own cyber forces. US allies such as Israel, the United Kingdom, and South Korea have similarly developed cadres of cyber warriors.

The race for cyber warriors might suggest a kind of arms race instability – a mutually reinforcing expansion of military capabilities. But cyber warriors are not the same as missiles or other technological artifacts; they are experts whose skills can be turned to a wide range of purposes. Whether and in what ways this surge in cyber warriors is stabilizing or destabilizing depends upon both what they do, and how those actions are perceived by others.

This chapter examines how the US military – arguably the world leader in cyber warfare capabilities – has developed the professional status, roles, and responsibilities of cyber warriors over the past thirty years. As we will see, many cyber warriors have been tasked with stabilizing the technological systems upon which US warriors and their allies rely. However, the activities that have brought cyber warriors the highest status and prestige focus less on stabilizing technology for allies and more on destabilizing adversary operations.

I argue that the greater status accorded to destabilizing adversary operations reflects the historical challenge of establishing cyber experts as "warriors." Advocates of military cyber capabilities have historically struggled to persuade military leadership that specialists in information-related fields such as intelligence, computing, and communications – which had long been regarded as warfighting support – should be regarded as warriors in their own right. And indeed, it might seem strange to consider cyber experts as warriors. Traditional warriors use physical force against adversaries, putting their bodies in harm's way; cyber warriors typically work at desks, and without substantial physical risk. Furthermore, while missiles, drones, combat aircraft, and other high technology have all changed how militaries fight and what it means to be a warrior, the technologies with which cyber warriors work are not unique to the military.[1] Every major civilian organization today relies on complex computer networks and experts who defend them. Indeed, the US Defense Department has leveraged the civilian US National Initiative on Cybersecurity Education workforce framework to build its own cyber workforce.[2] And the Department of Defense uses civilian contractors for both offensive and defensive cyber operations.

What most distinguishes military and civilian cyber experts is the military's offensive role. Under joint doctrine, offensive cyber operations aim to "project power by the application of force in and through cyberspace." US law prohibits civilian organizations from conducting offensive cyber operations unless they are operating under military authority. Offensive cyber operations thus have the greatest claim to "warfighting" and tend to have the highest status. They also tend to be the most destabilizing to adversary operations.

Yet under joint doctrine, offensive cyber operations are only the first of three missions for cyber warriors. The second mission, defensive cyber operations, focuses on destabilizing adversary operations that have breached Defense Department networks. These activities, including network monitoring and incident response, are very similar to defensive work within major corporations, civilian government, and other non-military organizations. Nonetheless, because defensive cyber operations disrupt adversaries, they have gained the status of "warfare."

The third mission, Department of Defense Information Network (DODIN) operations, focuses on mitigating vulnerabilities, and tends to be regarded as the least war-like activity. It includes "actions taken to secure, configure, operate, extend, maintain, and sustain [Defense Department] cyberspace." DODIN operations mitigate both technological and human vulnerabilities; for example, DODIN operators not only operate firewalls, but train users in good security practices. Not only are these activities commonplace in civilian organizations, but their focus on technology rather than adversaries tends to lower their claim to being "warfighting." In an effort to cast its work as warfighting, Joint Force Headquarters-DODIN describes its mission with the phrase "Fight the DODIN," not "secure," "maintain," or "sustain" the DODIN.[3] Joint doctrine seems to recognize the lower regard in which such operations might be held, noting that "although many DODIN operations activities are regularly scheduled events, they cannot be considered routine, since their aggregate effect establishes the framework on which most DOD [Department of Defense] missions ultimately depend."[4]

In other words, DODIN operations focus on stabilizing the technological systems upon which all US warriors and their allies critically rely, but they are generally regarded as lower in status than defensive or offensive cyber operations. However, the activities that bring cyber warriors the highest status and prestige focus less on stabilizing technology and more on destabilizing adversary operations. As discussed in more detail below, individuals engaged in offensive or defensive cyber operations tend to have greater professional opportunities and prestige than those engaged in DODIN operations.

The tendency to valorize threat-focused cyber operations, and particularly offensive cyber operations, is likely to contribute to intertwined forms of technological and political instability. The problem is not that cyber offense will necessarily escalate violence. On the contrary, as Jervis and Healey argue (in this volume), in times of relative peace, offensive cyber capabilities may serve as a kind of pressure release that reduces the propensity for violent escalation.[5] Nor is it the case that defensive cyber operations, which stabilize technology for friendly operators, inevitably decrease the propensity for international conflict. If kinetic operations contribute to international instability, the cyber defenses that enable those operations enable that instability. Nonetheless, as I will discuss further in the conclusion, the valorization of cyber offense creates multiple kinds of instability because it creates multiple kinds of uncertainty.

The remainder of this chapter is organized in four main sections, followed by a brief conclusion. First, I briefly outline the origins of computer network operations in the Defense Department, highlighting both vulnerability-oriented and threat-oriented approaches. This section extends previous accounts, which frame the rise of US cyber operations as a response to external threats, by showing that the rise of cyber operations was also a response to the growth of technological vulnerabilities within the US Defense Department.[6] Furthermore, while past accounts frame the establishment of cyber capabilities as a necessary innovation, this section highlights the growing necessity of mundane maintenance work, such as training users, patching software, and strengthening passwords.[7] In fact, as we will see, it was the pursuit of technological innovation, and neglect of vulnerability mitigation work, that created technological vulnerabilities. Innovation is thus not an unmitigated good; as one computer security researcher's tagline notes, "today's innovations are tomorrow's vulnerabilities."[8] Vulnerability-mitigation techniques aimed to maintain and recover the security that innovations destabilized.

The second section discusses the rise of "information warfare," which provided a conceptual and organizational context for further developing computer network operations during the 1990s. While computer network operations remained in a supporting role, efforts to elevate them tended to emphasize threat-oriented activities, and particularly offense.

Third, I discuss how the growing challenge of defending networks spurred the establishment of the first joint computer network operations in the mid- and late 1990s. Fourth, I discuss how the rise of joint operations led the services to elevate computer network operations in the new millennium. In conclusion, I briefly return to the question of how and in what ways cyber warriors contribute to stability and instability.

The Origins of US Computer Network Operations
Technological, Organizational, and Professional Vulnerability

The origins of what came to be called computer network operations can be found in US intelligence organizations, which tested the security of several state-of-the-art computer systems in the late 1960s and early 1970s by attempting to break in and take control of them.[9] These "tiger teams" were always successful, demonstrating pervasive vulnerabilities in even the best-designed systems.[10] It is reasonable to assume that intelligence agencies were also exploring ways of compromising adversaries' computer systems, although the existence of any such operations remains highly classified.[11]

By contrast, the need for computer network defense became a subject for public discussion after a panel of computer scientists addressed it at a 1967 conference and, for the first time, publicly acknowledged the existence of the National Security Agency, previously described as "No Such Agency."[12] For computer scientists, the ease with which computers could be penetrated by outsiders was partly a technological problem: hardware-software systems were so complex that they inevitably contained errors that could be exploited. With the sponsorship of the National Security Agency and the Air Force, computer scientists worked on developing techniques for reducing such errors and proving that computer systems actually enforced the security policies that they were programmed to enforce. These efforts failed to produce a provably secure computer, but succeeded in growing a community of government, industry, and academic computer security experts.[13]

This community recognized that security was also a market problem: companies had no incentive to design secure systems in the 1970s and 1980s, because there was little consumer demand for security. The personnel responsible for buying systems usually lacked the understanding needed to specify security requirements for new purchases.[14] Similarly, computing managers got "mostly 'arm waving' from the vendor," rather than an objective evaluation of the "secure-worthiness" of computer systems.[15] Accordingly, computer scientists convened by the National Bureau of Standards in 1978 proposed to develop "a process for evaluating the security of computer systems, and for accrediting particular systems for particular applications."[16]

These recommendations led to the creation of the Trusted Computer System Evaluation Criteria and the associated National Computer Security Center at the National Security Agency.[17] The center helped coordinate the development of these criteria and then used them to evaluate the security of commercial computer systems. But rapid innovation and the rise of computer networking threatened to make the criteria obsolete and led to a long series of "interpretations" to guide evaluations of new kinds of products.[18] Meanwhile, the slow process and high expense of evaluation deterred many organizations, including those in the Defense Department, from demanding high security ratings.[19] That changed somewhat after 1987, when the National Telecommunications and Information Systems Security Committee directed that, by 1992, all federal agencies must use only operating systems evaluated at level "C2" or higher to process national security information.[20] Evidence suggests that this mandate was indeed successful in improving security standards in the computer market.[21]

Nevertheless, C2 was still not a particularly high level of security, and communications and computing personnel did not typically demand more security than was required by the federal mandate. Furthermore, these personnel did not know how to use "trusted" systems to build secure networks.[22] Computer network vulnerabilities were thus also a result of training and management problems, in addition to being technological and market problems.

In 1990, the assistant secretary of defense for command, control, communications, and intelligence tasked the National Security Agency and Defense Communications Agency (soon to become the Defense Information Systems Agency) with developing means of better managing information security. This led to the creation of the Defense Information Systems Security Program, whose aim was to develop a comprehensive and integrated security architecture and policy for the Defense Department.[23]

However, the purchase, deployment, and management of computer networks remained highly decentralized across the military, and networks proliferated in the 1980s and early 1990s. This left the problem of configuring and maintaining such networks to disparate personnel in communications and computing fields throughout the services.[24] As I have discussed elsewhere, each of the services structured its computer and communications career fields differently, but the personnel charged with deploying and managing computer networks generally received insufficient training in computer security.[25]

To summarize, vulnerabilities in Defense Department networks were not just a matter of external technological changes nor insecurities in commercial products that the department could not control. The Defense Department actively drove many innovations in computer networking and security. But it was ultimately the Defense Department's inability to centrally manage the security of computer networks, combined with a lack of security skills and knowledge among its disparate communications–computing personnel, that made its networks so vulnerable.

Threat-oriented Approaches to Computer Network Defense

Computer scientists working with intelligence agencies recognized early on that even if they could create systems that would enforce security policies perfectly, an insider could wittingly or unwittingly compromise the system.[26] This recognition led to the development of one of the first threat-oriented approaches to computer network defense – intrusion detection systems – that would monitor computers and networks for suspicious behavior and alert security officers about potentially unauthorized activity. The National Security Agency, the Navy, and the Air Force all sponsored research into intrusion detection systems in the 1980s, and by the early 1990s they were using such systems to monitor select networks.[27] They also developed new kinds of expertise associated with intrusion detection systems, as security officers learned how to evaluate alerts about suspicious activity and determine what actions, if any, should be taken.[28]

Another early threat-oriented approach to computer network defense came in the form of computer emergency response teams, also known as computer incident response teams. These teams were first created in response to the Internet worm of 2 November 1988.[29] The Internet worm was the first to significantly disrupt the internet, which was then primarily a research network sponsored by the Defense Department. The Computer Emergency Response Team Coordinating Center, a federally funded, non-governmental organization based at Carnegie Mellon University, was established in January 1989 with the goals of preventing future incidents, providing a network of elite experts who could be called upon to diagnose future attacks, and facilitating the creation of a network of similar response teams.[30]

Defense Department units and the national nuclear laboratories were among the first organizations to form their own computer emergency response teams. In the early 1990s, the Defense Intelligence Agency formed an incident response team for its classified Intelligence Information Systems network, which, in late 1992, was renamed the Automated Systems Security Incident Support Team and moved to the Defense Information Systems Agency, where it was tasked with responding to incidents across the Defense Department.[31] Each of the services also began to form incident response capabilities.

In the early 1990s, response teams helped to identify and make visible intrusions that might otherwise have gone unnoticed. For example, the Department of Energy's Computer Incident Advisory Capability helped discover that between April 1990 and May 1991, at least thirty-four of the Defense Department's computers had been hacked.[32] Further investigation eventually concluded that the hackers were teenagers in the Netherlands who called themselves "High Tech for Peace" and had gained access to a computerized logistics management system. During preparations for Operation Desert Storm in Iraq, the hackers offered to sell the capabilities gained through that system to Saddam Hussein for $1 million. Had the Iraqi government responded to the offer, which fortunately it did not, the hackers could have disrupted the flow of supplies to US troops preparing for Desert Storm.[33]

Intrusion detection systems and incident response teams were important not only for identifying and stopping intruders, but also for making the argument that computer networks were increasingly under attack. Response teams tracked an exponential rise in incidents that paralleled the exponential rise in internet host sites in the 1990s.[34] Incident investigators also worked to identify the causes of the breaches and, in the process, repeatedly underscored the importance of a prior layer of defense: the systems administrators and personnel who were charged with deploying and maintaining secure networks. The 1988 Internet worm, the Dutch hacking incident, and many other breaches were enabled by a lack of security knowledge, skills, and practice among systems administrators.[35] In 1999, an analysis by the Air Force Office of Special Investigations showed that a majority of root intrusions in the previous year had resulted from non-compliance with security policies or emergency response team advisories. Only 13 percent were definitively determined to be "unpreventable."[36]

Thus, the Defense Department's threat-oriented approaches to network defenses became critical in the mid-1990s in no small part because of failings in the first line of defense: the systems administrators and maintainers who were uniquely positioned to prevent and mitigate vulnerabilities. Although both threat-oriented and vulnerability-oriented forms of expertise would eventually be incorporated into a new conception of warfighting, that transition was slower and more difficult for vulnerability-oriented expertise, as discussed in more detail below.

The Rise of Information Warfare and Information Assurance

In the mid-1990s, computer network operations began to find an organizational and conceptual home in "information warfare." To be clear, information warfare was not primarily about computer network operations. When military officers described Operation Desert Storm as the "first information war," they were discussing much older traditions of work such as gathering intelligence through satellites and airborne reconnaissance systems, using such intelligence to bomb command-and-control facilities, and setting up an in-theater communications system.[37]

Similarly, when the Department of Defense issued a top secret directive on information warfare in December 1992, it devoted little, if any, attention to the opportunities and risks inherent to using computer networks in military and intelligence operations.[38] The directive defined information warfare as the "competition of opposing information systems" through methods such as "signals intelligence and command and control countermeasures."[39] Such countermeasures, also known as command-and-control warfare, were defined as the "integrated use" of five elements – "operations security (OPSEC), military deception, psychological operations (PSYOP), electronic warfare (EW), and physical destruction" – all "mutually supported by intelligence."[40] Information warfare thus encompassed a very diverse range of military specializations, all of them long pre-dating computers.[41]

Nonetheless, information warfare provided the primary conceptual and organizational context for efforts to raise the status of computer network defense and attack in the mid-1990s.[42] As discussed further below, each of the services approached computer network operations somewhat differently, but they all built upon incident response and intrusion detection work that had begun in their signals intelligence organizations rather than their communications and computing units.

Air Force: Cyberspace as a New Warfighting Domain

The Air Force responded to the information warfare directive by merging the security functions of the Air Force Cryptologic Support Center with the Air Force's Electronic Warfare Center, thereby creating the Air Force Information Warfare Center at Kelly Air Force Base in San Antonio, Texas.[43] About half of the center's personnel had backgrounds in signals intelligence, while the rest came from a variety of fields.[44] The Information Warfare Center was established in the Air Force Intelligence Command in September 1993, which was demoted to become the Air Intelligence Agency the following month.[45]

The Information Warfare Center played a supporting role, helping integrate various information warfare methods into combat operations. Nonetheless, the Air Force began to formulate doctrine which treated computer network attack as a new form of warfare. In 1995, the Air Force published "Cornerstones of Information Warfare," which argued that information should be understood as a new "realm" or "domain" for operations, akin to land, sea, and air.[46] Based in part on this argument, in August 1995 the Air Force ordered the formation of the 609th Information Warfare Squadron under the 9th Air Force at Shaw Air Force Base. The squadron was charged with conducting both defensive and offensive missions in support of the 9th Air Force and Central Command's Air Operations Center.[47]

In keeping with an emphasis on warfighting, the squadron's work appears to have been focused on threat-oriented activities. Defensive operations focused on intrusion detection and response, rather than vulnerability mitigation, which would have included password management, configuration management, and training.[48] Furthermore, the majority of its mission time was actually spent on offensive operations.[49] The squadron also privileged offensive work by requiring individuals to do defensive duty before they were allowed to take the offensive.[50]

In the late 1990s, a review by a National Research Council committee critiqued the squadron's overall emphasis on offense:

> With a culture that values the taking of the offensive in military operations, the military may well have difficulty in realizing that defense against information attack is a more critical function than being able to conduct similar operations against an adversary, and indeed is more difficult and requires greater skill and experience than offensive information operations.[51]

The squadron's emphasis on offense, however, makes perfect sense from the perspective of a new unit eager to demonstrate its value to warfighters. Offensive operations could create dramatic military effects, at least in theory. By contrast, the effects of a successful defense are unremarkable: military operations and networks would continue to function as planned.

Navy: Net-centric Warfare

The Navy responded to the 1992 information warfare directive by establishing the Naval Information Warfare Activity in 1994, within the Naval Security Group, the Navy's cryptologic group.[52] The Navy also established the Fleet Information Warfare Center under Atlantic Command in October

1995 to help operationalize capabilities developed by the activity.[53] The Fleet Information Warfare Center had a defensive focus, and was a tiny organization comprised of warfighters – its first director was a former fighter pilot – along with cryptologists, electronic warfare technicians, and intelligence officers.[54]

While the Naval Information Warfare Activity and the Fleet Information Warfare Center remained in supporting roles, some leaders in the Navy argued that computer networking skills should be recognized as part of warfighting. The most influential articulation of what came to be called "net-centric warfare" came from Vice Adm. Arthur K. Cebrowski, a fighter pilot who had earned a master's degree in Information Systems Management from the Naval Postgraduate School in 1973.[55] In the mid-1990s, Cebrowski became the Navy director for space, information warfare, and command and control, and in this role he co-authored a *Proceedings* article outlining the concept of "network-centric warfare."[56] Cebrowski and his co-author, John Garstka, technical adviser to the Command, Control, Communications, and Computers Directorate, argued for shifting from platform-centric operations (that is, focusing on ships, submarines, and aircraft) to network-centric operations. They further argued that this shift entailed elevating the status of individuals with skills in information technology:

> "Operator" status frequently is denied to personnel with these critical talents, but the value of traditional operators with limited acumen in these processes is falling, and ultimately they will be marginalized . . . The services must both mainstream and merge those with technical skills and those with operational experience in these areas. These are the new operators.[57]

But while the Navy did make some changes to its information technology specializations in the late 1990s, it was not until after the rise of joint cyber operations that the Navy made cyber a warfare specialization.

Army: The Global Information Environment

The Army responded to the 1992 information warfare directive by establishing the Land Information Warfare Activity within the Intelligence and Security Command. This activity began with fifty-five personnel, including eleven enlisted, and roughly a dozen government civilians, and grew to about 250 by October 1997. The majority of the personnel were field-grade or higher-level officers from signals or intelligence. In the late 1990s, the Land Information Warfare Activity sought to incorporate more traditional operators, and it often augmented its technical capabilities by hiring contractors, with one member recalling that it was half contractors at one point in its history.[58] But the Land Information Warfare Activity remained in a supporting role; it helped commands plan information operations but did not conduct them.[59]

The Army also began to develop doctrine related to computer network operations. Perhaps most notably, Army "Field Manual 100-6: Information Operations," published in 1996, highlighted "database corruption" and "malicious software" as means of attacking information systems.[60] It also featured discussion of the Internet worm and Rome Labs breaches, which was excerpted in the Joint Doctrine for Command and Control Warfare, issued in February 1996.[61]

In 1998, the Army began creating a dedicated computer network operations force within Intelligence and Security Command's signals intelligence group. However, the Army struggled to grow a computer network operations capability because its personnel management system did not reward technical depth.[62] In the late 1990s it began to revise the Officer Personnel Management System to give technical specialists a path to promotion, and briefly created an "information operations" career field. However, when the Officer Personnel Management System was revised in 2006, this field was eliminated and most of the functional areas needed for cyber operations, including telecommunications engineering and information systems management, were firmly placed within operations support.[63]

The Problem of Defense

By the mid-1990s, efforts to elevate computer network operations from warfighting support to the level of "warfare" tended to emphasize threat-oriented activities, and particularly offense. Yet many observers were growing increasingly concerned about the challenge of defense, and particularly its reliance upon civilian assets that the US military could not control.

In 1994, the Joint Security Commission, which had been established by the secretary of defense and the director of central intelligence, highlighted the challenge of protecting information systems and networks "that are connected and depend upon an infrastructure we neither own nor control."[64] A 1994 Defense Science Board task force echoed these concerns, noting that "DoD [the Department of Defense] has tied its information systems to the private/commercial sector."[65] The task force was "persuaded that DoD is currently spending far too little on defensive IW [information warfare], and that the gravity and potential urgency of the problem deserves [sic] redress."[66]

Articles in the trade press at the time also suggest that defense was not a major focus in the early 1990s. An August 1994 *Defense Daily* article noted that "[a]ll of the services' information warfare tactics are currently focused more heavily on the offensive mission."[67] Reporting on an Information Warfare Conference in October 1995, one technology journalist described "Pentagon skeptics who joke that information warfare is just 'computer security with money.'"[68] As this suggests, computer security – a defensive activity – was seen as something that was different and less important than warfare.

Nonetheless, some military leaders worked to elevate the status of computer network defense.[69] In 1994, four years before the publication of his widely read article on "net-centric warfare," Cebrowski served as the director of the Joint Staff's Command, Control, Communications, and Computers Directorate, and established an information warfare division. Cebrowski brought in William Gravell, a captain in the Naval Security Group, to set it up.[70] As head of the Joint Staff's Information Warfare Division, Gravell aimed to persuade both military and private organizations to improve the security of computers and other information systems upon which military operations depended.[71] However, Gravell recalls that "private sector organizations and their lawyers and stockholders did not want to hear that they were engaged in 'warfare.'"[72] Accordingly, by 1995, the Joint Staff's Information Warfare Division had been officially renamed the Information Assurance Division, drawing on a term that was seeing increasing use in military and intelligence circles.[73]

Civilian control of infrastructure was just part of the challenge for information assurance.[74] In 1997, an Information Assurance Task Force led by the Office of the Assistant Secretary of Defense for Command, Control, Communications, and Intelligence and the Joint Staff's Information Assurance Division argued that the Defense Department's decentralized management of increasingly complex computer networks could not provide adequate security.[75] This led to a Defense-Wide Information Assurance Program, which was launched by the assistant secretary of defense for command, control, communications, and intelligence in his capacity as the Defense Department's chief information officer in January 1998.[76]

The Defense-Wide Information Assurance Program aimed to combine "centralized oversight with decentralized execution" of information assurance activities.[77] But it was not given the authority or resources needed to fulfill its charter.[78] Ultimately, elevating the status of computer network defense required more than an information assurance program from the Defense Department's chief information officer. The path to elevating computer network defense to the level of warfighting went through the Joint Staff's Operations Directorate.

The Need for a Joint Operational Defense

In June 1997, the Joint Staff's annual no-notice interoperability exercise, known as Eligible Receiver, included a computer network intrusion for the first time.[79] A National Security Agency red team comprised of about twenty-five personnel successfully broke into the computer systems of the US Pacific Command, the National Military Command Center, and a number of other joint command facilities. Eligible Receiver was set to run for two weeks, with an additional two weeks set aside, if necessary, but the National Security Agency red team was so successful that it ended after just four days.[80]

The Joint Staff had assigned a new Division for Information Operations to monitor the exercise around the clock and make recommendations. The division was spun off from the Joint Staff's Operations and Plans Division and was headed by Brig. Gen. John "Soup" Campbell, an Air Force fighter pilot. As Campbell's group began formulating recommendations for responding to the exercise, it quickly became clear that no single organization could be given primary responsibility for implementing them; nobody was in charge of defending computer networks.[81] Representatives of three directorates in the Joint Staff – intelligence; operations; and command, control, communications, and computers — and the Defense Information Systems Agency joined the operations deputies of each of the services in exploring who should be in charge.

By November of 1997, the services' operations deputies were considering several possible organizational structures, including the possibility of assigning the task to an agency such as the Defense Information Systems Agency or the National Security Agency.[82] However, Campbell recalls "resistance from the Services who didn't want any outside agency telling them how to run their networks, and having a Combat Support Agency ([for example] DISA [the Defense Information Systems Agency] or NSA [the National Security Agency]) do so was a non-starter."[83] Campbell and others eventually concluded that they should establish a new task force to direct computer network defense, and ensure that it had sufficient authority to get its work done.[84]

Efforts to establish the task force were made more urgent by the discovery of a new intrusion at Andrews Air Force base, just outside Washington, DC, on February 3, 1998. A task force that included members of the Joint Staff's Information Operations Directorate, the FBI, the Defense Information Systems Agency, and the National Security Agency began to investigate, and soon concluded that the hackers were three teenagers – two in the United States and one in Israel.[85] Although the hackers were soon apprehended, the breach demonstrated the ease with which the military's information systems could be compromised.

Not long after the discovery of the breach at Andrews Air Force Base, Deputy Secretary of Defense John Hamre called a meeting of about thirty people in the Pentagon. He asked the same question that had been looming since Eligible Receiver: who's in charge? Recounting the meeting fourteen years later, Campbell stated that he couldn't recall "if I raised my hand or if somebody poked me and I jumped," but as the director of the Joint Staff's Information Operations Division ("the J-39 Bubba"), he became the answer to Hamre's question.[86] Eventually Campbell became the commander of the new Joint Task Force-Computer Network Defense that the Information Operations Division was helping to organize.

What is Operational Computer Network Defense?

But what exactly would the new task force do? The answer to this question was shaped not only by analysis of the results of Eligible Receiver, but also by distinctive conceptions of the kinds of expertise and work that might constitute "warfighting."[87]

Eligible Receiver demonstrated the need for improvements in both mitigating vulnerabilities and responding to threats. Some vulnerabilities concerned poor security awareness and training: personnel at targeted units gave out their passwords over the phone or left them in the trash to be discovered by dumpster divers. Other vulnerabilities were well-known technological weaknesses that nonetheless remained unmitigated. Threat-oriented defenses had also failed. In an after-action report on Eligible Receiver, the National Security Agency red team targeting officer noted that intrusion detection systems had worked well but that reporting on intrusions came two weeks late: "They now know that the horse is out of the barn after it burned down and the ashes are cold."[88]

These weaknesses suggested that the new computer network defense task force needed to address both vulnerability mitigation and threat response. And, indeed, representatives from the Defense Information Systems Agency and the Joint Staff's Command, Control, Communications, and Computing Directorate argued that the task force should include vulnerability assessment, red teaming, and other kinds of work to prevent successful intrusions.[89] However, according to an October 1998 background paper by Air Force Capt. Jason Healey, an intelligence officer in the Air Staff, efforts to prevent intrusions "are not part of the JTF's [Joint Task Force's] computer network *warfighting* role and have been strongly resisted by the Services."[90]

In a later briefing, Healey described computer network defense as outwards-focused, engaging enemies, active, and requiring operational expertise. By contrast, he depicted information assurance as inwards-focused, not engaging enemies, passive, and requiring network management expertise.[91] Consistent with the services' preference for a warfighting focus, Healey noted that the task force would be staffed "mostly by traditional operators (pilots, combat arms, and so on), relying on DISA [the Defense Information Systems Agency] for technical comm-computer expertise."[92] Members of the task force distinguished their work from the technical support focus of the Defense Information Systems Agency. In October 1999, Army Col. Larry Frank, the chief of the task force's operations division, asserted, "we bring an operational focus" to defense and "we don't fix computers."[93]

This operational focus was partly driven by the need to persuade warfighters of the value of this new activity. As Campbell recalls: "[I]f you're going to have any credibility with the war fighters, you had to have operational people."[94] Specifically, the task force was projected to consist of nineteen billets, ten of which were dedicated to operations, four to communications, and five to intelligence.[95]

This tiny task force was officially "responsible for coordinating and directing the defense of the Department of Defense's computer systems and computer networks," a potentially enormous range of activities.[96] It functioned by relying on the services, contractors, and the Defense Information Systems Agency, where it was co-located. The services were each tasked with designating component forces and an associated commander that the Joint Task Force would have authority to coordinate and direct.[97] The Defense Department's computer emergency response team was also placed under the Joint Task Force-Computer Network Defense.[98] By 2000, it was composed of about one-third contractors, one-third military personnel, and one-third government civilian personnel.[99]

Significantly, many vulnerability mitigation activities were delegated to the Defense Information Systems Agency.[100] For example, the Defense Information Systems Agency developed the Information Assurance Vulnerability Alert process, wherein all of the Defense Department's systems administrators were required to receive, acknowledge, and report on their compliance with vulnerability alerts.[101] Nonetheless, in briefings before Congress, Campbell explicitly included red teaming and the Information Assurance Vulnerability Alert process within the category of "operations," alongside the Joint Task Force-Computer Network Defense. As this suggests, the concept of computer network operations was beginning to broaden to include vulnerability mitigation. And yet, this expanding concept of operations still excluded certain forms of vulnerability mitigation, such as training and certifying systems administrators and users.[102]

The Rising Status of Joint Cyber Operations and Service Responses

Computer network operations, both defensive and offensive, grew in influence, size, and authority in the twenty years following the establishment of the Joint Task Force-Computer Network Defense. Although the Joint Task Force-Computer Network Defense was initially chartered as a defensive organization, by January 1999 the Joint Chiefs of Staff had agreed that it would integrate both offensive and defensive operations and become part of US Space Command.[103] After the terrorist attacks of September 11, 2001, operations in Afghanistan and Iraq underscored the importance of defense. Thus, in 2004, the joint task force was returned to its initial defensive focus, with the new name, the Joint Task Force-Global Network Operations.[104] Offensive operations were moved to a new Joint Functional Component Command-Network Warfare within the National Security Agency. Both defensive and offensive components were commanded by Strategic Command, which had taken over several functions of Space Command when the latter dissolved in 2002.[105]

But the Joint Task Force-Global Network Operations did not discover the first-known breach of classified US military networks in October 2008. Instead, it was the National Security Agency's Information Assurance Directorate that first detected the intrusion, which was eventually attributed to the Russian Federal Security Service (FSB), Russia's national intelligence agency. Within a day the National Security Agency had devised a means of eliminating the intrusion, although cleaning up all of the Defense Department's networks would take well over a year.[106]

The National Security Agency's rapid response to the problem bolstered its case for unifying computer network attack and defense under the agency's authority. In June 2009, Secretary of Defense Robert Gates announced the formation of US Cyber Command, a unified command under Strategic Command that merged the Joint Task Force-Global Network Operations and the Joint Functional Component Command-Network Warfare. He also announced his intention to make the director of the National Security Agency dual-hatted as a four-star commander of US Cyber Command.[107] After decades of arguing for the importance of computer network operations, leaders in the intelligence community had finally gained the authority of a combatant command.

Gates also directed the services to establish component commands, which were expected to be three-star commands, to support US Cyber Command.[108] The elevation of joint computer network operations galvanized the services to elevate the professional and organizational status of computer network expertise. Each organized its supporting commands and associated career specializations slightly differently, but all gave greater status and priority to threat-oriented specializations than vulnerability-oriented work.

Air Force: Transforming Communications into "Operations"

The Air Force built its operational Cyber Command upon the earlier work of intelligence organizations while keeping communications organizations in a support role. However, when the Air Force finally established a new cyber operations career field, it drew most heavily on the communications career field. This was not because communications personnel were seen as warfighters, but because organizations specializing in electronic warfare and signals intelligence were unwilling to lose personnel to a field that it would not control. By contrast, computing-communications personnel were eager to raise their status by becoming the core of a new career field in cyber operations.[109] On April 30, 2010, the entire communications and information officer field, which included over 3,000 officers, changed to a new cyberspace officer field.[110] The cyberspace and information officer field quickly became a very broad career field that included both vulnerability reduction roles (for example, DODIN operations) and threat-oriented roles (for example offensive and defensive cyber operations).[111]

However, Air Force officers continue to view threat-oriented roles as preferable to vulnerability-oriented roles, by virtue of their greater warfighting status. For example, in a recent survey of the Air Force's cyberspace operations officers (17D), one officer asserted that "all 17Ds should be executing cyber operations, whether on the offensive line or defending a weapon system. Not supporting and maintaining."[112] Another argued that they were "making 'support' and 'maintenance' dirty words by calling everything 'operations,' and the true operational community sees that a huge portion of what we do is support or maintenance, and our marketing campaign costs us credibility."[113] Similarly, 1st Lt. Robert Lee, a cyber team leader in the Air Force Intelligence, Surveillance, and Reconnaissance Agency, has recognized that vulnerability-oriented roles were very important, but insisted on differentiating them from operational defense, that is warfighting: "Applying vendor-issued software patches is not defense; it is maintenance."[114]

Navy: Organizing an Information Warfare Community

To support US Cyber Command, in 2009, the Navy reactivated the 10th Fleet, which had played a critical role in anti-submarine warfare during the Second World War, and renamed it Fleet Cyber Command. The Navy moved all network organizations under Fleet Cyber Command/10th Fleet, empha-sizing that "victory will be predicated on intelligence and information rather than fire power."[115]

With growing demand for cyber warriors, the Navy also reorganized and elevated relevant career fields. Perhaps most significantly, in 2010 the Navy made information dominance a warfare specialization with an associ-ated qualification process and associated pin – something support fields typi-cally lacked.[116] In 2016, the Information Dominance Corps was renamed the Information Warfare Community to further "mainstream information warfare as one of four predominate warfare areas."[117]

Nonetheless, Navy personnel specializing in cyber operations have yet to gain the full opportunities available to traditional warfighters. The Information Warfare community is restricted line, meaning that officers within it are not eligible for command at sea.[118] Within the Information Warfare Community, the limitations have been particularly significant for the information profes-sional specialization – the Navy's network maintainers. Information profes-sionals saw dwindling command billets in the new millennium, not only due to technology and mission changes but because of civilian outsourcing.[119] By contrast, the cryptologic warfare specialization, which conducts defensive and offensive cyber operations, has been standing up new commands with asso-ciated opportunities.[120] This suggests that individuals specializing in threat-oriented work continue to have more opportunities than those focused on reducing vulnerabilities.

Army: Intelligence, Communications and the Creation of Cyber Branch

In October 2010, the Army established its component support to US Cyber Command at Fort Belvoir, Virginia, home to the Army's Computer Emergency Response Team.[121] The component, Army Cyber Command, assumed oper-ational control of the Army's communications and computing command, as well as computer network operations forces within the Army's intelligence command.[122]

The Army's Signals Branch and Intelligence Branches each created new career specializations to support the growing scale of joint cyber operations.[123] And, in 2014, the Army announced the new cyber branch as one "that will take its place alongside infantry, artillery and the other Army combat arms branches."[124] Officers within Cyber Branch were given the threat-oriented missions of defensive and offensive cyberspace operations.[125] By contrast, vulnerability-oriented work was assigned to warrant officers and enlisted personnel – a rank lower than commissioned officers – in the Army's Signals branch.[126] Thus, while Army cyber operations gained considerable status after the establishment of Cyber Command, threat-oriented roles continue to have greater warfighting status than vulnerability-oriented roles.

Conclusion: The Race for Cyber Warriors and Uncertainty in Cyberspace

By the time Cyber Command was elevated to become the 10th Unified Combatant Command in 2018, the professional identity and work roles of US cyber warriors had expanded to include not only threat-oriented activities, but also vulnerability-oriented activities. But it was the threat-focused activities, and particularly offensive cyber operations, that most readily gained warfighting status, and that continue to enjoy the most prestige and opportunity today.

Threat-focused activities, and particularly cyber operations, have also contributed most to an international race for cyber warriors. Shortly after the United States began developing information warfare capabilities, and placing a heavy emphasis on offense, China began to do the same. In 1997, China established a 100-person elite cyber warfare corps to launch attacks on US military networks, and it has grown its forces since then.[127] In 2015, China consolidated its cyber espionage and cyber attack forces into a single "Strategic Support Force," and established a network of training programs to train and recruit growing cadres of cyber warriors, moves similar to those undertaken in the United States.[128]

As noted above, it was partly the 2008 discovery of a Russian intrusion in US military networks that spurred the US to establish Cyber Command. And in turn US Cyber Command, along with revelations of US cyber attacks on Iran, encouraged Russia to build up its military cyber force, the GRU, which had languished for decades in the shadows of its intelligence agency.[129]

For its part, Iran responded to the cyber attacks on its nuclear enrichment facility by launching attacks on the Saudi Aramco oil company, and training its own force of cyber warriors. US officials in turn expressed concern about the growing threat from Iran as it learned from the US attack, and called for expanding cadres of US cyber warriors.[130]

These are just a few examples of how offensive operations by one nation have encouraged others to build up their own cyber warrior cadres. It is important to recognize that the organization and operational focus of cyber warriors vary in different nations. While US cyber warriors operate under formal command structures with official government authorization, and tend to focus on amplifying US military and intelligence operations, nations like North Korea,

China, and Russia rely more on volunteer or coerced citizen groups, and focus on stealing intellectual property or other financial resources.[131]

Nonetheless, as Healey and Jervis note (in this volume), offensive cyber operations appear to be ratcheting up in intensity. Once discovered, nations can build upon the exploits launched against them. For example, evidence suggests that Iran learned from the Stuxnet attacks, and one US industry expert recently warned that Iran's cyber warriors are "leapfrogging our defenses as they learn."[132] While these threat assessments at times may be inflated – and both industry leaders and military cyber forces have incentives to exaggerate threats as they make the case for investing more resources in their organizations – they amplify the race for cyber warriors, creating positive feedback and something akin to arms race instability.

It is important to recognize that offensive cyber operations do not necessarily escalate violence in any absolute sense. As Healey and Jervis also note, cyber operations can serve as an alternative to using force, de-escalating violent conflict. Nonetheless, offensive operations can create multiple kinds of instability simply because they create uncertainty. When military organizations find their computer networks behaving strangely, they may be quick to suspect other nations of an intrusion. Furthermore, once they discover an intrusion, they may be uncertain whether it was simply espionage, or preparation for an attack.

Additionally, cyber warriors cannot always predict the effects of their offensive operations. The physical effects of bombs and kinetic weapons are largely determined by physical laws; years of tests and experience have enabled relatively reliable predictions about destructiveness, collateral damage, and more. By contrast, the effects of cyber operations are shaped by the relatively unpredictable "arbitrary complexity" of information systems – the ad hoc ways in which humans and organizations have designed and interconnected computers and networks.[133]

Uncertainty about the impacts of cyber offense – whether intentional or unintentional – in turn increases anxiety and contributes to an international race for cyber warriors. Some of these investments focus on defense; intrusions in US computer networks have repeatedly led to investments in defensive technologies and personnel. But officials also have pointed to the offensive operations of other nations when arguing for expanding their own offensive capabilities. Furthermore, the race to train and deploy cyber warriors appears to be driven primarily by investments in offensive capabilities and associated uncertainties – not investments in defensive forces. It is difficult to find examples of officials expressing concern that they must expand offensive cyber capabilities because others have invested in defense.

In this respect, the race for cyber warriors is markedly different from nuclear arms races. With the exception of attacks on Hiroshima and Nagasaki, nuclear weapons have primarily served one purpose: to deter attack by threatening others with devastation. While nuclear threats are destabilizing insofar as they provoke international tensions and encourage further offensive build-up, deterrence is stabilizing insofar as it reduces the likelihood or destructiveness of attack. Nuclear defenses erode deterrence by creating uncertainty about the effectiveness of nuclear attack, giving nations incentives to invest in additional offense to overcome the defense, and thereby encouraging arms races.[134]

But cyber warriors carry out more variable and uncertain missions than nuclear weapons. Cyber warriors aim not only or even primarily at deterrence, but rather at subversion, espionage, and sabotage, all of which are destabilizing to adversaries.[135] Cyber defenses reduce uncertainty for defenders, both by preventing intrusions that have uncertain effects and by making them visible. And while cyber defenses may impose costs on attackers, they do not substantially increase uncertainty for attackers, who have always navigated uncertainty in the defenders' computer and information systems.

Of all the forms of defense undertaken by the United States, DODIN operations arguably are the most focused on maintaining stability – specifically, the stability of the technological systems upon which allied warriors rely. However, even DODIN operations do not necessarily contribute to stability in the ultimate sense. If the kinetic forces that they enable are deployed in ways that destabilize international relations, they too enable instability. The role of cyber warriors in stabilizing or destabilizing international order thus depends not only upon their technological capabilities, but also upon how national and military leaders use those capabilities to advance or undermine political objectives.

Acknowledgment

This chapter is based upon research supported by the National Science Foundation under grant number 1553069.

Notes

1. For discussion of the warfighting identity of missileers, see George L. Chapman, "Missileer: The Dawn, Decline, and Reinvigoration of America's Intercontinental Ballistic Missile Operators," Master's thesis (Air University, 2017): https://apps.dtic.mil/dtic/tr/fulltext/u2/10458 04.pdf. On drones and warfighting, see P. W. Singer, *Wired for War:*

The Robotics Revolution and Conflict in the 21st Century (New York: Penguin Press, 2009) and Hugh Gusterson, *Drone: Remote Control Warfare* (Cambridge, MA: The MIT Press, 2016).

2. William Newhouse et al., "National Initiative for Cybersecurity Education (NICE) Cybersecurity Workforce Framework," *National Institute of Standards and Technology*, Publication 800–181 (August 2017): https://doi.org/10.6028/NIST.SP.800-181

3. Jeffrey R. Jones, "Defense Department Cyber Requires Speed, Precision and Agility," *Signal*, May 1, 2019: https://www.afcea.org/content/defen se-department-cyber-requires-speed-precision-and-agility

4. Joint Chiefs of Staff, "Joint Publication 3-12: Cyberspace Operations," June 8, 2018, II-2–II-3.

5. TNSR and this volume.

6. The earliest books and papers to describe the rise of military cyber operations treated them as the necessary response to a series of "wake-up calls" that came in the form of computer network intrusions, by both real adversaries and penetration testers, in the 1990s and 2000s. This narrative first emerged in the 1990s among Defense Department insiders who advocated putting greater emphasis on cyber operations. See, for example, US Senate, "Security in Cyberspace," Hearings Before the Committee on Governmental Affairs, 104th Congress, 2nd Session, 1996; and Senate Armed Services Committee, "Department of Defense Authorization for Appropriations for Fiscal Year 2001 and the Future Years Defense Program, Part 5: Emerging Theats and Capabilities," 106th Congress, 2nd Session, 2000. Jason Healey, *A Fierce Domain: Conflict in Cyberspace, 1986 to 2012*, Kindle ed. (Vienna, VA: Cyber Conflict Studies Association, 2013) and Gregory J. Rattray, *Strategic Warfare in Cyberspace* (Cambridge, MA: The MIT Press, 2001). More recently, scholars have analyzed the rise of military cyber operations as a response to a broad set of technological changes that took place in the 1990s and early 2000s. Fred Kaplan, *Dark Territory: The Secret History of Cyberwar* (New York: Simon & Schuster, 2016); Thomas Rid, *Rise of the Machines: A Cybernetic History* (New York: W. W. Norton & Company, 2016); Myriam Dunn Cavelty, *Cyber-security and Threat Politics: US Efforts to Secure the Information Age* (New York: Routledge, 2007); Michael Warner, "Cybersecurity: A Prehistory," *Intelligence and National Security* 27, no. 5 (2012): https://cyb erdefensereview.army.mil/CDR-Content/Articles/Article-View/Arti cle/1136012/notes-on-military-doctrine-for-cyberspace-operations-in -the-united-states-1992/; "Notes on Military Doctrine for Cyberspace

Operations in the United States, 1992–2014," *Cyber Defense Review*, August 27, 2015.

7. David Edgerton, *The Shock of the Old: Technology and Global History Since 1900* (London: Profile Books, 2007); Andrew L. Russell and Lee Vinsel, "After Innovation, Turn to Maintenance," *Technology and Culture* 59, no. 1 (2018): 1–25, https://doi.org/10.1353/tech.2018.0004; and Rebecca Slayton and Brian Clarke, "Trusting Infrastructure: The Emergence of Computer Security Incident Response, 1989–2005," *Technology and Culture* 61, no. 1 (2020): 173–206, https://doi.org/10.1353/tech.2020.0036

8. Gary J. Finco, a Senior Advisory Engineer at Idaho National Laboratories, uses this in his signature line. Email sent to the SCADASEC listserve, March 2016: https://groups.io/g/scadasec. This observation is an important counterpoint to the assumptions of a vast literature on military innovation.

9. James P. Anderson, *Computer Security Technology Planning Study, Vol 1*, Electronic Systems Division of the Air Force Systems Command, October 1972: https://csrc.nist.gov/csrc/media/publications/conference-paper/1998/10/08/proceedings-of-the-21st-nissc-1998/documents/early-cs-papers/ande72a.pdf; *Computer Security Technology Planning Study, Vol 2*, Electronic Systems Division of the Air Force Systems Command, October 1972: https://apps.dtic.mil/dtic/tr/fulltext/u2/772806.pdf

10. For examples of early tests, see discussion in Jeffrey Yost, "Oral History Interview with Roger R. Schell," *Charles Babbage Institute*, May 1, 2012: http://hdl.handle.net/11299/133439; and Warner, "Cybersecurity: A Pre-history," 786.

11. Asked in 2012 whether penetration tests of US systems led to offensive work within the intelligence community, Roger Schell, an Air Force officer who played a leading role in developing more secure computer systems, responded that "we recognize that it would not be unexpected if an adversary were to take an offensive thing, and we didn't consider ourselves stupider than the adversary, you know, you can pretty well connect those dots." Yost, "Oral History Interview with Roger R. Schell."

12. Willis H. Ware, "Security and Privacy in Computer Systems," paper presented at the spring Joint Computer Conference, New York, April 18–20, 1967.

13. For an excellent summary of the research agendas begun to solve this problem, see Donald MacKenzie, *Mechanizing Proof: Computing, Risk, and Trust* (Cambridge, MA: The MIT Press, 2001).

14. For more on the *Privacy Act* and associated requirements, see Rebecca Slayton, "Measuring Risk: Computer Security Metrics, Automation, and Learning," *IEEE Annals of the History of Computing* 37, no. 2 (April–June 2015): 32–45, https://doi.org/10.1109/MAHC.2015.30

15. Clark Weissman, "Access Controls Working Group Report," in Susan K. Reed and Dennis K. Branstad (eds.), *Controlled Accessibility Workshop Report: A Report of the NBS/ACM Workshop on Controlled Accessibility*, December 10–13, 1972, Santa Fe, CA, 19.

16. Theodore M. P. Lee, "Processors, Operating Systems and Nearby Peripherals: A Consensus Report," in Zella G. Ruthberg, *Audit and Evaluation of Computer Security II: System Vulnerabilities and Controls*, Proceedings of the National Bureau of Standards Invitational Workshop Held at Miami Beach, FL, November 28–30, 1978, pp. 8–13.

17. Slayton, "Measuring Risk."

18. These became known as the "rainbow series." See discussion in M. Schaefer, "If A1 Is the Answer, What Was the Question? An Edgy Naïf's Retrospective on Promulgating the Trusted Computer Systems Evaluation Criteria," paper presented at the Annual Computer Security Applications Conference, Tucson, AZ, December 6–10, 1984.

19. Schaefer, "If A1 is the Answer"; Steven B. Lipner, "The Birth and Death of the Orange Book," *IEEE Annals of the History of Computing* 37, no. 2 (April–June 2015): 19–31, https://doi.org/10.1109/MAHC.2015.27

20. The National Security Telecommunications and Information Systems Security Committee (NTISSC) was first established as the US Communications Security Board in 1953 by NSC-168. Committee on National Security Systems, "CNSS History": https://www.cnss.gov /CNSS/about/history.cfm (accessed December 20, 2020).

21. Lipner, "The Birth and Death of the Orange Book."

22. John C. Nagengast, "Defining a Security Architecture for the Next Century," *Journal of Electronic Defense* 15, no. 1 (1992): 51–53.

23. Nagengast, "Defining a Security Architecture for the Next Century." The Defense Information Systems Security Program would be managed by a new Center for Information Systems Security and jointly staffed by personnel from the Defense Information Systems Agency and the National Security Agency. It is not clear from published records whether the Defense Information Systems Security Program ever produced the unified security architecture and policy. "Budget Plan Leaves Military Computers Vulnerable to Intrusion," *Defense Daily* 184, no. 54 (1994).

24. Although National Telecommunications and Information Systems Security Directive No. 500, "Telecommunications and Automated

Information Systems Security Education, Training, and Awareness," issued in June 1987, officially required agencies to implement security education and training programs, its effectiveness seems to have been limited. This directive is mentioned in the one that superseded it: National Security Telecommunications and Information Systems Security Committee, "NSTISS Directive 500: Information Systems Security (INFOSEC) Education, Training, and Awareness," Febuary 25, 1993: https://apps.dtic.mil/sti/pdfs/ADA362604.pdf

25. Rebecca Slayton, "What Is a Cyber Warrior? The Emergence of US Military Cyber Expertise, 1967–2018" (Winter 2021), *Texas National Security Review* (2021).

26. James P. Anderson, *Computer Security Threat Monitoring and Surveillance*, Fort Washington, PA, February 26, 1980, revised April 15, 1980: https://csrc.nist.gov/csrc/media/publications/conference-paper/1998/10/08/proceedings-of-the-21st-nissc-1998/documents/early-cs-papers/ande80.pdf. This is the earliest known study of threat monitoring. Anderson was an independent computer security expert who worked as a contractor primarily for military and intelligence agencies. While it is unclear what agency commissioned this report, it was very possibly the National Security Agency. And despite its opaque origins, the report was widely circulated and became very influential.

27. The early history of this work is described well in Jeffery R. Yost, "The March of IDES: Early History of Intrusion-Detection Expert Systems," *IEEE Annals of the History of Computing* 38, no. 4 (October–December 2016): 42–54, https://doi.org/10.1109/MAHC.2015.41. Systems were deployed by the Navy's Space and Naval Warfare Systems Command, the Air Force Cryptologic Support Center and the National Computer Security Center.

28. For example, one of the earliest such systems, the Intrusion Detection Expert System (IDES), had separate interfaces for systems administrators, security officers, and analysts. Yost, "The March of IDES."

29. "Internet" is capitalized here to highlight that it refers to a specific network developed under contract to the US Department of Defense. This was an important predecessor to the much larger and more public network that is known as the "internet." Internet is also capitalized throughout this chapter in references to this specific worm.

30. For a more detailed history, see Slayton and Clarke, "Trusting Infrastructure."

31. Author interview with Kenneth van Wyk, February 20, 2018, Alexandria, VA.

32. John Markoff, "Dutch Computer Rogues Infiltrate American Systems with Impunity," *The New York Times*, April 21, 1991: https://www.ny times.com/1991/04/21/us/dutch-computer-rogues-infiltrate-american -systems-with-impunity.html. The attackers had broken into computers at national laboratories that served as hosts for the MILNET, a non-classified military network.

33. John J. Fialka, "Pentagon Studies Art of 'Information Warfare' To Reduce Its Systems' Vulnerability to Hackers," *Wall Street Journal*, July 3, 1995; Jack L. Brock, *Hackers Penetrate DOD Computer Systems*, US General Accounting Office: https://nsarchive2.gwu.edu/NSAEBB/NS AEBB424/docs/Cyber-006.pdf; author phone interview with William Gravell, May 22, 2020.

34. See, for example, the testimony of Computer Emergency Response Team Coordination Center Director Richard Pethia in the hearing, "Security in Cyberspace," 306–323. Although Pethia was focused on civilian security incidents, he spoke in hearings that were motivated by intrusions of Department of Defense networks. Additionally, a presentation from January 1999 demonstrates that the Air Force Computer Emergency Response Team and Office of Special Investigations were collecting similar statistics by the late 1990s. See US Air Force, "Information Assurance Update," January 29, 1999: https://nsarchive.gwu.edu/dc.html?doc=61 68264-National-Security-Archive-US-Air-Force

35. US General Accounting Office, "Virus Highlights Need for Improved Internet Management," June 1989, pp. 20–21; Brock, "Hackers Penetrate DOD Computer Systems," 1; Government Accountability Office, "Information Security: Computer Attacks at Department of Defense Pose Increasing Risks," 6.

36. US Air Force, "Information Assurance Update."

37. Alan D. Campen (ed.), *The First Information War: The Story of Communications, Computers, and Intelligence Systems in the Persian Gulf War* (Fairfax, VA: AFCEA International Press, 1992). Edward Mann, "Desert Storm: The First Information War?," *AirPower Journal* VIII, no. 4 (Winter 1994): 4–14: https://www.airuniversity.af.edu/Portals/10/ASPJ/journa ls/Volume-08_Issue-1-Se/1994_Vol8_No4.pdf

38. It is possible that the directive mentioned attacking and defending computer systems – approximately fourteen lines of the four-page document remain classified – but computer network attack and defense are not mentioned in the declassified portion of the document, which is much larger than the classified portion. Donald J. Atwood, "Information Warfare," Department of Defense Directive TS 3600.1, December 21, 1992.

39. Atwood, "Information Warfare," 1.

40. Department of Defense, "Electronic Warfare (EW) and Command and Control Warfare (C2W) Countermeasures," Department of Defense Directive 3222.4, July 31, 1992, 1. Revisions issued on October 22, 1993 included replacing all references to "command, control, and communications countermeasures" with "command and control warfare."

41. In March 1993, the chairman of the Joint Chiefs of Staff issued a revised memorandum of policy on command-and-control warfare, calling it "the military strategy that implements information warfare." Department of Defense, "Memorandum of Policy Number 30: Command and Control Warfare," *Department of Defense*, March 1993, 3: https://archive.org/de tails/JCSMemoofPolicyNumber30CommandandControlWarfare. This was a revision to a 1990 memo on command, control, and communications countermeasures (C3CM). This revision replaced C3CM with C2W. It also added "psychological warfare" as one of five elements of C2W.

42. In December 1996, Directive S-3600.1, Information Operations, replaced the 1992 Directive on Information Warfare, and explicitly acknowledged the threat that "computer network attack" posed to command-and-control systems. The 1996 directive expanded the focus of the 1992 directive on winning in military conflict and included the goal of securing "peacetime national security objectives" through civil and public affairs activities. It was only in 1998 that the Joint Doctrine on Information Operations noted that offensive information operations "may include computer network attack." John P. White, "Department of Defense Directive S-3600.1: Information Operations," *Department of Defense*, December 9, 1996, 1–1: http://www.iwar.org.uk/iwar/resour ces/doctrine/DOD36001.pdf

43. "EW Expands Into Information Warfare," *Aviation Week & Space Technology* 141, no. 10 (October 1994): 47–48.

44. White, "Subcultural Influence on Military Innovation," 195.

45. The Information Warfare Center was co-located with the Joint Electronic Warfare Center, which became the Joint Command and Control Warfare Center in September 1994. "EW Expands Into Information Warfare," *Aviation Week & Space Technology.*

46. Department of the Air Force, "Cornerstones of Information Warfare," January 1 1995: 8, https://apps.dtic.mil/sti/citations/ADA307436

47. The potential legal problem of having the Air Force Information Warfare Center engaged in "warfighting" in Operation Uphold Democracy

was one rationale for creating an operational information warfare unit. Kaplan, *Dark Territory*.

48. See, for example discussion of Exercise Fort Franklin V in Ruffini, *609 IWS: A Brief History*, 14.

49. Atlantic Council, "Transcript: Lessons from Our Cyber Past – The First Military Cyber Units," March 5, 2012: https://www.atlanticcouncil.org /commentary/transcript/transcript-lessons-from-our-cyber-past-the-fir st-military-cyber-units/

50. *Realizing the Potential of C4I: Fundamental Challenges* (Washington, DC: National Academy Press, 1999), 161: http://nap.edu/6457

51. National Academy Press, *Realizing the Potential of C4I*, 161.

52. "Navy C4I Budget Safe for Now," *Defense Daily* 184, no. 41, (August 1994): 321.

53. Bryan Bender, "Navy Chief Commissions Fleet Information Warfare Center," *Defense Daily* 189, no. 17 (October 1995); also, "Implementing Instruction for Information Warfare/Command and Control Warfare," OPNAV Instruction 3430.26, Office of the Chief of Naval Operations, January 18, 1995: http://www.iwar.org.uk/iwar/resources/opnav/3430 _26.pdf

54. Bender, "Navy Chief Commissions Fleet Information Warfare Center." The exact size of the Fleet Information Warfare Center is difficult to establish. According to a 1996 Government Accountability Office report, only three of thirty personnel spots were granted for the Fleet Information Warfare Center. "Computer Attacks at Department of Defense Pose Increasing Risks," *Government Accountability Office* (May 1996), 38. On the other hand, NAVCIRT, formed at the same time within the Fleet Information Warfare Center, is described as having five people at its founding, growing to 250 people by 2003, and becoming the operational arm of the Fleet Information Warfare Center. Finley, "Navy Cyber Defense Operations Command Celebrates Past, Present, Future." One of White's interviewees states that the Fleet Information Warfare Center started as a "handful" of officers and contractors. White, "Subcultural Influence on Military Innovation," 306. Most likely, the discrepancies in numbers relate to the question of whether new billets were created or simply reassigned. Reportedly, the "Navy did not create new billets for the command, but rather, 'extracted' operation and main-tenance funds from facilities which have been stood down." Bender, "Navy Chief Commissions Fleet Information Warfare Center."

55. Naval Postgraduate School, "About the Cebrowski Institute": https:// nps.edu/web/cebrowski/about (accessed October 19, 2020).

56. According to the article, the term was introduced by Chief of Naval Operations Adm. Jay Johnson in an address to the US Naval Institute Annapolis Seminar and 123rd Annual Meeting on April 23, 1997, where Johnson described "a fundamental shift from what we call platform-centric warfare to something we call network-centric warfare." Arthur K. Cebrowski and John H. Garstka, "Network-centric Warfare: Its Origin and Future," *Proceedings* 124, no. 1 (January 1998): 28, https://www.usni.org/magazines/proceedings/1998/january/network-centric-warfare-its-origin-and-future

57. Cebrowski and Garstka, "Network-centric Warfare."

58. My discussion of the Land Information Warfare Activity draws primarily on White, "Subcultural Influence on Military Innovation," 61–71.

59. As noted previously, it appears that all of the services were involved in discussions about incident response by 1990, but the formalization of a coordinated incident response team came later. White cites a source that dates the formation of the Army Computer Emergency Response Team to September 1996. White, "Subcultural Influence on Military Innovation," 67. However, public announcements of the Army Computer Emergency Response Team only appeared in March 1997. Bryan Bender, "Army Stands Up Computer Security Coordination Center," *Defense Daily*, March 18, 1997; David L. Grange and James A. Kelley, "Victory Through Information Dominance," *Army* 47, no. 3 (March 1997).

60. US Army, "Field Manual 100-6: Information Operations," August 27, 1996: https://www.hsdl.org/?view&did=437397. The field manual broadened information operations to include civil and public affairs as well as command-and-control warfare, but did not expand the five elements of command-and-control warfare to include computer network operations.

61. Joint Chiefs of Staff, "Joint Pub 13-13.1: Joint Doctrine for Command and Control Warfare," February 7, 1996: https://www.bits.de/NRANEU/others/jp-doctrine/jp3_13_1.pdf. Although "Field Manual 100-6" was not formally published until August 1996, this discussion is quoted in the joint doctrine issued in February 1996, suggesting that "Field Manual 100-6" was far along in its development earlier in that year.

62. Stephanie Ahern, "Breaking the Organizational Mold: Why the Institutional U.S. Army Has Changed Despite Itself since the End of the Cold War," Doctoral dissertation (University of Notre Dame, 2009).

63. The exceptions were public affairs and information operations, which were moved to maneuver, fire, and effects. Ahern, "Breaking the Organizational Mold," 390–391.

64. Joint Security Commission, "Redefining Security: A Report to the Secretary of Defense and the Director of Central Intelligence," February 28, 1994: chapters 8 and 1, https://fas.org/sgp/library/jsc/

65. Office of the Undersecretary of Defense for Acquisition and Technology, "Report of the Defense Science Board Summer Study Task Force on Information Architecture for the Battlefield," 1994, 30: https://www.hs dl.org/?abstract&did=464955

66. Office of the Undersecretary of Defense for Acquisition and Technology, "Report of the Defense Science Board Summer Study Task Force," 32.

67. "Navy C4I Budget Safe for Now," *Defense Daily*.

68. Paul Constance, "From Bombs to Bytes: Era of On-line Weaponry Is Here," *Government Computer News* 14, no. 21 (October 1995).

69. In January 1995, the Defense Information Systems Agency elevated its Center for Information Systems Security out of the Joint Interoperability Engineering Organization and made it the operating arm of a new Information Warfare Division. The center included a focus on reducing vulnerabilities within the Defense Department. For example, it aimed to develop a standardized information security training program for the Defense Department. It also continued to include operational aspects of defense, such as the Defense Department's incident response team ASSIST, which was moved into the Defense Information Systems Agency's Global Control Center. Vanessa Jo Grimm, "In War on System Intruders, DISA Calls In Big Guns," *Government Computer News* 14, no. 3 (1995).

70. Gravell recalls a particularly well-received briefing to Chief of Naval Operations James Watkins in 1985. Cebrowski was present. Telephone interview with Gravell, May 22, 2020, and subsequent email correspondence.

71. See, for example, The Joint Staff, Department of Defense, "Information Warfare: Legal, Regulatory, Policy and Organizational Considerations for Assurance, 2nd Edition,"July 4, 1996: https://nsarchive.gwu.edu/dc .html?doc=5989661-National-Security-Archive-Joint-Chiefs-of-Staff

72. Phone interview with Gravell, May 22, 2020.

73. Email correspondence with Gravell, July 20, 2020.

74. By 1997, a report for the assistant secretary of defense for command, control, communications, and intelligence noted that "the complexity of managing DOD's information assurance efforts had increased due to the proliferation of networks across DOD and that its decentralized information assurance management could not deal with it adequately." Quoted in Li, "DOD's Information Assurance Efforts," US General Accounting Office: 4, https://www.gao.gov/assets/nsiad-98-132r.pdf

75. Quote is the summary of a November 1997 report from the assistant secretary of defense for command, control, communications, and intelligence, found in Li, "DOD's Information Assurance Efforts," 4. The interim report of the task force was presented on January 27, 1997, and the final report, "Improving Information Assurance: A General Assessment and Comprehensive Approach to an Integrated IA Program for the Department of Defense," is dated March 1997. These latter two documents are described in J. V. Gray, "Information Operations: A Research Aid," *Institute for Defense Analysis*, September 1997, 31.

76. In response to fiscal years 1999–2003 planning guidance, the assistant secretary of defense for command, control, communications, and intelligence developed "A Management Process for a Defense-wide Information Assurance Program (DIAP)," published November 15, 1997. See Li, "DOD's Information Assurance Efforts," 4, note 3. The assistant secretary of defense for command, control, communications, and intelligence was made the Defense Department chief information officer in response to the 1996 Clinger-Cohen Act, which required that all federal agencies appoint a chief information officer and use performance-based management to oversee information technology acquisition and use.

77. Government Accountability Office, *Serious Weaknesses Continue to Place Defense Operations at Risk*, August 26, 1999: 15, https://www.gao.gov/pr oducts/GAO/AIMD-99-107

78. Government Accountability Office, "Information Security: Progress and Challenges to an Effective Defense-wide Information Assurance Program," March 30, 2001: 22.

79. Kaplan, *Dark Territory*.

80. Ibid. 68. Kaplan states that "the entire defense establishment's network was penetrated" in four days, though the video briefing by the National Security Agency red team targeting officer Keith Abernethy indicates that one target was denied to the team.

81. Email to author from John Campbell, September 28, 2020.

82. Joint Chiefs of Staff, "DOD Organization for Computer Network Defense: Summary of Proposals," Slide 4, *National Security Archive*, June 1998: https://nsarchive.gwu.edu/dc.html?doc=6168257-National-Security-Archive-Joint-Chiefs-of-Staff. Kaplan states that the Information Operations Response Cell was formed shortly before Solar Sunrise, but slides showing the timeline for discussion of options for computer network defense show it starting earlier. Campbell recalls that it was established before Eligible Receiver. Email to author from Campbell, September 28, 2020.

83. Email to author from Campbell, September 28, 2020; emphasis in original.

84. Email to author from Campbell, September 28, 2020.

85. Kaplan, *Dark Territory*, 78.

86. Atlantic Council, "Transcript: Lessons from our Cyber Past."

87. Some documents related to Eligible Receiver, including an after-action report summarizing the major lessons of the exercise, have been declassified and are available at the Digital National Security Archive as part of an electronic briefing book. Michael Martelle (ed.), "Eligible Receiver 97: Seminal DOD Cyber Exercise Included Mock Terror Strikes and Hostage Simulations," *Department of Defense, Briefing Book* no. 634, August 1, 2018: https://nsarchive.gwu.edu/briefing-book/cyber-vault /2018-08-01/eligible-receiver-97-seminal-dod-cyber-exercise-included -mock-terror-strikes-hostage-simulations. Other weaknesses revealed by Eligible Receiver are based on interviews conducted by Fred Kaplan and reported in his book, *Dark Territory*.

88. "Eligible Receiver '97 After Action Report," in Martelle, "Eligible Receiver 97." Also available on YouTube: "Eligible Receiver '97 After Action Report," YouTube: https://youtu.be/iI3iZAq0Nh0 (accessed 22 December 2020).

89. Jason Healey, "Bullet Background Paper on Computer Network Defense-Joint Task Force (CND-JTF)," *Office of the Deputy Chief of Staff for Air and Space Operations*, October 14, 1998: 3, https://nsarchive.gwu.edu/dc.ht ml?doc=6168259-National-Security-Archive-Captain-Healey-US-Air; emphasis in original.

90. Healey, "Bullet Background Paper"; emphasis in original.

91. "Organizing for Information Warfare: An Air Staff Perspective," *U.S. Air Force Office of the Director of Intelligence, Surveillance, and Reconnaissance*, 1999, slide 25: https://nsarchive.gwu.edu/dc.html?doc=6168263-Natio nal-Security-Archive-US-Air-Force-Office-of. Jason Healey confirmed that he was the author of this presentation in an email to the author dated May 15, 2020.

92. "Organizing for Information Warfare," slide 2.

93. Dan Verton, "DOD Boosts IT Security Role," *Federal Computer Week*, October 3, 1999: https://fcw.com/articles/1999/10/03/dod-boosts-it -security-role.aspx

94. Atlantic Council, "Transcript: Lessons from our Cyber Past."

95. Jason Healey, "JTF Computer Network Defense Update," US Air Force Office of the Director of Intelligence, Surveillance, and Reconnaissance,

October 1998, slide 17: https://nsarchive.gwu.edu/dc.html?doc=61682 58-National-Security-Archive-US-Air-Force-Office-of

96. John H. Campbell, "Computer Network Defense: Computer Network Defense Update to the Defense Science Board', *National Security Archive*, January 18, 2000, slide 10: https://nsarchive.gwu.edu/dc.html?doc=314 5117-Document-03

97. Specifically, the Army's component was the Army Computer Emergency Response Team Coordination Center, directed by Land Information Warfare Activity. The Air Force's component was the Air Force Computer Emergency Response Team under the command of the Air Force Information Warfare Center. And the Navy formed a fourteen-person task force at the Naval Computer and Telecommunications Command, which worked in coordination with the Fleet Information Warfare Center and Navy Computer Incident Response Team. Marines also formed a new force. Each contribution to the Joint Task Force-Computer Network Defense is described in articles in the Fall 1999, volume 2, number 3 edition of *Information Assurance*, a newsletter for information assurance technology professionals published by the Information Assurance Technology Analysis Center within the Defense Information Systems Agency. See: https://assets.documentcloud.org/documents/579 8613/National-Security-Archive-Information-Assurance.pdf

98. The organization of the Joint Task Force for Computer Network Defense can be found in Campbell, "Computer Network Defense," slide 13: https://nsarchive.gwu.edu/dc.html?doc=3145117-Document-03

99. Atlantic Council, "Transcript: Lessons from our Cyber Past."

100. Ibid.

101. For a discussion of this process, including questions about the role that the Joint Task Force-Computer Network Defense should play in it, see DoD Inspector General, "DoD Compliance with the Information Assurance Vulnerability Alert Policy," *Department of Defense, Office of Inspector General*, December 1, 2000: https://www.dodig.mil/reports.ht ml/Article/1116364/dod-compliance-with-the-information-assurance -vulnerability-alert-policy/

102. Senate Armed Services Committee, "Department of Defense Authorization for Appropriations for Fiscal Year 2001 and the Future Years Defense Program," 19. In this testimony, Campbell presented "operations" as one part of "defense-in-depth," along with technology and people. Certifying systems administrators and users was in the "people" category, not "operations."

103. "Organizing for Information Warfare," slide 6. It became the Joint Task Force – Computer Network Operations in 2000, when it assumed responsibility for offense as well as defense. Senate Armed Services Committee, "Department of Defense Authorization for Appropriations for Fiscal Year 2001 and the Future Years Defnse Program," 42.

104. Atlantic Council, "Transcript: Lessons from our Cyber Past."

105. For an overview of the evolution of the Joint Task Force-Computer Network Defense into US Cyber Command, see US Cyber Command, "U.S. Cyber Command History,": https://www.cybercom.mil/About /History/ (accessed October 21, 2020).

106. Kaplan, *Dark Territory*, 180–185; Ellen Nakashima, "Cyber-intruder Sparks Response, Debate," *The Washington Post*, December 8, 2011: https://www.washingtonpost.com/national/national-security/cyber -intruder-sparks-response-debate/2011/12/06/gIQAxLuFgO_story .html; William J. Lynn III, "Defending a New Domain: The Pentagon's Cyberstrategy," *Foreign Affairs* 89, no. 5 (September/October 2010): 97, https://www.foreignaffairs.com/articles/united-states/2010-09-01/de fending-new-domain

107. Robert Gates, "Establishment of a Subordinate Unified U.S. Cyber Command Under U.S. Strategic Command for Military Cyberspace Operations," Memoranda, *Department of Defense*, June 23, 2009: https:// fas.org/irp/doddir/dod/secdef-cyber.pdf

108. Gates, "Establishment of a Subordinate Unified U.S. Cyber Command." The Army began by establishing Army Forces Cyber Command head-quarters within Army Space and Missile Defense Forces/Strategic Command, which had already been serving as a coordinating head-quarters for computer network operations, helping to meet the Army's requirements to support joint operations. White, "Subcultural Influence on Military Innovation," 105–106.

109. These developments are described in White, "Subcultural Influence on Military Innovation," 251–252.

110. This field was labeled 17D. Golembiewski, "From Signals to Cyber." Additionally, on November 1, 2009, roughly 43,000 enlisted and 8,800 civilian personnel in communications fields were transitioned into a new cyberspace support career field, the 3DXXX series. Rita Boland, "Military Branch Undertakes Massive Troop Conversion," *Signal*, February 2, 2010: https://www.afcea.org/content/military-branch-undertakes-massive-troop-conversion

111. Chaitra M. Hardison et al., *Attracting, Recruiting, and Retaining Successful Cyberspace Operations Officers* (Santa Monica, CA: RAND Corporation, 2019): https://www.rand.org/pubs/research_reports/RR2618.html

112. Ibid., 57.

113. Ibid., 56.

114. Robert M. Lee, "The Failing of Air Force Cyber," *Signal*, November 1, 2013: https://www.afcea.org/content/failing-air-force-cyber

115. US Department of Defense Information/Federal Information News Dispatch, "Navy Stands Up Fleet Cyber Command, Reestablishes U.S. 10th Fleet,", 2010: https://search.proquest.com/docview/190465152?accountid=10267

116. White, "Subcultural Influence on Military Innovation," 357.

117. Ted N. Branch, "The 'Information Dominance Corps' is now the 'Information Warfare Community,'" *CHIPS*, (January–March 2016): https://www.doncio.navy.mil/Chips/ArticleDetails.aspx?ID=7307

118. "Information Warfare Community Overview," *Navy Personnel Command*, last modified October 21, 2019: https://www.public.navy.mil/bupers-npc/officer/communitymanagers/active/restricted/Pages/Information_Warfare_Community.aspx; see also https://www.mynavyhr.navy.mil/Career-Management/Community-Management/Officer/Active-OCM/Restricted-Line/Information-Warfare/

119. Vincent A. Augelli, "Information-Dominance Officers Need to Command": https://www.bluetoad.com/publication/?i=102307&p=81&view=issueViewer

120. See, for example, US Department of Defense Information/Federal Information News Dispatch, "Cryptologic Warfare Group 6 Stands Up New Commands," 2018: https://www.dvidshub.net/news/288472/cryptologic-warfare-group-6-stands-up-new-commands

121. US Federal News Service, "Army Establishes Army Cyber Command," October 4, 2010: https://search.proquest.com/docview/756210143?accountid=10267

122. US Army, "Army Establishes Army Cyber Command," October 1, 2010: https://www.army.mil/article/46012/army_establishes_army_cyber_command

123. Similarly, the intelligence branch created the cryptologic cyberspace intelligence collector in 2012. In 2014, the Army finally created a new Cyber Branch, with three initial specializations: cyberspace officer, cyber operations technician (warrant officer), and cyber operations specialist (enlisted). Eventually all of the electronic warfare personnel were

converted to two new specializations in the Cyber Branch: electronic warfare officer and electronic warfare technician. US Army, "Army Cyber Branch Offers Soldiers New Challenges, Opportunities," *Fort Gordon Public Affairs Office,* November 25, 2014: https://www.army.mil/artic le/138883/army_cyber_branch_offers_soldiers_new_challenges_opport unities

124. US Army, "Army Cyber Branch Offers Soldiers New Challenges, Opportunities."

125. US Army, "Cyber Operations Officer (17A)": https://www.goarmy.com /careers-and-jobs/browse-career-and-job-categories/computers-and-te chnology/cyber-operations-officer.html (accessed October 25, 2020). Interestingly, however, the Army's Officer Personnel Management Directorate still classifies cyber operations officers as "operations support." United States Army Human Resources Command, "Officer Personnel Management Directorate," November 17, 2020: https://www.hrc.army .mil/Officer/Officer%20Personnel%20Management%20Directorate

126. Information protection technician warrant officers, a specialization created in Signal Branch in 2010, perform DODIN operations. US Army Recruiting Command, "Warrant Officer Prerequisites and Duty Description: 255S – Information Protection Technician," August 18, 2020: https://recruiting.army.mil/ISO/AWOR/255S/. Cyber network defenders, an enlisted specialization created in Signal Branch in 2014, conduct vulnerability assessments and other kinds of infrastructure support work, although they also conduct incident response, a threat-oriented activity. US Army, "Cyber Network Defender": https://www.go army.com/careers-and-jobs/browse-career-and-job-categories/compute rs-and-technology/cyber-network-defender.html (accessed October 26, 2020).

127. Desmond Ball, "China's Cyber Warfare Capabilites," *Security Challenges* 7, no. 2 (Winter 2011): 81–103, https://www.jstor.org/stable/26461991

128. On the Strategic Support Force, see Ben Buchanan and Fiona Cunningham, "Preparing the Cyber Battlefield: Assessing a Novel Escalation Risk in a Sino-American Crisis," *Texas National Security Review* 3, no. 4 (Fall 2020): 54–81, http://dx.doi.org/10.26153/tsw/10951. On training see Zi Yang, "China Is Massively Expanding Its Cyber Capabilities," *The National Interest*, October 13, 2017: https://nationalinterest.org/blog/the -buzz/china-massively-expanding-its-cyber-capabilities-22577

129. Bilyana Lilly and Joe Cheravitch, "The Past, Present, and Future of Russia's Cyber Strategy and Forces," in T. Jančárková, L. Lindström, M. Signoretti, I. Tolga, and G. Visky (eds.), *Proceedings of the 12th International*

Conference on Cyber Conflict (Tallinn: NATO CCD COE Publications, 2020), 129–155: https://ccdcoe.org/uploads/2020/05/CyCon_2020_8_Lilly_Cheravitch.pdf

130. Anthony Craig and Brandon Valeriano, "Conceptualizing Cyber Arms Races," in Proceedings of the 8th International Conference on Cyber Conflict, ed. N.Pissanidis, H.Rõigas, and M.Veenendaal (Tallinn: NATO CCD COE Publications, 2016), 141–158: https://ccdcoe.org/uploads/2018/10/Art-10-Conceptualising-Cyber-Arms-Races.pdf

131. See discussion for example in Ben Buchanan, *The Hacker and the State: Cyber Attacks and the New Normal of Geopolitics* (Cambridge, MA: Harvard University Press, 2020).

132. Eric Rosenbaum, "Iran is 'leapfrogging our defenses,'" CNBC, November 18, 2021: https://www.cnbc.com/2021/11/18/iran-leapfrogging-our-defenses-in-cyber-war-hacking-expert-mandia-.html. See also Collin Anderson and Karim Sadjadpour, "Iran's Cyber Threat: Espionage, Sabotage, and Revenge," *Carnegie Endowment for International Peace*, January 4, 2018: https://carnegieendowment.org/2018/01/04/iran-target-and-perpetrator-pub-75139

133. For more on this point, see Rebecca Slayton, "What Is the Cyber Offense-Defense Balance? Conceptions, Causes, and Assessment," *International Security* 41, no. 3 (2017): 72–109, https://doi.org/10.1162/ISEC_a_00267

134. For a history of arguments against defenses, see Rebecca Slayton, *Arguments that Count: Physics, Computing, and Missile Defense, 1949–2012* (Cambridge, MA: The MIT Press, 2013).

135. For more on this classification of cyber operations, see Thomas Rid, "Cyber War Will Not Take Place," *Journal of Strategic Studies* 35, no. 1 (2012): 5–32, DOI: 10.1080/01402390.2011.608939.

Part III

Infrastructures

7

Cyber Entanglement and the Stability of the Contemporary Rules-Based Global Order

Mark A. Raymond

This chapter examines the rapid emergence and expansion of the global cyber regime complex. It places particular emphasis on the role of the Internet of Things (IoT) in entangling the internet with an array of other issue-areas, and thus in generating potentially problematic interactions among the legacy internet governance regime, a host of other international regimes, and with domestic governance arrangements in highly networked countries. While the IoT exacerbates existing trends and underlying problems more than it creates them, it remains one of the most important drivers of change in this area, and one that has been underappreciated relative to issues such as social media disinformation. I use the IoT here to illustrate a larger argument about the effects of internet technologies on the stability of the international system.

The chapter argues that alongside the rapid penetration of the internet, we are seeing the metastasization of the global cyber regime complex, or the set of partially overlapping institutions and governance arrangements for cyberspace.[1] I use the word "metastasization" to convey three essential characteristics of the way that the internet and its legacy governance arrangements are becoming entangled with other institutions and governance arrangements in almost every country, and in almost every global issue-area. First, this entanglement is genuinely systemic, in that there is virtually no part of the international system that will remain untouched. Second, this growth is rapid and relatively unplanned from the perspective of the systems it affects, unfolding according to market-based and technical logics that are distinct from the core logics of diplomacy, international law, and international relations. Third, it is an enormously consequential development with the potential to fundamentally transform the operation and even the viability of those systems and arrangements.

As a result of this ongoing metastasization process, the viability of a variety of international regimes and domestic governance arrangements will increasingly depend on the effectiveness and legitimacy of the global cyber regime complex with which they are becoming inextricably entangled. The chapter briefly illustrates several examples of such entanglements across an array of distinct issue-areas. The chapter discusses these developments in light of their effects on the stability of the rules-based international order, identifying four challenges for international order exacerbated by the mass adoption of IoT systems and the continued diffusion of internet technologies more generally: an increased number and range of coordination problems with significant distributional implications; the potential for increased enforcement problems, mainly arising from a sharply increased number of relevant actors; problems of rule interpretation and application arising from the combination of complex, novel issues with multiple simultaneously valid rule sets; and challenges to maintaining democratic control and accountability over key domestic political issues subject to increasingly transnational and polycentric control. Under such conditions, cyber stability is not simply a matter of maintaining technical interoperability or reliability, or even the viability of international governance arrangements essential to cyberspace. Rather, the simultaneous ongoing development of internet technologies and related governance arrangements have crucial implications for the stability of rules-based international order. The chapter concludes by making the case for treating this regime complex as "critical governance infrastructure." Just as electric grids, water systems, and financial systems are systemically important components of modern societies, the global cyber regime complex is rapidly acquiring a singular importance as a condition of possibility for the remainder of the present system of rules-based global order and global governance.

IR literature has been concerned with international regimes for roughly forty years. This literature defines regimes as sets of "implicit or explicit principles, norms, rules and decision-making procedures around which actors' expectations converge in a given area of international relations."[2] For institutionalist scholars, these regimes shape the payoffs and incentives available to rational state actors seeking to achieve joint gains in an anarchic international system, and thus condition the behavior of those actors. For constructivists, regimes exert additional kinds of effects. They shape the choices actors see as appropriate, and rule certain options in or out based on a logic of appropriateness.[3] They also constitute the ways that actors see themselves and the world around them, exerting what Barnett and Duvall[4] call productive power. They do this in part by constituting various social practices,[5] including social practices pertaining to making, applying, and interpreting global rules.[6]

Early scholarship typically treated issue-specific international regimes as analytically distinct. For example, the international trade regime could be studied independently of the international human rights regime and the international environmental regime. Raustiala and Victor observed that the increasing institutional density of the international system entailed the emergence of regime complexes. They defined a regime complex as "a collective of partially overlapping and nonhierarchical regimes."[7] This observation was picked up by a range of scholars, examining a variety of issue-areas including plant genetic resources,[8] refugees,[9] climate governance,[10] energy,[11] and cyberspace.[12] The central insight of the regime complex literature is that the overlapping regimes that constitute a particular regime complex generate problematic interactions[13] as a result of "legal inconsistencies" that are created because "the rules in one regime are rarely coordinated closely with overlapping rules in related regimes."[14] This insight is consistent with constructivist work that starts from the premise that rules are a ubiquitous feature of social life and that demonstrates how the simultaneous existence of multiple overlapping valid rule sets shapes and regulates social interaction.[15]

The regime complex literature has thus far focused primarily on demonstrating the utility of the concept and on documenting individual cases. Realizing the promise of the concept for IR theory requires the investigation of processes of regime complex formation, as well as the dynamics and morphology of existing regime complexes. It is also essential to investigate the implications of increasing institutional density and regime complex formation for the operation and future trajectory of contemporary rules-based global order, including for the stability of that order. This chapter takes important preliminary steps in both of these directions.

It does so by examining the rapid emergence and expansion of the global cyber regime complex.[16] Rather than duplicating existing literature on internet governance,[17] I emphasize one particular contemporary trend within this regime complex with far-reaching and potentially transformative implications: the development and widespread deployment of a vast number of internet-connected devices in contexts well beyond traditional networked computing applications. This trend is colloquially referred to as IoT. Cisco, a leading global manufacturer of networking equipment, estimates that by 2023, there will be 29.3 billion networked devices and that 50 percent of global network connections will be machine-to-machine (M2M) connections.[18] These devices, and the associated growth of M2M communication, will further change the nature of the internet from a global communications facility to a means of control.[19] Internet-connected sensors and control devices will facilitate the remote monitoring and operation of physical devices and systems in real time and at large scale. In combination with expected advances in artificial intelligence and machine learning, it is anticipated that these monitoring and control applications of IoT systems will be accomplished with high levels of automation and relatively little direct human intervention.

The mass adoption of IoT systems is often thought of in terms of consumer products and services, but these systems will be as, or more, important in the context of industry and manufacturing, as well as in municipal infrastructure and the public sector more broadly. Notwithstanding the close relationship between IoT systems and the physical world, it is essential to note that there are crucial public policy concerns associated with these technologies that cannot be addressed by any single firm or country, no matter how powerful.[20] For example, many IoT products are likely to be produced by a small number of large firms located in Western countries; however, these same products are likely to be widely exported and operated in various legal jurisdictions around the world. As more and more countries adopt consumer privacy laws, lawful access statutes providing for law enforcement access to encrypted communications, and other similar legal and regulatory instruments, manufacturers and operators of IoT systems are likely to face significant compliance problems. In some cases, it may be impossible to simultaneously comply with relevant local laws and regulations in all jurisdictions. This problem is not unique to IoT systems, of course, but the scale of these technologies and the ways in which they will make data collection more pervasive and remote control of our physical world more common suggest that the mass adoption of IoT systems will effectively make the internet part of virtually every aspect of our economic, social, and political lives.

One important implication of this transition, from an internet dominated by communications to one in which remote sensing and control applications are pervasive and critically important, is that every part of human life will be increasingly dependent on internet connectivity. It follows from this that every aspect of governance will increasingly confront issues arising from and associated with internet policy. That is, the mass adoption of IoT systems should be expected to entangle the legacy internet governance regime with virtually every other international regime and with critical domestic institutions and governance processes.

This entanglement will be uneven in several respects. First, it will be uneven in temporal terms across different issue-areas and geographies. Industries experiencing the greatest potential benefits will likely adopt these systems most quickly, and adoption will likely be most rapid in advanced industrial democracies. Other factors affecting the speed, extent, and intensity of IoT adoption include the concentration of ownership in a particular industrial sector, and the perceived security of the technology itself. In the public sector, IoT adoption may be driven by potential environmental and health benefits associated with these technologies, as well as by the potential for gains in security provision. On the other hand, adoption may be curtailed in critical infrastructure sectors if geopolitical tensions create perceptions that available sources of supply for particular IoT systems are vulnerable to politically motivated interference or manipulation, or if the technologies themselves or the business practices of firms in the sector create concerns about negative effects on human rights. Despite the likely uneven adoption of IoT systems, over the medium to long term it seems virtually certain that the technology itself will be integrated into almost all major issue-areas currently governed by international regimes, as well as into a wide range of domestic public policy concerns. This uneven integration will pose challenges for both the stability of the internet and the stability of the international system.

The next section of the chapter examines the ways in which mass adoption of IoT systems will create overlaps and problematic interactions among the legacy internet governance regime on the one hand, and other international regimes, domestic institutions, and governance processes on the other hand. The metastasization of the global cyber regime complex will entangle vastly different cultures and modes of governance. The highly privatized and some-times multistakeholder governance arrangements typical of the legacy inter-net governance regime will be brought into close and regular contact both with multilateral governance modalities typical in international regimes and with various kinds of domestic governance modalities employed by individual states.[21] The result will be a global cyber regime complex characterized by per-vasive multilevel,[22] polycentric,[23] and multistakeholder[24] governance operated by a highly diverse group of participants with little experience in such social settings. The section then explores ways that this particular metastasization of the global cyber regime complex will make the viability of legacy international regimes and domestic governance arrangements dependent on the effective-ness and legitimacy of the enlarged and empowered global cyber regime com-plex that will emerge alongside the mass adoption of IoT systems. The chapter concludes by examining the implications of this scenario for the global cyber regime complex and for the stability of the contemporary rules-based global order writ large.

The Metastasization of the Global Cyber Regime Complex

I argued in the previous section that the mass global adoption of IoT systems will entangle the legacy internet governance regime with other international regimes and with domestic institutions and governance processes. That is, the adoption of IoT systems will drive what I refer to as the metastasization of the global cyber regime complex. As outlined above, the concept of a regime complex recognized that the growing institutional density of the international system made it antiquated and indefensible to maintain the previous approach of treating governance arrangements for specific issue-areas as analytically distinct. Grasping the reality of contemporary global internet and cyber security governance required understanding the legacy internet governance regime in the broader context of what Nye called the regime complex for global cyber activities, which included an array of actors, institutions, and processes for management of the international economy, human rights, and international security.[25]

My analysis here carries this argument one step further. The mass global adoption of IoT systems, and other drivers of internet adoption including continued growth in the global internet user base (which is still only slightly more than half the planet's population), will implicate at least parts of the global cyber regime complex in virtually every other international regime, as well as in the domestic governance arrangements of every state on the planet. The 2021 agreement among major economies on coordinating their corporate tax policies reflects the development not only of international trade and transportation, which have been evident for more than a century, but of a new level of economic integration enabled by internet technologies.[26]

One crucial mechanism for this process of metastasization will be the development, deployment, and operation of automated remote sensing and control systems that will collect vast amounts of data and that will exert meaningful control over important elements of individuals' daily lives. The development, deployment, and operation of such IoT systems at transnational scale will create situations in which elements of the legacy internet governance regime will apply much more broadly than they have in the past. As such, the legacy internet governance regime will overlap with many more international regimes and with many more domestic (national and subnational) legal and regulatory frameworks. These encounters between previously separate rule sets and governance processes will raise novel questions of how to resolve actual and potential conflicts. Such conflicts include whether to adopt the rules and norms associated with the global internet governance regime or with the relevant other international regime and/or domestic governance arrangement, and how to interpret and apply these distinct rule sets in combination with each other. They also include jurisdictional or competence conflicts between authorities from these disparate issue-areas that may wish to engage in oversight or enforcement actions. Finally, such conflicts include procedural disputes about how to handle or resolve incompatible rule sets drawn from different governance domains. All of these kinds of conflicts currently exist within the global cyber regime complex (as well as in other regime complexes), but in a world of pervasive IoT systems they will be more common and will apply to many more aspects of human social, political, and economic life. They will also tend to extend downward from the international system to the state and sub-state levels with much greater frequency than in the past, in part because of the local and material nature of IoT systems. The pervasive adoption of IoT systems will therefore increase the scale, scope, and complexity of the global cyber regime complex, and amplify and exacerbate a range of existing challenges for global and national governance.

One example of such complexity arises from concerns about supply-chain cyber security. Such concerns presently exist mainly with respect to hardware and software for 5G mobile broadband networks and sensitive government computer networks. The adoption and utilization of national security exceptions to international trade rules in the information technology sector would become a far larger concern in a world in which internet connectivity is present in a wide range of consumer products, industrial equipment, infrastructure, and other sectors. Managing these challenges will bring the global cyber regime complex into sustained contact both with the international trade regime more broadly and with the regime for managing international security affairs.

Another example arises from conflicts between the international trade regime and the international human rights regime. Different approaches to privacy protection led to the replacement of the United States–European Union Safe Harbor agreement with the Privacy Shield framework, which governs the conditions under which firms are permitted to transfer consumer data between legal jurisdictions. The future of the Privacy Shield agreement remains in doubt due to European concerns about American compliance.[27] The challenge in reconciling human rights and international trade concerns within the global cyber regime complex is underlined by the difficulty the United States and EU have experienced in creating a bilateral agreement in a context where a relatively limited number of firms (compared to the overall size of their economies) are affected. The mass global deployment of IoT systems will exacerbate these issues by affecting more firms, and by creating governance concerns around the deployment and operation of such systems that affect additional states.

Privacy and human rights concerns are not limited to the context of intra-firm transnational data transfers. Similar issues should be expected to arise with respect to secondary and tertiary markets in data, which will grow considerably as the volume of data collected is increased by the adoption of IoT systems.

European efforts to enforce the "right to be forgotten" on a global basis[28] will be particularly challenging in the context of mass IoT adoption if they are held to extend not only to publicly searchable information on the World Wide Web but also to data retained by firms and perhaps even civic authorities in other jurisdictions. Broadly, public demands for users to have more knowledge of, and control over, who possesses what kinds of data about them will challenge fundamental aspects of the internet economy, which Shoshana Zuboff has aptly described as "surveillance capitalism."[29]

The mass adoption of IoT systems also exacerbates the potential for conflict between the global environmental regime complex, the global cyber regime complex, and regimes for international security and international human rights. The deployment of IoT sensors offers potential for improving monitoring of global environmental conditions, such as greenhouse gases, air and water pollution, and other key indicators. However, these sensors may inadvertently collect data about individuals and about state military activities that could be utilized in ways that undermine human security and human rights, as well as international security. The deployment and operation of these systems would require state agencies and non-governmental organizations in the environmental protection sector to deal with concerns about data privacy and security, and other related policies with which they have little expertise, thereby enhancing the potential for inadvertent harms.

A final example arises from the intersection of the global cyber regime complex with the law of armed conflict and a loosely organized set of institutions and governance mechanisms for international security. The United Nations General Assembly's First Committee has dealt with issues relating to the state military use of information and communications technologies (ICTs) since the late 1990s. In 2013, the committee's Group of Governmental Experts (GGE) process issued a consensus report endorsed by a group of states that included all permanent members of the Security Council. This report included a candidate norm against the targeting of critical infrastructure in peacetime.[30] While this candidate norm (reiterated and expanded in the 2015 GGE report) represents an important step forward, it should be noted that Russia is believed to have conducted attacks against the Ukrainian electrical sector.[31] The US position is that these attacks did not violate the candidate GGE norm since they took place during a period of conflict between Russia and Ukraine. For its part, Russia has denied responsibility for the attacks.[32] The crucial point for the purpose of this chapter is that the candidate norm against targeting critical infrastructure during peacetime is of limited utility if states are willing to violate it and/or able to avoid credible attribution of the attacks. It is also of limited utility in the event of open military conflict. And, finally, it is important to note that both of these problems are exacerbated by the mass adoption of IoT systems, which will rapidly and significantly increase the size and significance of the attack surface, especially as IoT systems are adopted within critical infrastructure sectors ranging from energy, water, financial services, and other vital applications.

These kinds of situations associated with the mass global adoption of IoT systems cause at least four distinct kinds of difficulties for the global cyber regime complex and its component regimes and actors. First, they extend the range of issues on which global policy coordination is required. The resulting coordination problems are rendered more difficult to resolve by the presence of multiple equilibria with varied distributional consequences.[33] This kind of distributional problem is further exacerbated by the rapidly growing number of players involved[34] as a result of the diffusion of IoT systems across the globe and throughout the economy and by the varied conceptions of substantive and procedural justice held by those actors.[35]

Second, the growing number of actors creates other kinds of difficulties in situations characterized by enforcement problems, or incentives to defect.[36] Monitoring and ensuring the compliance of large numbers of actors involves significant transaction costs, particularly in an environment where some kinds of violations can be carried out anonymously. Enforcement efforts will also likely be complicated by ambiguities about jurisdiction, especially in cases where multiple sets of rules associated with different organizations and actors at different levels of analysis may be perceived as relevant. Here, the decentralization of governance creates difficulties for enforcement that are partially independent of the number of actors.[37]

Third, the necessity of interpreting and applying multiple sets of loosely related and partially overlapping rules to relatively novel empirical cases creates difficulties beyond those relating to determining who is authorized to enforce which set(s) of rules. In particular, the metastasization of the global cyber regime complex creates myriad opportunities for disputes about how a particular rule should be applied, which of multiple possible rules should be applied in a given case, and how to resolve conflicting rules applicable to the same issue. The final kind of difficulty of rule interpretation and application is likely to be particularly contentious when the conflicting rules originate in different international regimes and/or in different sovereign states. While these difficulties of interpretation and application are by no means limited to the global cyber regime complex or the mass adoption of IoT systems,[38] they are particularly important in this context given the large number of actors and the decentralized nature of governance, as well as the diversity of cultural perspectives on how to legitimately conduct social practices of rulemaking. In cases where participants have divergent views on practices of rulemaking, the ability to create and operate shared governance enterprises is limited.[39]

Fourth, the metastasization of the global cyber regime complex creates and exacerbates difficulties relating to democratic control and accountability. In a decentralized governance landscape, individual states are likely to make different choices about how to address issues such as antitrust regulation, encryption policy, net neutrality, and other matters. Power inequalities among states will mean that larger jurisdictions are likely to be much more able to enforce their policy preferences on large global technology firms, while smaller jurisdictions will effectively be rule-takers. Given global corporate concentration in many aspects of the internet economy, this means that even not so small states will exercise little effective control over technology policy matters that will shape the conditions of possibility not only for their economies but also for their public spheres – which have increasingly migrated to privately-owned online platforms. Parliaments in the United Kingdom and Canada have struggled to secure testimony from Facebook founder Mark Zuckerberg, for example. This difficulty has led parliamentarians to band together transnationally in efforts to exercise their oversight roles, so far without success.[40] It is striking that two G7 economies are unable to secure testimony from a firm with a major role in their domestic information ecosystems. Even aside from issues of oligopolistic market structure, some jurisdictions have disproportionate power in this regard as a result of their critical positionality in terms of physical internet infrastructure.[41] American policy on net neutrality has global importance in an internet landscape where, by some estimates, more than half of all internet routes originating in other countries pass through the United States.[42] This position of network centrality means that internet providers in other countries may be forced to seek transit arrangements with American network operators that guarantee top-priority treatment, or else be relegated to providing lower-quality internet service to their own customers due to the traffic management practices and pricing structures of American firms. American privacy policies have similar global implications, though in many respects American policy here results in higher protection for non-American users than their own governments would be likely to provide. While researchers have begun to develop "Region-Aware-Networking" tools to give users at least a semblance of control over the jurisdictions through which their data is routed, it is unclear whether these kinds of technical workarounds are sufficient to provide the level of democratic control and accountability citizens will prefer. People in countries other than the United States, for example, face limited options in the event that they prefer not to have their data routed through American infrastructure. Individual users are also likely to be limited by the routing control options offered by major global telecommunications providers, which may fall short of what is technologically possible. And addressing routing issues does nothing to prevent the further resale or transfer of accumulated data, including about people's internet history. It is also unclear whether these kinds of tools will scale well enough to permit the global internet to function as well as it currently does. These tools could also be used in conjunction with data localization requirements and other legislative initiatives to effectively fragment the internet and push global internet governance toward what Demchak and Dombrowski provocatively termed cyber Westphalia.[43]

At a macro level, these four kinds of challenges associated with the mass global adoption of IoT systems arise because this technological diffusion entangles a vast array of different cultures, institutions, processes, and modalities of governance. It brings the highly privatized[44] and sometimes multistakeholder[45] legacy internet governance regime into persistent contact both with other multilateral[46] regimes and also with a variety of democratic, authoritarian, and hybrid regime types for domestic politics and governance.[47] The result is a substantially enlarged global cyber regime complex that is difficult to disentangle from any particular area of global or domestic governance. As such, the effect of the mass global adoption of IoT systems is likely to be tantamount to the transformation of all governance arrangements into highly complex, multi-level, polycentric, and multistakeholder governance arrangements.

Such an outcome would have a further consequence worth noting. Namely, it would make the viability of legacy international regimes and of domestic governance arrangements (at least in highly networked societies) partially dependent on the effectiveness and legitimacy of the enlarged and empowered global cyber regime complex. This is likely to be problematic given that the complexity of the global cyber regime complex is itself likely to increase the odds of governance failures of various kinds, and given the necessity of a relatively significant level of global coordination on internet and cyber security governance. The mass global adoption of the internet, and especially IoT systems, raises difficult and yet largely unavoidable problems for which the international community presently lacks viable solutions. In the next section of the chapter, I discuss the implications of this scenario for global governance and for the contemporary rules-based global order.

The Global Cyber Regime Complex and the Stability of the Contemporary Rules-Based Global Order

The idea that the cyber domain, or internet technologies more generally, may affect international relations is hardly novel. However, there is also no

clear consensus about the nature and extent of any such effects. Demchak and
Dombrowski argued that the growing importance of the cyber domain would
effectively compel the creation of "cyber borders."[48] In contrast, Mueller has
argued that the nature of the technology renders such developments both
impractical and unwise.[49]

Most studies focus on the relationship between the state military use of
information technology and patterns of war and peace, which have been central concerns for IR scholars since the founding of the field. As I will argue
below, the focus on strategic military stability is myopic and risks occluding
important effects of the global adoption of internet technologies on the stability of the international system, like the ones outlined in the previous section
of this chapter. Even within this community, however, assessments differ –
including about how to define strategic military stability. Rovner and Moore
argue that the technical stability created by decentralized, redundant internet
architecture creates conditions in which hegemons can exploit their asymmetric advantages by playing offense without risking systemic instability.[50] This
assessment is in line with the desire within the American military and national
security community to adopt a more offensive posture in the cyber domain,
under the aegis of terms like persistent engagement.[51] Similarly, Borghard and
Lonergan suggest that escalation risks in the cyber domain are exaggerated.[52]

Not all analyses conclude that offense is required or feasible. Schneider
argues that new technologies for warfare can create a capability/vulnerability
paradox, in which countries that invest heavily in the technology experience
gains in relative power but also a heightened state of vulnerability that can
create first-strike incentives on both sides of a potential conflict.[53] Healey wor-
ries that proponents of persistent engagement and other more offense-oriented
approaches overlook the associated downside risks.[54] Nye and Slayton each
question a key premise of the argument for persistent engagement, seeking to
demonstrate that there are reasons to expect deterrence can be an important
part of an overall cyber security strategy and that offense dominance is less
certain than has been claimed.[55]

It is unlikely that something as complex as the set of technologies, practices,
and policies that collectively comprise the cyber domain will have a straightforward, easily discernible effect on the stability of the international system.
This is especially true given uncertainty about whether that stability should be
defined in terms of the likelihood of crisis escalation, the propensity for war
initiation, the severity of hostilities' effects on associated systems, or on some
combination of these and other factors. Given these uncertainties, the complexity of the cyber domain more generally, and the entanglement of the cyber
domain with nuclear command and control systems,[56] extreme caution should

be exercised in accepting and acting upon arguments for making use of offensive cyber capabilities. Mass adoption of IoT systems, and the concomitant metastasization of the global cyber regime complex, only increases the importance of such caution. It does so primarily by augmenting the potential for significant unintended consequences arising from state military use of information technologies on other socio-technical systems, as well as by increasing the possibility that interaction with other such systems may negatively affect critical military systems – such as those for the command and control of nuclear weapons.

Despite their clear importance, however, focus on questions of strategic military stability has tended to obscure other crucial dimensions of the relationship between the cyber domain on the one hand, and the international system or the contemporary rules-based global order on the other hand. The study of international organizations and regimes, in particular, has tended to be cantoned separately from the study of power politics and of the international system's structure. This is odd, given that constructivists and institutionalists have demonstrated that these organizations and regimes, and the deeper social structures that constitute them,[57] are in fact fundamental to and constitutive of the more surface-level questions addressed by the majority of the literature on the international system. Recognizing this, Goddard and Nexon articulated a framework for the study of power politics that explicitly treats contestation of rules and institutions in social settings as power political in nature, and therefore deserving of treatment alongside traditional questions in this literature, such as the issues of strategic military stability discussed previously in this section.[58] More recently, scholarship on the politics of hegemonic orders has begun to deliver on the promise of this analytical move. Internet and cyber security governance is the clearest contemporary example of the ways in which rulemaking, interpretation, and application are explicitly power political activities of the highest significance for the future trajectory of the international system.

Treating the international system in broader terms than simply its strategic military dimension expands the chessboard among major states to include cyber norms and diplomacy, as well as the relationship between ICTs and the global economy. Each of these are crucial aspects of power political competition in the twenty-first century but have not yet been fully considered by IR literature on the relationship between the cyber domain and the international system. Further, the increasing entanglement of cyber issues with every part of human society means that treating these dimensions of the international system in isolation will be less analytically defensible than in the past. Maintaining any specific rules-based global order requires far more than simply avoiding large-scale war. This is particularly true for an order like the current one that is predicated on the coexistence of a system of sovereign states with a complex global economy that includes highly transnational supply chains, relatively high capital mobility, and at least a modicum of labour mobility. The contemporary rules-based global order also depends on an architecture of international organizations and multistakeholder governance arrangements for managing shared global challenges such as climate change and global public health, in addition to maintaining the interoperability and stability of the internet and related technologies. Utilization of national security exceptions to international trade rules has clear potential to disrupt crucial global supply chains and perhaps set off trade wars that could undermine the overall health of the global economy and thus of the contemporary rules-based global order. Likewise, efforts to impose rules on network operators that enable monitoring for national security purposes are in tension with the international human rights regime, which has affirmed privacy as a technologically neutral right. Finally, efforts to shape technological standards and the broader digital economy are part of a status competition in the international system that states appear to believe will pay dividends in terms of soft power and broader global leadership. While these are not purely IoT issues, IoT systems have clear and important implications for each.

The metastasization of the global cyber regime complex should be expected to have at least two kinds of broad effects on the stability of the international system. First, it will substantially increase the degree of complexity facing policymakers on virtually every issue and at every level of analysis from local to global. This increase in complexity is likely to decrease the effectiveness of governance overall and may lead to governance failures that reverberate and cause wider effects than they would have done previously. In turn, such decreases in effectiveness and larger disruptions should be expected to have corrosive effects on perceptions of legitimacy. Second, there will also be a more direct negative effect on governance legitimacy arising from the collision of different views about who is entitled to govern and how they should do so. The metastasization of the global cyber regime complex creates new channels, and widens existing channels, by which the decisions made by one actor can potentially affect conditions experienced by other actors. This problem of interdependence is hardly unique to the cyber domain,[59] but the affordances of the technology create challenges in terms of speed and scale for the transmission of such effects. Effectively, the mass adoption of the internet and of cyberphysical systems and the metastasization of the associated regime complex will make externalities arising from everyday governance both more common and more consequential.[60] This should be expected to lead to additional disputes among actors, or a higher base level of friction in the international system. A world in which governance is less effective, less legitimate, and more contested should be expected to be less stable, especially because the international system generally lacks clear arrangements or procedures for handling disputes about who governs and how they should do so on the scale that will be required by mass adoption of these technologies.

The Global Cyber Regime Complex as Critical Governance Infrastructure for the Contemporary Rules-Based Global Order

The importance of protecting critical infrastructure from cyber security threats is widely recognized,[61] as are the challenges associated with the integration of IoT systems in critical infrastructure contexts.[62] The United States Department of Homeland Security already recognizes both the information technology and communications sectors as critical infrastructure in their own right, in large part because other critical infrastructure sectors are dependent upon them.[63] However, the analysis presented in this chapter suggests a further sense in which we need to think more broadly about the notion of critical infrastructure.

In particular, the mass adoption of IoT systems and the associated metastasization of the global cyber regime complex requires treating that regime complex as critical governance infrastructure. The United States Department of Homeland Security defines critical infrastructure as:

> Assets, systems, and networks, whether physical or virtual that are considered so vital to the United States that their incapacitation or destruction would have a debilitating effect on security, national economic security, national public health or safety, or any combination thereof.[64]

This national level definition can easily be repurposed to think more generically about critical infrastructure. As IoT systems are adopted more widely, the global cyber regime complex will take on this kind of importance because it will become a condition of possibility not only for the continued operation of the internet but also, by extension, for the operation of all systems that are highly integrated with internet technologies and – crucially – for the governance of any issue-areas that incorporate high degrees of internet connectivity.

The combination of pervasive IoT systems and the concomitant metastasization of the global cyber regime complex pushes the international system toward a state in which it has a single point of failure – a design in which that kind of failure prevents the entire system from operating. While designs with single points of failure are never desirable, this particular scenario is doubly undesirable because the global cyber regime complex – especially in the metastasized form envisioned in this chapter – is relatively likely to fail, for several reasons. The large, and rapidly growing, number of players poses a problem by itself.[65] This problem is compounded by participants' diverse views of legitimate practices of rulemaking.[66] Finnemore and Hollis correctly point out that cyber norms, and by extension cyber governance, must be understood in process terms rather than as an output.[67] But managing processes, and maintaining shared agreement on the legitimacy of those processes, is extremely difficult without agreement on how to do so. And insofar as there is agreement on legitimate governance procedures for cyberspace, it appears that the trend is toward nationalizing governance. But this is inherently complicated given the global nature of the technology itself, and the potential for negative externalities arising from attempts to govern aspects of the global internet at the national or subnational level.[68] Even more worrisome, empirical studies of actors motivated by justice concerns suggests that such actors are prone to fight harder and with less restraint,[69] and that those agreements perceived as unjust are less likely to last.[70] To the extent that actors in the cyber domain frame their disputes in justice terms and/or pursue maximalist positions, they are more likely to create lasting conflicts.[71] The prevalence of framing the internet as a source of threat is indicative of these kinds of dynamics, as are arguments downplaying the risks of conflict in and over the cyber domain.[72] Finally, such disputes are taking place in the context of a relative lack of knowledge about the consequences of internet technologies for global governance, and a relative lack of knowledge about how to operate anything like the global cyber regime complex.

This analysis suggests that the mass global adoption of IoT systems should be understood as a risk not only to the stability and interoperability of the global internet, but also as a systemic risk to the broader system of global – and even domestic – governance. Criticism of global technology firms and of internet governance has tended to focus on factors like the role of these firms in exacerbating economic inequality, undermining human rights, enabling authoritarianism, and stoking political division.[73] I am not suggesting that such risks are unimportant. In fact, I believe that further research should examine the ways in which these better-known risks interact with the additional source of systemic risk I have identified in this chapter. For instance, governance failure could exacerbate inequality, since those with greater resources are better able to absorb unanticipated crises or exogenous shocks. Governance failure may also encourage authoritarian populisms by creating a perception that the contemporary rules-based global order has not adequately delivered on its promises and may thereby exacerbate human rights violations. And governments may resort to othering strategies in an attempt to deflect blame for their inability to govern effectively in a complex, multilevel, polycentric, multistakeholder institutional landscape where participants struggle to agree on ways to manage a vast number of entanglements among legacy international regimes and domestic governance arrangements. In short, mass global adoption of IoT systems will exacerbate existing trends and pose a fundamental challenge to existing practices of global governance.[74] Unfortunately, this challenge is looming at a time when the contemporary rules-based global order has already been weakened.

Treating the global cyber regime complex as critical governance infrastructure suggests two key priorities for dealing with the challenges to international system stability that I have identified in this chapter. First, it directs attention to key gaps in existing capacity, while the notion of infrastructure also makes clear that these gaps are appropriately remedied by construction efforts to fill them. Without downplaying the importance of the continuing digital divide in terms of quantity and quality of physical internet infrastructure, my aim here is to point out an equally pressing need for constructing additional governance infrastructure. Among the highest priorities for new and expanded governance infrastructure is to develop rules, institutions, and practices for settling disputes about how to resolve differing interpretations of how to deal with governance challenges arising from the internet and from cyber-physical systems, particularly where these technologies and associated decentralized governance efforts create externalities for other parties. Far from affecting only the information technology sector itself, these disputes already encompass a huge range of public issues, ranging from public safety to law enforcement investigation, taxation, media content governance, intellectual property rights, consumer protection, and more. What were formerly domestic issues in individual countries will increasingly affect firms, governments, and even individuals in other states. These effects will occur not only when those firms or individuals travel or do business in other countries, but often in the course of their normal domestic lives. Handling these kinds of disputes requires thinking far beyond traditional diplomacy as a means of dispute resolution, even though foreign ministries and international organizations are likely to be involved as means of last resort for the most serious disputes.

Finally, treating the global cyber regime complex as critical governance infrastructure highlights the need to treat the global cyber regime complex with considerable caution. The discourse around critical infrastructure emphasizes, rightfully, the importance of its protection. Placing the global cyber regime complex in this category makes clear that states, as public authorities, have an important stake in these rules, institutions, and practices. However, it makes equally clear that states have obligations to their citizens and to their fellow states to refrain from taking actions that place shared critical governance infrastructure in jeopardy. It demands that states recognize more completely than many have to date that military conflict is not the only way that their actions in the cyber domain can negatively affect the stability of the international system or undermine the operation of the contemporary rules-based global order. Responsible state behavior in cyberspace requires not only a considerable degree of restraint in the military and espionage uses of information technology, but also a more robust, good-faith engagement in basic tasks of shared governance and peaceful dispute resolution.

Notes

1. Kal Raustiala and David G. Victor, "The Regime Complex for Plant Genetic Resources," *International Organization* 58, no. 2 (2004): 277–309; Joseph S. Nye, *The Regime Complex for Managing Global Cyber Activities* (Centre for International Governance Innovation, 2014).

2. Stephen D. Krasner, "Structural Causes and Regime Consequences: Regimes as Intervening Variables," *International Organization* 36, no. 2 (1982): 185–205.

3. Martha Finnemore and Kathryn Sikkink, "International Norm Dynamics and Political Change," *International Organization* 52, no. 4 (1998): 887–917.

4. Michael Barnett and Raymond Duvall, "Power in International Politics," *International Organization* 59, no. 1 (2005): 39–75.

5. Vincent Pouliot and Jean-Philippe Thérien, "Global Governance in Practice," *Global Policy* 9, no. 2 (2018): 163–172.

6. Wayne Sandholtz, "Dynamics of International Norm Change: Rules against Wartime Plunder," *European Journal of International Relations* 14, no. 1 (2008): 101–131; Mark Raymond, *Social Practices of Rule-Making in World Politics* (New York: Oxford University Press, 2019).

7. Raustiala and Victor, "The Regime Complex for Plant Genetic Resources," 277.

8. Ibid.

9. Alexander Betts, "The Refugee Regime Complex," *Refugee Survey Quarterly* 29, no. 1 (2010): 12–37.

10. Robert O. Keohane and David G. Victor, "The Regime Complex for Climate Change," *Perspectives on Politics* 9, no. 1 (2011): 7–23.

11. Jeff D. Colgan et al., "Punctuated Equilibrium in the Energy Regime Complex," *Review of International Organizations* 7, no. 2 (2012): 117–143.

12. Nye, *The Regime Complex for Managing Global Cyber Activities*.

13. Amandine Orsini, Jean Frédéric Morin, and Oran Young, "Regime

Complexes: A Buzz, a Boom, or a Boost for Global Governance?," *Global Governance: A Review of Multilateralism and International Organizations* 19, no. 1 (2013): 27–39, 29.

14. Raustiala and Victor, "The Regime Complex for Plant Genetic Resources," 277.
15. Nicholas Greenwood Onuf, *World of Our Making: Rules and Rule in Social Theory and International Relations* (Columbia: University of South Carolina Press, 1989); Wayne Sandholtz, "Dynamics of International Norm Change: Rules against Wartime Plunder," *European Journal of International Relations* 14, no. 1 (2008): 101–131; Mark Raymond, *Social Practices of Rule-Making in World Politics* (New York: Oxford University Press, 2019).
16. Nye, *The Regime Complex for Managing Global Cyber Activities*.
17. See for example Laura DeNardis, *The Global War for Internet Governance* (New Haven, CT: Yale University Press, 2014); Mark Raymond and Laura DeNardis, "Multistakeholderism: Anatomy of an Inchoate Global Institution," *International Theory* 7, no. 3 (2015): 572–616; Roxana Radu, *Negotiating Internet Governance* (Oxford: Oxford University Press, 2019).
18. Cisco, "Cisco Annual Internet Report (2018–2023) White Paper," 2020: https://www.cisco.com/c/en/us/solutions/collateral/executive-perspectives/annual-internet-report/white-paper-c11-741490.html
19. Laura DeNardis, *The Internet in Everything: Freedom and Security in a World with No Off Switch* (New Haven, CT: Yale University Press, 2020).
20. Raymond and DeNardis, "Multistakeholderism: Anatomy of an Inchoate Global Institution."
21. Ibid.
22. Liesbet Hooghe and Gary Marks, "Unraveling the Central State, but How? Types of Multi-Level Governance," *American Political Science Review* 97, no. 2 (2013): 233–243.
23. Elinor Ostrom, "Beyond Markets and States: Polycentric Governance of Complex Economic Systems," *American Economic Review* 100, no. 3 (2010): 641–672.
24. Raymond and DeNardis, "Multistakeholderism: Anatomy of an Inchoate Global Institution."
25. Nye, *The Regime Complex for Managing Global Cyber Activities*.
26. David J. Lynch, "130 Countries Sign on to Global Minimum Tax Plan, Creating Momentum for Biden Push," *The Washington Post*, July 1, 2021: https://www.washingtonpost.com/us-policy/2021/07/01/global-corporate-tax-oecd/
27. Hayley Evans and Shannon Togawa Mercer, "Privacy Shield on Shaky Ground: What's Up with EU-U.S. Data Privacy Regulations," *Lawfare*,

September 2, 2018: https://www.lawfareblog.com/privacy-shield-shaky-ground-whats-eu-us-data-privacy-regulations

28. Stephanie Bodoni, "Google Clash Over Global Right to Be Forgotten Returns to Court. Bloomberg," 2019: https://www.bloomberg.com/news/articles/2019-01-09/google-clash-over-global-right-to-be-forgotten-returns-to-court

29. Shoshana Zuboff, *The Age of Surveillance Capitalism: The Fight for a Human Future at the New Frontier of Power* (London: Profile Books, 2019); Ronald J. Deibert, "The Road to Digital Unfreedom: Three Painful Truths about Social Media," *Journal of Democracy* 30, no. 1 (2019): 25–39.

30. Mark Raymond, *Social Practices of Rule-Making in World Politics* (New York: Oxford University Press, 2019).

31. Scott Shackelford, Michael Sulmeyer, Amanda Craig, Ben Buchanan, and Biran Micic, "From Russia with Love: Understanding the Russian Cyber Threat to U.S. Critical Infrastructure and What to Do about It," *Nebraska Law Review*, 96, no. 2 (2017): 320–338.

32. Natalia Zinets, "Ukraine Charges Russia with New Cyber Attacks on Infrastructure," *Reuters*, 2017: https://www.reuters.com/article/us-ukraine-crisis-cyber-idUSKBN15U2CN

33. Stephen D. Krasner, "Global Communications and National Power: Life on the Pareto Frontier," *World Politics* 43, no. 3 (1991): 336–366; Samantha Bradshaw et al., *The Emergence of Contention in Global Internet Governance* (Centre for Internet Governance Innovation, 2015).

34. Barbara Koremenos, Charles Lipson, and Duncan Snidal, "The Rational Design of International Institutions," *International Organization* 55, no. 4 (2001): 761–799.

35. David A. Welch, *Justice and the Genesis of War* (Cambridge: Cambridge University Press, 1993); Cecilia Albin, *Justice and Fairness in International Negotiation* (Cambridge: Cambridge University Press, 2001); Mark Raymond, "Cyber Futures and the Justice Motive: Avoiding Pyrrhic Victory," *Military Cyber Affairs* 3, no. 1 (2018): 1–23.

36. Koremenos, Lipson, and Snidal, "The Rational Design of International Institutions."

37. Mark Raymond, "Managing Decentralized Cyber Governance: The Responsibility to Troubleshoot," *Strategic Studies Quarterly* 10, no. 4 (2016): 123–149.

38. Sandholtz, "Dynamics of International Norm Change: Rules against Wartime Plunder"; Jutta Brunnée and Stephen J. Toope, *Legitimacy and Legality in International Law* (Cambridge: Cambridge University Press, 2010); Raymond, *Social Practices of Rule-Making in World Politics*.

39. Ostrom, "Beyond Markets and States: Polycentric Governance of Complex Economic Systems"; Raymond, *Social Practices of Rule-Making in World Politics*.

40. Sara Salinas, "Facebook's Zuckerberg is Asked to Speak Before UK Parliament Again, and This Time Canada is Joining In," CNBC October 31, 2018: https://www.cnbc.com/2018/10/31/uk-canada-invite-facebooks-zuckerberg-to-speak-before-parliaments.html

41. Henry Farrell and Abraham L. Newman, "Weaponized Interdependence: How Global Economic Networks Shape State Coercion," *International Security* 44, no. 1 (2019): 42–79.

42. Molly Sharlach, "New Tool Helps Users Decide Which Countries Their Internet Traffic Transits," *Tech Xplore*, 2018: https://techxplore.com/news/2018-08-tool-users-countries-internet-traffic.html

43. Chris C. Demchak and Peter Dombrowski, "Rise of a Cybered Westphalian Age," *Strategic Studies Quarterly* 5, no. 1 (2011): 32–61.

44. Tim Büthe and Walter Mattli, *The New Global Rulers: The Privatization of Regulation in the World Economy*, (Princeton, NJ: Princeton University Press, 2011).

45. Raymond and DeNardis, "Multistakeholderism: Anatomy of an Inchoate Global Institution."

46. John Gerard Ruggie, "Multilateralism: The Anatomy of an Institution," *International Organization* 46, no. 3 (1992): 561–598; Christian Reus-Smit, *The Moral Purpose of the State: Culture, Social Identity, and Institutional Rationality in International Relations* (Princeton, NJ: Princeton University Press, 1999).

47. Mikael Wigell, "Mapping the 'Hybrid Regimes': Regime Types and Concepts in Comparative Politics," *Democratization* 15, no. 2 (2008): 230–250.

48. Demchak and Dombrowski, "Rise of a Cybered Westphalian Age."

49. Milton Mueller, "Against Sovereignty in Cyberspace," *International Studies Review* 22, no. 4 (2020): 779–801.

50. Joshua Rovner and Tyler Moore, "Does the Internet Need a Hegemon?," *Journal of Global Security Studies* 2, no. 3 (2017): 184–203.

51. Michael P. Fischerkeller and Richard J. Harknett, "Persistent Engagement, Agreed Competition, and Cyberspace Interaction Dynamics and Escalation," (Washington, DC: Institute for Defense Analyses, May 2018).

52. Erica D. Borghard and Shawn W. Lonergan, "Cyber Operations as Imperfect Tools of Escalation," *Strategic Studies Quarterly* 13, no. 3 (2019): 122–145.

53. Jacquelyn Schneider, "The Capability/Vulnerability Paradox and Military Revolutions: Implications for Computing, Cyber, and the Onset of War," *Journal of Strategic Studies* 42, no. 6 (2019): 841–863.

54. Jason Healey, "The Implications of Persistent (and Permanent) Engagement in Cyberspace," *Journal of Cybersecurity* 5, no. 1 (2019): 1–15.

55. Joseph S. Nye, "Deterrence and Dissuasion in Cyberspace," *International Security* 41, no. 3 (Winter 2016): 44–71; Rebecca Slayton, "What is the Cyber Offense-Defense Balance? Conceptions, Causes, and Assessment," *International Security* 41, no. 3 (2017): 72–109.

56. Erik Gartzke and Jon R. Lindsay, "Thermonuclear Cyberwar," *Journal of Cybersecurity* 3, no. 1 (2017): 37–48.

57. Christian Reus-Smit, *The Moral Purpose of the State: Culture, Social Identity, and Institutional Rationality in International Relations* (Princeton, NJ: Princeton University Press, 1999).

58. Stacie E. Goddard and Daniel H. Nexon, "The Dynamics of Global Power Politics: A Framework for Analysis," *Journal of Global Security Studies* 1, no. 1 (2016): 4–18.

59. Robert Owen Keohane and Joseph S. Nye, *Power and Interdependence*, 3rd edition (London: Longman, 2001); Farrell and Newman, "Weaponized Interdependence."

60. Mark Raymond, "Puncturing the Myth of the Internet as a Commons," *Georgetown Journal of International Affairs, International Engagement on Cyber III* (2013/2014): 53–64.

61. Rid, "Cyber War Will Not Take Place"; Martha Finnemore and Duncan B. Hollis, "Constructing Norms for Global Cybersecurity," *The American Journal of International Law* 110, no. 3 (2016): 425–479; Scott Shackelford et al., "From Russia with Love: Understanding the Russian Cyber Threat to U.S. Critical Infrastructure and What to Do About It."

62. Laura DeNardis and Mark Raymond, "The Internet of Things as a Global Policy Frontier," *U.C. Davis Law Review* 51, no. 2 (2017): 475–497; Rebecca Slayton and Aaron Clark-Ginsberg, "Beyond Regulatory Capture: Coproducing Expertise for Critical Infrastructure Protection," *Regulation & Governance* 12, no. 1 (2018): 115–130.

63. Cybersecurity and Insfrastructure Security Agency, "Critical Infrastructure Sectors," 2020: https://www.cisa.gov/critical-infrastructure-sectors

64. Ibid.

65. Koremenos, Lipson, and Snidal, "The Rational Design of International Institutions."

66. Raymond, *Social Practices of Rule-Making in World Politics*.

67. Finnemore and Hollis, "Constructing Norms for Global Cybersecurity."

68. Raymond, "Puncturing the Myth of the Internet as a Commons."

69. Welch, *Justice and the Genesis of War*; David A. Welch, "The Justice Motive in International Relations: Past, Present, and Future," *International Negotiation* 19, no. 3 (2014): 410–425.

70. Albin, *Justice and Fairness in International Negotiation*.

71. Mark Raymond, "Cyber Futures and the Justice Motive: Avoiding Pyrrhic Victory," *Military Cyber Affairs* 3, no. 1 (2018): 1–23.

72. For the former, see Myriam Dunn Cavelty, "From Cyber-Bombs to Political Fallout: Threat Representations with an Impact in the Cyber-Security Discourse," *International Studies Review* 15, no. 1 (2013): 105–122; for an example of the latter, see Rovner and Moore, "Does the Internet Need a Hegemon?"

73. Seva Gunitsky, "Corrupting the Cyber-Commons: Social Media as a Tool of Autocratic Stability," *Perspectives on Politics* 13, no. 1 (2015): 42–54; Deibert, "The Road to Digital Unfreedom: Three Painful Truths about Social Media."

74. Pouliot and Thérien, "Global Governance in Practice."

8

The Negative Externalities of Cyberspace Insecurity and Instability for Civil Society

Siena Anstis, Sophie Barnett, Sharly Chan, Niamh Leonard, and Ron Deibert

It has long been assumed that civil society[1] has benefitted from cyberspace. Initial research focused on how digital technologies provided innovative and much-needed mechanisms by which civil society could communicate and conduct advocacy work while evading repressive state policies. These views were reinforced during the Arab Spring when new digital technologies, in particular social media, provided civil society with means to circumvent government censorship and mobilize protest movements.[2] However, as repressive regimes became aware of the disruptive potential of digital technologies, many took measures to neutralize them.[3] Sophisticated information controls increased over time, with a growing number of states deploying surveillance, targeted espionage, and other types of covert disruptions against civil society targets.[4] Authoritarianism now routinely takes place online (referred to as "digital authoritarianism" or "networked authoritarianism") as well as in person.[5]

Yet, civil society continues to depend on the international communications ecosystem to facilitate national and transnational advocacy. This ecosystem is constantly mutating, invasive by design, poorly regulated, and prone to abuse. Surveillance capitalism, the products and services of the cyber warfare industry, and increasingly aggressive offensive cyber policies yield an insecure structure, contributing to an unstable environment for civil society. No single regulation, policy, technology, or application will resolve these issues. Further, these conditions will worsen as the center of gravity of "cyberspace" shifts to China, India, and the Global South, where human rights are fragile, exploitation of digital technologies to repress global civil society is increasingly *de rigeur*, and institutionalized safeguards against abuses of power are either weak or altogether absent.

In this chapter, we shift the focus from the benefits of cyberspace for civil society to how the central characteristics of our evolving communications ecosystem produce mounting insecurities for the work of civil society. We adopt a narrow definition of the word "insecurity," focused on technical insecurities that arise in devices, protocols, applications, and telecommunications networks. These insecurities have, in turn, led to greater instability by facilitating the activities of state – and non-state – actors to surveil and silence civil society, both nationally and transnationally. In the first section, we define the notions of insecurity and instability. While there is a substantial corpus of literature on various dimensions of international stability[6] and cyber stability,[7] we propose to engage with these concepts through a different "human-centric" lens that makes civil society the focal point of the analysis.[8] We then consider two underlying key features of our insecure global communications ecosystem: surveillance capitalism and states' growing adoption of aggressive offensive cyber policies. In the second section, we take a closer look at a third feature of the global communications ecosystem: the surveillance industry. This industry is dependent on, and a significant contributor to, continued insecurity in global communications. It feeds the ability of state and non-state actors to abuse digital technologies and repress civil society. We describe different surveillance products for sale, highlight select companies in the industry, and outline how these technologies contribute to human rights abuses. We also note key aspects of the surveillance industry that contribute to a lack of accountability, especially limited transparency in the development of surveillance technologies, export transactions, procurement, and the market for zero-days. Finally, in the third section, we consider one particular surveillance technology in more detail: spyware. This technology is intimately reliant on the "accidental megastructure" described by Benjamin Bratton and its security failings. It leads to significant and even lethal harms for civil society. In closing, we step back and evaluate what these features of the global landscape mean for the future of civil society and instability in international relations.

Central Features of the Digital Communications Ecosystem

Innovation has been a central feature of our digital communications environment over the last several decades. Much of the world's population is now collectively immersed in a constantly mutating, networked environment: always on; increasingly indispensable; and intimately intertwined with the most intimate details of our personal lives.[9] The term "cyberspace" is often used to describe interconnected technology, but without precision; there are countless definitions of cyberspace. However, cyberspace is not fixed, nor is it a single "thing." It is better described as an ecosystem that is a "continuously evolving mixture of elements, some slow-moving and persistent and others quickly mutating."[10] As new technologies and infrastructures are introduced, they are built "on top of legacy systems and then patched backwards haphazardly, leaving persistent and sometimes gaping vulnerabilities up and down the entire environment for a multitude of bad actors to exploit."[11] This communications ecosystem was not developed with a single well-thought-out design plan, and computer, network, and data security has largely been an afterthought. Bratton aptly describes the communications ecosystem not as disparate systems but "as forming a coherent and interdependent whole . . . an accidental megastructure, one that we are building both deliberately and unwittingly and is in turn building us in its own image."[12] Within this system, data breaches flow through the cracks, leaving many opportunities for exploitation. Bratton notes how understanding the communications ecosystem as an accidental megastructure allows us to see how "these different machines are parts of a greater machine" which allows us to "make the composition of alternatives – including new sovereignties and new forms of governance – both more legible and more effective."[13] Tackling these issues in the communications ecosystem requires a holistic approach to reform the innovation and development landscape from the infrastructure to the socioeconomic system around it.

Instability and Insecurity in our Digital Ecosystem: Focusing on Civil Society

In this section, we outline two terms used throughout this chapter: insecurity and instability. We adopt a human-centric approach to cyber security and focus the discussion of insecurity and instability in cyberspace on the perspective of civil society.

First, we adopt a narrow, focused definition of the term "insecurity" centered on "the protection of connected users" and one that puts "humans at the center of cyber security."[14] In doing so, we set aside definitions of cyber security that have traditionally been dominated by private sector and state actors.[15] We are concerned with insecurity in the sense of lack of safety in users' computers, networks, and data and how this facilitates human rights violations. As we discuss in more depth in the subsequent section, our global digital ecosystem is organized around the exploitation of a power imbalance that facilitates the (often non-consensual) collection of data from the public. The surveillance industry profits off this infrastructure by exploiting flaws in software code and our communications infrastructure to facilitate state surveillance and other authoritarian practices. We thus conceive of the depth and breadth of insecurity in cyberspace as a conduit for rights violations against civil society.

Second, we argue that this narrow notion of "insecurity" in computers, networks, and data is related to a lack of "stability" in cyberspace for civil society. In using the term "stability," we adopt a definition that is focused on civil society, rather than the traditional concern for interstate and intrastate relations. "Stability" in international relations literature – and without delving into granular detail – has generally been understood as referring to "a desired outcome of international order and a pre-condition of peaceful international and domestic life."[16] Thus, "stability, for a single state, represents the probability of its 'continued political independence and territorial integrity without any significant probability of becoming engaged in a war for survival.'"[17] In short, "stability concerns an entity's capacity to resist unavoidable threats and accommodate to inevitable changes."[18] The focus of "stability" has been largely state-centric. "Stability" in international relations literature also abstracts away from how state actors achieve and acquire stability, for example through authoritarian means and the violation of the rights of those seeking to change the status quo. State actors are likely to argue that a measure of insecurity in cyberspace is a mechanism that allows for stability to persist in intrastate affairs (and, by extension, facilitating regional stability). For example, insecurities in the digital ecosystem provide (for now) relatively low-cost mechanisms to exert authoritarian practices domestically and internationally as a means to silence dissent and maintain regime stability.

However, we argue that – when viewed through the lens of civil society – what state actors may consider to be beneficial for "stability" can perversely end up being a threat to civil society – the very subjects of state security, at least in theory. The continued overt and covert violation of rights by state actors creates instability for civil society and undermines its efforts. For example, it creates a chilling effect by using digital surveillance technology that leads to digital self-censorship among advocacy communities, by undertaking surveillance to detect and shut down online advocacy networks, or even by tracking the location of activists and committing extrajudicial killings. Through this chapter, we urge for a different concept of stability that adopts the perspective of civil society actors as the primary concern. Viewed through this "human-centric" lens, we draw the inescapable conclusion that our digital ecosystem is deeply flawed and in need of an overhaul: the agenda of state actors and the private sector has dominated, generating and perpetuating insecurity and instability for civil society.

Surveillance Capitalism: A Business Model Premised on Insecurity

The digital communications ecosystem's primary characteristics are derived from the underlying business model of many social media applications and other sectors of the economy. Shoshana Zuboff defines this business model as "surveillance capitalism," in which the goal is to "predict and modify human behaviour as a means to produce revenue and market control."[19] In exchange for the use of their products, companies engaged in surveillance capitalism gather as much personal information as they can monetize and sell to advertisers, other businesses, and, increasingly, to governments. Personal human experiences have become the new raw materials that can be mined and turned into what Zuboff calls "behavioural surplus" to produce prediction products. Under the regime of surveillance capitalism, the customers of social media are not the users per se, but rather the businesses (and other clients) who seek predictions about human behavior.[20]

In the race to innovate, gain market shares, and increase profits, social media companies collect as much personal data as fast as they can from as many human subjects and machine-based data points as possible. In Facebook's 2012 initial public offering (IPO), CEO Mark Zuckerberg noted that Facebook operates on a mantra of "move fast and break things."[21] This mantra is not unique to Facebook. It defines the personal data surveillance industry as a whole: rapid innovation alongside gross negligence for user security and the protection of user data. The current legal and market structure favors this strategy, as companies pass the cost of insecurity on to users and others in a rush to move products and applications first to the market. This system's pathologies are reflected in a daily abundance of data breaches and security failures – ultimately leaving the burden of insecurity on users with little to no meaningful avenues of redress.

Civil society is affected by this data sharing frenzy. High-risk individuals depend on the same applications and networked platforms as billions of other users do, but the routine collection of personal information combined with generalized insecurity presents a much greater personal risk for this category of users.[22] Even principal tools that are used to access the internet, such as browsers, can pose risks to civil society because they can collect and store a lot of data about a user. For example, browser tracking can include data about your hardware and software, as well as your Internet Protocol (IP) address, browsing history, mouse movements, social media accounts, installed fonts, and other kinds of data.[23] These data generate a unique fingerprint that data brokers and third parties can use to build profiles and sell to other actors, such as governments or companies.[24] While seemingly innocuous, everyday privacy risks can be especially dangerous for high risk members of civil society, such as human rights defenders. For example, if a human rights defender uploads a YouTube video, the IP address, which identifies your location, is stored and could be traced back to an Internet Service Provider (ISP).[25] The ISP may be compelled to provide the subscriber information to the relevant authorities. Government access to such data can have dangerous consequences. For example, a report prepared for the United Nations (UN) Special Rapporteur on Extrajudicial, Summary, or Arbitrary Executions found that the physical safety of human rights defenders is closely linked to their digital security.[26]

These types of insecurities are not "bugs," they are "features" of an industry constituted on the basis of surveillance capitalism.[27] When profits depend on gleaning data from users, companies do not put in place adequate protections to prevent data from leaking. Moreover, businesses constituted on the basis of surveillance capitalism are driven by a relentless logic; they aim to become more invasive and "closer" to users through sensors deployed on smart home devices, personal artificial intelligence (AI) assistants, personal health applications, and a growing number of other embedded applications. As technology and services offered by companies inch closer to users, their bodies, their habits, and the places they inhabit, the insecurities inherent to the sector are amplified.

This massive data extraction process yields huge volumes of fine-grained data that circulate widely among a growing number of third parties, "turning our digital lives inside out."[28] Data brokers, location tracking companies, and other data analytic service providers are ubiquitous in this digital ecosystem. They amass and monetize granular data points around specific categories of individual behavior, which themselves are gleaned from a growing number of embedded devices, applications, and software development kits. An investigation into one internet advertising company, Quantcast, revealed a massive trove of data for a single person in one week: "5,300 rows and more than 46 columns worth of data including URLs, time stamps, IP addresses, cookies IDs, browser information and much more."[29] Most users are unaware of their data going to these data brokers and advertising companies.[30]

The data analytics industry emerged suddenly and spread widely, leaving the sector poorly regulated. In 2018, Privacy International argued these kinds of third parties do not comply with the *General Data Protection Regulation* in the European Union (EU) and filed complaints against a number of data brokers, credit reference agencies, and data protection authorities in Europe.[31] While these and other cases move slowly through EU and United Kingdom courts, the businesses' parasitic data-gathering and selling practices flourish largely unimpeded in the regulatory equivalent of *terra nullius*.

Of even greater concern is the growing proclivity of companies in this sector to sell their data services to governments (in particular, law enforcement, intelligence, and other security agencies). Collected through a myriad of device manufacturers, application developers, data brokers, and other third parties, government agencies purchase detailed data on the public, often without judicial authorization, arguing that such data are in the "public domain."[32] For example, in the US, government contractor Venntel gathers location data from advertisers and other entities and "sells location data of smartphones to US law enforcement agencies including ICE [Immigration and Customs Enforcement], CBP [Customs and Border Protection], and the FBI [Federal Bureau of Investigation]."[33]

In Canada, the Calgary Police Service uses Palantir Gotham from Palantir Technologies to store "individuals' information about physical characteristics, relationships, interactions with police, religious affiliation, and 'possible involved activities,' in addition to using Palantir to map out the location of purported crime and calls for services."[34] Palantir Gotham has the capability to incorporate open source, third-party, and email and telecommunication information but at the time of writing, Palantir was not being used by the Calgary Police Services for predictive policing.[35] Despite these disturbing cases, there is no comprehensive detail on which governments are purchasing these types of capabilities and why.

The large, growing, and poorly regulated marketplace of data analytics, location tracking, and advertising companies creates an environment ripe for malicious exploitation and subversion. We face greater personalized insecurity as our lives increasingly move online, particularly with the push for sensors closer to users and the data extracted from those sensors circulating widely in a poorly regulated marketplace. The "accidental megastructure" of the communications ecosystem and its proclivity to surveillance capitalism provides bad actors with an endless and multiplying number of vulnerabilities to be exploited and a growing and poorly regulated sector of data vendors whose services can be used to target civil society.

The Growth of Offensive Cyber Operations

This environment of pervasive insecurity, combined with huge volumes of highly revealing data, has led governments to develop so-called "offensive capabilities" in cyberspace – in short, to "militarize" the space.[36] One critical but understudied aspect of this militarization[37] has been the proliferation of institutions and funding dedicated to the development and implementation of offensive cyber operations by state actors against both perceived foreign and domestic threats. In 2017, the former Deputy Director of the US National Security Agency (NSA), Richard Ledgett, estimated that "well over 100 countries around the world are now capable of launching cyberattacks."[38] Given the increasing climate of instability, this figure has likely grown since then. Although the size of commands and military intelligence units does not necessarily correlate with their level of operational activity, the sheer amount of resources that states are dedicating to these ends indicates the importance attached to them. For instance, the US Cyber Command (USCYBERCOM) was established in 2010 as a sub-unified command under the Strategic Command to direct and conduct "integrated electronic warfare, information and cyberspace operations as authorized, or directed, to ensure freedom of action in and through cyberspace and the information environment, and to deny the same to our adversaries."[39] Citing the increasing importance of cyberspace to US national security, USCYBERCOM was elevated to a Unified Combatant Command in 2018, making it the 11th joint military command of the Department of Defense (DOD).

Offensive cyber operations embody several features that make them attractive options for infiltrating or controlling targets. Importantly, they are easy to execute and difficult to attribute to a specific state. Undertaken remotely and behind a computer screen, offensive cyber operations are less likely to directly endanger the life of the perpetrator. Furthermore, they are generally conducted in secret,[40] making them hard to identify and regulate. The growing demand to attack and surveil in this way has also created a market in which products and services tailor-made for such operations can be purchased easily and at low cost, thus carrying greater capacity to provoke instability. We are, as a consequence, living in the golden age of cyber espionage: the benefits gained by choosing information operations over other means makes it unlikely that states would decline to participate.

Some states have specifically outlined the intent and purpose behind their integration of offensive cyber policies. For example, Canada's 2017 *National Defence Policy* states that the Canadian Armed Forces (CAF) will invest in capabilities including "offensive cyber operations capabilities to target, exploit, influence and attack in support of military operations."[41] Further, the Department of National Defence and the CAF work closely with the Communications Security Establishment (CSE) to develop "active" cyber capabilities – which the CAF concedes may refer to offensive operations – and the CSE assists them in the operations themselves (Supplementary Estimates A 2019–2020). Section 19 of the 2019 *CSE Act* also broadly authorizes the CSE to conduct "active cyber operations" – activities to "degrade, disrupt, influence, respond to or interfere with the capabilities, intentions or activities of a foreign individual, state, organisation or terrorist group as they relate to international affairs, defence or security" – abroad.[42]

In the US, the persistent engagement approach has informed the conduct of cyber operations since 2018. This approach is an element of DOD's defend forward concept, under which USCYBERCOM operations are "defending forward as close as possible to the origin of adversary activity extends our reach to expose adversaries' weaknesses, learn their intentions and capabilities, and counter attacks close to their origins."[43] Cyber operations taken below the level of armed conflict thus pursue "attackers across networks and systems to render most malicious cyber and cyber-enabled activity inconsequential while achieving greater freedom of manoeuvre to counter and contest dangerous adversary activity before it impairs our national power."[44] Indeed, the confidential 2018 "National Security Presidential Memorandum 13" allows the US military to more easily engage in "actions that fall below the 'use of force' or a level that would cause death, destruction or significant economic impacts."[45]

Moreover, the *Joint Publication 3-12 on Cyberspace Operations* establishes that offensive cyber operations "may exclusively target adversary cyberspace functions or create first-order effects in cyberspace to initiate carefully controlled cascading effects into the physical domains" or compromise actions that constitute the use of force, including physical damage.[46] The 2019 *National Defense Authorization Act* further expands USCYBERCOM authority to execute offensive cyber operations – including in areas beyond conflict zones – as part of the US policy to "employ all instruments of national power, including the use of offensive cyber capabilities" to deter malicious cyber activities of foreign states. Under section 1642, Russia, China, North Korea, and Iran are explicitly identified as permissible targets where one of them conducts an "active, systematic and ongoing campaign of attacks" against the US.[47]

Although authoritarian regimes are not so explicit in their adoption of offensive cyber capabilities, it is possible to identify certain cyber operations, including against civil society.[48] For example, Nate Schenkkan and Isabel Linzer observe how states engage in campaigns "across national borders to silence dissent among their diaspora and exile communities."[49] Although these actions can include physical acts of repression, digital technologies are increasingly making these activities much easier to execute. Acts of digital transnational repression – identified by the authors as part of the repression tactic of executing "threats from a distance" – are particularly popular "because [of] their ease for the origin state and degree to which they can affect the target," leading Freedom House and other civil society groups to call it an "everyday" form of transnational repression.[50] Digital transnational repression is particularly harmful to civil society, whose modes of advocacy are increasingly conducted online by dissidents who are careful of the fate of remaining family members in the country of origin as a consequence of their actions.

Alongside the temptations presented by huge volumes of insecure data generated on a daily basis, and institutional shifts toward offensive hacking by states, the rise and spread of end-to-end encryption in the face of mounting digital insecurity has provided even more incentives for governments to develop hacking means and methods. Indeed, the general assumption amongst states appears to be that stability is enhanced by uses of such technology (for example, greater control over the population). As Herpig observes, the increased use of encryption technologies has led some states – including Germany and the US – to allow law enforcement to conduct investigations via hacking tools.[51] "Lawful hacking," as it is called, refers to the interference "with the integrity of software – including online services – or hardware to access data in transit, data at rest, and sensors to manipulate a target's device by law enforcement for the purpose of criminal investigations."[52] The growth of lawful hacking by governments has, in turn, precipitated a concomitant growth of private companies offering such services (a sector that will be profiled in more depth below).

Evidently, the development of norms for state behavior in cyberspace has largely revolved around the stability of the international system. In the result, regime type has not mattered so long as the international order is "stable" – in other words, so long as there is no armed conflict between nation states in cyberspace.[53] The focus is on achieving "systemic stability" in the international system, which occurs where no single nation state can become dominant, while survival of most states is ensured and there is no large-scale war.[54] This view is reflected in the US Department of Energy's approach to cyber stability, which "is undermined when actors behave aggressively in the cyber realm in ways that undermine US national interests and the post-World War II liberal democratic order."[55]

However, the state-centric nature of existing discourse surrounding cyber stability obscures a different type of instability that emerges from the insecurities of the cyber domain: instability around civil society. In particular, the militarization of cyberspace means that "[n]umerous governments have used the exigencies of cybersecurity to justify vast internet censorship regimes, extensive surveillance programs, international cyber espionage, [and] disinformation campaigns targeting regime critics."[56] This "sense of alarm" in the narrative "has clouded the need to objectively and evidentially substantiate the likelihood and nature of the dangers at hand."[57] While most state-centric approaches to cyber stability condone domestic repression as a by-product of international stability, stability for civil society necessitates different norms altogether – affirming the ability to exercise human rights without reprisal. Of particular importance are the rights to privacy, freedom of expression, and freedom of assembly, all of which depend on responsible state behavior in cyberspace, as well as human rights-friendly regimes, for effectiveness. However, only modest effort has been made to clarify the scope of international human rights in cyberspace.[58]

The solution is an alternative approach to cyber stability under which humans, rather than state sovereignty, are the "primary objects of security."[59] A human-centric approach promotes the protection of networks as "as part of the essential foundation for the modern exercise of human rights," rather than as part of the "territorial sovereignty" of states. States are important only as "supporting institutions whose purpose is the protection of individuals' rights and wellbeing."[60] When it comes to network security, this approach "would strive to ensure that all laws, policies, and practices uphold the integrity of communication systems worldwide . . . [thereby] preventing government policies that would deliberately impede technological developments that protect data and users' security."[61] It would also prioritize unrestricted internet access, control of individuals over their personal data, and investigation of human rights violations online.[62] In the end, cyber stability means:

> Everyone can be reasonably confident in their ability to use cyberspace safely and securely, where the availability and integrity of services and information provided in and through cyberspace are generally assured, where change is managed in relative peace, and where tensions are resolved in a non-escalatory manner.[63]

A Closer Look at The Surveillance Industry

In the prior section, we reviewed two underlying features of our digital communications infrastructure: surveillance capitalism – where business models premised on insecurity in computers, networks, and data are able to thrive – and the growth in offensive cyber policies among state actors, which are premised on this digital insecurity. In this section, we take a closer look at the features and components of the surveillance industry. We define the surveillance industry broadly to include a wide range of products that can facilitate the following types of activities to the detriment of human rights: data analysis, audio and video surveillance, phone, location and internet-monitoring, monitoring centers, intrusion software, biometrics, counter-surveillance, equipment, and forensics.[64] These technologies have significant implications for international human rights, and are emerging in a marketplace that is secretive, lightly regulated and exploited by state actors. This section, which provides an overview of central features of the growing surveillance marketplace, as well as a review of products sold to state actors, illustrates the growing diversity of products that exploit insecurities in our global ecosystem to the detriment of civil society. This insecurity, in turn, generates significant instability for civil society actors operating in cyberspace.

A Growing Industry Marked by a Lack of Accountability

The picture painted by existing data and research on the surveillance industry is that of a marketplace – with a strong footprint in the Global North[65] – growing at a rapid rate and with few constraints despite the harmful effects. Privacy International's Surveillance Industry Index, with data up to May 2016, shows an increase in surveillance companies being created from the late 1970s onwards. These companies are primarily located within Organisation for Economic Co-operation and Development (OECD) member countries (87 percent), with 75 percent of companies located in North Atlantic Treaty Organization (NATO) countries.[66] Other reporting on the surveillance industry confirms a continued expansion. In 2019, *The New York Times* reported that the marketplace for digital espionage services was valued at $12 billion.[67] In early 2021, NSO Group, a notorious producer of spyware technology that has been used against civil society, floated the possibility of an IPO. The company was reported to be valued by market sources at $2 billion.[68] Meanwhile, the Chinese surveillance industry is also growing, and expanding.[69] Chinese companies are not only exporting intrusive surveillance products abroad, but also sustaining the entrenchment of a system of digital control and surveillance within China.[70] Persecuted minorities, in particular Uyghurs, are bearing the brunt of this deepening form of digital control, which has alarming consequences because of its ability to facilitate and enable human rights violations.[71]

A number of features of the surveillance industry lead to a lack of regulation and accountability, which in turn contributes to the continued expansion of the surveillance industry and its growing profitability. Secrecy, in particular, is key: a highly secretive marketplace is a challenge to regulate. Secrecy permeates numerous dimensions of the market.[72] The sampling of surveillance technology takes place at specialized non-public events, such as the Intelligence Support System (ISS) World Meeting, as well as similar events like Milipol Paris where state actors come to shop for new surveillance wares. These events are closed to the public and remain exclusive and closed affairs.[73] Surveillance companies keep their client lists confidential. The little information known to the public in the past few years regarding the surveillance industry's client base has been primarily due to public interest research by organizations using advanced methods of internet scanning and malware and spyware detection, investigations by journalists, freedom of information requests and associated litigation, as well as data breaches.[74] There are obvious incentives for companies to keep their clients out of the public eye. For example, one company may sell the same vulnerability and associated malware to states with opposed political and security interests, creating a conflict of interest that might discourage business. Further, such public disclosure may attract the attention of state authorities in the company's jurisdiction, leading to potential sanctions or the cancelation of export authorizations.[75] Although marketed for use principally in law enforcement investigations, it is an open secret that these services are widely deployed for international espionage. States may also require secrecy as a condition of sale, to hide from the public that they are acquiring and using surveillance technologies. Companies are also engaged in selling surveillance technologies to authoritarian regimes, which attracts negative public attention. Hiding such sales is in the company's reputational interests and protects its business model.

Another dimension of secrecy in the surveillance industry is how surveillance companies structure the sale of their products. For example, public documents show that companies producing spyware – such as NSO Group – use intermediary business entities.[76] In selling spyware technology to the Ghanaian government, for instance, NSO Group did not enter into a contract directly with the Ghanian government, but rather provided its products to the state through a third-party entity in Ghana called Infraloks Development Limited.[77] This sale structure creates complications in tracking the sale of spyware technology, the relevant business actors, and whether export laws are being complied with. Similarly, Hacking Team used an intermediary reseller company called CICOM USA in the US in its sale of spyware technology to the US Drug Enforcement Agency (DEA). As Motherboard noted, this "allowed the existence of the contract with the spy tech company to go unnoticed for three years."[78] A 2021 investigation by *Al Jazeera* into the sale of surveillance equipment to Bangladesh showed that company and client entered into a non-disclosure agreement and that the sale was structured with the use of an intermediary and was designed to "disguise the true nature of the deal and involved front companies."[79]

While surveillance companies may publicly state a commitment to human rights, their internal operations and practices are largely obfuscated from the public. As David Kaye, former UN Special Rapporteur on the promotion and protection of the right to freedom of opinion and expression, noted in his 2019 report on the surveillance industry, "[b]ecause the companies in the private surveillance industry operate under a cloak of secrecy, the public lacks any information about the way in which they may – if at all – consider the human rights impacts of their products."[80] For example, Israeli-based NSO Group claims to be running its business in compliance with the UN Guiding Principles on Business and Human Rights. However, citing legal provisions in Israel that prevent disclosure and commercial confidentiality, it continues to refuse to provide specific and verifiable information regarding its operations that would allow the public to hold it to account for its business activities.[81]

There are also significant hurdles in accessing information regarding the purchase and sale of surveillance technology from government agencies.[82] This is particularly true not only of sales to authoritarian regimes, but also to government entities in democratic regimes with more robust rule of law systems, which purchase such technologies with little to no democratic debate and use it with insufficient legal controls. Even in countries with freedom of information laws in place and an independent judiciary within which to litigate them, the process of acquiring information regarding state hacking practices can be lengthy and contentious.[83]

As numerous scholars and human rights practitioners have noted, there is only limited regulation affecting the expansion of the surveillance industry.[84] For example, in response to allegations of abuse of mass surveillance and commercial spyware, Wassenaar Arrangement member states agreed to add clauses restricting items related to IP network communications surveillance systems and intrusion software to the Arrangement's control lists, which are then to be implemented in domestic law given that the Arrangement itself is a non-binding framework. Yet, despite being the principal instrument referred to in the "regulation" of international trade in the surveillance industry, the Arrangement remains insufficient to regulate trade and prevent human rights abuses. In particular, the Arrangement does not ban trade, but rather establishes "a licensing framework" and is "designed to account for security considerations while also facilitating commerce to the extent possible."[85] In short, "[t]here is simply no guarantee that licensing parameters and decisions in any given state will properly account for human rights concerns."[86] There are numerous examples of export licenses being approved for the export of surveillance equipment implicated in human rights abuses by states who are participating in the Arrangement.[87] There are also significant challenges in defining the items to be regulated, in ensuring sufficient and timely coverage of novel surveillance technologies, and in ensuring that legitimate uses (for example security research) are adequately protected.[88]

The Functions, Features, and Harms of Surveillance Technologies

Having reviewed some of the key features of the surveillance industry that contribute to an environment of lawless development, this section gives an overview of a selection of surveillance technologies that are being developed and sold to state actors (while also being acquired, at times, by non-state actors), as well as associated dangers to civil society and human rights in the deployment of these technologies. Further, this section underlines how insecurities in our digital ecosystem lead to significant instability for civil society actors, evidenced through how these technologies facilitate a range of human rights violations. For example, data analytics used by policing agencies entail the application of discriminatory algorithms which further entrench existing racist policing practices. Location-tracking technology and the ability to access target communications and networks facilitates the detention and prosecution of civil society targets in authoritarian regimes.

Data analytics

Data analytics software involves using data to "map relationships, recognize patterns, and analyse words' meaning."[89] An example of the harms that can flow from the usage of powerful data analytics software is exemplified by Palantir, an American public company. Palantir markets itself as creating "software that lets organizations integrate their data, their decisions, and their operations into one platform."[90] While this may sound innocuous, the company's software has been linked to the facilitation of multiple human rights abuses by government agencies. In 2020, for example, Amnesty International highlighted Palantir's provision of its Integrated Case Management (ICM) and FALCON software to the US Department of Homeland Security (DHS) for products and services for ICE, an agency involved in numerous human rights abuses in the US. According to Amnesty International's research, Palantir's technologies enabled ICE operations by facilitating the identification, sharing of information, investigation, and tracking of migrants and asylum seekers to effect arrests and workplace raids.[91] Palantir software is also being used by police departments in the context of harmful and controversial predictive policing activities. For example, in 2018 it was revealed that the Los Angeles Police Department (LAPD) uses Palantir software to analyse LAPD data in order to target "chronic offenders." This use-case has been characterized by the Stop LAPD Spying Coalition as creating a "racist feedback loop" as the data being analyzed is based on the police's own racist policing.[92] Palantir continues to strengthen its relationship with government agencies worldwide, raising questions about human rights, data privacy, and government transparency regarding relationships with the corporation.[93] While Palantir is not the only company engaged in data analytics, it serves as a useful case study to show how the deployment of data analytics software by government agencies facilitates harmful surveillance practices with serious human rights impacts.

Location tracking, data interference, and more: IMSI-catchers
International Mobile Subscriber Identity catchers (or "IMSI-catchers") permit operators to undertake "indiscriminate surveillance" of mobile phones and users.[94] IMSI-catchers emulate mobile phone towers and "entice mobile phones to reveal their IMSI and International Mobile Equipment Identity (IMEI) data. They can be used to track and locate all phones that are switched on in a specific area without user consent," and for the interception of text messages, calls, and internet traffic.[95] Some IMSI-catchers can "re-route or edit communications and data sent to and from" a mobile or jam service so that a phone can no longer be used, even in an emergency.[96] The purchase and use of IMSI-catchers by a range of states – from the US to Canada, Bangladesh and the UK – raises serious concerns in light of their surreptitious and intrusive nature, and particularly where there is an absence of a legal framework in the jurisdictions in which they are deployed.[97] IMSI-catchers present a significant threat to a range of human rights, including freedom of expression, freedom of assembly and association, and the right to privacy.

A "spy in your pocket": spyware technology
Spyware – which is discussed in more detail in the third section of this chapter – is a highly intrusive surveillance technology that permits the operator access to a range of functions on a device. For example, the Pegasus spyware produced by NSO Group is marketed as allowing the operator to "remotely and covertly extract valuable intelligence from virtually any mobile device."[98] The software facilitates the extraction and secure transmission of collected data for analysis, and installation is done remotely and without necessarily requiring user interaction (so called "zero-click" spyware). The data collected from the device can include texts, emails, calendar entries, call history, messaging, contacts, browsing history, and more, as well as accessing audio and visual files and allowing location tracking.[99] As with IMSI-catchers, spyware technology can threaten a number of human rights, including the rights to privacy, free expression, and assembly and association.[100] These human rights harms – flowing from spyware produced by different companies, such as Hacking Team, Cyberbit, and NSO Group – have been documented by a number of research bodies and advocacy organizations. Targets have included journalists, human rights defenders, members of political opposition movements, dissi-

dents exiled abroad, and more.[101] In the third section, we review how spyware has been specifically deployed against global civil society.

Internet-monitoring: deep packet inspection and internet-filtering technologies
Deep-packet inspection and internet-filtering technologies can be used by private companies for traffic management, but also by ISPs to prevent entire populations from accessing politically sensitive information online and/or be used for mass surveillance. Research by the Citizen Lab has shed a spotlight on a number of companies providing these services, namely Blue Coat, Sandvine, and Netsweeper.[102] For example, in 2018, the Citizen Lab documented how Netsweeper's internet-filtering products were used by clients to block political content sites and LGBTQ+ content, among other political and social online materials. In 2015, the Citizen Lab also documented how Netsweeper technology was being used to block internet content during the armed conflict in Yemen following the dictates of the Houthis, a Yemeni rebel group.[103] These technologies infringe a range of rights. For example, former UN Special Rapporteur David Kaye noted that the "multiple uses" of network monitoring equipment and technology raise freedom of expression and privacy concerns where they are used for internet-filtering, interception, and throttling data.[104]

Even more location-tracking: insecurity in global Signaling System 7 (SS7)
Long known – yet still unaddressed – insecurities in our global mobile communications infrastructure are another prime example of how state actors benefit from and exploit the collective insecurity of global civil society. Signaling System 7 (SS7) is a protocol suite developed in 1975 for the exchange of information and routing phone calls between wireline telecommunications companies. Because of SS7's continued lack of authentication features, any attack that interconnects with the SS7 network can send commands to a subscriber's home network, falsely indicating that the subscriber is roaming. These commands allow the attacker to track the victim's location and intercept voice calls and SMS text messages. They can also be used to intercept codes for two-factor authentication sent via SMS. At present, SS7 is used primarily in 2G and 3G mobile networks. While 4G uses the Diameter protocol, which includes features for authentication and access control, they are optional features and the need for 4G users to interconnect with older mobile networks introduces security concerns.[105] The growth of a private surveillance industry has made access to technology exploiting SS7 vulnerabilities much easier. In 2020, the Bureau of Investigative Journalism and *The Guardian* found that private companies were using phone networks in the Channel Islands to facilitate their clients' surveillance operations, which targeted British and US cit-

izens, among others.[106] More specifically, such companies were "able to rent access from mobile phone operators," which then exploit SS7 vulnerabilities to "allow the tracking of the physical location of users across the world" (as well as potentially facilitating interception of calls and data).[107] The Citizen Lab has also documented how Circles, an Israeli cyber espionage company that exploits SS7 weaknesses, has clients around the world, including among states with poor rule of law and human rights records, like Mexico, Honduras, and Nigeria, to name a few.[108]

Biometrics: the use of facial recognition software
Facial recognition is a biometric identification technology that uses "computer algorithms to pick out specific, distinctive details about a person's face."[109] These collected details are "converted into a mathematical representation and compared to data on other faces previously collected and stored in a face recognition database."[110] Importantly, facial recognition takes the risks inherent to biometric technology "to a new level because it is much more difficult to prevent the collection of your face" and it "allows for covert, remote, and mass capture and identification of images."[111] This technology is being deployed by a variety of state actors. Facial recognition technology notably poses a threat to freedom of expression, assembly and association, and the right to privacy. For example, it has reportedly been deployed by the police in the context of protests[112] and by Chinese authorities to facilitate the brutal persecution of Uighurs.[113] The risks around facial recognition technology are especially acute and growing because digital networked cameras have proliferated at an exponential rate, ranging from applications on mobile devices, social media platforms, to CCTV cameras located in public and private spaces. Compounding these risks, as with many other applications in the surveillance capitalism ecosystem, many of these sources of digital imagery are poorly secured and open to malicious exploitation or unregulated data gathering. While biometric technologies are deployed by state actors in order to ensure a level of internal stability (for example, in attempting to track protest and quell internal dissent), this technology leads to greater instability when viewed from the perspective of civil society actors whose ability to engage in free expression and protect their own security and liberty is severely impaired.

A Spotlight on Spyware Abuse Against Global Civil Society

The unlawful use of spyware technology to surveil human rights defenders, journalists, civil society and related actors is a particularly pernicious example of the abuse of power in cyberspace. Once downloaded, spyware can provide an operator with a complete window into a target's life via their digital device. It includes a range of functions, from secretly downloading files from a device to covertly activating and using a device's audio recording and video functions. The continued uptick in cases of spyware abuse, combined with the growing availability of spyware technology and associated zero-days to facilitate such activities, means that such instances of abuse will likely multiply. The following section illustrates a handful of instances of spyware abuse, with a specific focus on the deployment of spyware against global civil society. While a complete review of all publicly documented instances of spyware abuse is beyond the scope of this chapter, the selected case studies illustrate how spyware can be abused by states (and non-state actors), the troubling impact of such surveillance on targets, and how this technology can enable transnational repression by authoritarian states, which in turn contributes to closing spaces for transnational advocacy by civil society.

Mexico: Spyware Sold into the Hands of a Notorious Government

Mexico has a long track record of serious human rights violations. Journalists, in particular, have been the victim of countless horrific acts, including kidnappings and assassinations. In 2020, the country was declared by the Committee to Protect Journalists (CPJ) as the world's most dangerous country in which to be a journalist.[114] Human rights defenders are subjected to "intimidation, criminalization, and violence," as reported by Human Rights Watch in its 2020 World Report.[115] Despite this clear track record of human rights violations by the authorities and as mentioned above, NSO Group sold its Pegasus spyware to the Mexican government, which subsequently used it against a range of human rights and civil society targets.[116]

Between 2017 and 2019, the Citizen Lab published a series of reports documenting the use of Pegasus spyware in Mexico against numerous targets, including: a scientist at the Mexican National Institute for Public Health and employees at non-governmental organizations working on obesity and soda consumption; journalists and lawyers working on a range of issues including investigations of corruption by the Mexican president and the government's participation in human rights abuses, along with a minor child of one of the targets; senior politicians with the National Action Party; investigators into the 2014 Iguala Mass Disappearance; lawyers representing the families of three slain Mexican women; the director of a Mexican anti-corruption group; and the director of the publication *Río Doce*, a colleague of slain journalist Javier Valdez Cárdenas (who was also a journalist with that same paper as well as its founder), and Javier Valdez Cárdenas' wife.[117] In 2021, *The Guardian* revealed that Mexico had targeted 15,000 numbers for infection with the Pegasus software, the most of any country using the software.[118]

In addition to illustrating how government purchasers of spyware technology are prone to abusing such capabilities in violation of international human rights law, the trajectory of NSO Group's Pegasus spyware in Mexico is a cautionary tale regarding the broader potential for abuse of spyware technology by non-state or other malicious actors. Not only has spyware technology been used with impunity by government authorities against various targets, but *The Guardian* has reported that spyware technology has ended up in the hands of non-state actors: Mexico's infamous cartels.[119] Officials from the US Drug Enforcement Administration confirmed in an interview that "[a]s many as 25 private companies" have courted and sold spyware technology to Mexican federal and state police forces. They described the situation as a "free-for-all," noting that there was "little or no regulation of the sector – and no way to control where the spyware ends up."[120] They also confirmed that "[c]orrupt Mexican officials have helped drug cartels in the country obtain state-of-the-art spyware."[121]

The 2019 WhatsApp Hack and the 2021 "Pegasus Project": The Spread of Commercially Available Spyware and its Impact on Targets

In addition to the numerous documented instances of abuse of NSO Group's Pegasus spyware by the Citizen Lab, two significant events in the past few years illustrate the spread of spyware and its impact on civil society. In 2019, Facebook and WhatsApp filed a suit in the United States alleging that NSO Group helped state actors hack into the accounts of "at least 100 human–rights defenders, journalists and other members of civil society across the world."[122] The complaint sets out in detail allegations of how NSO Group exploited WhatsApp servers without authorization to inject malware components into the targeted devices.[123] In 2021, investigations by a consortium of media organizations and Amnesty International revealed numerous additional cases of the abusive deployment of NSO Group's Pegasus spyware (the "Pegasus Project").[124] WhatsApp and Pegasus Project intrusions targeted residents of a number of states, including Rwanda, India, Morocco, and Togo. The geographical range of this hack illustrates how commercially available spyware technology is becoming increasingly accessible to a broad swathe of actors, and thus facilitates the abuse of power in cyberspace.

The impact on victims is notable. In 2020, Access Now published a compilation of interviews with victims of NSO Group's WhatsApp hack.[125] Among the interviewees was Bela Bhatia, a human rights lawyer and activist in India, who believes that she was targeted because of her work against police and paramilitary impunity. The WhatsApp hack was not the first abuse Bhatia was subjected to, and forms part of a continuum of other forms of physical attacks she has suffered in the past. Asked about the impact of this surveillance, Bhatia explained that she was "forced to work in an environment of suspicion and live a restricted life." She noted that "[b]uilding trust among community members for any joint activity has become all the more difficult," that she has not been able to live where she wants, and that she lives with the "constant apprehension of possible arrest based on false charges."[126] She also described that being targeted with the Pegasus spyware made her "even more controversial and vulnerable."[127] Aboubakr Jamaï, a Moroccan journalist and winner of the CPJ's Journalists' International Press Freedom Award and another victim of the WhatsApp hack, explained that this surveillance ruined his professional relationships and "reduc[ed] . . . his social circle." In particular, it meant putting "at risk . . . relatives and friends [at risk] by the mere fact of freely talking to them on the phone."[128] Fouad Abdelmoumni, a Moroccan human rights and democracy activist working with Human Rights Watch and Transparency International, stated that the WhatsApp hack made him feel "invaded, harassed, and severely violated." Abdelmoumni has also been subjected to other abuses, including torture, imprisonment, and enforced disappearance, and described himself as "experiencing [the recent surveillance] as much more violent."[129]

These interviews illustrate that digital targeting with technologies like spyware can have serious impacts. It generates fear, apprehension, self-censorship, and other behavioral modifications among targets, harming their ability to engage in transnational advocacy efforts online.[130] The significant number of targets of software like NSO Group's Pegasus and the range of countries in which they are located show a growing appetite for this technology. They also demonstrate a willingness to use it in contravention of international human rights law, for example by targeting journalists and human rights defenders.

The Long Reach of the Authoritarian Regime: The Use of Spyware Against Dissidents in Exile

A final example of the pernicious effects of the abuse of cyberspace through the deployment of intrusive spyware technology is that of authoritarian states using this technology to reach outside their borders and pursue dissidents in exile and others in the diaspora. This transnational digital repression illustrates the dangers associated with the unchecked proliferation of spyware technology: it enables authoritarian regimes who undermine democratic spaces and interfere with transnational political and social advocacy by civil society.

Over the past few years, we have seen a number of such cases. For example, Omar Abdulaziz, a Saudi dissident who arrived in Canada as a refugee and is now a permanent resident, was targeted by Saudi operators using Pegasus in October 2018.[131] This targeting happened in the months before Jamal Khashoggi − also a dissident and a friend of Abdulaziz − was kidnapped and murdered by Saudi officials in Turkey. In the UK, several dissident Bahrainis have instituted a legal action against Gamma Group for allegedly having sold their spyware technology to the Bahraini government, which was then used against the dissidents in exile.[132] The Citizen Lab has also documented the use of spyware technology against Ethiopian dissidents in the US, the UK, and other countries.[133] Targets of the 2019 WhatsApp hack were also living in exile, such as Rwandan victim Faustin Rukondo.[134]

The availability of spyware technology provides another mechanism by which authoritarian states can gather information against an extraterritorial target, discover what individuals are participating in a transnational advocacy network, and identify activists who may still be within a country's borders for persecution, among other outcomes. The known availability of such technology has a chilling effect on civil society in and of itself, hampering advocacy efforts. It may also accompany more sinister forms of transnational repression, such as kidnappings, forcible disappearances, and murders. As Schenkkan and Linzer note, the use of spyware and other forms of transnational repression at a distance "are intimately connected to physical attacks."[135] Ultimately, "[t]he very digital technologies that enable cross-border communication also present opportunities for interference by an authoritarian regime. States use spyware, social media monitoring, and online harassment to disrupt and surveil exiles' networks from thousands of miles away."[136]

Conclusion

The previous sections of this chapter have described in some detail the all-encompassing and multifaceted nature of digital insecurity, as well as the variety of technologies, companies, and state actors that thrive in our disorganized and unregulated digital ecosystem. While traditional discussion around security and stability in cyberspace has focused on state actors (and to some extent private sector actors), we have reoriented this discussion to factor in the experience of civil society actors. As we illustrate, we are long past the days of uncritically hailing the revolutionary effects of digital communications in fueling the national and transnational advocacy efforts of civil society. The structure of our digital ecosystem, dominated by surveillance capitalism and a thriving surveillance marketplace, has become one of the most important sources of insecurity for civil society actors. This insecurity creates significant instability for civil society actors through its ability to facilitate widespread and severe human rights violations.

Unfortunately, there is no simple remedy to these problems. Fixing the internet's inherent insecurities is a heavy lift, and it would require a fundamental shift in the innovation and development landscape and a concerted effort to rein in surveillance capitalism. The large and growing sector of data brokers, location trackers, and advertising analytics firms has deeply burrowed its way into everyday applications. Extracting and monetizing the data they collect is now a major revenue generator, and a service highly sought after by government agencies, particularly in law enforcement and intelligence. However, malicious despots and other actors intent on subverting the rule of law and civil society are reaping systematic benefits from the instabilities of cyberspace we have identified. Absent strong regulations to the contrary (which, at present, seem unlikely to materialize) these trends will continue.

While wholesale reform of the entire ecosystem is unlikely to come soon, a number of targeted strategies, policies, laws, and regulations could be adopted to reform some elements of this digital ecosystem and, in particular, to begin to better constrain and regulate the actors within the surveillance industry. For example, the inclusion of human rights as a justification for export control in the recent amendments to the EU's Dual-Use Regulations and steps toward greater transparency regarding export authorizations present a hopeful expansion of the regulation of surveillance technologies, although how this will play out in reality remains to be seen.[137] A similar approach might be adopted for export legislation in national jurisdictions. Governments can also take significant steps toward ensuring greater transparency regarding the business practices of surveillance companies within national jurisdictions.[138] Legislation could require that surveillance industry companies engage in detailed transparency reporting and be subject to mandatory human rights due diligence legislation with significant consequences for failure to comply. Governments could ensure transparency in contracting with surveillance companies by proactively identifying and disclosing contracts and complying with freedom of information requests without engaging in litigation. They could also adopt a broad definition of the "surveillance technology" and publish detailed statistics regarding export licenses granted for the industry's products heading abroad. Further, states could ensure that public procurement processes for surveillance products are public, actively engage civil society, and categorically exclude tenders from companies with histories of providing technology to regimes that violate human rights or which have insufficient internal and independent oversight structures to ensure compliance with human rights.[139] Finally, states could take a categorical position against the transnational targeting of civil society within their borders, including by facilitating and pursuing litigation to deter state actors from undertaking such transnational repression and companies from facilitating it.

More broadly, targeted regulation could help reign in the free-wheeling data broker, location tracking, and data analytics sector. In 2020 alone, data brokers in the US "rivaled the spending of individual Big Tech firms like Facebook and Google" on lobbying congress.[140] Of particular importance to curb the harms from these sectors would be regulations that clarify the legality of sales for these and other services to state agencies, and whether law enforcement and intelligence agencies should be able to purchase them without judicial oversight and approval. As these industries globalize, the challenges around effective legal controls grow significantly – especially as the center of gravity of innovation moves to the Global South and states like China, where the rule of law and public accountability is weak.

The analysis we have presented in this chapter highlights a tension between state-centric and human-centric approaches to cyber security, and by extension among differing conceptions of "stability" in international relations. Those approaching the topic from a realist perspective perceive international system stability as the primary value, which in turn privileges a state-centric approach to cyber security. Perversely, securing "the state" and the "international system" in this manner has been a major contributor to different kinds of both insecurity and instability for other sectors of global politics. In the context of a digital ecosystem that is already deeply insecure, poorly regulated, and prone to abuse, this state-centric paradigm is producing enormous and growing "negative externalities" for human rights and for global civil society.

Notes

1. Unless specified otherwise, "civil society" is broadly defined here as the national and transnational assemblage of individuals and organizations that is distinct from governments and businesses and which includes, for example, human rights defenders, activists, and journalists.
2. Molly K. Land, "Networked Activism," *Harvard Human Rights Journal* 22, no. 2 (2009): 205–244: https://heinonline.org/HOL/P?h=hein .journals/hhrj22&i=209; Henry Farrell, "The Consequences of the Internet for Politics," *Annual Review of Political Science* 15 (2012): 35–52, https://doi.org/10.1146/annurev-polisci-030810-110815; Larry Diamond, "Liberation Technology," *Journal of Democracy* 21, no. 3 (2010): 69–83, https://www.journalofdemocracy.org/articles/liberation

-technology/; Stephanie Hankey and Daniel Ó Clunaigh, "Rethinking Risk and Security of Human Rights Defenders in the Digital Age," *Journal of Human Rights Practice* 5, no. 3 (2013): 535–547, https://doi.org /10.1093/jhuman/hut023

3. Adel Iskandar, "Egyptian Youth's Digital Dissent," *Journal of Democracy* 30, no. 3 (2019): 154–164, https://doi.org/10.1353/jod.2019.0049

4. Ronald Deibert, "Authoritarianism Goes Global: Cyberspace Under Siege," *Journal of Democracy* 26, no. 3 (2015): 64–78, 65, 66, 68, https:// doi.org/10.1353/jod.2015.0051

5. Molly K. Land and Jay D. Aranson, "Human Rights and Technology: New Challenges for Justice and Accountability," *Annual Review of Law and Social Science* 16 (2020): 223–240, https://www.annualre views.org/doi/pdf/10.1146/annurev-lawsocsci-060220-081955; Rebecca MacKinnon, "Liberation Technology: China's 'Networked Authoritarianism'," *Journal of Democracy* 22, no. 2 (2011): 32–46, http:// doi.org/10.1353/jod.2011.0033; Seva Gunitsky, "Corrupting the Cyber-commons: Social Media as a Tool of Autocratic Stability," *Perspectives on Politics* 13, no. 1 (2015): 42–54, http://individual.utoronto.ca/seva/cor rupting_cybercommons.pdf; Ronald Deibert, "Authoritarianism Goes Global: Cyberspace Under Siege," *Journal of Democracy* 26, no. 3 (2015): 64–78, https://doi.org/10.1353/jod.2015.0051; Ronald Deibert, "The Road to Digital Unfreedom: Three Painful Truths About Social Media," *Journal of Democracy* 30, no. 1 (2015): 25–39, https://www.jo urnalofdemocracy.org/articles/the-road-to-digital-unfreedom-three-pa inful-truths-about-social-media/; Justin Sherman, "The Long View of Digital Authoritarianism," *New America*, June 20, 2019: https://www .newamerica.org/weekly/edition-254/long-view-digital-authoritaria nism/; Human Rights Council, General Assembly, *Report of the Special Rapporteur on the Promotion and Protection of the Right to Freedom of Opinion and Expression* (New York: UN Headquarters, 2019): https://documents -dds-ny.un.org/doc/UNDOC/GEN/G19/148/76/PDF/G1914876 .pdf?OpenElement

6. William C. Wohlforth, "The Stability of a Unipolar World," *International Security* 24, no. 1 (1999): 5–41; Glenn Snyder, *Deterrence and Defense* (Princeton, NJ: Princeton University Press, 1961); Karl W. Deutsch and David J. Singer, "Multipolar Power Systems and International Stability," *World Politics* 16, no. 3 (1964): 390–406.

7. See for example Mika Kerttunen and Eneken Tirk, "The Politics of Stability: Cement and Change in Cyber Affairs," *NUPI Report 4/2019*: https://nupi.brage.unit.no/nupi-xmlui/bitstream/handle/11250/259

8287/NUPI_Report_4_2019_KerttunenTikk.pdf?sequence=1&isAl lowed=y; Alexander Klimburg and Virgilio A. F. Almeida, "Cyber Peace and Cyber Stability: Taking the Norm Road to Stability," *IEEE Internet Computing* 23, no. 4 (2019): 61–66, https://ieeexplore.ieee.org /document/8874985; Jason Healey and Robert Jervis, "The Escalation Inversion and Other Oddities of Situational Cyber Stability," *Texas National Security Review* 3, no. 4 (Fall 2020): 30–53; Edward M. Roche, "The Search for Global Cyber Stability," *Journal of Information Technology Case and Application Research* 29, no. 2 (2019): 68–73, https://doi.org /10.1080/15228053.2019.1636570; Franklin D. Kramer, "Achieving International Cyber Stability," *Georgetown Journal of International Affairs* (International Engagement on Cyber 2012: Establishing Norms and Improving Security): 121–137.

8. Ronald Deibert, "Towards a Human-Centric Approach to Cyber-security," *Ethics and International Affairs* 32, no. 4 (2018): 411–424, https://doi.org/10.1017/S0892679418000618

9. There is still vast digital inequality in the world, with about 40 percent of the world not using the internet. See Statista, "Global Digital Population as of January 2021," *Statista*, 2021: https://www.statista.com/statistics /617136/digital-population-worldwide/; however, infrastructure devel-opment and adoption is rising quickly and many populations are leap-frogging older landline connections for mobile connectivity. United Nations Conference on Trade and Development, 2018, Leapfrogging: Look Before you Leap, UNCTAD, December 2018: https://unctad .org/system/files/official-document/presspb2018d8_en.pdf; Deibert, *Reset: Reclaiming the Internet for Civil Society. The Unabridged Bibliography* (Toronto: House of Anansi Press, 2020): https://reset-bibliography.ca/

10. Ibid.

11. Ibid., 12.

12. Benjamin Bratton, *The Stack* (Cambridge, MA: The MIT Press, 2015), 5.

13. Ibid., 5.

14. Alex Comninos and Gareth Seneque, "Cyber Security, Civil Society, and Vulnerability in an Age of Communications Surveillance," *GIS Watch*, 2014: https://giswatch.org/en/communications-surveillance/cyber-se curity-civil-society-and-vulnerability-age-communications-sur; Ronald Deibert, "Towards a Human-Centric Approach to Cybersecurity."

15. Ibid.

16. Kerttunen and Tikk, "The Politics of Stability," 7.

17. Ibid., 7.

18. Ibid., 8.

19. Shoshana Zuboff, "Big Other: Surveillance Capitalism and the Prospects of an Information Civilization," *Journal of Information Technology* 30, no. 1 (2015): 75–89, https://doi.org/10.1057/jit.2015.5

20. While there are critiques of Zuboff's definition of surveillance capitalism, these debates are not addressed in this chapter. See Morozov Evgeny, "Capitalism's New Clothes," *The Baffler*, 2019: https://thebaffler.com/latest/capitalisms-new-clothes-morozov; Deibert, *Reset: Reclaiming the Internet for Civil Society*, chapter 1. These debates are not addressed in this chapter. Rather, we focus on the generally accepted characteristics of the business model of surveillance capitalism, and especially its many well-known pathologies. Zuboff, "Big Other"; Deibert, *Reset: Reclaiming the Internet for Civil Society*.

21. Facebook, Inc., "Form S-1 Registration Statement (no. 333)," *SEC Archives*, February 1, 2012: https://www.sec.gov/Archives/edgar/data/1326801/000119312512034517/d287954ds1.htm#toc287954_10

22. See Tanya Notley and Stephanie Hankey, "Human Rights Defenders and the Right to Digital Privacy and Security," in *Human Rights and Information Communication Technologies: Trends and Consequences of Use*, ed. John Lannon and Edward Halpin (Hershey, PA: IGI Global, 2013): https://doi.org/10.4018/978-1-4666-1918-0.ch010

23. Ronald Deibert, *Reset: Reclaiming the Internet for Civil Society*, 58. See also Bennet Cyphers and Gennie Gebhart, "Behind the One-Way Mirror: A Deep Dive into the Technology of Corporate Surveillance," *EFF*, 2019: https://www.eff.org/wp/behind-the-one-way-mirror

24. Fingerprinting techniques: R. Upathilake, Y. Li, and A. Matrawy, "A Classification of Web Browser Fingerprinting Techniques," in 2015 7th International Conference on New Technologies, Mobility and Security (NTMS) (1–5), IEEE; D. Fifield and S. Egelman, "Fingerprinting Web Users through Font Metrics." In *International Conference on Financial Cryptography and Data Security* (Springer, Berlin, Heidelberg, 2015): 107–124.

25. Notley and Hankey, "Human Rights Defenders and the Right to Digital Privacy and Security."

26. Ella McPherson, "ICTs and Human Rights Practice: A Report Prepared for the UN Special Rapporteur on Extrajudicial, Summary, or Arbitrary Executions," *University of Cambridge Centre of Governance and Human Rights* (2015): https://doi.org/10.17863/CAM.16807

27. Deibert, *Reset: Reclaiming the Internet for Civil Society*, 74.

28. Ronald Deibert, *Black Code: Inside the Battle for Cyberspace* (Toronto: Signal, McLelland & Steward, 2013), xvi.

29. Frederike Kaltheuner, "I Asked an Online Tracking Company for All of My Data and Here's What I Found," *Privacy International*, November 7, 2018: https://privacyinternational.org/long-read/2433/i-asked-online-tracking-company-all-my-data-and-heres-what-i-found

30. For example, "Quantcast has no direct relationship with the people whose data they collect. Therefore, most people have never heard of the company's name, do not know that they process their data and profile them, whether this data is accurate, for what purposes they are using it, or with whom it is being shared and the consequences of this processing." Kaltheuner, "I Asked an Online Tracking Company for All of My Data and Here's What I Found."

31. Privacy International, "Challenge to Hidden Data Ecosystem," *Privacy International*, 2018: https://privacyinternational.org/legal-action/challenge-hidden-data-ecosystem

32. Joseph Cox, "How an ICE Contractor Tracks Phones Around the World," *Vice Motherboard*, March 12, 2020: https://www.vice.com/en/article/epdpdm/ice-dhs-fbi-location-data-venntel-apps

33. Ibid.

34. Kate Robertson, Cynthia Khoo, and Yolanda Song, "To Surveil and Predict: A Human Rights Analysis of Algorithmic Policing in Canada – The Current Landscape," *Citizen Lab*, September 29, 2020: https://citizenlab.ca/wp-content/uploads/2021/01/AIPolicing_factualfindings_v6.pdf

35. Ibid.: 47–48.

36. Paul Meyer, "Norms of Responsible State Behaviour in Cyberspace," in *The Ethics of Cybersecurity*, ed. Markus Christen, Bert Gordijn, and Michele Loi (Cham: Springer, 2020), 347–360, 349, https://library.oapen.org/bitstream/handle/20.500.12657/22489/1007696.pdf?sequence=1#page=352

37. Germany, for example, outlined plans in 2016 to establish the Cyber and Information Space Command, complete with 13,500 soldiers. (Nina Werkhäuser, "German Army Launches New Cyber Command," *DW*, April 1, 2017: https://www.dw.com/en/german-army-launches-new-cyber-command/a-38246517. In France, the 2018 Military Programming Law for 2019–2025 dedicated €1.6 billion for cyber operations along with a total of 4,000 cyber combatants by 2025 (Hassan Meddah, "Pourquoi la France se dote d'une cyber-armée," *L'usine Nouvelle*, December 13, 2016: https://www.usinenouvelle.com/article/pourquoi-la-france-se-dote-d-une-cyber-armee.N476239; Nathalie Guibert, "L'armée française consolide son commandement cyber," *Le*

Monde, December 12, 2016: https://www.lemonde.fr/international/ar
ticle/2016/12/12/l-armee-francaise-consolide-son-commandement-cy
ber_5047780_3210.html; Arthur Laudrain, "France's New Offensive
Cyber Doctrine," *Lawfare*, February 26, 2019: https://www.lawfareblog
.com/frances-new-offensive-cyber-doctrine. In China, Unit 61398 of
the People's Liberation Army – one of China's cyber espionage units –
has been linked to an array of cyber espionage operations targeting US
nuclear, metal, and solar companies to access trade secrets, leading the
FBI to indict five Chinese military officers for hacking in 2014 (Megha
Rajagopalan, "Chinese Military Force to Take Lead on Cyber, Space
Defense," *Reuters*, January 29, 2016: https://www.reuters.com/article
/us-china-military-idUSKCN0V714B

38. Mike Levine, "Russia Tops List of 100 Countries that Could Launch
    Cyberattacks on US," *ABC News*, May 18, 2017: https://abcnews.go
    .com/US/russia-tops-list-100-countries-launch-cyberattacks-us/story?id
    =47487188

39. United States Cyber Command, "Army Cyber Command," *United States
    Cyber Command*, undated: https://www.cybercom.mil/Components.aspx

40. Meyer, "Norms of Responsible State Behaviour in Cyberspace," 348.

41. Canadian Department of National Defence, "Strong, Secure, Engaged:
    Canada's Defence Policy," *Canadian Department of National Defence*, 2017:
    https://www.canada.ca/content/dam/dnd-mdn/documents/reports/20
    18/strong-secure-engaged/canada-defence-policy-report.pdf

42. *Communications Security Establishment Act*, SC 2019, c 13, s 76 at s 19.

43. United States Cyber Command, "The Elevation of Cyber Command,"
    United States Cyber Command, undated: https://www.cybercom.mil/Abo
    ut/History/

44. Ibid.

45. Ellen Nakashima, "White House Authorizes 'Offensive Cyber Operations'
    to Deter Foreign Adversaries," *The Washington Post*, September 20, 2018:
    https://www.washingtonpost.com/world/national-security/trump-aut
    horizes-offensive-cyber-operations-to-deter-foreign-adversaries-bolton
    -says/2018/09/20/b5880578-bd0b-11e8-b7d2-0773aa1e33da_story
    .html

46. United States Joint Chiefs of Staff, "Joint Publication 3-12: Cyberspace
    Operations," June 8, 2018: https://www.jcs.mil/Portals/36/Documents/
    Doctrine/pubs/jp3_12.pdf

47. United States Congress, "National Defense Authorization Act for the
    Fiscal Year 2019," 2019: https://www.congress.gov/bill/115th-congress
    /house-bill/5515/text

48. The use of offensive cyber by authoritarian regimes is not limited to activities specifically aimed at their nationals and, more specifically, civil society. For example, we have seen offensive cyber used with the goal of foreign interference, for example cyber-enabled foreign election interference (O'Connor et al., "Cyber-enabled Foreign Interference in Elections and Referendums," *International Cyber Policy Centre, ASPI,* Policy Brief 4 (2020): https://www.aspi.org.au/report/cyber-enabled-foreign-interference-elections-and-referendums), or industrial espionage, for example cyber espionage in the manufacturing sector (Phil Neray, "Industrial Espionage is a Major Threat to the Manufacturing Sector," *IIoT World,* August 29, 2017: https://iiot-world.com/ics-security/cybersecurity/industrial-espionage-is-a-major-threat-to-the-manufacturing-sector/).

49. Nate Schenkkan and Isabel Linzer, "Out of Sight, Not Out of Reach: The Global Scale and Scope of Transnational Repression," *Freedom House,* 2021: https://freedomhouse.org/sites/default/files/2021-02/Co mplete_FH_TransnationalRepressionReport2021_rev020221.pdf

50. Schenkkan and Linzer, "Out of Sight, Not Out of Reach," 1–9.

51. Sven Herpig, "A Framework for Government Hacking in Criminal Investigations," *Stiftung Neue Verantwortung,* November 2, 2018: https://www.stiftung-nv.de/en/publication/framework-government-hacking-criminal-investigations

52. Ibid., 4–6.

53. Kerttunen and Tikk, "The Politics of Stability," 4–5; Klimburg and Almeida, "Cyber Peace and Cyber Stability: Taking the Norm Road to Stability," 61–66, 61; Jason Healey and Robert Jervis," The Escalation Inversion and Other Oddities of Situational Cyber Stability," *Texas National Security Review* 3, no. 4 (2020): 30–53, 33.

54. Kerttunen and Tikk, "The Politics of Stability," 7.

55. R. Goychayev et al., "Cyber Deterrence and Stability," *US Department of Energy,* 2017: https://www.pnnl.gov/main/publications/external/techn ical_reports/PNNL-26932.pdf

56. Ronald Deibert, "Towards a Human-Centric Approach to Cyber-security."

57. Anja Kovacs and Dixie Hawtin, "Cybersecurity, Cyber Surveillance and Online Human Rights," *Global Partners Digital,* January 31, 2013: https://www.gp-digital.org/publication/second-pub/

58. The UN General Assembly Resolution A/RES/68/169, for instance, clarifies that international human rights law applies online as well as offline. Further, the UN Office of the High Commissioner for Human

Rights 2018 reports on the right to privacy in the digital age states that human rights law "applies where a State exercises its power or effective control in relation to digital communications infrastructure, wherever located" and "where a State exercises regulatory jurisdiction over a third party that controls a person's information." It also imposes duties on states to "adopt legislative and other measures to give effect to the prohibition of and protection against unlawful or arbitrary interference and attacks" and to "protect persons within their jurisdiction from extraterritorial interference with their right to privacy, such as means of interception of communications or hacking." The UN Human Rights Committee's General Comment No. 37 on the right of peaceful assembly further states that Article 21 of the International Covenant on Civil and Political Rights "protects peaceful assemblies wherever they take place," including online, and warns that any legal framework for this provision should be informed by the reality that surveillance technologies can "infringe on the right to privacy and other rights of participants and bystanders and have a chilling effect."

59. Deibert, "Towards a Human-Centric Approach to Cybersecurity," 412.
60. Ibid., 412.
61. Ibid., 415.
62. Ibid., 416–420.
63. Global Commission on the Stability of Cyberspace, "Advancing Cyber Stability: Final Report": https://cyberstability.org/report/#2-what-is-meant-by-the-stability-of-cyberspace
64. Privacy International, "The Global Surveillance Industry," *Privacy International*: https://privacyinternational.org/sites/default/files/2017-12/global_surveillance_0.pdf
65. While the focus of research to date has been primarily on the development of surveillance technology by companies in Europe and Israel, many unknowns remain regarding the development of these companies in other jurisdictions. For example, there have been a number of reports over the past few years regarding increasing concern with the export of Chinese surveillance technology. Sheena Chestnut Greitens, "Dealing with Demands for China's Global Surveillance Exports," in *Global China: Assessing China's Growing Role in the World*, April 2020: https://www.brookings.edu/wp-content/uploads/2020/04/FP_20200428_china_surveillance_greitens_v3.pdf
66. Privacy International, "The Global Surveillance Industry," 18.
67. Mark Mazzetti et al., "A New Age of Warfare: How Internet Mercenaries Do Battle for Authoritarian Governments," *The New York Times*, March

21, 2019: https://www.nytimes.com/2019/03/21/us/politics/govern ment-hackers-nso-darkmatter.html

68. "Israli Cyber Firm NSO Group Mulls Tel Aviv IPO at $2 Billion Value – Reports," *Reuters*, January 6, 2021: https://www.reuters.com/article /israel-cyber-nso-ipo-int-idUSKBN29B0WU

69. Greitens, "Dealing with Demands for China's Global Surveillance Exports."

70. Kenneth Roth and Maya Wang, "Data Leviathan: China's Burgeoning Surveillance State," *Human Rights Watch:* https://www.hrw.org/news /2019/08/16/data-leviathan-chinas-burgeoning-surveillance-state

71. Chris Buckley and Paul Mozur, "How China Uses High-Tech Surveillance to Subdue Minorities," *The New York Times*, May 22, 2020: https://www.nytimes.com/2019/05/22/world/asia/china-surveillance -xinjiang.html

72. For a detailed discussion regarding the marketplace for offensive cyber capabilities, see Winnona DeSombre et al., "A Primer on the Proliferation of Offensive Cyber Capabilities," *Atlantic Council*, March 1, 2021: https://www.atlanticcouncil.org/in-depth-research-reports/issue-brief/ a-primer-on-the-proliferation-of-offensive-cyber-capabilities/#markets

73. Collin Anderson, "Monitoring the Lines: Sanctions and Human Rights Policy Considerations of TeleStrategies ISS World Seminars," July 31, 2014: https://cda.io/notes/monitoring-the-lines/

74. For example, the notorious spyware company Hacking Team was hacked in 2015, which in turn confirmed a host of authoritarian countries as the company's clients after the company persistently refused to confirm its client list and despite repeated findings by research organizations that it was providing spyware to authoritarian states. Katie Collins, "Hacking Team's Oppressive Regimes Customer List Revealed in Hack," *Wired*, July 6, 2015: https://www.wired.co.uk/article/hacking-team-spyware -company-hacked

75. DeSombre et al., "A Primer on the Proliferation of Offensive Cyber Capabilities."

76. For further discussion regarding the structuring of sales of offensive cyber capabilities, see James Shires, *The Politics of Cybersecurity in the Middle East* (London: Hurst, 2021).

77. WhatsApp Inc. v. NSO Group Technologies Limited, "Exhibit 1 through 11 – Document #1, Attachment #1," 2019: 67, https://www .courtlistener.com/docket/16395340/1/1/whatsapp-inc-v-nso-group -technologies-limited/ (accessed February 25, 2021).

78. Lorenzo Franceschi-Bicchierai, "Here's the DEA Contract for Hacking

Team's Spyware," *Vice*, February 19, 2016: https://www.vice.com/en/article/yp3v8y/dea-contract-with-hacking-team-spyware-foia

79. Al Jazeera Investigative Unit, "Bangladesh Bought Mass Spying Equipment from Israeli Company," *Al Jazeera*, February 2, 2021: https://www.aljazeera.com/news/2021/2/2/bangladesh-bought-surveillance-equipment-from-israeli-company. Also see: Hannah Beech, "Myanmar's Military Deploys Digital Arsenal of Repression in Crackdown," *The New York Times*, March 1, 2021: https://www.nytimes.com/2021/03/01/world/asia/myanmar-coup-military-surveillance.html

80. Human Rights Council, General Assembly, *Report of the Special Rapporteur on the Promotion and Protection of the Right to Freedom of Opinion and Expression* (New York: UN Headquarters, 2019): https://documents-dds-ny.un.org/doc/UNDOC/GEN/G19/148/76/PDF/G1914876.pdf?OpenElement

81. Stephen Peel, "Response to Open Letter to Novalpina Capital on 15 April 2019," *Citizen Lab*: https://citizenlab.ca/wp-content/uploads/2019/05/Novalpina-reply-May-15.pdf

82. There also remain open questions regarding the relationship between spyware companies and the jurisdictions in which they operate. For example, it is common knowledge that ex-members of the Israeli Defense Force transition into the technology industry in Israel (DeSombre et al., "A Primer on the Proliferation of Offensive Cyber Capabilities"); however, less is known about whether domestic governments provide support to the local surveillance industry under a type of quid pro quo agreement to receive access to the technology being produced, companies' client lists, individuals being targeted by clients, and more.

83. For example, Privacy International, ACLU and the Civil Liberties and Transparency Clinic of the University at Buffalo School of Law had to file a lawsuit in 2018 to acquire information from American federal law enforcement and immigration authorities regarding the nature and extent of their hacking activities (Privacy International, "IMSI Catchers: PI's Legal Analysis," *Privacy International*, 2020: https://privacyinternational.org/report/3965/imsi-catchers-pis-legal-analysis). This is just one recent example among many others.

84. Ronald Deibert et al, "Champing at the Cyberbit: Ethiopian Dissidents Targeted with New Commercial Spyware," *Citizen Lab*, 2017: https://citizenlab.ca/2017/12/champing-cyberbit-ethiopian-dissidents-targeted-commercial-spyware/; Human Rights Council, General Assembly, *Report of the Special Rapporteur on the Promotion and Protection of the Right to Freedom of Opinion and Expression* (2019).

85. Deibert et al., "Champing at the Cyberbit," 7.

86. Ibid.

87. Ibid., 7.

88. Ibid., 6–9.

89. Privacy International, "The Global Surveillance Industry, *Privacy International*, 2016: 20, https://privacyinternational.org/sites/default/files/2017-12/global_surveillance_0.pdf

90. Palantir n.d., "Home page," *Palantir.* https://www.palantir.com/#:~:text=At%20Palantir%2C%20we%20build%20software,the%20people%20who%20need%20it (accessed March 31, 2021).

91. Amnesty International found that "[u]sing ICM, ICE can access a vast range of personal data from U.S. agencies and law enforcement." FALCON Search and Analysis "is an information management system to allow ICE and other DHS personnel to 'search, analyze and visualize' existing ICE data." The FALCON Tipline permits "ICE and other DHS personnel to link information from tips to existing databases, and create profiles based on these tips." Amnesty International documents ICE's use of ICM and Falcon to various ICE operations, such as the 2017 arrest of more than 400 people "in an operation targeting parents and caregivers of unaccompanied children, leading to detentions and harming children's welfare" and workplace raids leading to numerous arrests and family separations. Amnesty International, "Failing to Do Right: The Urgent Need for Palantir to Respect Human Rights," *Amnesty International*, September 2020: 4–6, https://www.amnestyusa.org/wp-content/uploads/2020/09/Amnest-International-Palantir-Briefing-Report-092520_Final.pdf

92. George Joseph, "The LAPD Has a New Surveillance Formula, Powered by Palantir," *The Appeal*, May 8, 2018: https://theappeal.org/the-lapd-has-a-new-surveillance-formula-powered-by-palantir-1e277a95762a/; Sarah Brayne, *Predict and Surveil* (Oxford: Oxford University Press, 2020).

93. See, for example, Privacy International, "All Roads Lead to Palantir," *Privacy International*, 2020: https://www.privacyinternational.org/report/4271/all-roads-lead-palantir

94. Privacy International, "IMSI Catchers: PI's Legal Analysis," *Privacy International*, 2020: 1, https://privacyinternational.org/report/3965/imsi-catchers-pis-legal-analysis

95. Ibid., 4.

96. Ibid.

97. Ibid.

98. WhatsApp Inc. v. NSO Group Technologies Limited, "Exhibit 1 through 11 – Document #1, Attachment #1," 33.

99. Ibid., 40.

100. Siena Anstis, Sharly Chan, Adam Senft, and Ron Deibert, "Annotated Bibliography: Dual-Use Technologies: Network Traffic Management and Device Intrusion for Targeted Monitoring," *Citizen Lab*, October 2020: https://citizenlab.ca/wp-content/uploads/2020/11/Annotated -Bibliography-Network-Traffic-Management-and-Device-Intrusion -for-Targeted-Monitoring.pdf

101. Anstis et al., "Annotated Bibliography."

102. Ibid.

103. Jakub Dalek, Ron Deibert, Sarah McKune, Phillipa Gill, Adam Senft, and Naser Noor, "Information Controls During Military Operations: The Case of Yemen During the 2015 Political and Armed Conflict," *Citizen Lab*: https://citizenlab.ca/2015/10/information-controls-milita ry-operations-yemen/

104. Human Rights Council, General Assembly, *Report of the Special Rapporteur on the Promotion and Protection of the Right to Freedom of Opinion and Expression* (New York: UN Headquarters, 2017): https://undocs.org/pdf ?symbol=en/a/hrc/35/22, 13

105. Billet Marczak al., "Running in Circles: Uncovering the Clients of Cyberespionage," *Citizen Lab*, December 1, 2020: https://citizenlab.ca /2020/12/running-in-circles-uncovering-the-clients-of-cyberespionage -firm-circles/

106. Crofton Black, "Spy Companies Using Channel Islands to Track Phones Around the World," *Bureau of Investigative Journalism*, December 16, 2020: https://www.thebureauinvestigates.com/stories/2020-12-16/spy -companies-using-channel-islands-to-track-phones-around-the-world

107. Ibid.

108. Marczak et al., "Running in Circles."

109. Jennifer Lynch, "Face Off: Law Enforcement Use of Face Recognition Technology," *Electronic Frontier Foundation,* February 2018: 9, https:// www.eff.org/files/2018/02/15/face-off-report-1b.pdf

110. Ibid., 9.

111. Ibid.

112. James Vincent, "NYPD Used Facial Recognition to Track Down Black Lives Matter Activist," *The Verge*, August 18, 2020: https://www.thever ge.com/2020/8/18/21373316/nypd-facial-recognition-black-lives-mat ter-activist-derrick-ingram

113. Darren Byler, "China's Hi-Tech War on Its Muslim Minority," *The*

Guardian, April 11, 2019: https://www.theguardian.com/news/2019/apr/11/china-hi-tech-war-on-muslim-minority-xinjiang-uighurs-surveillance-face-recognition

114. Associated Press, "More Journalists Killed in Mexico in 2020 Than Anywhere Else in the World," *LA Times*, December 22, 2020: https://www.latimes.com/world-nation/story/2020-12-22/mexico-sees-most-journalists-killed-in-2020-group-says

115. Human Rights Watch, "World Report 2020: Mexico," 2021: https://www.hrw.org/world-report/2020/country-chapters/mexico

116. Azam Ahmed, "Mexican President Says Government Acquired Spyware But He Denies Misuse," *The New York Times*, June 22, 2017: https://www.nytimes.com/2017/06/22/world/americas/mexico-pena-nieto-hacking-pegasus.html

117. John Scott-Railton, "Reckless Reports," *Citizen Lab*, February 11, 2017: https://citizenlab.ca/2017/02/bittersweet-nso-mexico-spyware/

118. Stephanie Kirchgaessner et al. "Revealed: Leak Uncovers Global Abuse of Cyber-Surveillance Weapon," *The Guardian*, July 18, 2021: https://www.theguardian.com/world/2021/jul/18/revealed-leak-uncovers-global-abuse-of-cyber-surveillance-weapon-nso-group-pegasus

119. Cecile Schilis-Gallego and Nina Lakhani, "It's a Free-For-All: How Hi-Tech Spyware Ends Up in the Hands of Mexico's Cartels," *The Guardian*, December 7, 2020: https://www.theguardian.com/world/2020/dec/07/mexico-cartels-drugs-spying-corruption

120. Ibid.

121. Ibid.

122. Will Cathcart, "Why WhatsApp is Pushing Back on NSO Group Hacking," *The Washington Post*, October 29, 2019: https://www.washingtonpost.com/opinions/2019/10/29/why-whatsapp-is-pushing-back-nso-group-hacking/

123. WhatsApp Inc. v. NSO Group Technologies Limited, "Exhibit 1 through 11 – Document #1, Attachment #1."

124. Laurent Richard and Sandrine Rigaud, "Spyware Can Make Your Phone Your Enemy: Journalism is Your Defense," *The Guardian*, July 19, 2021: https://www.theguardian.com/world/commentisfree/2021/jul/19/spyware-can-make-your-phone-your-enemy-journalism-is-your-defence

125. Access Now, "Access Now Tells the Ninth Circuit Court: NSO Group Cannot Escape Accountability in US Courts," *Access Now*, December 23, 2020: https://www.accessnow.org/nso-group-whatsapp-lawsuit-civil-society-amicus-brief/

126. Ibid.

127. Ibid.

128. Ibid.

129. Ibid.

130. Dana M. Moss, "The Ties That Bind: Internet Communication Technologies, Networked Authoritarianism, and 'Voice' in the Syrian Diaspora," *Globalizations* 15, no. 2 (2018): 265–282. Marcus Michaelsen, "Far Away, So Close: Transnational Activism, Digital Surveillance and Authoritarian Control in Iran," *Surveillance & Society* 15, no. 3/4 (2017): 465–470, https://doi.org/10.24908/ss.v15i3/4.6635.https://doi.org/10.1080/14747731.2016.1263079; Marcus Michaelsen, "Exit and Voice in a Digital Age: Iran's Exiled Activists and the Authoritarian State," *Globalizations*, 15, no. 2 (2018): 248–264, https://doi.org/10.1080/14747731.2016.1263078

131. Marczak et al., "The Kingdom Came to Canada: How Saudi-Linked Digital Espionage Reached Canadian Soil," *Citizen Lab*, October 1, 2018: https://citizenlab.ca/2018/10/the-kingdom-came-to-canada-how-saudi-linked-digital-espionage-reached-canadian-soil/

132. David Pegg and Rob Evans, "Controversial Snooping Technology 'Used By At Least Seven Policy Forces,'" *The Guardian*, October 10, 2016: https://www.theguardian.com/world/2016/oct/10/controversial-phone-snooping-technology-imsi-catcher-seven-police-forces

133. Marczak et al., "Champing at the Cyberbit."

134. Joe Tidy, "I Was a Victim of the WhatsApp Hack," *BBC News*, October 31, 2019: https://www.bbc.com/news/technology-50249859

135. Nate Schenkkan and Isabel Linzer, "Out of Sight, Not Out of Reach: The Global Scale and Scope of Transnational Repression," *Freedom House*, 2021: 4, https://freedomhouse.org/sites/default/files/2021-02/Complete_FH_TransnationalRepressionReport2021_rev020221.pdf

136. Ibid., 6.

137. However, even with these amendments, there remains widespread criticism that the draft does not go far enough. Beatrix Immenkamp, "Review of Dual-Use Export Controls," *European Parliament Think Tank*, January 2021: https://www.europarl.europa.eu/RegData/etudes/BRIE/2016/589832/EPRS_BRI(2016)589832_EN.pdf

138. DeSombre et al., "Countering Cyber Proliferation: Zeroing in on Access-as-a-Service," *Atlantic Council*, March 1, 2021: https://www.atlanticcouncil.org/in-depth-research-reports/report/countering-cyber-proliferation-zeroing-in-on-access-as-a-service/#nso

139. Ibid.

140. Alfred Ng and Maddy Verner, "The Little-Known Data Broker Industry Is Spending Big Bucks Lobbying Congress," *The Markup,* April 1, 2021: https://themarkup.org/privacy/2021/04/01/the-little-known-data-bro ker-industry-is-spending-big-bucks-lobbying-congress

Part IV

Subaltern and Decolonial Perspectives

9

Infrastructure, Law, and Cyber Instability: An African Case Study

Mailyn Fidler

Cyber stability for African countries is unique. Where dominant views of cyber stability tend to center technological and regulatory openness, interoperability, and internationality, African countries can view global integration as fostering cyber instability through dependence. Where dominant views of cyber stability tend to focus on within-domain threats, African states have heightened sensitivity to a wider range of cross-domain threats. Both of these differences mean that, for African countries, attaining cyber stability can initially require actions that the global community might view as destabilizing.

This chapter challenges dominant conceptions of cyber stability from a subaltern perspective, drawing on research of African states. These arguments about cyber stability are a small part of a larger argument I make in a forthcoming book, which argues that we should conceive emerging African rules about cyberspace as a kind of political resistance. I draw on two specific sets of policy decisions African countries have made with respect to the cyber realm: investment patterns in cyber infrastructure, and the legal architecture of cyber security. First, African states have demonstrated preferences for certain international investors in their undersea fiber optic cable infrastructure, even if that comes at the cost of decreasing the diversity of investors overall or at the cost of maximizing technological elements such as bandwidth. African states have demonstrated a preference for investments from other African countries or from non-African countries – including China – without a history of African colonialism. Although some argue that China is a neo-colonial power, or, at the least, an exploitative power, perception of China as a historical non-colonial power in Africa matters here.[1] Again, these investment patterns contrast with dominant views of cyber security that associate stability with openness and maximizing international investment, not with selecting a few key partners.

Second, African states have turned to authoring their own cyber security laws and regulations through the African Union, rather than joining dominant external legal mechanisms, as a response to perceived threats and vulnerability in the cyber realm. This splintering of rules is viewed by dominant states as destabilizing but by African states as stabilizing. This example particularly highlights how more than just cyber vulnerability informs subaltern conceptions of cyber stability: both infrastructurally and *historically* vulnerable African states tend to support this pan-African legal authorship effort more strongly.

My approach focuses on the *perception* of these elements by African states. As Robert Jervis articulated, "it is often impossible to explain crucial decisions and policies without reference to the decision-makers' beliefs about the world and their images of others."[2] The empirical record on the effects of globalization or colonial investment in Africa, or on cyber attacks on the continent, may be mixed, but I contend that African state perception of associated threats is the important factor in assessing cyber stability.

Subalternity in International Relations

Two introductory notes on terminology: "subaltern" is a term that emerged from postcolonial, critical, and Gramscian scholarship to denote populations occupying marginalized positions and typically excluded from the core of decision-making to the periphery.[3] I use this term in a statist manner, following international relations scholars such as Mohammad Ayoob, to denote states occupying marginalized positions in the international system.[4] It does not connote a value judgment; rather, it takes its origins in the international relations tradition of assessing the relative material power of states with respect to each other and invokes a kind of material core and periphery.[5] It is worth noting that using the term subaltern in a statist manner elides some of the complexity and heterogeneity its originators intended it to hold.[6] Crucially, it is important to note that decision-makers within subaltern states might be considered more or less subaltern themselves – say, someone part of a transnational elite would not be considered a subaltern voice by original subaltern scholars – and that subaltern states also have varying experiences of colonialism, affecting their subaltern status.[7] As one way of combating this elision, my research disaggregates the colonial experience of the subaltern states I examine by identity of the colonial power. Overall, I use this term, despite these drawbacks, as an alternative to terms such as the "Third World" or "developing nations," as a way of centring the agency of the relevant states more fully, viewing them as subjects rather than as objects of international relations.[8]

This chapter speaks of states and organizational units like the African Union as unitary actors. This unitary actor approach simplifies complex dynamics in any study of international relations and does so specifically in African politics. My forthcoming book explores the internal dynamics of the African Union and member states in further detail, especially the roles that intergovernmental, supranational, and elite experts played in driving the development of the relevant African Union convention, drawing on Thomas Tieku's three-pronged analysis of the African Union.[9] This tripartite analysis is especially important in isolating the important role that elites have in the formation of African Union cyber policy.[10] I focus in particular on the African Union as the regional body of African states because this is the body that developed the African Union Convention, but many other regional identities exist across Africa and are active on cyber matters, too, which I also explore further in my book.

This chapter proceeds as follows: First, I give an overview of African state perceptions of cyber stability. Second, I analyze and critique two dominant concepts from the cyber stability literature from an African subaltern state perspective. First, I show how the dominant view of interdependence as central to cyber stability misses important aspects of the African experience, using investments in undersea fiber optic cables as an example. Second, I show how African state perceptions about threats are cross-domain, using regional cyber security laws as an example. Overall, African states are pursuing cyber stability through control of laws and through selectivity in infrastructural investments, both of which cut against typical expectations of subaltern states.

An Overview of African State Experiences of Cyber Stability

For African states, cyber stability is primarily about African control of both the laws governing and the infrastructure comprising a new sphere of influence – the cyber realm. African states have turned to selecting who invests in infrastructure and building their own legal governance systems as responses to perceived vulnerabilities and threats in the cyber arena, rather than responding purely within the cyber domain. Again, this conception of cyber stability runs counter to the dominant view, which considers such inward-looking governance and selective trade strategies to be destabilizing.[11] Control, legal and otherwise, is not a unique goal of African states.[12] But this seeking of control when material and historical conditions weigh against it is unusual, and African states in particular have rarely done so.[13] Especially surprising is that African states with the most vulnerable internet infrastructures seem more disposed to support African-led legal mechanisms.

This desire for control affects international policy, on which this chapter focuses, as well as domestic policy. My book explores the domestic side in more detail, but to briefly address it here: for many African states, negotiations on the international stage also serve a second goal of increasing government control and regime stability at home. This duality is not a phenomenon unique to Africa; many countries utilize this strategy.[14] Domestic implementations of international laws, domestic laws, and technical tools all form part of this strategy. For instance, the frequent internet shutdowns of the last decade in African countries demonstrate the use of a technical tool to this end.[15]

Part of this focus on control stems from hard facts about cyber capabilities: African states generally cannot match the cyber arsenals of dominant countries, and so turn to other methods of asserting themselves that are more available to them.[16] But a second part of this prioritization of control comes from African state experiences with conflict and governance by proxy. As decolonization and the Cold War progressed, African states experienced the politics of world powers playing out in their domestic affairs in two ways: "imperial powers hoped to transfer the reins of government to neo-colonial regimes that would continue to serve their political and economic interests" and "Cold War powers strove to shape a new international order that catered to their interests."[17] Part of this second effort involved small conflicts in African states transforming into full-scale wars with the backing of outside interests.[18]

The cyber domain is "attractive as a way to shape conflict in other domains."[19] African states' historical backdrop means they are particularly sensitized to such proxy conflicts. African states thus embody, perhaps to an extreme, a pattern cyber scholars have observed: "victims of aggression can and likely will look to responses not only in kind but also through whatever other means they possess."[20] Although "whatever means" usually means "military retaliation, irregular warfare and covert subversion, trade and financial sanctions," the African experience shows that those means range further – to authorship of legal rules and to ownership of infrastructure – all the more unexpected because of the existing material conditions that make this more challenging for African states.[21] And, importantly, the African experience demonstrates that those particularly vulnerable on the infrastructural front are more likely to turn to legal rule authorship as a way of seeking cyber stability. To explore this African experience of cyber stability, this chapter next investigates two key traditional components of cyber stability – interdependence and threat perception – and how they differ in the African context. Namely, African states tend to prioritize independence over global interdependence, and engage in wide-ranging, cross-domain threat perception.

Stability, Through Interdependence or Independence?
Dominant Views

Dominant views of cyber stability tend to prioritize technological and governance openness, interoperability, and internationality. Lu Chuanying argues, for instance, that cyber stability is only possible if state cyber strategies avoid cyberbalkanization.[22] The United States has traditionally taken this viewpoint, arguing that multilateral cooperation and multistakeholder governance are the keys to a secure internet.[23] The US State Department Deputy Coordinator for Cyber Issues, Michele Markoff, summarized the United States' approach in 2015 as follows: regarding the internet, "we view the role of states as one of many stewards – that is, caretakers, who work with all other stakeholders to ensure that this resource is available to all to reap positive benefits and rewards."[24]

The success of this vision relies on all states viewing the internet similarly, as a kind of commons, rather than as a threat to domestic stability (see Kerr, Chapter 3 this volume). This view tends to consider state over-involvement in the cyber governance realm as destabilizing. Christopher Painter, the State Department's Coordinator for Cyber Issues, expressed this view in his testimony to a Committee on Foreign Relations subcommittee in 2016.[25] He identified China's and Russia's approach to cyberspace in the international context as a key "challenge to the implementation of our cyberspace strategy."[26] Specifically, China's "desire to maintain internal stability, [and] maintain sovereignty over its domestic cyberspace" and Russia's "focus . . . on the maintenance of internal stability, as well as sovereignty over its 'information space'" posed a threat to the US vision of an internationally stable internet.[27] These "alternative concepts of cyberspace policy" needed to be countered to preserve such stability.[28]

Another key component of this stability-through-openness view is the free flow of the global tech trade. Countries risk destabilizing cyberbalkanization, Chuanying argues, when they "reject . . . foreign products and investments in ways that undermine global trade."[29] Under this view, developing country acceptance of foreign investments in telecommunications promotes, rather than undermines, stability.

This dominant account misses several important considerations – namely, perceptions – that are relevant to subaltern states. First, it neglects the possibility that, for such states, greater interdependence can foster a sense of dependence. Critics of globalization have long articulated this view. Major elements of globalization as implemented – trade relations, foreign direct investment, and direct aid – created, in the eyes of some, "persistent forms of dependency."[30]

Under this lens, globalization's "promised bounties have not materialized."[31] Instead, globalization "has proved to be inimical to the vulnerable majority especially in the poor sub-Saharan African countries."[32] Rather than stability and prosperity, "North-South integration failed in laying a more viable, fair and equal partnership between the developing and developed countries and arguably restricted and purposely took advantage of countries on the periphery."[33] This view of globalization is contested, certainly, but the prevalent narratives of cyber stability fail to take into account the possibility that certain subaltern actors might not share a view of interdependence as stabilizing. For subaltern states, it is precisely this kind of integration that can be destabilizing.

The African Experience: Selective, Non-colonial Investments in Cable Infrastructure as Stability-enhancing

Investment choices for cyber infrastructure show one way in which African state choices to maximize cyber stability counter dominant narratives. Across the board, African states have favored non-colonial financiers in undersea cable infrastructure, especially in the past five years. Preferred investors have included those who lack historical colonial ties with African countries, including other African countries, China, and the US – meaning cable infrastructure projects have moved away from (although not abandoned) European financing. Out of the six major cable projects in Africa completed or in progress 2017–2021, only one is primarily funded by companies with ties to a former colonial power.[34] This shift in funders represents a change from earlier investments in undersea cables in Africa. Many existing "backbone" cables are funded by former colonial powers, sometimes in conjunction with African partners. For instance, the 2000 Atlantis-II cable received substantial support from French telecom companies, and the 2001 SAT3 cable was funded by French and US companies with additional support from Indian and Singaporean companies. A decade later, the major Africa Coast to Europe Cable (ACE) (2012) was also funded primarily by French companies in conjunction with African partners.

In contrast, the most ambitious cable projects in Africa now primarily draw their funding from African countries themselves, in conjunction with other Global South companies, US companies, or Chinese companies. Chinese companies are heavily involved in the Pakistan and East Africa Connecting Europe (PEACE) cable, launching in 2021 with landing points in Egypt, Somalia, Djibouti, Kenya, and the Seychelles. Chinese companies are also the only investors in the 2021 regional Senegal Horn of Africa Regional Express (SHARE) cable. Google is building a solely owned cable along the West Coast of Africa, with African landing points in Nigeria, the Democratic Republic of the Congo, South Africa, and Namibia. And Facebook, along with China Mobile, are key investors in the pan-African cable project Africa2, scheduled for completion in 2023 – although its co-investors look suspiciously like the old guard, with companies from the United Kingdom and France also investing.[35]

It might seem like African countries are simply swapping one source of outside investment for another, especially if one considers China a neo-colonial power.[36] But maintaining a diversity of outside investments as a hedge against unfavorable terms by former colonial powers matters to African countries, as does the source of the investment in and of itself.[37] As one African Union official commented with respect to alleged espionage by the Chinese telecom company Huawei – "at least they never colonized us."[38]

Since 2017, African countries are also increasingly funding cable projects solely or with partnerships with non-colonizer nations. The 2018 South Atlantic Cable System connects Angola to Brazil and is solely funded by Angolan telecom companies. The 2018 South Atlantic InterLink connects Cameroon with Brazil and is a joint venture between Chinese and Cameroonian telecom companies. On the regional side, a consortium of exclusively African companies funded the Djibouti Africa Regional Express 1 (DARE1) to connect Kenya, Djibouti, and Somalia. The CEIBA2 project connects Cameroon and Equatorial Guinea, funded by an Equatorial Guinean company. And Maroc Telecom, a Moroccan company, solely funded the 2021 Maroc Telecom West Africa cable connecting Morocco, Côte d'Ivoire, Benin, Gabon, and Togo. These investment patterns run precisely counter to what dominant cyber stability literature considers to be stabilizing.

Cross-domain Threat Perception and Response
Dominant Views

The primary account of cyber stability also vastly simplifies cyber threat and vulnerability perception of subaltern states. For instance, this account tends to view strong states as more materially vulnerable, because more networked states have more cyber attack surfaces. Lindsay and Gartzke, for example, state flatly that "poor states are not vulnerable" because they lack the attack "surface" to be as damaged by cyber operations as states more dependent on internet infrastructure.[39] But the notion of cyber vulnerability cannot be considered in isolation. Perceptions of and responses to vulnerability are informed by considerations across domains – not just cyber-related factors.

One of the critical and overlooked cross-domain considerations is a country's experiences with colonialism. Many, if not most, threats are evaluated by African states with reference to this historical fact and its lingering effects. Consider the concept of conflict escalation, as used in the cyber realm. Scholars often characterize escalation as "an increase in the intensity or scope of conflict that crosses threshold(s) considered significant by one or more of the participants."[40] The conflict escalation ladder looks different for postcolonial countries because the logic of colonialism continues to operate even today, both within states and between states.[41] Just as Western countries might view an autocracy's views about cyber openness as a threat to their vision of stability, postcolonial states might view a former colonizer's views of cyber openness as a threat to theirs.

The issue of foreign investment in cyber infrastructure is an illustrative example of the complexities of threat perception in the postcolonial environment. As described above, the prevalent cyber stability view considers free trade and investment in cyber infrastructure a key component of cyber stability. But this view fails to recognize the ways in which countries reliant on such outside investments are cognizant of the foreign influence and control such investments can bring.[42] This view also conveniently elides details about great power influence on technological standards and covert interference with certain products; as the Snowden disclosures indicated, subaltern states are right to be concerned about backdoor influence.[43] For subaltern, postcolonial, states, foreign products and investments from certain countries inculcate vulnerability of one kind in exchange for the promise of what, in the dominant state's view, builds stability.[44]

Cyber skirmishes present another example. Jason Healey and Robert Jervis argue that small cyber skirmishes can either be stabilizing, if there is relative peace or strong desires on both sides to limit conflict, or destabilizing, if there is "tension in cyberspace between states."[45] This calculus misses a key consideration for subaltern states: the ability to respond. A threat that other states might be willing to leave unanswered might appear to have a non-escalatory effect. But, for subaltern states, choosing not to respond versus being unable to respond results in different cumulative effects on threat perception; over time, even if relative peace and strong desires exist between states, an imbalance in ability to respond can exert a destabilizing effect.

On a similar note, perceptions of cyber escalation in subaltern states go beyond the standard "effects of an attack, the means by which an attack was conducted, and the physical location of the attack or effect."[46] To give a very cursory look at the internet landscape in Africa, only about 20 percent of the sub-Saharan African population used the internet as of 2017, according to the most recently available World Bank statistics.[47] According to a 2016 report prepared jointly by the African Union and Symantec Security, only 1 percent of global attacks targeted Africa and three percent originated in Africa.[48] Given this comparatively low level of penetration and threat activity, both outgoing and incoming, Lindsay and Gartzke's assessment that African states are not vulnerable might look accurate.[49] But an actual cyber attack need not have occurred at all to increase an African state's threat perceptions in the cyber realm. The next section of this chapter examines how considerations in the legal systems governing cyber security affect threat perceptions – specifically, how African states perceive dominant state efforts to assert legal primacy in the cyber area as a threat, and how African development of their own legal rules in this area serves as a form of threat response.

Rule Authorship and Threat Perception: Legal Splintering as Stabilizing

In 2014, the African Union launched its Convention on Cybersecurity and Data Protection. The African Union was the fifth regional organization to develop such an international mechanism – a step unusual at all for a region usually subject to an expectation or pressure to go along with Western attempts to promote international cooperation on a given subject.[50] The European Commission had positioned its 2001 Budapest Convention on Cybercrime to become the global gold standard of cyber security governance. But its dominance was challenged from the start, first by the 2001 Russia-led Commonwealth of Independent States' agreement on the same topic, then by the 2009 Russia- and China-led Shanghai Cooperation Organization agreement, the 2010 League of Arab States convention, and the African Union Convention.

In interviews I conducted, interviewees invariably cast the African Union's launch of this Convention as a kind of response to a perceived sense of vulnerability in a new issue area – cyberspace – and a desire to assert some form of control. Moses Karanja, then at the Centre for Intellectual Property and Information Technology Law at Strathmore University in Kenya said, "The problem came with the whole sovereignty thing. We can't just borrow or join another Convention." He continued, "anything that is – I don't want to use the word colonial – dependent on international forces isn't workable." Arthur Gwagwa, then of the Zimbabwe Human Rights NGO Forum, was direct about the source of this sense of vulnerability: "it's a non-starter to convince African governments to join a European mechanism . . . It's the colonial legacy." Emilar Vushe, then of the Association for Progressive Communications, continued this theme: the Convention could be characterized as an attempt to assert "that we've done this ourselves. It's an African Convention, from an African perspective, a pan-African approach." 'Gbenga

Sesan, then Director of Paradigm Initiative Nigeria, described the Convention as coming "from a sense of pride – we did this." African ownership of the rules really mattered to African actors.

African ownership of rules matters, in particular, to the most vulnerable African states. Vulnerability is a complex concept to measure. I use two proxies: colonial history and subsea fiber optic infrastructural development. Of these two factors, infrastructural development is easier to measure: I examine number of fiber optic cables, coastal landing points, and growth in these metrics. For colonial history, I use the identity of the colonizing country as a proxy for historical vulnerability. Former French colonies, as well as colonies of smaller nations such as Portugal and the Netherlands, are widely regarded as more economically vulnerable than former British colonies.[51] To present a few of many reasons for this imbalance, French colonies continued to experience comparatively more dependence on France during the postcolonial era than other former colonies depended on their respective colonizer countries. France viewed its former colonies as a key economic and global political asset, maintaining strong personal, financial, and security ties with former colonies and extending support to pro-French leaders.[52] Former French colonies used the CFA Franc, pegged at a fixed rate and fully convertible with the French Franc, until 1994, which favored elites with French ties over indigenous producers.[53] The French aid budget was also huge: in the late 1980s, it was 50 percent larger than the World Bank's sub-Saharan allocations.[54] All of these factors contributed to overall higher perceptions of vulnerability in Francophone Africa – as well as worse economic realities. In contrast, scholars point to aspects including the indirect nature and lack of forced labor of British colonial rule, as well as arguably positive economic effects of Commonwealth membership for former colonies, as contributing to an overall less acute – although not absent – sense of economic vulnerability.[55]

A clear pattern emerges on both measures of vulnerability: more vulnerable states tend to support the African Union convention. Forty-seven percent of the nineteen member states that have acceded (of a possible total of fifty-five) are former French colonies.[56] Thirty-two percent are from Portuguese or other smaller colonial powers.[57] Only 21 percent are British.[58] Among non-signatories, in contrast, 44 percent are former British colonies, 31 percent are former French colonies, 14 percent are former colonies of smaller countries, and 11 percent have non-standard colonial histories (see Table 9.1).[59]

Signatories share another common vulnerability: on average, signatories have fewer undersea fiber optic cable landing points than coastal non-signatories. Undersea cables are critical components of internet connectivity: they carry most of the internet's data across borders quickly and reliably.[60]

Table 9.1 Signatory status by colonial history

	French (%)	British (%)	Other (%)	Non-standard (%)
Signatories	47	21	32	0
Non-signatories	31	44	14	11

Note: "Other" indicates a colonial history with any other non-French or non-British colonizer. "Non-standard" indicates that (1) different areas of the country were under control by different nations at decolonization or (2) the country does not have a history of colonization.

Table 9.2 Signatories by undersea fiber optic cable data

Coastal countries	Cables	Landing points	Cable growth 2017–2021
Signatories	2.58	1.16	0.58
Non-signatories	3.66	1.57	1.08

Countries generally classify these cables as critical infrastructure, since they are vulnerable to threats ranging from being cut by ocean-going ships to espionage and sabotage. For scale, the continental United States has between forty and fifty cities with landing points, with about twice that many entering cable branches. Boca Raton, Florida, alone, has six entering cables, more than the average African country.[61] In 2021, coastal signatories of the African Union Convention had an average of 2.58 cables at 1.16 landing points, with an average growth of 0.58 cables over the last five years.[62] In 2021, coastal non-signatories had an average of 3.66 cables at 1.57 landing points, with an average growth of 1.08 cables over the past five years (see Table 9.2). (Note that the comparison class here is to coastal non-signatories because, by definition, only coastal states can have undersea cable landing points.) Supporters of the Convention are, on average, more vulnerable in terms of the scale and growth rate of their undersea fibre optic infrastructure than comparable non-signatories.

The African Union's decision to develop an alternative to the dominant global legal regime runs counter to mainstream notions of cyber stability. Dominant states consider global mechanisms more conducive to cyber stability. Here, we see more infrastructurally vulnerable nations, and more historically vulnerable nations, supporting a legal effort that dominant states consider destabilizing. And these states are factoring more than just cyber vulnerability into their decision to support the African Union cyber legal mechanism: colonial history has powerful echoes. These states are not supporting a "splintered" legal mechanism because they benefit from instability; conversely, these states are supporting the Convention precisely because it contributes to their view of cyber stability. If a state cannot set the terms of its historical and economic relationships with dominant states, and it cannot achieve the infrastructural independence and diversity it would like, it can at least control the rules of the game on its own turf, seeking (if not achieving) a sense of legal cyber stability.

Conclusion

Cyber stability looks different for subaltern states. Dominant states have pursued their vision of cyber stability in ways that subaltern states perceive as destabilizing, namely, authoring "global" rules and expanding global infrastructural investments. Subaltern states have pursued their own vision of cyber stability that dominant states perceive as destabilizing, by developing their own rules and selectively choosing infrastructural investors. The experience of African states, as presented here, underscores that cyber stability is fundamentally socio-technical in nature – it depends on more than just the contents of a state's digital arsenal, including authorship of laws.[63] Taking a subaltern view demonstrates that stability is a goal states share with respect to the cyber realm – but one that is difficult to achieve, given competing conceptions of what contributes to stability.

Notes

1. See infra note 56 and accompanying text.
2. Robert Jervis, *Perception and Misperception in International Relations* (Princeton, NJ: Princeton University Press, 1976), 28.
3. Antonio Gramsci, *Subaltern Social Groups* (New York: Columbia University Press, 2021).
4. See Mohammed Ayoob, "Inequality and Theorizing in International Relations: The Case for Subaltern Realism," *International Studies Review* 4, no. 3 (2002): 27–48.
5. Gramsci, *Subaltern Social Groups*, note 4.
6. Gayatri Chakravorty Spivak, "Can the Subaltern Speak?," in *Marxism and the Interpretation of Culture*, ed. Cary Nelson and Lawrence Grossberg (Champaign: University of Illinois Press, 1988).
7. Mumford, Chapter 10 this volume.
8. Dipesh Chakrabarty, "Subaltern Studies and Postcolonial Historiography," *Nepantla: Views from South* 9, no. 15 (2000): 1. "The declared aim of Subaltern Studies was to produce historical analyses in which the subaltern groups were viewed as the subjects of history."

9. For example, Thomas Kwasi Tieku, *Governing Africa: 3D Analysis of the African Union's Performance* (Lanham, MD: Rowman & Littlefield, 2017).

10. Mumford, Chapter 10 in this volume. Mumford discusses the role of transnational technical elites in internet governance.

11. See previous sections of this volume for examples.

12. Laura DeNardis, "Governance by Infrastructure," in *The Turn to Infrastructure in Internet Governance*, ed. Francesca Musiani et al. (Basingstoke: Palgrave Macmillan, 2016); Kenneth Merrill, "Domains of Control: Governance of and by the Domain Name System," in *The Turn to Infrastructure in Internet Governance*, ed. Musiani et al.; Daniel R. Headrick, *The Invisible Weapon: Telecommunications and International Politics* 1851–1945 (Oxford: Oxford University Press, 1991).

13. African states rarely formulate their own legal mechanisms when international bodies offer an alternative; for exceptions, see the African Charter on Human and People's Rights (1981) and the Bamako Convention on the Ban on the Import Into Africa and the Control of Transboundary Movement and Management of Hazardous Wastes within Africa (1991). For one account of why weak states tend to join international efforts, see Christina Schneider, "Weak States and Institutionalized Bargaining Power in International Organizations," *International Studies Quarterly* 55, no. 2 (2011); see also Eyal Benvenisti and George Downs, "The Empire's New Clothes: Political Economy and the Fragmentation of International Law," *Stanford Law Review* 60, no. 2 (2007): 595, 620.

14. See generally "Abuse of Cybercrime Measures Taints UN Talks," *Human Rights Watch*, May 5, 2021; Ronald Deibert et al. (eds.), *Access Controlled: The Shaping of Power, Rights, and Rule in Cyberspace* (Cambridge, MA: The MIT Press, 2010); Bassant Hassib and James Shires, "Co-opting Cybersecurity in Egypt," Atlantic Council, May 11, 2021.

15. "Internet Shutdowns in Africa: 'It's Like Being Cut Off from the World,'" Association for Progressive Communications, January 16, 2019; see generally Nanjala Nyabola, *Digital Democracy, Analogue Politics: How the Internet Era is Transforming Politics in Kenya* (London: Zed Books, 2018), 231–260.

16. Nigeria appears to be the only African country with a cyber command as of June 2021. See Kate O'Flaherty, "The Nigerian Cyber Warfare Command: Waging War in Cyberspace," *Forbes*, November 26, 2018: https://www.forbes.com/sites/kateoflahertyuk/2018/11/26/the-niger ian-cyber-warfare-command-waging-war-in-cyberspace/?sh=448f4c5f 2fba

17. Elizabeth Schmidt, *Foreign Intervention in Africa: From the Cold War to the War on Terror* (Cambridge: Cambridge University Press, 2013), 1.

18. Ibid., 8. See generally Odd Arne Westad, *The Global Cold War: Third World Intervention and the Making of Our Times* (Cambridge: Cambridge University Press, 2005).

19. Jon R. Lindsay and Eric Gartzke, "Coercion through Cyberspace: The Stability-Instability Paradox Revisited," in *Coercion: The Power to Hurt in International Politics*, ed. Kelly M. Greenhill and Peter Krause (New York: Oxford University Press, 2018), 179.

20. Ibid., 194.

21. Ibid.

22. Lu Chuanying, "Forging Stability in Cyberspace," *Survival* 62, no. 2 (2020).

23. Testimony of Christopher Painter: "International Cybersecurity Strategy: Deterring Foreign Threats and Building Cyber Norms," Hearings before the Subcommittee on East Asia, the Pacific, and International Cybersecurity Policy, Senate, 114th Congress (May 2016): https://www .govinfo.gov/content/pkg/CHRG-114shrg28853/html/CHRG-114 shrg28853.htm; M. Hathaway, "Cyberspace Policy Review: Assuring a Trusted and Resilient Information and Communications Infrastructure," *Report United States Office of the White House*, 2019.

24. Michelle Markoff, "Remarks for Panel Session 'Developments of Cyberspace and Emerging Challenges,'" report prepared for ASEAN Regional (ARF) Cyber Capability Workshop, 2009: 2, https://2009-2017.state.gov/s/ cyberissues/releasesandremarks/245720.htm

25. Testimony of Christopher Painter: "International Cybersecurity Strategy." At the time of this interview, Painter was also involved in the Global Forum on Cyber Expertise, a key multistakeholder cyber capacity-building institution founded in 2015. See "Foundation Board," *Global Forum on Cyber Expertise*: https://thegfce.org/foundation_board/chris-painter/ (accessed June 24, 2021).

26. Ibid.

27. Ibid.

28. Ibid.

29. Chuanying, "Forging Stability in Cyberspace," 132.

30. Elisabeth Farny, "Dependency Theory: A Useful Tool for Analyzing Global Inequalities Today," *E-ir* (2016): 7, https://www.e-ir.info/2016/11/23/ dependency-theory-a-useful-tool-for-analyzing-global-inequalities- today/.

31. Alfred J. López, "Introduction: The (Post) Global South," *The Global South* 1, no. 1 (2007): 1–11.

32. Luke Amadi, "Africa: Beyond the 'New' Dependency: A Political

Economy," *African Journal of Political Science and International Relations* 6, no. 8 (2012): 191–203.

33. Farny, "Dependency Theory," 7; Also see J. E. Stiglitz, *Globalization and its Discontents* (New York: Norton, 2012), 224.

34. The Meltingpot Indianoceanic Submarine System (METISS) is funded by two French companies and companies from Mauritius, Madagascar, and Réunion. Mauritius and Madagascar have former colonial ties with France, and Réunion is still a French territory.

35. Companies from South Africa, Mauritius, Egypt, and Saudi Arabia round out the list. Facebook is also partnering with Liquid Telecom in an ambitious project to bring overland fiber to the Democratic Republic of the Congo and its neighbors. See: Liquid Intelligent Technologies "Liquid Intelligent Technologies and Facebook Partner to Build a Fibre Network in the Democratic Republic of Congo," *Liquid Telecom*, July 5, 2021.

36. Whether China is or is not neo-colonial in its orientation toward Africa is the subject of intense debate that this chapter does not fully address. For a selection of relevant literature, see Zhao Suisheng, "A Neo-Colonialist Predator or Development Partner? China's Engagement and Rebalance in Africa," *Journal of Contemporary China* 23, no. 90 (2014): 1039; Ivar Kolstad and Arne Wiig, "Better the Devil you Know? Chinese Foreign Direct Investment in Africa," *Journal of African Business* 12, no. 31 (2011); Osman Antwi-Boateng, "New World Order Neo-Colonialism: A Contextual Comparison of Contemporary China and European Colonization in Africa," *Africology: The Journal of Pan African Studies* 10, no. 177 (2017); Ishan Sharma, "China's Neocolonialism in the Political Economy of A.I. Surveillance," *Cornell International Affairs Review* 8, no. 4 (2020).

37. Japan's investment in African states in the 1980s and 1990s is an example of this trend. Kweku Ampiah, "Japan and the Development of Africa: A Preliminary Evaluation of the Tokyo International Conference on African Development," *African Affairs* 104, no. 97 (2005); Christian M. Rogerson, "Japan's Hidden Involvement in South African Manufacturing," *GeoJournal* 30, no. 99 (1993); "Annex Table 4: FDI Outflows from Selected OECD Countries to Africa, 1983–1997," in "Foreign Direct Investment in Africa: Performance and Potential," *UNCTAD*, 1999.

38. Mailyn Fidler, "African Union Bugged by China: Cyber Espionage as Evidence of Strategic Shifts," *Council on Foreign Relations*, March 6, 2018, quoting the French original: Galia Khadiri and Joan Tilouine, "A Addis-Abeba, le siège de l'Union africaine espionné par Pékin," *Le Monde Afrique*, January 26, 2018.

39. Lindsay and Gartzke, "Coercion through Cyberspace: The Stability-Instability Paradox Revisited."

40. Forrest E. Morgan et al., *Dangerous Thresholds: Managing Escalation in the 21st Century* (Santa Monica, CA: RAND Corporation, 2008), 8.

41. Nathan Nunn, "Historical Legacies: A Model Linking Africa's Past to its Current Underdevelopment," *Journal of Development Economics* 83, no. 157 (2007); Samuel O. Oloruntoba, "Breaking the Incubus? The Tripartite Free Trade Agreements and the Prospects of Developmental Integration in Africa," in *The Development of Africa*, ed. Olayinka Akanle and Jimi Olalekan Adesina (Cham: Springer International Publishing, 2018) (discussing how the logic of colonialism continues to operate, including in the very borders of African states themselves); Charis Enns and Brock Bersaglio, "On the Coloniality of 'New' Mega-Infrastructure Projects in East Africa," *Antipode* 101, no. 56 (2020); Daron Acemoglu, Simon Johnson, and James Robinson, "The Colonial Origins of Comparative Development: An Empirical Investigation," *American Economic Review* 91, no. 1369 (2001).

42. Kwame Nkrumah, *Neo-Colonialism, the Last Stage of Imperialism* (London: Thomas Nelson and Sons, 1965); Keith Glaister, Nigel Driffield, and Yupu Lin, "Foreign Direct Investment to Africa: Is There a Colonial Legacy?" *Management International Review* (2020); Todd Moss, Vijaya Ramachandran, and Manju Kedia Shah, "Is Africa's Skepticism of Foreign Capital Justified? Evidence from East African Firm Survey Data," *Working Paper Series* 41, no. 1 (2004); Ian Taylor, "France à Fric: The CFA Zone in Africa and Neocolonialism," *Third World Quarterly* 40, no. 6 (2019).

43. Susan Landau, "On NSA's Subversion of NIST's Algorithm," *Lawfare*, July 25, 2014; Glenn Greenwald, "How the NSA Tampers with US-Made Internet Routers," *The Guardian*, May 12, 2014.

44. *Supra* note 23.

45. Jason Healey and Robert Jervis, "The Escalation Inversion and Other Oddities of Situational Cyber Stability," *Texas National Security Review* 3, no. 4 (2020).

46. Ibid.

47. "Individuals Using the Internet (% of population) – Sub-Saharan Africa," *World Bank*, 2017. Author's note: the lack of more recent comprehensive statistics about internet usage and cyber attacks (see next footnote) demonstrates another way in which African countries are subaltern.

48. African Union and Symantec, "Cyber Crime and Cyber Security Trends in Africa," 2016: https://thegfce.org/cybercrime-and-cybersecurity-trends-in-africa/; many cyber attacks in Africa also go unreported.

49. See *supra* note 20.
50. See *supra* note 36.
51. This view does not speak to what would have happened absent colonialism. Alexander Lee and Kenneth Schultz, "Comparing British and French Colonial Legacies: A Discontinuity Analysis of Cameroon," *Quarterly Journal of Political Science* 7, no. 1 (2012); F. Hayek, *The Constitution of Liberty* (Chicago: University of Chicago Press, 1960); Seymour M. Lipset, "The Social Requisites of Democracy Revisited: 1993 Presidential Address," *American Sociological Review* 59, no. 1 (1994); Douglass North, *Understanding the Process of Economic Change* (Princeton, NJ: Princeton University Press, 2005); Rafael La Porta et al., "Law and Finance," *Journal of Political Economy* 106, no. 1113 (1998).
52. Christopher Clapham, *Africa and the International System* (Cambridge: Cambridge University Press, 1996), 38; Kaye Whiteman, "The Rise and Fall of Eurafrique: From the Berlin Conference of 1884/1885 to the Tripoli EU-Africa Summit of 2010," in *The EU and Africa: From Eurafrique to Afro-Europa*, ed. Adekeye Adebajo and Kaye Whiteman (New York: Columbia University Press, 2012), 31; Michael C. Reed, "Gabon: A Neo-Colonial Enclave of Enduring French Interest," *The Journal of Modern African Studies* 25, no. 2 (June 1987): 297; Daniel Bon and Karen Mingst, "French Intervention in Africa: Dependency or Decolonization," *Africa Today* 27, no. 2 (1980): 16.
53. Adedeji Adedeji, "Comparative Strategies of Economic Decolonization in Africa," *General History of Africa* 8 (1993): 395; Roland Marchal, "France and Africa: The Emergence of Essential Reforms?" *International Affairs* 74, no. 2 (2002): 355–372; Clapham, *Africa and the International System*, 94.
54. Clapham, *Africa and the International System*, 95.
55. Lee and Shultz, *supra* note 50, 11–12; See also Matthew Lange, "British Colonial Legacies and Political Development," *World Development* 32, no. 905 (2004); Sarianna M. Lundan and Geoffrey Jones, The *"Commonwealth" Effect and the Process of Internationalisation The World Economy* 24, no. 1 (2001): 99–118; Joana Bennett et al., "Trading Places: The 'Commonwealth Effect' Revisited," *Royal Commonwealth Society*, working paper, September 30, 2010.
56. Colonial status determined by identify of colonizer at decolonization. If mixed or not colonized, I counted the country as having a non-standard colonial history. Signatories with French colonial history: Benin, Chad, Comoros, the Republic of Congo, Guinea, Mauritania, Senegal, Togo, and Tunisia.
57. Signatories with histories of colonization by other countries: Angola,

Guinea-Bissau, Mozambique, São Tomé and Principe (Portugal); Namibia (German and others), and Rwanda (Dutch).

58. Signatories with British colonial history: Ghana, Mauritius, Sierra Leone, and Zambia.

59. Non-signatories with British colonial history: Botswana, Egypt, Eswatini, The Gambia, Kenya, Lesotho, Libya, Malawi, Nigeria, the Seychelles, South Africa, South Sudan, Sudan, Tanzania, Uganda, and Zimbabwe. Non-signatories with French colonial history: Côte d'Ivoire, Djibouti, Gabon, Burkina Faso, Central African Republic, Madagascar, Mali, Morocco, Sahwari Arab Democratic Republic, Niger, and Algeria. Non-signatories with other colonial histories: Equatorial Guinea (Spain), DRC (Belgium), Eritrea (Italy), Cabo Verde (Portugal). Countries with non-standard colonial histories: Cameroon (British-French), Somalia (Italy-UK), Liberia (none), and Ethiopia (none with Italian occupation).

60. NATO Cooperative Cyber Defense Center of Excellence, "Strategic Importance of, and Dependence On, Undersea Cables," 2019: https://cc dcoe.org/uploads/2019/11/Undersea-cables-Final-NOV-2019.pdf

61. As of June 2021, Boca Raton hosted docking points for the Bahamas Internet Cable System, Colombia-Florida Subsea Fiber, GigNet-1, GlobeNet, Monet, and South America-1. See Submarine Cable Map, *PriMectra, Inc.* (2021).

62. My forthcoming book completes more statistical comparisons than I present here. These numbers represent data from coastal, non-Mediterranean, non-island member nations of the African Union. They include only global cable data, excluding any intra-country cables or regional cables connecting a few nations. Island nations are excluded because they tend to have higher numbers of cables, given their positions in the ocean, but greater vulnerability in other areas; Mediterranean-bordering African countries are also excluded from this comparison because their cable histories are radically different, given their proximity to the Mediterranean and Europe. These data are drawn primarily from TeleGeography's Submarine Cable Map: https://submarine-cable-map-2021.telegeography.com/

63. Sandra Braman, "Instability and Internet Design," *Journal of Internet Regulation* 5, no. 1 (2016); See also Jon R. Lindsay, "Restrained By Design: The Political Economy of Cybersecurity," *Digital Policy, Regulation and Governance* 19, no. 6 (2017): 493–514 (investigating the socio-technical determinants of the consequences of cyber attack).

10

Confronting Coloniality in Cyberspace:
How to Make the Concept of (In)Stability Useful

Densua Mumford

Reflecting on the narrowly legal human rights framework through which her activist community operates, Gracie May Bradley, Interim Director of Liberty, considers the possibilities that have opened up by thinking about digital surveillance in terms of "abolition":

> And I understand abolition to be concerned not simply with reacting to harm, but as I say, kind of transforming the conditions in which harm occurs. And rather than sort of just getting rid of stuff, if we think about how Angela Davis talks about prisons, it's about making them obsolete . . . What would need to happen for surveillance tech to be obsolete? . . . We often do find it difficult to get out of the mode of "how do we just constrain this thing?" And I think abolition is really challenging, but it really pushes us to widen the frame of the debate and to look for transformative solutions that would get to the root, to look at what non-punitive policy solutions might be on the table when often we end up laser focused on when we can use facial recognition, *not what else might solve the problems that facial recognition claims to solve* without any of the rights harms."[1]

Abolition as a frame of thought emerges from the epistemes of the subaltern[2] in the United States, specifically, African American knowledges rooted in the lived experience of slavery and incarceration.[3] This is decolonial thinking. A decolonial approach to conceptualizing cyberspace is about escaping limited Eurocentric epistemic frames that constrain what we conceive of as possible. Especially important is the shift away from resisting power while still standing on its epistemic turf, to adopting entirely new epistemic foundations that make obsolete the dominant modes of thinking. Adopting epistemes rooted in the experiences of silenced groups (border thinking) to entirely reinterpret an issue and the range of possible solutions will foster pluralistic knowledge that is useful[4] for a plurality of communities and augment human creativity and knowledge production about cyberspace.

I wish to emphasize that there is no such thing as a definitive decolonial conceptualization of (in)stability, nor is there ever likely to be. Decoloniality is not a uniform theory about the (social) world that generates universal concepts to craft a systematized notion of reality. It is also not an ideology or a catch-all term for "critical" perspectives wanting to change bad or unpleasant conditions. Rather, it is "an *epistemic stance* that struggles against the ignorance of monocultural approaches" to knowledge production.[5] As an epistemic stance, its key purpose is to, firstly, offer critiques about how idiosyncratic epistemes (cosmologies, ontologies, epistemologies, knowledges, understandings, concepts, constructs) rooted in specifically Euro-American communities have come to dominate how we make sense of the world and, secondly, to dismantle this domination through forming coalitions (purposive collaborative action) amongst various communities and making visible their non-modern knowledges.

The important question from a decolonial perspective is *whose* knowledge operates unquestioned and whose knowledge is systematically excluded from setting the terms of the debate about (social) reality in the first place. Many perspectives invite challengers into a fully furnished room to join in a supposedly open conversation about this or that topic. Decoloniality, on the other hand, questions this presumed openness by asking who built and furnished the room in the first place, how this determines the atmosphere and trajectory of the conversation, and who has been prevented from helping to build or furnish the room and therefore can never be at home in the conversation. It goes beyond this to suggest what decolonial rooms might look like instead.[6] Decoloniality thus exposes the non-obvious silences; it aims to connect with communities whose epistemes have been marginalized in processes that shape the world. What makes it explicitly *de*colonial is that it sees this silencing or "epistemic violence" – the eradication, marginalization, delegitimization, or hierarchization of non-modern epistemes – as rooted in 500 years of colonialism, and it argues that redressing this requires a continuing process of decolonization.

Therefore, in contrast to most chapters in this volume, I will not provide a substantive conceptualization of (in)stability. Instead, I offer decolonial warnings about approaching conceptualization without first critically "positioning" such an endeavor, i.e. without first acknowledging the cultural, socio-economic, epistemological, historical, and spatial context of this book project and the ways in which these particular contexts may limit its ability to develop a concept that speaks to the lives of those positioned differently. I also reveal how even critics and activists struggling against domination in cyberspace may still end up operating within the fundamental epistemic framings of those they are challenging. As an exercise in knowledge production, this book project will be enriched by decolonial insights. That is, a decolonial approach to conceptualizing cyberspace generally, and (in)stability specifically, will strengthen the quality of our knowledge by making it more useful for a plurality of communities.

This chapter will first introduce the decolonial perspective, outlining its most important distinguishing propositions. It will then contextualize this volume's focus on (in)stability in cyberspace as existing within a broader pattern of coloniality, thereby highlighting the dangers of uncritically extending idiosyncratic understandings to all of cyberspace as though they were epistemically neutral. I argue that conceptualizations of (in)stability reproduce coloniality by reifying the epistemes, problem definitions, and understandings of dominant Euro-American states, educational and research institutions, and civil society groups. Assumptions of epistemic neutrality will backfire by creating a worse experience of cyberspace for the global majority, no matter how well-meaning. Engaging more directly with the focal concept of this volume, I next problematize *what* exactly is meant to become (un)stable and for *whom* these conceptualizations intend to establish (in)stability. Mitigating coloniality will require sustained reflection about the positionality of this project and its authors, a shift in consciousness to what I term "self-aware humility," and, most importantly, sustained dialogue with the epistemes of subaltern communities through border thinking. Finally, the chapter will summarize the main argument and reflect on some useful ways forward.

The Epistemic Stance of Decoloniality

Decoloniality, at its core, is a practice of theorizing from the margins: it is concerned with exposing and undoing the epistemic violence eradicating or marginalizing the knowledges of subaltern communities in the world, thereby opening space for those silenced knowledges to shape dialogues about the human condition. It asserts that in thinking with knowledges from a plurality of communities, that is, delinking from narrow hegemonic forms of knowing, our understanding of the world will be richer and we may conceive of, and institute, radically alternative ways of living.[7] Moreover, the knowledge generated will be more useful for a greater plurality of communities. Decoloniality is not simply about exercising epistemic justice but equally about ensuring more robust knowledge that serves the many and not just a few. Knowledge is power: therefore, knowledge created by and for the few will only empower the few.

Decoloniality is connected to a rich and varied "family" of Global South philosophies and political theories that broadly call for the decoloni*zation* of knowledge. Thus, many scholars from Africa, Asia, Latin America, and elsewhere over the decades have acknowledged the continuing oppressive effects of colonialism on the knowledges of peoples from those regions. Pioneers and seminal contemporaries calling for decolonization include Ngugi wa Thiong'o, Syed Hussein Alatas, Anibal Quijano, Maria Lugones, Walter Mignolo, Achille Mbembe, Gurminder Bhambra, Sabelo Ndlovu-Gatsheni, and others.[8] Amongst this broad range of perspectives, decolon*iality* specifically – also known as the modernity/coloniality school – originating in Latin America with Anibal Quijano,[9] and which provides the main framing of this chapter, offers in my view the most systematized set of concepts.

According to decoloniality, the global political economy of knowledge production privileges the ontologies and epistemologies of Euro-American subjects. That is, European and North American definitions of knowledge as objective, neutral, and founded on Western rationality have dominated global debates on (social) reality at the expense of the epistemes of others.[10] This domination was achieved through colonialism's deliberate and systematic displacement of the knowledges of the colonized.[11] The assertion is not just that Euro-American knowledges have marginalized the knowledges of other communities, but that they have simultaneously masked their own idiosyncrasy, thereby casting themselves as emerging from nowhere in particular, what Mignolo calls the "the zero point epistemology,"[12] and serving no agenda in particular while rendering all other knowledges as relativist and particular and therefore not worthy of general promulgation. This phenomenon of Eurocentrism may be understood as an "arrogant ignorance," i.e. "pretending to be wide-ranging, or even claiming universal validity, while remaining oblivious to the epistemic diversity of the world."[13]

One of the important notions shaping decoloniality is that of conceiving of the last 500 years of history as shaped by modernity/coloniality. Modernity is understood as a set of conditions and norms related to individual rationality, the rationalization of communities through the emergence of the modern bureaucratic sovereign state, a belief in perpetual linear progress, and capitalism. It constructs itself especially in opposition to tradition, backwardness, and the historical past.[14] An important feature of modernity is the division of the world especially into racial and gendered categories (or "constructs") that allow for hierachization and silencing in ways that elevate Euro-America.[15]

Modernity has been assumed by Euro-America to be the sole lens through which to understand historical development (thereby, for example, constituting notions of pre-modernity and post-modernity).

Coloniality, on the other hand, includes the

> long-standing patterns of power that emerge in the context of colonialism, which redefine culture, labor, intersubjective relations, aspirations of the self, common sense, and knowledge production in ways that accredit the superiority of the colonizer. Surviving long after colonialism has been overthrown, coloniality permeates consciousness and social relations in contemporary life."[16]

Coloniality, then, includes oppressive conditions that continue in cultural, socio-economic, and epistemic practices despite the ending of formal political colonialism. The slash both connecting and dividing modernity and coloniality indicates that they are co-constitutive: we cannot logically conceive of the emergence of a belief in linear progress and objective rationality without reference to the fact that such notions developed by way of Euro-America contrasting itself with the barbaric and irrational Other who exists in the backwards past, and practicing these distinctions through colonialism.[17] Therefore, it is not possible to understand the Euro-American experience of modernity without understanding the subaltern experience of coloniality, and vice versa (thus Maria Lugones prefers the language of non-modernity, i.e. the notion that there are ways of making sense of the world that are entirely divorced from modernity and instead emerge from the subjects of coloniality[18]).

Decoloniality seeks to form solidarity among marginalized groups such that they can delink from the knowledges propagated by dominant groups and (re)evaluate their lived experiences through their own epistemes. As Ramon Grosfoguel argues,

> The fact that one is socially located in the oppressed side of power relations does not automatically mean that he/she is epistemically thinking from a subaltern epistemic location. Precisely, the success of the modern/colonial world-system consists in making subjects that are socially located in the oppressed side of the colonial difference, to think epistemically like the ones on the dominant positions.[19]

This is a crucial reminder that even opposition to power can still fall short of decolonial aims by relying on dominant epistemes. It is this problem of being constrained by conceptualizations derived from Euro-American knowledges

that prompted Ngugi wa Thiong'o, the Kenyan scholar and author of the seminal *Decolonising the Mind*,[20] to dedicate himself to writing in his native language
of Gikuyu. Practicing useful epistemes and generating radically new ways of
conceiving of the human condition for Ngugi means utilizing native Kenyan
constructs, which are best expressed through Kenyan languages.

At this point, it is vitally important to not conflate decoloniality with calls
for diversity and inclusion. They reinforce each other and are usually complementary. However, in very crude terms, decoloniality privileges diversity
of epistemes over diversity of identities. It is not a perspective primarily concerned with bringing more racial or gender identities to powerful positions,
but with the inclusion of a plurality of epistemes in knowledge production (the
latter of which is itself a vital site of power). These aims may overlap to the
extent that diverse identities act as superficial proxies for diverse knowledges.
However, as illustrated above, diverse racial, gendered, and socio-economic
groups may nevertheless still share fundamental epistemes. Conversely, people
sharing similar superficial identities may have radically different epistemic positions. Epistemes and identities, like decoloniality and diversity, must therefore
not be conflated. While standard calls for diversity are imperative and supported by the decolonial position, they do not go far enough. It is insufficient
to invite someone into an epistemically predetermined room to join in a conversation (diversity and inclusion), but rather it is crucial that they co-decide
which epistemic room the debate should be held in and how it should be
furnished (decoloniality).

The above account in no way suggests that decolonial scholarship is limited
to the humanities and social sciences. In fact, decolonial scholarship also challenges the Euro-American ontologies and epistemologies that underpin much
of the natural sciences. Again, this should not be conflated with debates about
the representation of marginalized groups in STEM disciplines.[21] Rather,
decoloniality challenges the very notion that Euro-American epistemes in the
natural sciences uniquely hold the keys to unlocking universal truths. Other
knowledges must be equally engaged in questions about the natural world.[22]
For example, indigenous communities have developed centuries of knowledge
about how to understand and live with the natural world that has allowed them
not just to survive but also to thrive.[23] This chapter is thus relevant to both
the technical and cultural wings of the debate on (in)stability in cyberspace.
Having provided a brief outline of decoloniality, the next section will show
the relevance of coloniality to cyberspace and will thereby position attempts to
conceptualize (in)stability.

Coloniality and the Question of (In)Stability in Cyberspace

This volume has the laudable objective of conceptualizing (in)stability in cyberspace through diverse perspectives, thereby avoiding overly simplistic narratives. Decoloniality can contribute important and unique insights that highlight non-obvious limitations and offer approaches for mitigating them. In this section, I use the decolonial perspective to characterize the modernity/coloniality duality present in cyberspace debates (across government, industry, and academia) and the silences that are created as a result, thereby revealing the Eurocentric, colonial context in which conceptualizations of (in)stability are occurring. Reading cyberspace debates through a modernity/coloniality lens reveals the ways in which dominant communities – primarily Euro-American state and non-state actors – rearticulate modernity while at the same time masking the colonial underbelly that allows for their rearticulation in the first place.

Decoloniality, though still sparsely applied to questions of the digital age, potentially has much to say about cyberspace. This is because cyberspace itself represents a continuation of coloniality. Typically, practices in cyberspace privilege masculine Euro-American subject-positions and epistemes (while at once masking their particularity), thereby elevating the voices of a narrow set of dominant communities while simultaneously marginalizing, silencing, and delegitimizing the epistemes of a plurality of others such as indigenous communities, LGBTQ people, and Global South women, among others. For example, it has been pointed out how Massively Multiplayer Online Role-Playing Games (MMORPG) such as World of Warcraft create worlds that are coded white, not just in the racial make-up of the playable and non-playable characters, but in the very fact that fantasy worlds are based on European mythologies. Eurocentric cultural understandings of humanity are naturalized while non-European conceptualizations are erased or marginalized as deviations through the game.[24] From a decolonial perspective, this practice merely continues the centuries-long habit of assuming Europe as the subject, the sole objective perspective through which humanity in its entirety can be unproblematically explored.[25] There is thus a marginalization of non-European subjectivities in MMORPGs.

Syed Mustafa Ali, speaking specifically of internet governance, diagnoses the reproduction of coloniality in cyberspace as located in the following condition:

> . . . there is far too much taken for granted – politically, economically, socially, culturally, ethically etc. – in discussions about Internet governance;

far too many assumptions and predispositions that remain hegemonically and tacitly operative in the background, shaping the boundaries (limits, borders) and contours (landscape, topology) of this discourse, not to mention setting its terms (that is, its "logic" or grammar and "lexicon" or vocabulary) . . . .[26]

Coloniality in cyberspace, that is the silencing of the ontologies and epistemologies of various communities in debates about cyberspace, occurs through myriad taken-for-granted assumptions. Too many understandings, constructs, concepts, and principles are left implicit, which allows dominant voices to represent their epistemes, problem definitions, and technical solutions as neutral, natural, and universally valid – as quite literally coming from the objective nowhere and therefore relevant everywhere. Thus, the fact that debates regarding cyberspace have focused on questions such as "network neutrality, openness, standards and interoperability, stability and universality (as against instability and fragmentation), must be understood as potentially informed and inflected by the . . . orientations of those generating this discourse."[27] Notably, that includes this very volume on (in)stability, which is being constructed within a Eurocentric framework. Non-reflexive conceptualizations of (in)stability will therefore represent a continuation of coloniality in the sense that they reproduce the epistemes of dominant Euro-American societal groups who have the power to shape these debates in the first place.

Revealing these assumptions and exposing them as idiosyncratic, as opposed to universal and objective, requires positioning the ideas and their authors. This means recognizing the cultural, socio-economic, epistemic, historical, and spatial contexts that have given rise to these ways of knowing and being. Speaking explicitly of computing, Ali states that "decolonial computing, as a 'critical' project, is about interrogating *who* is doing computing, *where* they are doing it, and, thereby, *what* computing means both epistemologically (i.e. in relation to knowing) and ontologically (i.e. in relation to being)."[28] This echoes Mignolo's own assertions that "in order to call into question the modern/colonial foundation of the control of knowledge, it is necessary to focus on the knower rather than on the known."[29] Why (in)stability matters in the first place is determined by who is conceptualizing and from what position they are doing it. In the following, I reveal coloniality in the overwhelmingly Euro-American subjects present in the debates on cyberspace, the geographical and communal spaces in which they tend to be located, and the Eurocentric understandings they generate to make sense of cyberspace. I thereby contextualize this volume's focus on (in)stability in cyberspace as existing within a broader logic of coloniality.

Who Dominates Cyberspace Debates and Guides our Intellectual Inquiry to Prioritize Questions of (In)Stability? Where are they Located?

The community that epistemically dominates cyberspace is what I call the transnational techno-elite (TTE). This community somewhat mirrors what Bhupinder Chimni calls the transnational capitalist class (TCC), a diffuse community with shared interests, ideologies, control over the means of production, and unrivalled access to powerful institutions in the Global North and South.[30] Another neighbouring concept may be McKenzie Wark's "vectoralist class" who "control the vectors along which information circulates. They own the means of realizing the value of information. Information emerges as a concept precisely because it can be quantified, valued and owned."[31] Instead of land (feudal lords) or capital (the bourgeoisie), they own and commodify information (vectoralists). Tech (mostly male) billionaires like Bill Gates and Elon Musk may come to mind because of their prominence in the media.[32] However, I argue that they are mere figureheads for a general class composed of diverse actors aspiring to propagate certain ideals: perpetual progress, meritocracy, neoliberal entrepreneurship, rationalization of processes and people for profit, and beliefs of technology transcending politics. Chimni's global governance concept is therefore too broad from a decolonial perspective while Wark's Marxist one is too narrow.

The transnational techno-elite do not just exist in Silicon Valley, they also populate government agencies such as foreign ministries and the military; they shape global governance policies at the UN and EU; they exchange ideas in departments in Stanford and Harvard; they spread best practices while working for consultancy firms like Deloitte; and they foster a tech-based popular culture as high-profile (social) media influencers.[33] Moreover, this community includes critics within those debates who position themselves as fighting for privacy rights and user control. While the critics oppose the commercialization of data and the loss of rights to tech corporations and governments, their resistance is often fought on similar epistemic grounds as their opponents. For example, the founders of ProtonMail, a dominant player in the private email industry started in 2013, are Caltech, Harvard, and CERN alumni. Had Edward Snowden not created the necessary Zeitgeist for their successful business venture, they might just as likely have worked for Microsoft, Mozilla, McKinsey, or MIT. They are disproportionately male, young, and English-speaking.[34]

Another less obvious example of resistance fought from within Eurocentric frameworks may be found in the Association for Progressive Communication (APC). This network of organizations has a strong focus on the Global South and other marginalized communities, countering the patriarchy to support gender equality, and ensuring equitable access to the internet. Notably, this NGO, which is incorporated in the US but headquartered in South Africa, and has a globally diverse membership, has a vision for "people to use and shape the internet and digital technologies to create a just and sustainable world."[35] These specific aims align well enough with decolonial aims. At the same time, the APC predominantly couches these struggles in terms of defending human rights as opposed to fostering non-modern forms of knowing and being in cyberspace that would render these injustices obsolete. What is missing from their core objectives is an explicit acknowledgment of the coloniality, or epistemic injustice, shaping cyberspace debates in the first place.[36] This again suggests that the framing chosen for resistance is still a decidedly Eurocentric one. While working to diversify and decentralize the governance of the internet and digital technologies, which are indispensable efforts, the APC and other civil society organizations like the EFF,[37] Access Now,[38] and Citizen Lab,[39] nevertheless reproduce the silencing of subaltern epistemes. This is not to argue that their work does not make an important difference in people's lives, but rather that their core concerns and approaches overlook decolonial questions of epistemic violence. Indirectly, of course, their focus on giving voice to the dispossessed in cyberspace may open ad hoc opportunities for subaltern epistemes to be recognized, but such outcomes would be a by-product at best.

While diffuse and networked, the transnational techno-elite often converges on important agenda-setting and decision-making bodies, such as the Internet Engineering Task Force (IETF) or the United Nations. The United Nations Group of Governmental Experts (GGE) and the Open-ended Working Group (OEWG) are tasked with studying and developing recommendations related to international law and norms on cyberspace. While the OEWG is open to all UN member states – as opposed to the GGE's limited membership of twenty-five – this has been inconsequential for the question of epistemic plurality. Both groups, comprised of experts from member states, and occasionally supported by consultants drawn from elite academic institutions and think tanks, have developed highly securitized and statist notions of (in)stability, with a focus on infrastructure.[40]

Notable are the communities whose subjectivities are systematically marginalized or missing in those debates. Vast swathes of the Global South, women, LGBTQ persons, indigenous communities facing settler colonialism, the working class, and labor, amongst others. This is the case despite the fact that they make up the majority of users of the internet.

What Knowledges do Dominant Groups Promulgate about Cyberspace and How do Questions of (In)Stability Cohere with these Knowledges?

This transnational techno-elite has generated particular Eurocentric understandings about cyberspace and its own role in it, which in turn have shaped practices to disproportionately benefit them while representing their actions as a universal benefit to humanity. These understandings have significantly determined the disadvantageous terms upon which marginalized communities are assimilated into cyberspace and led to their silencing in debates about cyberspace. Most notable (but not exhaustive) are understandings of linear progress that suggest Euro-America has won the (technological) race to the utopian future and the rest must merely catch up; a neoliberal myth of post-racial and gender-equal meritocracy; and, relatedly, a radical scientism that represents technology as a neutral solution for highly complex social ills. These understandings are further elaborated and demonstrated in the following paragraphs.

First, cyberspace is seen as a space of linear progress.[41] Alfred Yen intervenes in the early 2000s debate on internet governance by examining the metaphors of the "Western Frontier," which continue to shape thinking on cyberspace today. This metaphor evokes an innocent United States free of stifling government regulation, which generated entrepreneurship and innovation and an uninterrupted forward march toward progress. For Yen, this metaphor is misguided as the US Wild West also harbored social ills such as "[g]enocide, racism, and personal exploitation in the name of progress."[42] A better metaphor for cyberspace, he argues, is that of a European feudal system, because while cyberspace is decentralized, there are overlapping local authorities and sites of power, including actors such as ISPs and ICANN, some of which may exploit the powerless. He invokes the image of a feudal cyberspace to argue for the importance of law in bringing justice to the disadvantaged.[43] However, both of these metaphors converge on the characterization of cyberspace as unruly and therefore treacherous by relying on idealized images of the past, i.e. of tradition and backwardness. Beyond the fact that both metaphors project onto cyberspace specifically Euro-American constructs, they also reinforce the notion of linear progress and time. For the Western Frontier proponents, the very wildness of cyberspace fosters the seeds of future progress; for Yen, the feudal backwardness of cyberspace, its confusion of privatized powers, must be tamed through (Eurocentric notions of) law, must be rationalized and made stable. Both mobilize the myth of modernity whereby an ancient and undisciplined past must or will inevitably be transcended by a rationalized and superior future.

Second, cyberspace is understood as a post-racial and gender-equal space where, in a sense, Rawls' veil of ignorance has once more been restored. Scholars have noted the promulgation of a post-racial myth in Silicon Valley culture, for example.[44] Post-racialism suggests that race has been effectively neutralized as a socio-political force shaping people's chances in life. All this despite mounting evidence that, from the algorithms, to their coders, to the data gathered, to the business and political practices in which they are embedded, racial and gender stereotypes remain pervasive.[45]

Third, technology as a pure product of science, and therefore of course its creators, are free of bias and therefore able to take the god's eye view of the world. Hubristic belief in technology as a neutral hammer for every nail is what allowed Google executives Jared Cohen and Eric Schmidt to assume the mantle of reimagining how the world could be refashioned into a tech paradise, from education to preventing terrorism, in their book *The New Digital Age* (as though that job were not up to citizens themselves).[46]

Together, Eurocentric notions of linear progress, post-racial and gender-equal meritocracy, and uncritical faith in technology help to constitute and legitimize coloniality. For example, cyber security capacity-building has become one industry predicated on the discourse of a mature vs. immature society, the former being one that adheres to (Western) technological and technocratic standards.[47] The dynamic generated as a result is one of outside expertise, predominantly from Europe, America, and also South Asia, educating Global South communities and integrating them into "advanced" ways of thinking about and practicing cyber security. As a result of this linear understanding of technological progress, the transnational techno–elite construct themselves as neutrally intervening to hoist backwards communities to the frontiers of modernity.[48] Thus, from an objective epistemic stance, beneficent technology is created, which must then be indiscriminately applied to all societies for their own betterment.

For example, observers have noted how attempts by Big Tech to make inroads into Global South communities consolidate the domination of American tech corporations over local competitors and lead to a new "corporate colonisation."[49] Their control over the structures and networks, including search, major platforms, advertising, etc., that make up the main components of cyberspace means they not only dominate in terms of shaping the market but also generate dominant framings of inevitable modernity and progress that shape how cyberspace is understood and practiced. When, in 2015, the South African ANC government entered a deal with Big Tech to bring digital technologies to the country's public schools, it was doing so within a broader logic characterized by a belief in teleological technological progress, the resulting need to catch up with developments in the Global North, and adoption of technologies without critical investigation of whether they are suitable for the local context. Using the education of children as a channel, especially, ensures that a new generation of South Africans are integrated into American understandings of technology and therefore elevated to modernity.[50]

Similarly, Facebook's attempts to connect India's rural poor to the internet through its Free Basics program illustrates the logic of applying technological fixes to complex problems of inequality. This practice represents underlying ideologies of linear progress and neoliberal understandings of market actors as an important moral force. Notably, even resistance to Free Basics, which eventually succeeded, was mobilized on countervailing principles of the elite that fit within this logic: appeals were made to net neutrality in a manner that echoed the debates in the United States and thereby empowered the transnational techno-elite *within* India over and above the rural poor.[51] In this manner, the debate about the role of technology in Indian society was rooted in Eurocentric epistemes and understandings rather than framed through the perspectives of the rural poor who were the supposed beneficiaries.

In this context, it is important to ask how the very act of raising the question of (in)stability may echo such coloniality. Eurocentric notions of objectivity and progress that legitimize the self-identities and practices of the transnational techno-elite are operating to inform questions of (in)stability, because they are being raised by those very same actors. One organization tackling matters of (in)stability in cyberspace is the Global Commission on the Stability of Cyberspace (GCSC), headquartered in The Hague, whose founders are security think thanks in the Global North, and whose partners and funders include several states' foreign affairs departments, the Microsoft Corporation, Google, the European Union (EU), and the African Union (AU), among others. Its recommended six norms for a stable cyberspace focus solely on maintaining infrastructural integrity and setting standards of responsible behavior amongst state and non-state actors in narrow security terms. Participants of the conference that produced these norms included an array of powerful agencies, from state ministries to academics to ICANN to JPMorgan Chase.

Subaltern communities with non-modern epistemes are glaringly absent from the event. Especially stark is the high likelihood of (de)stabilizing cyberspace in ways that are comfortably familiar for this transnational techno-elite and adhering to their particular notions of the good life while disempowering the vast plurality of communities that exist in cyberspace. We are witnessing this already with Big Tech's prioritization of platform stability over other values and states' use of cyberspace to stabilize their rule, both of which will be discussed further in the following sections. Of course, the subaltern's continuing silence is not inevitable, but neither is simple awareness of this dynamic sufficient. Avoiding coloniality in cyberspace requires active dialoguing amongst a plurality of epistemes.

This section has contextualized conceptualizations of (in)stability in cyberspace as occurring within an ongoing condition of coloniality. A useful conceptualization of (in)stability should proceed from an explicit acknowledgment that even the choice to focus on this concept implies particular dominant subject-positions and epistemes, and therefore is likely to reproduce longstanding logics. Critically confronting the coloniality operating behind conceptualizations of (in)stability will strengthen the conceptual exercise. In keeping with the aim of decolonial approaches to foster just and pluralistic knowledge, the next section will explore Ali's questions of who, where, and what as a means of positioning this volume's exercise in knowledge production. By raising critical questions to expose and explore deep-seated assumptions about (in)stability, the aim is to at least prompt positioned conceptualizations and to open up space for subaltern epistemes to engage equally in conceptualizations.

Thinking Decolonially about (In)Stability in Cyberspace

In this section, I shift away from characterizing coloniality in cyberspace to addressing specifically the question of conceptualizing (in)stability. Given the coloniality inherent to many debates about cyberspace and the epistemic violence that results from them, how can conceptualizations generated from dominant subject-positions integrate decolonial insights? I argue that this is made possible, though not necessarily easy, through continuous reflection on the assumptions underpinning epistemic practices and acknowledging them as particular or positioned. Conceptualizations of (in)stability should be reviewed in light of the ways in which they embody Eurocentrism and thereby reproduce the modernity/coloniality duality. I highlight two specific approaches.

First, I draw on the notion of border thinking, which is one important approach to decolonial knowledge production.[52] It requires conceptualizing the world using the epistemes of subaltern communities, i.e. the knowledges of those struggling through the violence of coloniality.[53] That is, it requires taking a subaltern subject-position, thereby decentring the Euro-American subject in knowledge production and de-linking from modernity. Hence the importance of engaging in critical dialogue with communities that embody subaltern epistemes in order to ensure radically new and useful conceptualizations. The alternative of maintaining a self-referential debate amongst Eurocentric scholars, practitioners, and policymakers will worsen, and not improve, the plurality of lives inside and outside cyberspace.

Second, from the position of narrowly Euro-American epistemes, an attitude of self-aware humility – as opposed to arrogant ignorance (Eurocentrism) – will matter most as an initial step. Elsewhere, this has been called epistemic vulnerability, whereby "the safety of what is known is relinquished,"[54] or the humbling of modernity, in the sense that modernity is understood as "a specific genealogy of the West, but we need to recognize that there are other worlds of meaning that are not reducible to modernity's history."[55] These terms suggest a transformation of consciousness, such that "researchers who become aware of the positionality of knowledge become humble knowledge practitioners."[56] Being *self-aware* means recognizing that there exists a plurality of epistemes and acknowledging the particularities and situatedness of Euro-American knowledges; practicing *humility* means dialoguing with a plurality of epistemes with an attitude of equal co-learning instead of paternalism. By positioning knowledge production and practicing self-aware humility we can enter into dialogue with different knowledges about cyberspace. The following three questions are prompts for further reflection to facilitate explicit awareness of some of the particularities and inherent limitations of any conceptualization of (in)stability.

Why (In)Stability and Not Something Else?

This is not about tritely questioning the value of conceptualizing (in)stability. Evidently, it is useful and meaningful for the particular community of scholars engaged in this project, including myself, and the (largely elite Euro-American) target audience that may read these efforts.[57] Instead, I raise this question to invite explicit debate about how it is that (in)stability has attracted *our* scholarly attention as opposed to alternative constructs – for example, justice or spiritual well-being or love – that may be important to marginalized communities that participate in cyberspace but are receiving less or even no attention. It is an invitation to not take for granted that *our* concern about (in)stability is natural, universal, and unproblematic, but to acknowledge this choice as rooted in our particular epistemes and our particular problem definitions. For example, Burton and Stevens (Chapter 4 this volume) show how NATO's shaping of conceptions of (in)stability remains in keeping with the preferred framings of Euro-American states such as the United States and the United Kingdom. Furthermore, these definitions shift over time to remain in keeping with the interests of dominant states.

Notions of stability are related closely to notions of order, of freezing in place a state of being that is presumed (always by someone particular) to be good or adequate. However, it leaves implicit assumptions about *who* would benefit from investigations of (in)stability and *whose* subject-position is reinforced through a focus on (in)stability. For example, this is likely to be well-resourced actors with sufficient control over the infrastructures of cyberspace to conceive of *making* it (un)stable in the first place, such as the GCSC. When we reinforce the salience of (in)stability amongst groups that dominate cyberspace, we must acknowledge that it will reinforce the silence of others who are *not* empowered to speak using their epistemes about alternative concepts that matter more to their lives. Using border thinking, i.e. thinking from the margins, we may find other concerns regarding cyberspace to be far more crucial than (in)stability. The possibilities regarding this are endless; the main point being that we must not assume (in)stability as the only important concern simply because it has been adopted by the transnational techno-elite. In a world where knowledge production is skewed in favor of dealing with the problems of Euro-American elites more than the rest, a conceptualization exercise that comes from a place of self-aware humility, and recognizes (positions) itself as emerging from some-where and serving a specific someone, is a small but important step.

(In)Stability of What?

An important step in positioning any conceptualization of (in)stability is to explicitly justify *what* exactly should be considered (un)stable. Even in a hypo-thetical world where (in)stability may be assumed to be an important concept for a plurality of communities in cyberspace, the diversity of lived experiences will nevertheless lead to diverging and possibly competing understandings of what should or should not be stable.

In the realm of modernity, (in)stability of market conditions may be of special interest to corporations. Maintaining a stable user base that continually produces the raw data to be commodified is key to profitability. Platforms of various kinds, ranging from social media platforms to entire technologi-cal ecosystems such as that belonging to Apple, aim to exploit the "network effect" whereby users find it difficult to leave because it also means leaving social networks or services that are important to them. For example, delet-ing a Facebook account may come at the cost of exclusion and isolation. No longer owning an Apple device means being unable to use iMessage. The net-work effect ensures a stable source of data, and creates a level of predictability and security for the corporation and a steady base from which to continue expansion and growth. Nevertheless, stability for the transnational techno-elite means significant costs for the user. A user of Facebook concerned with the use of their data or simply unhappy with the service as a whole may find it difficult to migrate elsewhere without abandoning long-established networks. Many discovered the challenge of migrating their entire networks after wanting to leave WhatsApp for alternatives such as Telegram and Signal once the former updated its data sharing policies in 2021.[58]

Though there is high-profile contestation on this front, it is still fought within narrowly Eurocentric frameworks. According to the Electronic Frontier Foundation (EFF), a highly influential NGO located in the United States, platform stability is detrimental for the majority of users and for competition in the marketplace. In their campaign to enshrine the principle of interoperability in government regulation and cyberspace norms, they argue for a package of changes:

> "**Data portability** gives users the right to access and transfer their data from the companies that hold it. **Back-end interoperability** would require very large companies – those that dominate a particular market segment – to maintain interfaces that allow their users to interact fluidly with users on other services. Finally, **delegability** would require those large companies to build interfaces that allow third-party software to interact with their services on a user's behalf.[59]

Such proposals are designed to introduce greater instability and fragmentation, i.e. to make it easier for users to change services or become less reliant on any single platform and to support competitors, all of which would undermine the stability of powerful platforms to the benefit of users.

Even in their differences, the EFF and Facebook share many constructs and assumptions that render invisible the lived experiences and epistemes of the subaltern. The EFF still speaks the language of Western rationality and predicates its arguments with an assumption of technology as a unique driver of linear progress:

> Interoperability fosters competition, and with competition comes more choice, and the chance to improve the quality of our online lives. An Internet with more competition will allow users to express themselves more freely and craft their online identities more deliberately.[60]

Their justifications rely on Eurocentric arguments about individual freedom, competitive markets, and win–win technological progress. Identities are invoked in the sense of individual privacy and security, e.g. as pertains to identity fraud. The implication is that we may occupy the position of the Euro-American subject and still help the marginalized. The differences between the principles of the EFF and Facebook mirror Yen's narrow distinctions between the Western Frontier and European feudalism metaphors.

In the realm of coloniality, however, people may experience very differently how (in)stability interacts with their identities and exacerbates personal vulnerabilities. For LGBTQ youth, constructing an unstable online identity can be protective. The ephemerality or anonymity of the account may determine the choice of social media platform. A stable online identity can be easily found and publicly outed, with the threat of reprisals from family members or friends unaware of the individual's sexuality. It can also risk connections being made across different life domains, such as work and school and friendship circles. LGBTQ youth may prefer a context where they may explore their own sexualities with an anonymous identity and via more fluid interactions. Maintaining different and fluid identities also makes it possible to maintain distinctions between different areas of life.[61]

However, some platforms such as Facebook maintain a real name policy, which induces stability of identity. This in fact may make it *more* difficult for LGBTQ youth to express themselves authentically as they have no area of life that is protected. Transgender people are especially affected by demands for a stable and singular identity on social media, with real implications for their lives and livelihoods when transphobic family members or employers discover their true identities.[62] "This design bias includes baked-in normativities that rehearse a standpoint that being-in-public is somehow neutral, low-risk, unraced, ungendered, and unsexed."[63] The Eurocentrism informing the imposition of stable identities is also predicated on the invisibility of LGBTQ subjects located in non-Western contexts, especially those in societies where trans- and homophobia are written into law, and where enforcement agencies use digital technologies to surveil and entrap citizens.[64] Such struggles are not captured well by debates about (in)stability of platforms and interoperability. Practicing border thinking – that is, using the knowledges of marginalized communities – to re-evaluate cyberspace (in)stability will reshape and decolonize *what* we even believe to be at stake. All this is to say that positioning conceptualizations of (in)stability and practicing self-aware humility means being explicit about what specifically should be kept stable and what should not, opening up these choices to scrutiny, and not assuming that they remain relevant across all societal domains.

(In)Stability for Whom?

Also integral to a positioned conceptualization exercise is to justify *whose* life (located where) we want to make (un)stable. I use "for whom" to mean "from whose perspective," as it is important to avoid paternalistic logics of conceptualizing on behalf of others whose lived experiences we do not share. In sum, from whose subjectivity can we imagine this or that particular conception of (in)stability being useful? This question matters because the persons in whose service we place our concept will be empowered. Occupying a particular Euro-American subject-position that masquerades as objective and neutral means that knowledge generated to supposedly serve the world is in fact generated to reinforce the dominant position of a narrow set of powerful actors. Mailyn Fidler (Chapter 9 this volume) shows that even amongst states there is significant divergence in understandings: African states' understandings of (in)stability are significantly shaped by their history of colonialism, manifesting in greater suspicion of universalist attempts to define the concept. From a decolonial perspective, however, statist responses to the question of "for whom" are typical of Eurocentric debates. Though rarely explicit, statism – that is, reducing discussion to the perspective of the modern state – operates as a systematic assumption that underpins dominant scholarship and policy recommendations and reproduces modernity/coloniality.[65]

To offer a prominent example, speaking specifically of deterrence – the nuclear version of which was key to Cold War thinking about (in)stability – Joseph Nye's work discusses whether this may be achieved in cyberspace.[66] His understanding of the merits, strengths, and means of deterrence in cyberspace is unmistakably statist and militarized:

> In 2007, after a dispute with Russia about moving a World War II memorial to Soviet soldiers, Estonia suffered a series of denial-of-service attacks that disrupted its access to the Internet for several weeks. Similar attacks accompanying the 2008 Russian invasion of Georgia interfered with Georgia's defense communications. In 2010 the Stuxnet virus attack that led to the destruction of more than 1,000 Iranian centrifuges and delayed Iran's enrichment program was widely attributed to the United States and Israel.[67]

Government agencies such as the Pentagon and specific world leaders are mentioned at times. Otherwise, Nye's conception of cyberspace in this article is decidedly statist. While others have pointed out the technological, political, and normative difficulties of constructing a state-based, territorially bound cyberspace,[68] the point I am making is more simply that too often the subjects of such theorizing remain the standard powerful states. We may see another example of this in the chapter by Goldman (Chapter 5 this volume), in which attempts to understand cyberspace from the perspective of the interests of the United States arguably lead to securitized and marketized ("competitive mindset") understandings of (in)stability: primarily manifesting in the aim to keep the United States' security and economic conditions stable.

Even those who recognize a multiplicity of actors – through the language of multistakeholderism, for example – refer to the usual dominant players in global governance, including international organizations such as the UN, NGOs, and private companies, who are often merely alternative sites for that same transnational techno-elite.[69] All of these entities represent Eurocentric conceptions of actorness, namely rationalized, bureaucratized, and neoliberalized group actors that already dominate governance outside of cyberspace (instead of, say, self-identified communities such as ethnic groups, family groups, religious communities, linguistic groups, etc.). As a result, Euro-American subjectivities are given voice and those of subaltern groups are rendered silent.

The value to humanity of conceptualizing (in)stability to serve these actors is uncertain. There is evidence that when states try to establish stability for themselves in cyberspace, various societal groups experience more instability.[70] Kurowska and Reshetnikov illuminate how the Russian state mobilizes state-funded trolls to destabilize online discussions such that a coherent radical discourse that constructs the state as a threat cannot emerge amongst opposition groups in the first place (what the authors call "neutrollisation"). "Somewhere in the process, the possibility of securitizing a politically pressing issue vanishes. Political energy is no longer refuted or even closed down in a traditional authoritarian manner but is instead eroded."[71] In sum, the Russian state has learned to destabilize opposition discourses, as opposed to using naked repression, in order to stabilize its own rule. Further examples can be seen in Anstis et al.'s discussion (Chapter 8 this volume) on states' offensive cyber operations such as hacking and disinformation against ordinary citizens and civil society.[72]

On the other hand, subaltern epistemes are either entirely silenced or marginalized in debates on cyberspace.[73] Those whose experience is one of coloniality may simply not exist in the imaginations of dominant cyberspace theorists and policymakers, most likely because they are themselves located in Euro-American spaces and operate through networks of colleagues who share their Eurocentric epistemic positions.

Cyberspace is partly being experienced as a destabilizing force in the social fabric of Innuit communities in Canada, by changing social norms and eroding interpersonal relations necessary for transmitting traditional knowledge.[74] Unstable access to the internet has also ensured a trade-off between staying at home where internet connections are more reliable or going hunting and visiting elders, social activities through which the experiential and relational Innuit knowledge is transmitted. Textual, video, and photographic knowledges that dominate cyberspace are a poor replacement for the "dynamic, interactive, embodied, and experiential" approach of learning by doing.[75] By conceptualizing (in)stability from the subject-position of indigenous communities, it may be possible to ensure that cyberspace further nurtures, rather than displaces (i.e. erases), non-modern knowledges.

Cyberspace debates can be decolonial if they involve the knowledges of the subaltern. In proposing a decolonization of the digital humanities, Roopika Risam points to projects that explicitly engage marginalized groups such as Chicana feminists and indigenous groups in the development and execution of societal and scientific digital projects. Not only their lived experiences, but their very knowledges, shape the inputs and outputs.[76] Taking seriously subaltern subjectivities, one academic article offers activist Yaseen Aslam a platform to recount in first-person narration his experience of fighting Uber for workers' rights for app drivers in the courts of the United Kingdom.[77] Instability of the gig economy, in apt metaphorical language, is the feature and not the bug, and it interacts with racial divides to trap the already disadvantaged in a life of significant precarity (ethnic minorities make up 94 percent of the private hire cabs such as Uber while whites dominate in the more privileged black cabs' industry in London).[78]

These examples of border thinking, which is (re)thinking from the margins, reveal a powerful approach for decentring the transnational techno-elite from our knowledge production regarding cyberspace, instead making visible and un-silencing lives rendered irrelevant by dominant approaches to cyberspace. Future conceptualizations of (in)stability should avoid the trap of equating Euro-American subject-positions with universality by also positioning themselves and explicating for whom they are developing their concepts.

Conclusion

Why confront coloniality in cyberspace? The risk embedded in Eurocentric conceptualizations of (in)stability — that is, conceptualizations that assume the perspective of the predominantly white, cis-male, Euro-American transnational techno-elite — is that they will reproduce forms of (in)stability that are comfortably familiar for dominant communities and oppressive for the subaltern. From the position of Eurocentric epistemes, other ways of knowing the world are rendered either inconceivable or peculiarly exotic and therefore unworthy of participating equally in dialogues about important topics such as the fate of cyberspace. According to the decolonial perspective, cyberspace should instead be constructed in accordance with a plurality of epistemes, not just narrow Euro-American ones. A thriving cyberspace that supports and nurtures a plurality of communities will require that these various communities define using their own knowledges and in equal dialogue with others what cyberspace means and the logics by which it should operate. This reminder is especially relevant for activists and other critics of domination, such as the EFF and other privacy and human rights advocates, who nevertheless build their challenges on the same epistemic foundations promulgated by the transnational techno-elite.

Delinking from modernity/coloniality is a significant challenge. Future attempts to (re)conceptualize cyberspace will benefit from border thinking, i.e. adopting subaltern epistemes, and using methodologies that avoid their marginalization or erasure. At minimum, mitigating the epistemic violence caused by coloniality in cyberspace requires positioning conceptualizations of (in)stability: that means confronting the colonial logics in which such con-ceptualizations are embedded and the particular subject-positions of the the-orists, as well as explicitly justifying *what* it is we want to make (un)stable and for *whom* we want to generate this (in)stability. Practicing self-aware humility means making plain that the knowledge created comes from somewhere and is serving someone, as opposed to emanating from an objective nowhere. In doing so, we can better acknowledge the silences still left. Positioned con-ceptualizations welcome critique and scrutiny and create space for subaltern communities to set their own epistemic agendas; that is, to build and furnish their own rooms for conversation, and to engage in equal dialogue by visiting rooms occupied by others across the hallway.

Notes

1. Sarah Chander, "Decolonising Data Panel" (Digital Freedom Fund, February 17, 2021): https://www.youtube.com/watch?v=WRobUCm13m4

2. My use of the term "subaltern" differs significantly from the way Mailyn Fidler (Chapter 9 this volume) uses it when she discusses African Union member states. While Fidler adapts the term to include states that are mate-rially marginalized, I use the term in a decolonial sense to mean decidedly non-state communities that are epistemically invisibilized/silenced, i.e. whose ways of knowing and being are ignored, marginalized, or even under threat of eradication. From the perspective of decoloniality, Global South states are merely extensions and bulwarks of modernity and not marginalized alternatives. Thus, the modern state, whatever its geograph-ical location, is a major product and source of coloniality.

3. Liat Ben-Moshe, "Dis-Epistemologies of Abolition," *Critical Criminology* 26, no. 3 (September 2018): 341–355, https://doi.org/10.1007/s10612-018-9403-1

4. By "useful" I mean knowledge that helps a plurality of communities navi-

gate their particular problems, aspirations, and values in cyberspace in ways that are specifically beneficial to them. This is to emphasize that plurality in circumstances requires plurality in knowledges. It also helps to avoid the conflation of knowledge that benefits a narrow elite with knowledge that is equally useful for everyone.

5. Emphasis added. Rosalba Icaza and Rolando Vasquez, "Diversity or Decolonisation? Researching Diversity at the University of Amsterdam," in *Decolonising the University*, ed. Gurminder K. Bhambra, Dalia Gebrial, and Kerem Nisancioglu (London: Pluto Press, 2018), 116.

6. I thank Rosalba Icaza of Rotterdam Erasmus University, The Netherlands, for this metaphor.

7. Walter D. Mignolo, "DELINKING: The Rhetoric of Modernity, the Logic of Coloniality and the Grammar of de-Coloniality," *Cultural Studies* 21, no. 2–3 (2007): 449–514, https://doi.org/10.1080/095023806 01162647

8. For important reviews of the lineages of decolonization and decoloniality, see Leon Moosavi, "The Decolonial Bandwagon and the Dangers of Intellectual Decolonisation," *International Review of Sociology* 30, no. 2 (2020): 332–354, https://doi.org/10.1080/03906701.2020.1776919; Breny Mendoza, "Coloniality of Gender and Power: From Postcoloniality to Decoloniality," in *The Oxford Handbook of Feminist Theory*, ed. Lisa Disch and Mary Hawkesworth (Oxford: Oxford University Press, 2015), https://doi.org/10.1093/oxfordhb/9780199328581.013.6; Emma D. Velez and Nancy Tuana, "Toward Decolonial Feminisms: Tracing the Lineages of Decolonial Thinking through Latin American/Latinx Feminist Philosophy," *Hypatia* 35, no. 3 (2020): 366–372, https://doi.org/ 10.1017/hyp.2020.26

9. Aníbal Quijano, "Coloniality and Modernity/Rationality," *Cultural Studies* 21, no. 2–3 (2007): 168–178, https://doi.org/10.1080/095 02380601164353

10. This decolonial challenge pertains to Western critical theories, too. Many poststructuralists, feminists, Marxists, and scholars of the Frankfurt School maintain a fundamental assumption that particular epistemes rooted in Euro-American scholarship such as Michel Foucault, Karl Marx, and Judith Butler are nevertheless epistemologically neutral. Eurocentrism in knowledge production is therefore endemic not just in mainstream perspectives but also in those who position themselves as the traditional challengers within Western scholarly debates. While decoloniality draws extensively from postcolonialism and has many overlaps with it, some have extended this critique to parts of postcolonial scholarship. Thus "postcolonial theory

ultimately constitutes, at least epistemologically, a Eurocentric critique of Eurocentrism" according to Syed Mustafa Ali, "A Brief Introduction to Decolonial Computing," *XRDS: Crossroads, The ACM Magazine for Students* 22, no. 4 (June 13, 2016): 3, https://doi.org/10.1145/2930886; for further discussion see also Ramon Grosfoguel, "Decolonizing Post-Colonial Studies and Paradigms of Political-Economy: Transmodernity, Decolonial Thinking, and Global Coloniality," *TRANSMODERNITY: Journal of Peripheral Cultural Production of the Luso-Hispanic World* 1, no. 1 (2011): 2, https://escholarship.org/uc/item/21k6t3fq; Meera Sabaratnam, "Avatars of Eurocentrism in the Critique of the Liberal Peace," *Security Dialogue* 44, no. 3 (2013): 259–278, https://doi.org/10.1177/0967 010613485870; Robbie Shilliam, "Decolonising the Grounds of Ethical Inquiry: A Dialogue between Kant, Foucault and Glissant," *Millennium: Journal of International Studies* 39, no. 3 (2011): 649–665, https://doi .org/10.1177/0305829811399144

11. Sabelo J. Ndlovu-Gatsheni, "The Dynamics of Epistemological Decolonisation in the 21st Century: Towards Epistemic Freedom," *Strategic Review for Southern Africa* 40, no. 1 (2018): 23–26; Ngugi wa Thiong'o, *Decolonising the Mind: The Politics of Language in African Literature*, reprint, Studies in African Literature (Oxford: Currey [u.a.], 2005), 10–13; Oyèrónkẹ́ Oyěwùmí, *The Invention of Women: Making an African Sense of Western Gender Discourses* (Minneapolis, MN and London: University of Minnesota Press, 1997).

12. Walter D. Mignolo, "Epistemic Disobedience, Independent Thought and Decolonial Freedom," *Theory, Culture & Society* 26, no. 7–8 (2009): 160, https://doi.org/10.1177/0263276409349275

13. Icaza and Vasquez, "Diversity or Decolonisation? Researching Diversity at the University of Amsterdam," 112. Heteronormativity and anthropocentricity are not problems *only* of Euro-American knowledge, but Euro-American epistemes requires special attention from the decolonial perspective because they are hegemonic.

14. Mignolo, "DELINKING," 453–484; Jean Baudrillard, "Modernity," *Canadian Journal of Political and Social Theory* 11, no. 3 (1987): 63–72.

15. Marìa Lugones, "Toward a Decolonial Feminism," *Hypatia* 25, no. 4 (2010): 742–759, https://doi.org/10.1111/j.1527-2001.2010.01137.x; Walter D. Mignolo and Madina V. Tlostanova, "Theorizing from the Borders: Shifting to Geo- and Body-Politics of Knowledge," *European Journal of Social Theory* 9, no. 2 (2006): 205–206, https://doi.org/10.1177/ 1368431006063333

16. Mendoza, "Coloniality of Gender and Power: From Postcoloniality to

Decoloniality," 114; Nelson Maldonado-Torres, "On the Coloniality of Being: Contributions to the Development of a Concept," *Cultural Studies* 21, no. 2–3 (2007): 243, https://doi.org/10.1080/09502380601162548

17. Edward Said, *Orientalism*, repr. with a new preface, Penguin Classics (London: Penguin, 2003); Arturo Escobar, *Encountering Development: The Making and Unmaking of the Third World* (Princeton, NJ: Princeton University Press, 2012); Roxanne Lynn Doty, *Imperial Encounters: The Politics of Representation in North-South Relations* (Minneapolis: University of Minnesota Press, 1996): http://site.ebrary.com/id/10159633

18. Lugones, "Toward a Decolonial Feminism," 743.

19. Grosfoguel, "Decolonizing Post-Colonial Studies and Paradigms of Political-Economy," 5.

20. Ngugi, *Decolonising the Mind*. Please note that Ngugi is not of the decolonial tradition, but the broader and older one of decolonization.

21. Maureen Mauk, Rebekah Willett, and Natalie Coulter, "The Can-Do Girl Goes to Coding Camp: A Discourse Analysis of News Reports on Coding Initiatives Designed for Girls," *Learning, Media and Technology* 45, no. 4 (2020): 395–408, https://doi.org/10.1080/17439884.2020.1781889

22. Linda Nordling, "How Decolonization Could Reshape South African Science," *Nature* 554, no. 7691 (2018): 159–162, https://doi.org/10.1038/d41586-018-01696-w; Robert P. Crease, Joseph D. Martin, and Richard Staley, "Decolonizing Physics: Learning from the Periphery," *Physics in Perspective* 21, no. 2 (June 2019): 91–92, https://doi.org/10.1007/s00016-019-00240-1; Rohan Deb Roy, "Science Still Bears the Fingerprints of Colonialism," *Smithsonian Magazine* (blog), 2018: https://www.smithsonianmag.com/science-nature/science-bears-fingerprints-colonialism-180968709/

23. See the Decolonizing Light project hosted by Concordia University, Canada, which engages indigenous knowledges in the study of natural light: https://decolonizinglight.com/

24. Tanner Higgin, "Blackless Fantasy: The Disappearance of Race in Massively Multiplayer Online Role-Playing Games," *Games and Culture* 4, no. 1 (2008): 9–11, https://doi.org/10.1177/1555412008325477

25. Meera Sabaratnam, "Is IR Theory White? Racialised Subject-Positioning in Three Canonical Texts," *Millennium: Journal of International Studies* 49, no. 1 (2020): 3–31, https://doi.org/10.1177/0305829820971687

26. Syed Mustafa Ali, "Prolegomenon to the Decolonization of Internet Governance," in *Internet Governance in the Global South: History, Theory and Contemporary Debates*, ed. Daniel Oppermann (São Paulo: NUPRI University of São Paulo, 2018), 110–111.

27. Ibid., 118.

28. Ali, "A Brief Introduction to Decolonial Computing," 5.

29. Mignolo, "Epistemic Disobedience, Independent Thought and Decolonial Freedom," 162.

30. Bhupinder S. Chimni, "International Institutions Today: An Imperial Global State in the Making," *European Journal of International Law* 15, no. 1 (2004): 4–6; Peter M. Haas, "Introduction: Epistemic Communities and International Policy Coordination," *International Organization* 46, no. 1 (1992): 1–35.

31. McKenzie Wark, "INFORMATION WANTS TO BE FREE (BUT IS EVERYWHERE IN CHAINS)," *Cultural Studies* 20, no. 2–3 (2006): 172, https://doi.org/10.1080/09502380500495668

32. The fact that they are billionaires and newsworthy is not a spurious connection but a causal one, given the special legitimacy of material wealth in Eurocentric and modernist narratives of progress.

33. See media outlets like TechCrunch.com as well as prominent YouTube celebrities such as MKBHD, iJustine, and Unbox Therapy.

34. I acknowledge the significant role of actors from China, and to a lesser extent from Southeast Asia and Eastern Europe. Mignolo suggests that they represent de-Westernizing forces, not decolonial ones – instead of delinking from modernity/coloniality, they are merely taking over the reins of the modern epistemes, institutions, and agendas set in place by Euro-America. The logic of coloniality, according to Mignolo, would therefore still hold. See Mignolo, "Epistemic Disobedience, Independent Thought and Decolonial Freedom," 161; Walter D. Mignolo, "The Way We Were. Or What Decoloniality Today Is All About," *Anglistica AION: An Intersciplinary Journal* 23, no. 2 (2019): 21. However, I am more ambivalent about the role of China specifically because this large, complex community may possess particular understandings that may yet lead to non-modern conceptualizations of cyberspace. Still, instead of ushering in a decolonial future that encourages plurality in ways of knowing and being, the Chinese state's alternatives may simply create new, non-modern forms of domination. It is an empirical question whether Chinese users of cyberspace understand or make sense of cyberspace in the same way as users in Euro-America.

35. Association for Progressive Communications, "About APC," *Association for Progressive Communications* (blog), June 30, 2021: https://www.apc.org /en/about

36. See, for example, the description of their values and objectives in the APC's governance manual. Association for Progressive Communications,

"APC Governance Manual: Version 8" (2017): https://www.apc.org/sites/default/files/APC_GovernanceManual_Version_8_April_2017.pdf

37. Located in the United States with a focus on user privacy, free expression, and innovation. Electronic Frontier Foundation, "About EFF," *Electronic Frontier Foundation* (blog), 2021: https://www.eff.org/about

38. Located in the United States with a focus on privacy, net neutrality, and the digital and human rights of marginalized communities across the world. See Access Now, "Access Now Defends and Extends the Digital Rights of Users at Risk around the World," *Access Now* (blog), 2021: https://www.accessnow.org/about-us/

39. Located in Canada with a focus on privacy rights, freedoms, and threats to civil society. See Citizen Lab, "About the Citizen Lab," *The Citizen Lab* (blog), 2021: https://citizenlab.ca/about/

40. United Nations General Assembly, "Report of the Group of Governmental Experts on Developments in the Field of Information and Telecommunications in the Context of International Security," A/70/174 (2015); United Nations General Assembly, "Open-Ended Working Group on Developments in the Field of Information and Telecommunications in the Context of International Security. Final Substantive Report," A/AC.290/2021/CRP.2 (2021).

41. Kieron O'Hara, "The Contradictions of Digital Modernity," *AI & Society* 35, no. 1 (March 2020): 197–208, https://doi.org/10.1007/s00146-018-0843-7; Tim Stevens, *Cyber Security and the Politics of Time* (Cambridge: Cambridge University Press, 2015): https://doi.org/10.1017/CBO9781316271636

42. Alfred C. Yen, "Western Frontier or Feudal Society?: Metaphors and Perceptions of Cyberspace," *Berkeley Technology Law Journal* 17, no. 4 (2002): 1230.

43. Ibid.: 1232–1261.

44. Safiya Noble and Sarah Roberts, "Technological Elites, the Meritocracy, and Postracial Myths in Silicon Valley," in *Racism Postrace*, ed. Roopali Mukherjee, Sarah Banet-Weiser, and Herman Gray (Durham, NC: Duke University Press, 2019), 113–132.

45. Safiya Umoja Noble, *Algorithms of Oppression: How Search Engines Reinforce Racism* (New York: NYU Press, 2018); Cathy O'Neil, *Weapons of Math Destruction: How Big Data Increases Inequality and Threatens Democracy* (London: Penguin Books, 2017); Mario Koran, "Black Facebook Staff Describe Workplace Racism in Anonymous Letter," *The Guardian*, November 13, 2019: https://amp.theguardian.com/technology/2019/nov/13/facebook-discrimination-black-workers-letter; Mimi Onuoha,

"What Is Missing Is Still There": https://www.youtube.com/watch?v=5
7Lgztk62uY&t=6s

46. Rex Troumbley, "Colonization.Com-Empire Building For a New Digital
    Age," *East-West Affairs* 1, no. 4 (2013): 96–97.

47. James Shires, *The Politics of Cybersecurity in the Middle East* (London: Hurst,
    2021), chapter 3.

48. For a similar argument made about the field of international development,
    see Escobar, *Encountering Development*.

49. Michael Kwet, "Digital Colonialism: US Empire and the New Imperialism
    in the Global South," *Race & Class* 60, no. 4 (2019): 6, https://doi.org/10.
    1177/0306396818823172

50. Kwet, "Digital Colonialism."

51. Revati Prasad, "Ascendant India, Digital India: How Net Neutrality
    Advocates Defeated Facebook's Free Basics," *Media, Culture & Society* 40,
    no. 3 (2018): 415–431, https://doi.org/10.1177/0163443717736117

52. Gloria Anzaldúa, *Borderlands: The New Mestiza = La Frontera* (San Francisco,
    CA: Aunt Lute, 1987); Mignolo and Tlostanova, "Theorizing from the
    Borders"; Walter D. Mignolo, *Local Histories/Global Designs: Coloniality,
    Subaltern Knowledges, and Border Thinking* (Princeton, NJ and Oxford:
    Princeton University Press, 2012): https://doi.org/10.1515/978140084
    5064

53. Grosfoguel, "Decolonizing Post-Colonial Studies and Paradigms of
    Political-Economy," 26.

54. Rosalba Icaza, "Decolonial Feminism and Global Politics: Border Thinking
    and Vulnerability as a Knowing Otherwise," in *Vulnerability and the Politics
    of Care: Transdisciplinary Dialogues*, ed. Victoria Browne, Jason Danely, and
    Dörthe Rosenow (Oxford: Oxford University Press, 2021), 49.

55. Rosa Wevers, "Decolonial Aesthesis and the Museum: An Interview with
    Rolando Vazquez Melken," *Stedelijk Studies*, no. 8 (2019): 6.

56. Icaza and Vasquez, "Diversity or Decolonisation? Researching Diversity at
    the University of Amsterdam," 112.

57. An important innovation of the project is that it aims to conceptualize sta-
    bility and instability conjointly rather than focusing just on stability (often
    presumed to be the natural good), thereby acknowledging the ambiguous
    ways in which they relate.

58. Kate O'Flaherty, "Is It Time to Leave WhatsApp – and Is Signal the
    Answer?," *The Guardian*, January 24, 2021: https://www.theguardian
    .com/technology/2021/jan/24/is-it-time-to-leave-whatsapp-and-is-sig
    nal-the-answer

59. Bold type in original. Bennett Cyphers and Cory Doctorow, "Privacy

Without Monopoly: Data Protection and Interoperability" (Electronic Frontier Foundation, 2021), 5: https://www.eff.org/wp/interoperability -and-privacy

60. Ibid., 7.

61. Alexander Cho, "Default Publicness: Queer Youth of Color, Social Media, and Being Outed by the Machine," *New Media & Society* 20, no. 9 (September 2018): 3183–3200, https://doi.org/10.1177/146144481774 4784

62. Jillian C. York and Dia Kayyali, "Facebook's 'Real Name' Policy Can Cause Real-World Harm for the LGBTQ Community," *Electronic Frontier Foundation* (blog), September 16, 2014: https:// www.eff.org/deeplinks/2014/09/facebooks-real-name-policy-can-cause-real-world-harm-lgbtq-community

63. Cho, "Default Publicness," 3190.

64. Afsaneh Rigot, "Egypt's Dangerous New Strategy for Criminalizing Queerness," *Slate* (blog), December 30, 2020: https://slate.com/technolo gy/2020/12/egypt-lgbtq-crime-economic-courts.html

65. For examples of statist conceptions of cyberspace, see Jon R. Lindsay and Erik Gartzke, "Coercion Through Cyberspace: The Stability-Instability Paradox Revisited," in *Coercion: The Power to Hurt in International Politics*, ed. Kelly M. Greenhill and Peter Krause (New York: Oxford University Press, 2018), 179–203; Sergei Boeke and Dennis Broeders, "The Demilitarisation of Cyber Conflict," *Survival* 60, no. 6 (2018): 73–90, https://doi.org/10.1080/00396338.2018.1542804; Chris C. Demchak and Peter Dombrowski, "Cyber Westphalia: Asserting State Prerogatives in Cyberspace," *Georgetown Journal of International Affairs* (2013): 29–38; Rex Hughes, "A Treaty for Cyberspace," *International Affairs* 86, no. 2 (2010): 523–541, https://doi.org/10.1111/j.1468-2346.2010.00894.x

66. Joseph S Nye Jr., "Deterrence and Dissuasion in Cyberspace," *International Security* 41, no. 3 (Winter 2016): 44–71.

67. Ibid.: 48.

68. Gus Swanda, "The Deficiencies of a Westphalian Model for Cyberspace: A Case Study of South Korean Cyber Security," *International Journal of Korean Unification Studies* 25, no. 2 (2016): 77–103.

69. Mark Raymond and Laura DeNardis, "Multistakeholderism: Anatomy of an Inchoate Global Institution," *International Theory* 7, no. 3 (November 2015): 572–616, https://doi.org/10.1017/S1752971915000081; Myriam Dunn Cavelty, "Aligning Security Needs for Order in Cyberspace," in *The Rise and Decline of the Post-Cold War International Order*, ed. Hanns W. Maull (Oxford: Oxford University Press, 2018), 104–119; Duncan B.

Hollis and Jens David Ohlin, "What If Cyberspace Were for Fighting?," *Ethics & International Affairs* 32, no. 4 (2018): 441–456, https://doi.org/10.1017/S089267941800059X

70. Netina Tan, "Digital Learning and Extending Electoral Authoritarianism in Singapore," *Democratization* 27, no. 6 (2020): 1073–1091, https://doi.org/10.1080/13510347.2020.1770731; Aim Sinpeng, "Digital Media, Political Authoritarianism, and Internet Controls in Southeast Asia," *Media, Culture & Society* 42, no. 1 (2020): 25–39, https://doi.org/10.1177/0163443719884052; Florian Toepfl, "Innovating Consultative Authoritarianism: Internet Votes as a Novel Digital Tool to Stabilize Non-Democratic Rule in Russia," *New Media & Society* 20, no. 3 (2018): 956–972, https://doi.org/10.1177/1461444816675444

71. Xymena Kurowska and Anatoly Reshetnikov, "Neutrollization: Industrialized Trolling as a pro-Kremlin Strategy of Desecuritization," *Security Dialogue* 49, no. 5 (2018): 353, https://doi.org/10.1177/0967010618785102

72. States also use destabilizing strategies against each other. See James Shires, "The Simulation of Scandal: Hack-and-Leak Operations, the Gulf States, and US Politics," *Texas National Security Review* 3, no. 4 (2020): 10–28, https://doi.org/10.26153/TSW/10963

73. For rare exceptions, see Marianne I. Franklin, "Inside Out: Postcolonial Subjectivities and Everyday Life Online," *International Feminist Journal of Politics* 3, no. 3 (January 2001): 387–422, https://doi.org/10.1080/14616740110078194; Francesca Sobande, Anne Fearfull, and Douglas Brownlie, "Resisting Media Marginalisation: Black Women's Digital Content and Collectivity," *Consumption Markets & Culture* 23, no. 5 (2020): 413–428, https://doi.org/10.1080/10253866.2019.1571491; Hang Yin, "Chinese-Language Cyberspace, Homeland Media and Ethnic Media: A Contested Space for Being Chinese," *New Media & Society* 17, no. 4 (2015): 556–572, https://doi.org/10.1177/1461444813505363; Wendy Willems and Winston Mano (eds.), *Everyday Media Culture in Africa: Audiences and Users*, Routledge Advances in Internationalizing Media Studies (New York and Abingdon: Routledge, 2017).

74. Jason C. Young, "The New Knowledge Politics of Digital Colonialism," *Environment and Planning A: Economy and Space* 51, no. 7 (2019): 1431–1434, https://doi.org/10.1177/0308518X19858998

75. Ibid.: 1435.

76. Roopika Risam, "Decolonizing The Digital Humanities in Theory and Practice," in *English Faculty Publications*, vol. 7 (2018): 81–84, https://digitalcommons.salemstate.edu/english_facpub/7

77. Yaseen Aslam and Jamie Woodcock, "A History of Uber Organizing in the UK," *South Atlantic Quarterly* 119, no. 2 (April 1, 2020): 412–421, https://doi.org/10.1215/00382876-8177983
78. Ibid.: 419.

Bibliography

Abraham, Chon and Sally Daultrey, "Considerations For NATO In Reconciling Barriers To Shared Cyber Threat Intelligence: A Study Of Japan, The UK And The US," in Amy Ertan et al. (eds.), *Cyber Threats and NATO 2030*, Tallinn, Estonia: NATO CCD COE Publications, 2020, 194–214.

"Abuse of Cybercrime Measures Taints UN Talks," *Human Rights Watch*, May 5, 2021, https://www.hrw.org/news/2021/05/05/abuse-cybercrime-meas ures-taints-un-talks.

Access Now, "Access Now Tells the Ninth Circuit Court: NSO Group Cannot Escape Accountability in US Courts," *Access Now*, December 23, 2020, https://www.accessnow.org/nso-group-whatsapp-lawsuit-civil-soci ety-amicus-brief/

Access Now, "Access Now Defends and Extends the Digital Rights of Users at Risk around the World," *Access Now* (blog), 2021, https://www.accessn ow.org/about-us/

Acemoglu, Daron, Simon Johnson, and James Robinson, "The Colonial Origins of Comparative Development: An Empirical Investigation," *American Economic Review* 91, no. 1369 (2001).

Acton, James M., "Escalation Through Entanglement: How the Vulnerability of Command-and-Control Systems Raises the Risks of an Inadvertent Nuclear War," *International Security* 43, no. 1 (Summer 2018), https://doi .org/10.1162/isec_a_00320

Acton, James M., "Cyber Warfare & Inadvertent Escalation," *Daedalus* 149, no. 2 (Spring 2020): 133–149, https://doi.org/10.1162/daed_a_01794

Adamsky, Dmitry, *The Culture of Military Innovation: The Impact of Cultural Factors on the Revolution in Military Affairs in Russia, the US, and Israel*, Stanford, CA: Stanford University Press, 2010.

Adamsky, Dmitry, "Cross-Domain Coercion: The Current Russian Art of

Strategy," Institut Français des Relations Internationales, Paris, France, November 2015.

Adedeji Adedeji, "Comparative Strategies of Economic Decolonization in Africa," *General History of Africa* 8 (1993): 393–431.

Adler, Emmanuel, "The Spread of Security Communities: Communities of Practice, Self-Restraint, and NATO's Post-Cold War Transformation," *European Journal of International Relations* 14, no. 2 (2008): 195–230.

Adler, Emmanuel and Michael Barnett, *Security Communities*, Cambridge: Cambridge University Press, 1998.

Admiral Michael S. Rogers, "Statement of Admiral Michael S. Rogers Commander United States Cyber Command Before the Senate Armed Services Committee," § Senate Armed Services Committee (2015), https://fas.org/irp/congress/2015_hr/031915rogers.pdf

African Union and Symantec, "Cyber Crime and Cyber Security Trends in Africa," 2016, https://thegfce.org/cybercrime-and-cybersecurity-trends-in-africa/

Ahern, Stephanie, "Breaking the Organizational Mold: Why the Institutional U.S. Army Has Changed Despite Itself since the End of the Cold War," Doctoral dissertation, (University of Notre Dame, 2009).

Ahmed, Azam, "Mexican President Says Government Acquired Spyware But He Denies Misuse," *The New York Times*, June 22, 2017, https://www.nytimes.com/2017/06/22/world/americas/mexico-pena-nieto-hacking-pegasus.html

Al Jazeera Investigative Unit, "Bangladesh Bought Mass Spying Equipment from Israeli Company," *Al Jazeera*, February 2, 2021, https://www.aljazeera.com/news/2021/2/2/bangladesh-bought-surveillance-equipment-from-israeli-company

Albin, Cecilia, *Justice and Fairness in International Negotiation*, Cambridge: Cambridge University Press, 2001.

Alexander, Keith B., "Building a New Command in Cyberspace," *Strategic Studies Quarterly* 5, no. 2 (Summer 2011): 3–12, https://www.jstor.org/stable/26270554?seq=2#metadata_info_tab_contents

Ali, Syed Mustafa, "A Brief Introduction to Decolonial Computing," *XRDS: Crossroads, The ACM Magazine for Students* 22, no. 4 (13 June 2016), https://doi.org/10.1145/2930886

Ali, Syed Mustafa, "Prolegomenon to the Decolonization of Internet Governance," in Daniel Oppermann (ed.), *Internet Governance in the Global South: History, Theory and Contemporary Debates*, São Paulo: NUPRI University of São Paulo, 2018.

Allison, Graham and Philip Zelikow, "Essence of Decision," *Foreign Policy*, no. 114 (1999): 234–237, https://doi.org/10.2307/1149596

Amadi, Luke, "Africa: Beyond the 'New' Dependency: A Political Economy," *African Journal of Political Science and International Relations* 6, no. 8 (2012): 191–203.

Amnesty International, "Failing to Do Right: The Urgent Need for Palantir to Respect Human Rights," *Amnesty International*, September 2020, https://www.amnestyusa.org/wp-content/uploads/2020/09/Amnest-International-Palantir-Briefing-Report-092520_Final.pdf

Ampiah, Kweku, "Japan and the Development of Africa: A Preliminary Evaluation of the Tokyo International Conference on African Development," *African Affairs* 104, no. 97 (2005).

Anderson, Collin, "Monitoring the Lines: Sanctions and Human Rights Policy Considerations of TeleStrategies ISS World Seminars," July 31, 2014, https://cda.io/notes/monitoring-the-lines/

Anderson, Collin and Karim Sadjadpour, "Iran's Cyber Threat: Espionage, Sabotage, and Revenge," *Carnegie Endowment for International Peace*, January 4, 2018, https://carnegieendowment.org/2018/01/04/iran-target-and-perpetrator-pub-75139

Anderson, James P., *Computer Security Technology Planning Study, Vol 1*, Electronic Systems Division of the Air Force Systems Command, October 1972, https://csrc.nist.gov/csrc/media/publications/conference-paper/1998/10/08/proceedings-of-the-21st-nissc-1998/documents/early-cs-papers/ande72a.pdf

Anderson, James P., *Computer Security Technology Planning Study, Vol 2*, Electronic Systems Division of the Air Force Systems Command, October 1972, https://apps.dtic.mil/dtic/tr/fulltext/u2/772806.pdf

Anderson, James P., *Computer Security Threat Monitoring and Surveillance*, Fort Washington, PA, February 26, 1980, revised April 15, 1980, https://csrc.nist.gov/csrc/media/publications/conference-paper/1998/10/08/proceedings-of-the-21st-nissc-1998/documents/early-cs-papers/ande80.pdf

Anderson, Jeffrey, G. John Ikenberry, and Thomas Risse-Kappen, *The End of the West? Crisis and Change in the Atlantic Order*, Ithaca, NY: Cornell University Press, 2008.

Angstrom, Jan and Peter Haldén, "The Poverty Of Power In Military Power: How Collective Power Could Benefit Strategic Studies," *Defense & Security Analysis* 35, no. 2 (2019): 170–189.

Anstis, Siena, Sharly Chan, Adam Senft and Ronald Deibert, "Annotated Bibliography: Dual-Use Technologies: Network Traffic Management and Device Intrusion for Targeted Monitoring," *Citizen Lab*, October 2020,

https://citizenlab.ca/wp-content/uploads/2020/11/Annotated-Bibliogra
phy-Network-Traffic-Management-and-Device-Intrusion-for-Targeted
-Monitoring.pdf

Antian Shiyan Shi [Antiy Labs], "Wukelan Tingdian Shijian Qishilu
[Revelations from the Ukrainian Power Outage Incident]," *Zhongguo Xinxi
Anquan [China Information Security]* 4 (2016), http://www.cnki.com.cn/
Article/CJFDTotal-CINS201604021.htm

Antwi-Boateng, Osman, "New World Order Neo-Colonialism: A Contextual
Comparison of Contemporary China and European Colonization in
Africa," *Africology: The Journal of Pan African Studies* 10, no. 177 (2017).

Anzaldúa, Gloria, *Borderlands: The New Mestiza = La Frontera*, San Francisco,
CA: Aunt Lute, 1987.

Aslam, Yaseen and Jamie Woodcock, "A History of Uber Organizing in the
UK," *South Atlantic Quarterly* 119, no. 2 (April 1, 2020): 412–421, https://
doi.org/10.1215/00382876-8177983

Associated Press, "More Journalists Killed in Mexico in 2020 Than Anywhere
Else in the World," *LA Times*, December 22, 2020, https://www.latim
es.com/world-nation/story/2020-12-22/mexico-sees-most-journalists-kil
led-in-2020-group-says

Association for Progressive Communications, "APC Governance Manual:
Version 8" (2017), https://www.apc.org/sites/default/files/APC_Governa
nceManual_Version_8_April_2017.pdf

Association for Progressive Communications, "About APC," *Association for
Progressive Communications* (blog), June 30, 2021, https://www.apc.org/en
/about

Atlantic Council, "Transcript: Lessons from Our Cyber Past – The First
Military Cyber Units," March 5, 2012, https://www.atlanticcouncil.org
/commentary/transcript/transcript-lessons-from-our-cyber-past-the-first
-military-cyber-units

Atwood, Donald J., "Information Warfare," Department of Defense Directive
TS 3600.1, December 21, 1992.

Auerswald, David P. and Stephen Saideman, *NATO in Afghanistan: Fighting
Together, Fighting Alone*, Princeton, NJ and Oxford: Princeton University
Press, 2014.

Augelli, Vincent A., "Information-Dominance Officers Need to Command,"
https://www.bluetoad.com/publication/?i=102307&p=81&view=issue
Viewer

Ayoob, Mohammed, "Inequality and Theorizing in International Relations:
The Case for Subaltern Realism," *International Studies Review* 4, no. 3
(2002): 27–48.

Ball, Desmond, "China's Cyber Warfare Capabilites," *Security Challenges* 7, no. 2 (Winter 2011): 81–103, https://www.jstor.org/stable/26461991

Barnes, Julian E. and Thomas Gibbons-Neff, "U.S. Carried Out Cyberattacks on Iran," *The New York Times*, June 22, 2019, US section, https://www.nytimes.com/2019/06/22/us/politics/us-iran-cyber-attacks.html

Barnes, Julian E., Matthew Rosenberg, and Edward Wong, "As Virus Spreads, China and Russia See Openings for Disinformation," *The New York Times*, March 28, 2020, https://www.nytimes.com/2020/03/28/us/politics/china-russia-coronavirus-disinformation.html

Barnes, Julian, David Sanger, Ronen Bergman, and Lara Jakes, "As U.S. Increases Pressure, Iran Adheres to Toned-Down Approach," *The New York Times*, September 19, 2020, https://www.nytimes.com/2020/09/19/us/politics/us-iran-election.html

Barnett, Michael and Raymond Duvall, "Power in International Politics," *International Organization* 59, no. 1 (2005): 39–75.

Bate, Laura et al., "Defending Forward by Defending Norms," *Lawfare*, March 11, 2020, https://www.lawfareblog.com/defending-forward-defending-norms

Baudrillard, Jean, "Modernity," *Canadian Journal of Political and Social Theory* 11, no. 3 (1987): 63–72.

Beck, Lindsay, "China and U.S. Sign Accord on Defense Hotline," *Reuters*, February 29, 2008, https://www.reuters.com/article/us-china-us-defence-idUSPEK7130320080229

Beech, Hannah, "Myanmar's Military Deploys Digital Arsenal of Repression in Crackdown," *The New York Times*, March 1, 2021, https://www.nytimes.com/2021/03/01/world/asia/myanmar-coup-military-surveillance.html

Bender, Bryan, "Navy Chief Commissions Fleet Information Warfare Center," *Defense Daily* 189, no. 17 (October 1995).

Bender, Bryan, "Army Stands Up Computer Security Coordination Center," *Defense Daily* (March 18, 1997).

Ben-Moshe, Liat, "Dis-Epistemologies of Abolition," *Critical Criminology* 26, no. 3 (September 2018): 341–355, https://doi.org/10.1007/s10612-018-9403-1

Bennett, Joana et al., "Trading Places: The 'Commonwealth Effect' Revisited," *Royal Commonwealth Society*, working paper, September 30, 2010.

Benvenisti, Eyal and George Downs, "The Empire's New Clothes: Political Economy and the Fragmentation of International Law," *Stanford Law Review* 60, no. 2 (2007).

Betts, Alexander, "The Refugee Regime Complex," *Refugee Survey Quarterly* 29, no. 1 (2010): 12–37.

Betts, Richard K., *Surprise Attack: Lessons for Defense Planning*, Washington, DC: Brooking Institution, 1982.

Black, Crofton, "Spy Companies Using Channel Islands to Track Phones Around the World," *Bureau of Investigative Journalism*, December 16, 2020, https://www.thebureauinvestigates.com/stories/2020-12-16/spy-compani es-using-channel-islands-to-track-phones-around-the-world

Blainey, Geoffrey, *Causes of War* (New York: Free Press, 1973).

Blank, Stephen, "Cyber War and Information War À La Russe," in George Perkovich and Ariel E. Levite (eds.), *Understanding Cyber Conflict: 14 Analogies*, Washington, DC: Georgetown University Press, 2017, 81–98.

Bodoni, Stephanie, "Google Clash Over Global Right to Be Forgotten Returns to Court. Bloomberg," 2019, https://www.bloomberg.com/news /articles/2019-01-09/google-clash-over-global-right-to-be-forgotten-retu rns-to-court

Boeke, Sergei and Dennis Broeders, "The Demilitarisation of Cyber Conflict," *Survival* 60, no. 6 (2018): 73–90, https://doi.org/10.1080/00396338. 2018.1542804

Boland, Rita, "Military Branch Undertakes Massive Troop Conversion," *Signal*, February 2, 2010, https://www.afcea.org/content/military-branch -undertakes-massive-troop-conversion

Bon, Daniel and Karen Mingst, "French Intervention in Africa: Dependency or Decolonization," *Africa Today* 27, no. 2 (1980): 5–20.

Borghard, Erica D. and Shawn W. Lonergan, "The Logic of Coercion in Cyberspace," *Security Studies* 26, no. 3 (July 3, 2017): 452–481, https://doi .org/10.1080/09636412.2017.1306396

Borghard, Erica D. and Shawn W. Lonergan, "Confidence Building Measures for the Cyber Domain," *Strategic Studies Quarterly* 12, no. 3 (2018): 10–49.

Borghard, Erica D and Shawn W. Lonergan, "Cyber Operations as Imperfect Tools of Escalation," *Strategic Studies Quarterly* 13, no. 3 (2019), https:// www.airuniversity.af.edu/Portals/10/SSQ/documents/Volume-13_Issue -3/Borghard.pdf

Boutin, Paul, "Slammed!" *Wired*, July 1, 2003, https://www.wired.com/20 03/07/slammer/

Bracken, Paul, "The Cyber Threat to Nuclear Stability," *Orbis* 60, no. 2 (2016): 188–203.

Bradshaw, Samantha et al., *The Emergence of Contention in Global Internet Governance*, Centre for Internet Governance Innovation, 2015.

Braman, Sandra, "Instability and Internet Design," *Journal of Internet Regulation* 5, no. 1 (2016).

Branch, Ted N., "The 'Information Dominance Corps' is now the 'Information Warfare Community'" *CHIPS* (January-March 2016), https://www.don cio.navy.mil/Chips/ArticleDetails.aspx?ID=7307

Brandt, Jessica, "How Democracies Can Win an Information Contest Without Undercutting Their Values," Carnegie Endowment, August 2, 2021, https:// carnegieendowment.org/2021/08/02/how-democracies-can-win-info rmation-contest-without-undercutting-their-values-pub-85058

Brantly, Aaron (ed.), *The Cyber Deterrence Problem*, New York: Rowman & Littlefield, 2020.

Brantly, Aaron F., Nerea M. Cal, and Devlin P. Winkelstein, "Defending the Borderland: Ukrainian Military Experiences with IO, Cyber, and EW," January 7, 2017, https://vtechworks.lib.vt.edu/handle/10919/81979

Bratton, Benjamin, *The Stack*, Cambridge: The MIT Press, 2015.

Brauchle, Jan-Philipp et al., "Cyber Mapping the Financial System," *Carnegie Endowment for International Peace*, April 7, 2020, https://carnegieendowment .org/2020/04/07/cyber-mapping-financial-system-pub-81414

Brayne, Sarah, *Predict and Surveil*, Oxford: Oxford University Press, 2020.

Brock, Jack L., *Hackers Penetrate DOD Computer Systems*, US General Accounting Office, https://nsarchive2.gwu.edu/NSAEBB/NSAEBB424 /docs/Cyber-006.pdf

Brunnée, Jutta and Stephen J. Toope, *Legitimacy and Legality in International Law*, Cambridge: Cambridge University Press, 2010.

Buchanan, Ben, *The Cybersecurity Dilemma: Hacking, Trust and Fear between Nations*, Oxford University Press, 2017, https://doi.org/10.1093/acprof:o so/9780190665012.001.0001

Buchanan, Ben, "How North Korean Hackers Rob Banks Around the World," February 28, 2020, https://www.wired.com/story/how-north-ko rea-robs-banks-around-world/

Buchanan, Ben, *The Hacker and the State: Cyber Attacks and the New Normal of Geopolitics*, Cambridge, MA: Harvard University Press, 2020.

Buchanan, Ben and Fiona Cunningham, "Preparing the Cyber Battlefield: Assessing a Novel Escalation Risk in a Sino-American Crisis," *Texas National Security Review* 3, no. 4 (Fall 2020): 54–81, http://dx.doi.org/10 .26153/tsw/10951

Buckley, Chris and Paul Mozur, "How China Uses High-Tech Surveillance to Subdue Minorities," *The New York Times*, May 22, 2020, https:// www.nytimes.com/2019/05/22/world/asia/china-surveillance-xinjiang. html

"Budget Plan Leaves Military Computers Vulnerable to Intrusion," *Defense Daily* 184, no. 54 (1994).

Burton, Joe, *NATO's Durability in a Post-Cold War World*, New York: State University of New York Press, 2018.

Büthe, Tim and Walter Mattli, *The New Global Rulers: The Privatization of Regulation in the World Economy*, Princeton, NJ: Princeton University Press, 2011.

Byler, Darren, "China's Hi-Tech War on Its Muslim Minority," *The Guardian*, April 11, 2019, https://www.theguardian.com/news/2019/apr/11/china-hi-tech-war-on-muslim-minority-xinjiang-uighurs-surveillance-face-recognition

Campbell, John H., "Computer Network Defense: Computer Network Defense Update to the Defense Science Board," *National Security Archive*, January 18, 2000, slide 13, https://nsarchive.gwu.edu/dc.html?doc=3145117-Document-03

Campbell, Kurt M. and Ali Wyne, "The Growing Risk of Inadvertent Escalation Between Washington and Beijing," *Lawfare*, August 16, 2020, https://www.lawfareblog.com/growing-risk-inadvertent-escalation-between-washington-and-beijing

Campen, Alan D. (ed.), *The First Information War: The Story of Communications, Computers, and Intelligence Systems in the Persian Gulf War*, Fairfax, VA: AFCEA International Press, 1992.

Canadian Department of National Defence, "Strong, Secure, Engaged: Canada's Defence Policy," *Canadian Department of National Defence*, 2017, https://www.canada.ca/content/dam/dnd-mdn/documents/reports/2018/strong-secure-engaged/canada-defence-policy-report.pdf

Carson, Austin, *Secret Wars: Covert Conflict in International Politics*, Princeton, NJ: Princeton University Press, 2018.

Cathcart, Will, "Why WhatsApp is Pushing Back on NSO Group Hacking," *The Washington Post*, October 29, 2019, https://www.washingtonpost.com/opinions/2019/10/29/why-whatsapp-is-pushing-back-nso-group-hacking/

Cebrowski, Arthur K. and John H. Garstka, "Network-centric Warfare: Its Origin and Future," *Proceedings* 124, no. 1 (January 1998), https://www.usni.org/magazines/proceedings/1998/january/network-centric-warfare-its-origin-and-future

Chairman of the Joint Chiefs of Staff (CJCS), "National Military Strategy of the United States of America 2004: A Strategy for Today; A Vision for Tomorrow," Department of Defense, 2004.

Chakrabarty, Dipesh, "Subaltern Studies and Postcolonial Historiography," *Nepantla: Views from South* 9, no. 15 (2000).

Chander, Sarah, "Decolonising Data Panel" (Digital Freedom Fund, February 17, 2021), https://www.youtube.com/watch?v=WRobUCm13m4

Chapman, George L., "Missileer: The Dawn, Decline, and Reinvigoration of America's Intercontinental Ballistic Missile Operators," Master's thesis (Air University, 2017), https://apps.dtic.mil/dtic/tr/fulltext/u2/1045804.pdf

Chen, John, Joe McReynolds, and Kieran Green, "The PLA Strategic Support Force: A 'Joint' Force for Information Operations," in Joel Wuthnow et al. (eds.), *The PLA Beyond Borders: Chinese Military Operations in Regional and Global Context*, Washington, DC: National Defense University Press, 2021.

Chimni, Bhupinder S, "International Institutions Today: An Imperial Global State in the Making," *European Journal of International Law* 15, no. 1 (2004).

"China Exports AI Surveillance Tech to Over 60 Countries: Report," *Nikkei Asian Review*, December 16, 2019, https://asia.nikkei.com/Business/China-tech/China-exports-AI-surveillance-tech-to-over-60-countries-report

"China's Guidelines on Joint Operations Aim for Future Warfare: Defense Spokesperson," *China Military Online*, November 27, 2020, http://english.scio.gov.cn/pressroom/2020-11/27/content_76954237.htm

Cho, Alexander, "Default Publicness: Queer Youth of Color, Social Media, and Being Outed by the Machine," *New Media & Society* 20, no. 9 (September 2018): 3183–3200, https://doi.org/10.1177/1461444817744784

Christensen, Thomas J., "The Meaning of the Nuclear Evolution: China's Strategic Modernization and US-China Security Relations," *Journal of Strategic Studies* 35, no. 4 (2012): 482–484, https://doi.org/10.1080/01402390.2012.714710

Christou, George, *Cybersecurity in the European Union: Resilience and Adaptability in Governance Policy*, Basingstoke: Palgrave Macmillan, 2016.

Cisco, "Cisco Annual Internet Report (2018–2023) White Paper," 2020, https://www.cisco.com/c/en/us/solutions/collateral/executive-perspectives/annual-internet-report/white-paper-c11-741490.html

Citizen Lab, "About the Citizen Lab," *The Citizen Lab* (blog), 2021, https://citizenlab.ca/about/

Clapham, Christopher, *Africa and the International System*, Cambridge: Cambridge University Press, 1996.

Clark, Ian, "International Society and China: The Power of Norms and the Norms of Power," *The Chinese Journal of International Politics* 7, no. 3 (Autumn 2014): 315–340, https://doi.org/10.1093/cjip/pot014

Clinton, Hillary Rodham, "Internet Freedom: The Prepared Text of U.S. of Secretary of State Hillary Rodham Clinton's Speech, Delivered at the Newseum in Washington, D.C.," *Foreign Policy*, January 21, 2010.

Colgan, Jeff D. et al., "Punctuated Equilibrium in the Energy Regime Complex," *Review of International Organizations* 7, no. 2 (2012): 117–143.

Collins, Katie, "Hacking Team's Oppressive Regimes Customer List Revealed in Hack," *Wired*, July 6, 2015, https://www.wired.co.uk/article/hacking-team-spyware-company-hacked

Committee on National Security Systems, "CNSS History," https://www.cnss.gov/CNSS/about/history.cfm

Comninos, Alex and Gareth Seneque, "Cyber Security, Civil Society, and Vulnerability in an Age of Communications Surveillance," *GIS Watch*, 2014, https://giswatch.org/en/communications-surveillance/cyber-security-civil-society-and-vulnerability-age-communications-sur

Constance, Paul, "From Bombs to Bytes: Era of On-line Weaponry Is Here," *Government Computer News* 14, no. 21 (October 1995).

Corn, Gary, "Punching on the Edges of the Grey Zone: Iranian Cyber Threats and State Cyber Responses," *Just Security*, February 11, 2020, https://www.justsecurity.org/68622/punching-on-the-edges-of-the-grey-zone-iranian-cyber-threats-and-state-cyber-responses/

Corn, Gary, "Coronavirus Disinformation and the Need for States to Shore Up International Law," *Lawfare*, April 2, 2020, https://www.lawfareblog.com/coronavirus-disinformation-and-need-states-shore-international-law

Costello, John K. and Joe McReynolds, *China's Strategic Support Force: A Force for a New Era*, Washington, DC: Institute for National Strategic Studies, National Defense University, September 2018.

Cox, Joseph, "How an ICE Contractor Tracks Phones Around the World," *Vice Motherboard*, March 12, 2020, https://www.vice.com/en/article/epdpdm/ice-dhs-fbi-location-data-venntel-apps

Craig, Anthony and Brandon Valeriano, "Conceptualizing Cyber Arms Races," in N. Pissanidis, H. Rõigas, and M. Veenendaal (eds.), *Proceedings of the 8th International Conference on Cyber Conflict*, Tallinn: NATO CCD COE Publications, 2016, 141–158, https://ccdcoe.org/uploads/2018/10/Art-10-Conceptualising-Cyber-Arms-Races.pdf

Crease, Robert P., Joseph D. Martin, and Richard Staley, "Decolonizing Physics: Learning from the Periphery," *Physics in Perspective* 21, no. 2 (June 2019), https://doi.org/10.1007/s00016-019-00240-1

Crowther, Glenn Alexander, "The Cyber Domain," *The Cyber Defense Review* 2, no. 3 (Fall 2017): 63–72.

Cunningham, Fiona S., "China's Search for Coercive Leverage in the Information Age," working paper.

Cunningham, Fiona S. and M. Taylor Fravel, "Assuring Assured Retaliation:

China's Nuclear Strategy and U.S.-China Strategic Stability," *International Security* 40, no. 2 (Fall 2015): 7–50, https://doi.org/10.1162/ISEC_a_0 0215

Cunningham, Fiona S. and M. Taylor Fravel, "Dangerous Confidence? Chinese Views of Nuclear Escalation," *International Security* 44, no. 2 (2019): 61–109, https://doi.org/10.1162/isec_a_00359

Cyber Security Intelligence, "The British Cyber Command," January 22, 2020, https://www.cybersecurityintelligence.com/blog/the-british-cyber-command-4748.html

Cybersecurity and Insfrastructure Security Agency, "Critical Infrastructure Sectors," 2020, https://www.cisa.gov/critical-infrastructure-sectors

Cyphers, Bennett and Cory Doctorow, "Privacy Without Monopoly: Data Protection and Interoperability," Electronic Frontier Foundation, 2021, https://www.eff.org/wp/interoperability-and-privacy

Cyphers, Bennet and Gennie Gebhart, "Behind the One-Way Mirror: A Deep Dive into the Technology of Corporate Surveillance," *EFF*, 2019, https://www.eff.org/wp/behind-the-one-way-mirror

Dalek, Jakub, Ron Deibert, Sarah McKune, Phillipa Gill, Adam Senft, and Naser Noor, "Information Controls During Military Operations: The Case of Yemen During the 2015 Political and Armed Conflict," *Citizen Lab*, https://citizenlab.ca/2015/10/information-controls-military-operations-yemen/

Daniel, Michael and Joshua Kenway, "Repairing The Foundation: How Cyber Threat Information Sharing Can Live Up To Its Promise And Implications For NATO," in Amy Ertan, Kathryn Floyd, Piret Pernik, and Tim Stevens (eds.), *Cyber Threats and NATO 2030: Horizon Scanning and Analysis*, Tallinn, Estonia: NATO CCD COE Publications, 2020, 178–193.

de Tomas Colatin, Samuele, "A Surprising Turn of Events: UN Creates Two Working Groups on Cyberspace," *NATO Cooperative Cyber Defence Centre of Excellence*, https://ccdcoe.org/incyder-articles/a-surprising-turn-of-events-un-creates-two-working-groups-on-cyberspace/

Defense Science Board, "Task Force Report: Resilient Military Systems and the Advanced Cyber Threat," January 2013, https://apps.dtic.mil/dtic/tr/fulltext/u2/1028516.pdf

Defense Science Board, *DSB Summer Study Report on Strategic Surprise*, 2015.

Deibert, Ronald J., *Black Code: Inside the Battle for Cyberspace*, Toronto: Signal, MccLelland & Steward, 2013.

Deibert, Ronald J., "Authoritarianism Goes Global: Cyberspace Under Siege,"

Journal of Democracy 26, no. 3 (2015): 64–78, https://doi.org/10.1353/jod
.2015.0051

Deibert, Ronald J., "Towards a Human-Centric Approach to Cybersecurity,"
Ethics and International Affairs 32, no. 4 (2018): 411–424. https://doi.org/10
.1017/S0892679418000618

Deibert, Ronald J., "The Road to Digital Unfreedom: Three Painful Truths
about Social Media," *Journal of Democracy* 30, no. 1 (2019): 25–39.

Deibert, Ronald J., *Reset: Reclaiming the Internet for Civil Society. The Unabridged
Bibliography*, Toronto: House of Anansi Press, 2020, https://reset-bibliogra
phy.ca/

Deibert, Ronald J. et al. (eds.), *Access Controlled: The Shaping of Power, Rights,
and Rule in Cyberspace*, Cambridge, MA, The MIT Press, 2010, https://
library.oapen.org/bitstream/handle/20.500.12657/26076/1004009.pdf;jses
sionid=E86AF42D3F71A442FB7B79A68290F5EB?sequence=1

Deibert, Ronald J. et al, "Champing at the Cyberbit: Ethiopian Dissidents
Targeted with New Commercial Spyware," *Citizen Lab*, 2017, https://citi
zenlab.ca/2017/12/champing-cyberbit-ethiopian-dissidents-targeted-com
mercial-spyware/

Demchak, Chris C., "Three Futures for a Post-Western Cybered World,"
Military Cyber Affairs 3, no. 1 (2018), https://scholarcommons.usf.edu/cgi
/viewcontent.cgi?article=1044&context=mca

Demchak, Chris C. and Peter Dombrowski, "Rise of a Cybered Westphalian
Age," *Strategic Studies Quarterly* 5, no. 1 (Spring 2011): 32–61, https://www
.jstor.org/stable/26270509

Demchak, Chris C. and Peter Dombrowski, "Cyber Westphalia: Asserting
State Prerogatives in Cyberspace," *Georgetown Journal of International Affairs*
(2013): 29–38.

DeNardis, Laura, *The Global War for Internet Governance*, New Haven, CT:
Yale University Press, 2014.

DeNardis, Laura, "Governance by Infrastructure," in Francesca Musiani et al.
(eds.), *The Turn to Infrastructure in Internet Governance*, Basingstoke: Palgrave
Macmillan, 2016.

DeNardis, Laura and Mark Raymond, "The Internet of Things as a Global
Policy Frontier," *U.C. Davis Law Review* 51, no. 2 (2017): 475–497.

DeNardis, Laura, *The Internet in Everything: Freedom and Security in a World with
No Off Switch*, New Haven, CT: Yale University Press, 2020.

Denning, Dorothy E., "Rethinking the Cyber Domain and Deterrence," *Joint
Forces Quarterly* 77 (2015): 8–15.

Department of the Air Force, "Cornerstones of Information Warfare," January
1, 1995: 8, https://apps.dtic.mil/sti/citations/ADA307436

Department of Defense, "Electronic Warfare (EW) and Command and Control Warfare (C2W) Countermeasures," Department of Defense Directive 3222.4, July 31, 1992.

Department of Defense, "Memorandum of Policy Number 30: Command and Control Warfare," *Department of Defense*, March 1993, https://archive.org /details/JCSMemoofPolicyNumber30CommandandControlWarfare

Department of Defense, *Quadrennial Roles and Missions Review Report*, January 2009.

Department of Defense, *Department of Defense Strategy for Operating in Cyberspace*, July 2011.

Department of Defense, "The Department of Defense Cyber Strategy," 2015, https://archive.defense.gov/home/features/2015/0415_cyber-strategy /final_2015_dod_cyber_strategy_for_web.pdf.pdf

Department of Defense, *Department of Defense Cyber Strategy 2018: Summary*, September 2018.

Department of Defense, Defense Science Board, "Task Force on Cyber Deterrence" (February 2017): 1–44, https://www.armed-services.senate .gov/imo/media/doc/DSB%20CD%20Report%202017-02-27-17_v18 _Final-Cleared%20Security%20Review

Department of Justice, "United States of America v. Ahmad Fathi, Hamid Firoozi, Amin Shokohi, Sadegh Ahmadzadegan, Omid Ghaffarinia, Sina Keissar, and Nader Saedi," March 24, 2016, https://www.justice.gov/opa /file/834996/download

Department of Justice, "United States of America v. Park Jin Hyok," June 8, 2018: 45–53, from "Cyber Brief: DOJ's Park Jin Hyok Criminal Complaint and North Korean Cyber Operations," *National Security Archive*, September 6, 2018: https://nsarchive.gwu.edu/news/cyber-vault/2018-09-06/cyber -brief-dojs-park-jin-hyok-criminal-complaint-north-korean-cyber-oper ations

DeSombre, Winnona et al., "A Primer on the Proliferation of Offensive Cyber Capabilities," *Atlantic Council*, March 1, 2021, https://www.atlanticcouncil .org/in-depth-research-reports/issue-brief/a-primer-on-the-proliferation -of-offensive-cyber-capabilities/#markets

DeSombre, Winnona et al., "Countering Cyber Proliferation: Zeroing in on Access-as-a-Service," *Atlantic Council*, March 1, 2021, https://www.at lanticcouncil.org/in-depth-research-reports/report/countering-cyber-proli feration-zeroing-in-on-access-as-a-service/#nso

Deutsch, Karl W. and David J. Singer, "Multipolar Power Systems and International Stability," *World Politics* 16, no. 3 (1964): 390–406.

Devanny, Joe, "'Madman Theory' or 'Persistent Engagement'? The Coherence of US Cyber Strategy Under Trump," *Journal of Applied Security Research* (2021), https://doi.org/10.1080/19361610.2021.1872359

Diamond, Larry, "Liberation Technology," *Journal of Democracy* 21, no. 3 (2010): 69–83, https://www.journalofdemocracy.org/articles/liberation-te chnology/

Díaz-Plaja, Rubén, "Projecting Stability: An Agenda for Action," March 13, 2018, https://www.nato.int/docu/review/articles/2018/03/13/projecting -stability-an-agenda-for-action/index.html

Director of National Intelligence Clapper, James R., "Worldwide Threat Assessment of the US Intelligence Community," § Senate Armed Services Committee (2015), https://www.armed-services.senate.gov/imo/media /doc/Clapper_02-26-15.pdf

DoD Inspector General, "DoD Compliance with the Information Assurance Vulnerability Alert Policy," *Department of Defense, Office of Inspector General*, December 1, 2000, https://www.dodig.mil/reports.html/Article/1116364 /dod-compliance-with-the-information-assurance-vulnerability-alert-po licy/

Donnelly, D. A. et al., "A Technical and Policy Toolkit for Cyber Deterrence and Stability," *Journal of Information Warfare* 18, no. 4 (2019): 53–69.

Dorfman, Zach et al., "Secret Trump Order Gives CIA More Powers to Launch Cyberattacks," *Yahoo News*, July 15, 2020, https://news.yahoo.com /secret-trump-order-gives-cia-more-powers-to-launch-cyberattacks-0900 15219.html

Doty, Roxanne Lynn, *Imperial Encounters: The Politics of Representation in North-South Relations*, Minneapolis: University of Minnesota Press, 1996, http:// site.ebrary.com/id/10159633

Dunn Cavelty, Myriam, *Cyber-security and Threat Politics: US Efforts to Secure the Information Age*, New York: Routledge, 2007.

Dunn Cavelty, Myriam, "From Cyber-Bombs to Political Fallout: Threat Representations with an Impact in the Cyber-Security Discourse," *International Studies Review* 15, no. 1 (2013): 105–122.

Dunn Cavelty, Myriam, "Aligning Security Needs for Order in Cyberspace," in Hanns W. Maull (ed.), *The Rise and Decline of the Post-Cold War International Order*, Oxford: Oxford University Press, 2018, 104–119.

Dunn Cavelty, Myriam and Florian J. Egloff, "The Politics of Cybersecurity: Balancing Different Roles of the State," *St. Antony's International Review* 15, no. 1 (2019).

Edgerton, David, *The Shock of the Old: Technology and Global History Since 1900*, London: Profile Books, 2007.

Electronic Frontier Foundation, "About EFF," *Electronic Frontier Foundation* (blog), 2021: https://www.eff.org/about

Elgin, Ben and Michael Riley, "Now at the Sands Casino: An Iranian Hacker in Every Server," *Bloomberg*, December 11, 2014, https://www.bloomberg.com/news/articles/2014-12-11/iranian-hackers-hit-sheldon-adelsons-sands-casino-in-las-vegas

Emmott, Robin, "NATO Cyber Command to Be Fully Operational in 2023," *Reuters*, October 16, 2018, https://www.reuters.com/article/us-nato-cyber-idUSKCN1MQ1Z9

Enns, Charis and Brock Bersaglio, "On the Coloniality of 'New' Mega-Infrastructure Projects in East Africa," *Antipode* 101, no. 56 (2020).

Ensmenger, Nathan, "The Environmental History of Computing," *Technology and Culture* 59, no. 4 (2018): 7–33.

Escobar, Arturo, *Encountering Development: The Making and Unmaking of the Third World*, Princeton, NJ: Princeton University Press, 2012.

European Commission, "The EU's Cybersecurity Strategy for the Digital Decade," *European Commission*, December 16, 2020, https://ec.europa.eu/digital-single-market/en/news/eus-cybersecurity-strategy-digital-decade

European Council, "Declaration by the High Representative on Behalf of the European Union – Call to Promote and Conduct Responsible Behaviour in Cyberspace," February 2020, https://www.consilium.europa.eu/en/press/press-releases/2020/02/21/declaration-by-the-high-representative-on-behalf-of-the-european-union-call-to-promote-and-conduct-responsible-behaviour-in-cyberspace/

Evans, Hayley and Shannon Togawa Mercer, "Privacy Shield on Shaky Ground: What's Up with EU-U.S. Data Privacy Regulations," *Lawfare*, September 2, 2018, https://www.lawfareblog.com/privacy-shield-shaky-ground-whats-eu-us-data-privacy-regulations

Evgeny, Morozov, "Capitalism's New Clothes," *The Baffler*, 2019, https://thebaffler.com/latest/capitalisms-new-clothes-morozov

"EW Expands Into Information Warfare," *Aviation Week & Space Technology* 141, no. 10 (October 1994): 47–48.

Facebook, Inc., "Form S-1 Registration Statement (no. 333)," *SEC Archives*, February 1, 2012, https://www.sec.gov/Archives/edgar/data/1326801/000119312512034517/d287954ds1.htm#toc287954_10

Farny, Elisabeth, "Dependency Theory: A Useful Tool for Analyzing Global Inequalities Today," *E-ir* (2016), https://www.e-ir.info/2016/11/23/dependency-theory-a-useful-tool-for-analyzing-global-inequalities-today/.

Farrell, Henry, "The Consequences of the Internet for Politics," *Annual Review of Political Science* 15 (2012): 35–52, https://doi.org/10.1146/annurev-polisci-030810-110815

Farrell, Henry and Abraham L. Newman, "Weaponized Interdependence: How Global Economic Networks Shape State Coercion," *International Security* 44, no. 1 (2019): 42–79.

Feldstein, Steven, "The Global Expansion of AI Surveillance," *Carnegie Endowment for International Peace*, September 17, 2019, https://carnegieendowment.org/2019/09/17/global-expansion-of-ai-surveillance-pub-79847

Fialka, John J., "Pentagon Studies Art of 'Information Warfare' To Reduce Its Systems' Vulnerability to Hackers," *Wall Street Journal*, July 3, 1995.

Fifield, D. and S. Egelman, "Fingerprinting Web Users through Font Metrics," in *International Conference on Financial Cryptography and Data Security*, Springer, Berlin, Heidelberg, 2015.

Finnemore, Martha and Duncan B. Hollis, "Constructing Norms for Global Cybersecurity," *The American Journal of International Law* 110, no. 3 (2016): 425–480.

Finnemore, Martha and Kathryn Sikkink, "International Norm Dynamics and Political Change," *International Organization* 52, no. 4 (Autumn 1998), https://www.jstor.org/stable/2601361

Fischerkeller, Michael P. and Richard J. Harknett, "Deterrence Is Not a Credible Strategy for Cyberspace," *Orbis* 61, no. 3 (2017): 381–393, https://doi.org/10.1016/j.orbis.2017.05.003

Fischerkeller, Michael P. and Richard J. Harknett, "Persistent Engagement, Agreed Competition, and Cyberspace Interaction Dynamics, and Escalation," Washington, DC: Institute for Defense Analyses, May 2018.

Fischerkeller, Michael P. and Richard J. Harknett, "Persistent Engagement and Tacit Bargaining: A Path Toward Constructing Norms in Cyberspace," *Lawfare*, November 9, 2018, https://www.lawfareblog.com/persistent-engagement-and-tacit-bargaining-path-toward-constructing-norms-cyberspace

Fischerkeller, Michael P. and Richard J. Harknett, "What is Agreed Competition in Cyberspace?" *Lawfare*, 2019), https://www.lawfareblog.com/what-agreed-competition-cyberspace

Fischerkeller, Michael P., Emily O. Goldman, and Richard J. Harknett, *Cyber Persistence: Redefining National Security in Cyberspace*, New York: Oxford University Press, 2022.

"Foundation Board," *Global Forum on Cyber Expertise*, https://thegfce.org/foundation_board/chris-painter/

Franceschi-Bicchierai, Lorenzo, "Here's the DEA Contract for Hacking Team's Spyware," *Vice*, February 19, 2016, https://www.vice.com/en/article/yp3v8y/dea-contract-with-hacking-team-spyware-foia

Franklin, Marianne I., "Inside Out: Postcolonial Subjectivities and Everyday Life Online," *International Feminist Journal of Politics* 3, no. 3 (January 2001): 387–422, https://doi.org/10.1080/14616740110078194

Fravel, M. Taylor, "China's 'World Class Military' Ambitions: Origins and Implications," *The Washington Quarterly* 43, no. 1 (2020): 85–99.

Freedberg, Sydney, "Trump Eases Cyber Ops, but Safeguards Remain: Joint Staff," *Breaking Defense*, September 17, 2018, https://breakingdefense.com/2018/09/trump-eases-cyber-ops-but-safeguards-remain-joint-staff/

Freedman Lawrence, "Beyond Surprise Attack," *The US Army War College Quarterly* 47, no. 2 (Summer 2017).

Fridman, Ofer, *Russian Hybrid Warfare: Resurgence and Politicisation*, London: Hurst and Company, 2018.

"Full Text: International Strategy of Cooperation on Cyberspace," *Xinhua News Agency*, March 1, 2017: http://news.xinhuanet.com/english/china/2017-03/01/c_136094371_2.htm

Futter, Andrew, *Hacking the Bomb: Cyber Threats and Nuclear Weapons*, Washington, DC: Georgetown University Press, 2018.

"G7 Declaration on Responsible States Behavior In Cyberspace," April 11, 2017, https://www.mofa.go.jp/files/000246367.pdf

Gallagher, Ryan, "U.S. Military Bans The Intercept," *The Intercept* (blog), August 20, 2014, https://theintercept.com/2014/08/20/u-s-military-bans-the-intercept/

Gallagher, Sean, "US, Russia to Install 'Cyber-Hotline' to Prevent Accidental Cyberwar," *Ars Technica*, June 18, 2013, https://arstechnica.com/information-technology/2013/06/us-russia-to-install-cyber-hotline-to-prevent-accidental-cyberwar/

Gartzke, Erik, "The Myth of Cyberwar: Bringing War in Cyberspace Back Down to Earth," *International Security* 38, no. 2 (Fall 2013): 41–73, https://doi.org/10.1162/ISEC_a_00136

Gartzke, Erik and Jon R. Lindsay, "Weaving Tangled Webs: Offense, Defense, and Deception in Cyberspace," *Security Studies* 24, no. 2 (April 3, 2015): 316–348, https://doi.org/10.1080/09636412.2015.1038188

Gartzke, Erik and Jon R. Lindsay, "Thermonuclear Cyberwar," *Journal of Cybersecurity* 3, no. 1 (2017): 37–48, https://academic.oup.com/cybersecurity/article/3/1/37/2996537

Gartzke, Erik and Jon R. Lindsay, "The Cyber Commitment Problem and the Destabilization of Nuclear Deterrence," in Herbert Lin and Amy Zegart (eds.), *Bytes, Bombs, and Spies: The Strategic Dimensions of Offensive Cyber Operations*, Washington, DC: Brookings Institution Press, 2019, 195–234.

Gartzke, Erik and Jon R. Lindsay, "Politics by Many Other Means: The

Comparative Strategic Advantages of Operational Domains," *Journal of Strategic Studies* (2020): 23–24, https://doi.org/10.1080/01402390.2020.17 68372

Gates, Robert, "Establishment of a Subordinate Unified U.S. Cyber Command Under U.S. Strategic Command for Military Cyberspace Operations," Memoranda, *Department of Defense*, June 23, 2009, https://fas.org/irp/dod dir/dod/secdef-cyber.pdf

Geist, Edward, "Deterrence Stability in the Cyber Age," *Strategic Studies Quarterly* 9, no. 4 (2015): 44–61.

Gerasimov, Valery, "The Value of Science is in the Foresight: New Challenges Demand Rethinking the Forms and Methods of Carrying out Combat Operations," *Military Review* (January–February 2016): 23–29.

Gheciu, Alexandra, (2005) "Security Institutions as Agents of Socialization? NATO and the 'New Europe,'" *International Organization* 59, no. 4 (2005): 973–1012.

Giles, Keir, "Chapter 5. 'Information Troops' – A Russian Cyber Command?" in Katharina Ziolkowski, Christian Czosseck and Rain Ottis (eds.), *2011 3rd International Conference on Cyber Conflict*, Tallin, Estonia: CCDCOE Publications, 2011: 45–60, https://ccdcoe.org/uploads/2018/10/Inform ationTroopsARussianCyberCommand-Giles.pdf

Giles, Keir, *Handbook of Russian Information Warfare*, Rome: NATO Defense College, November 2016.

Glaister, Keith, Nigel Driffield, and Yupu Lin, "Foreign Direct Investment to Africa: Is There a Colonial Legacy?" *Management International Review* 60 (2020): 315–349.

Glaser, Charles L. and Chaim Kaufmann, "What Is the Offense-Defense Balance and How Can We Measure It?" *International Security* 22, no. 4 (1998), https://doi.org/10.1162/isec.22.4.44

Global Commission on the Stability of Cyberspace, "Advancing Cyber Stability: Final Report," https://cyberstability.org/report/#2-what-is-mea nt-by-the-stability-of-cyberspace

Global Commission on the Stability of Cyberspace, "The Commission," https://cyberstability.org/about/

Goddard, Stacie E. and Daniel H. Nexon, "The Dynamics of Global Power Politics: A Framework for Analysis," *Journal of Global Security Studies* 1, no. 1 (2016): 4–18.

Goldman, Emily O., John Surdu, and Michael Warner, "The Cyber Pearl Harbor: The Attacker's Perspective," in Emily O. Goldman and John Arquilla (eds.), *Cyber Analogies*, Monterey, CA, Naval Postgraduate School, 2014, https://apps.dtic.mil/dtic/tr/fulltext/u2/a601645.pdf

Goldsmith, Jack (ed.), *The United States' Defend Forward Cyber Strategy: A Comprehensive Legal Assessment*, New York: Oxford University Press, 2022.

Goldstein, Avery, "First Things First: The Pressing Danger of Crisis Instability in U.S.-China Relations," *International Security* 37, no. 4 (2013): 49–89.

Goldstein, Avery, "US-China Rivalry in the Twenty-First Century: Deja vu and Cold War II," *China International Strategy Review* 2, no. 1 (2020): 48–62.

Gompert, David C. and Martin Libicki, "Cyber Warfare and Sino-American Crisis Instability," *Survival* 56, no. 4 (2014): 7–22, https://doi.org/10.1080/00396338.2014.941543

Goodman, Michael S., "Applying the Historical Lessons of Surprise Attack to the Cyber Domain: The Example of the United Kingdom," in Emily O. Goldman and John Arquilla (eds.), *Cyber Analogies*, Monterey, CA, Naval Postgraduate School, 2014, https://apps.dtic.mil/dtic/tr/fulltext/u2/a601645.pdf

Gorman, Lindsay, "5G is Where China and the West Finally Diverge," *The Atlantic*, January 5, 2020, https://www.theatlantic.com/ideas/archive/2020/01/5g-where-china-and-west-finally-diverge/604309/

Gosling, William, *Helmsmen and Heroes: Control Theory as a Key to Past and Future*, London: Weidenfeld and Nicolson, 1994.

Government Accountability Office, *Serious Weaknesses Continue to Place Defense Operations at Risk*, August 26, 1999, https://www.gao.gov/products/GAO/AIMD-99-107

Government Accountability Office, "Information Security: Progress and Challenges to an Effective Defense-wide Information Assurance Program," March 30, 2001.

Goychayev, R. et al., "Cyber Deterrence and Stability," *US Department of Energy*, 2017, https://www.pnnl.gov/main/publications/external/technical_reports/PNNL-26932.pdf

Goździewicz, Wiesław (2019), "Cyber Effects Provided Voluntarily By Allies (SCEPVA)," *Cyber Defense Magazine*, November 11, 2019, https://www.cyberdefensemagazine.com/sovereign-cyber/

Gramsci, Antonio, *Subaltern Social Groups*, New York: Columbia University Press, 2021.

Grange, David L. and James A. Kelley, "Victory Through Information Dominance," *Army* 47, no. 3 (March 1997).

Gray, J. V., "Information Operations: A Research Aid," *Institute for Defense Analysis*, September 1997.

Greenberg, Andy, "The Untold Story of NotPetya, the Most Devastating

Cyberattack in History," *Wired*, August 22, 2018, https://www.wired.com /story/notpetya-cyberattack-ukraine-russia-code-crashed-the-world/

Greenberg, Andy, "Inside Olympic Destroyer, the Most Deceptive Hack in History," *Wired*, October 17, 2019, https://www.wired.com/story/untold -story-2018-olympics-destroyer-cyberattack/

Greenwald, Glenn, "How the NSA Tampers with US-Made Internet Routers," *The Guardian*, May 12, 2014.

Greenwood Onuf, Nicholas, *World of Our Making: Rules and Rule in Social Theory and International Relations*, Columbia: University of South Carolina Press, 1989.

Greitens, Sheena Chestnut, "Dealing with Demands for China's Global Surveillance Exports," in *Global China: Assessing China's Growing Role in the World*, April 2020, https://www.brookings.edu/wp-content/uploads/2020 /04/FP_20200428_china_surveillance_greitens_v3.pdf

Grimm, Vanessa Jo, "In War on System Intruders, DISA Calls In Big Guns," *Government Computer News* 14, no. 3 (1995).

Grosfoguel, Ramon, "Decolonizing Post-Colonial Studies and Paradigms of Political-Economy: Transmodernity, Decolonial Thinking, and Global Coloniality," *TRANSMODERNITY: Journal of Peripheral Cultural Production of the Luso-Hispanic World* 1, no. 1 (2011), https://escholarship.org/uc/item /21k6t3fq

Guibert, Nathalie, "L'armée française consolide son commandement cyber," *Le Monde*, December 12, 2016, https://www.lemonde.fr/international/ar ticle/2016/12/12/l-armee-francaise-consolide-son-commandement-cyber _5047780_3210.html

Gunitsky, Seva, "Corrupting the Cyber-Commons: Social Media as a Tool of Autocratic Stability," *Perspectives on Politics* 13, no. 1 (2015): 42–54.

Gusterson, Hugh, *Drone: Remote Control Warfare*, Cambridge, MA: The MIT Press, 2016.

Haas, Peter M., "Introduction: Epistemic Communities and International Policy Coordination," *International Organization* 46, no. 1 (1992): 1–35.

Hankey, Stephanie and Daniel Ó Clunaigh, "Rethinking Risk and Security of Human Rights Defenders in the Digital Age," *Journal of Human Rights Practice* 5, no. 3 (2013): 535–547, https://doi.org/10.1093/jhuman/hut023

Hanson, Victor David, "Lord Ismay, NATO, and the Old-New World Order," *National Review*, July 5, 2017, https://www.nationalreview.com/ 2017/07/nato-russians-out-americans-germans-down-updated-reversed/

Hardison, Chaitra M. et al., *Attracting, Recruiting, and Retaining Successful Cyberspace Operations Officers*, Santa Monica, CA: RAND Corporation, 2019, https://www.rand.org/pubs/research_reports/RR2618.html

Harknett, Richard, "United States Cyber Command's New Vision: What It Entails and Why It Matters," *Lawfare*, March 23, 2018, https://www.law fareblog.com/united-states-cyber-commands-new-vision-what-it-entails -and-why-it-matters

Harknett, Richard J. and Michael P. Fischerkeller, "Through Persistent Engagement, the U.S. Can Influence 'Agreed Competition,'" *Lawfare*, April 15, 2019, https://www.lawfareblog.com/through-persistent-enga gement-us-can-influence-agreed-competition

Harknett, Richard J. and Max Smeets, "Cyber Campaigns and Strategic Outcomes," *Journal of Strategic Studies* 45, no. 4 (2020), https://doi.org/10.10 80/01402390.2020.1732354

Harold, Scott Warren, Martin C. Libicki, and Astrid Stuth Cevallos, "Getting to Yes with China in Cyberspace," Santa Monica, CA: RAND, 2016, https://www.rand.org/content/dam/rand/pubs/research_reports/RR13 00/RR1335/RAND_RR1335.pdf

Hassib, Bassant and James Shires, "Co-opting Cybersecurity in Egypt," *Atlantic Council*, May 11, 2021.

Hathaway, Melissa E., "Toward a Closer Digital Alliance," *SAIS Review of International Affairs* 36, no. 2 (2016).

Hathaway, Melissa E., "Cyberspace Policy Review: Assuring a Trusted and Resilient Information and Communications Infrastructure," *Report United States Office of the White House*, 2019.

Hattem, Julian, "Ex-CIA Head: 'Shame on Us' for Allowing Government Hack," *The Hill*, June 16, 2015, https://thehill.com/policy/national-secur ity/245101-ex-cia-head-shame-on-us-for-allowing-government-hack

Hayek, Friedrich, *The Constitution of Liberty*, Chicago: University of Chicago Press, 1960.

Headrick, Daniel R., *The Invisible Weapon: Telecommunications and International Politics 1851–1945*, Oxford: Oxford University Press, 1991.

Healey, Jason, "A Fierce Domain: Conflict in Cyberspace, 1986 to 2012," Vienna, VA: Cyber Conflict Studies Association, 2013.

Healey, Jason, "A Nonstate Strategy for Saving Cyberspace," *Atlantic Council Strategy Papers*, 2017, http://www.atlanticcouncil.org/images/publications /AC_StrategyPapers_No8_Saving_Cyberspace_WEB.pdf

Healey, Jason, "Cyber Warfare in the 21st Century: Threats, Challenges, and Opportunities," § House Armed Services Committee (2017), https://do cs.house.gov/meetings/AS/AS00/20170301/105607/HHRG-115-AS00 -Bio-HealeyJ-20170301-U1.pdf

Healey, Jason, "What Might Be Predominant Form of Cyber Conflict?," in *2017 International Conference on Cyber Conflict (CyCon US)* (2017 International

Conference on Cyber-Conflict, Washington, DC: IEEE, 2017): 36–44, https://doi.org/10.1109/CYCONUS.2017.8167511

Healey, Jason, "The Implications of Persistent (and Permanent) Engagement in Cyberspace," *Journal of Cybersecurity* 5, no. 1 (2019): tyz008, https://doi.org/10.1093/cybsec/tyz008

Healey, Jason, "Getting the Drop in Cyberspace," *Lawfare*, August 19, 2019, https://www.lawfareblog.com/getting-drop-cyberspace

Healey, Jason and Neil Jenkins, "Rough-and-Ready: A Policy Framework to Determine If Cyber Deterrence Is Working or Failing," in *2019 11th International Conference on Cyber Conflict (CyCon)*, 2019 11th International Conference on Cyber Conflict, Tallinn, Estonia: IEEE, 2019, 1–20, https://doi.org/10.23919/CYCON.2019.8756890

Healey, Jason and Robert Jervis, "The Escalation Inversion and Other Oddities of Situational Cyber Stability," *Texas National Security Review* 3, no. 4 (Fall 2020): 30–53.

Healey, Jason and Tim Maurer, "What It'll Take to Forge Peace in Cyberspace," *CSM Passcode*, March 20, 2017, https://www.csmonitor.com/World/Passcode/Passcode-Voices/2017/0320/What-it-ll-take-to-forge-peace-in-cyberspace

Healey, Jason, "Bullet Background Paper on Computer Network Defense-Joint Task Force (CND-JTF)," *Office of the Deputy Chief of Staff for Air and Space Operations*, October 14, 1998, https://nsarchive.gwu.edu/dc.html?doc=6168259-National-Security-Archive-Captain-Healey-US-Air

Healey, Jason, "JTF Computer Network Defense Update," U.S. Air Force Office of the Director of Intelligence, Surveillance, and Reconnaissance, October 1998, slide 17: https://nsarchive.gwu.edu/dc.html?doc=6168258-National-Security-Archive-US-Air-Force-Office-of

Heftye, Erik, "Multi-Domain Confusion: All Domains Are Not Equal," *Real Clear Defense*, May 26, 2017.

Heginbotham, Eric, Michael Nixon, Forrest E. Morgan, Jacob L. Heim, Sheng Tao Li, Jeffrey Engstrom, Martin C. Libicki, Paul DeLuca, David A. Shlapak, David R. Frelinger, Burgess Laird, Kyle Brady, and Lyle J. Morris, *The U.S.-China Military Scorecard: Forces, Geography, and the Evolving Balance of Power, 1996–2017*, Santa Monica, CA: RAND Corporation, 2015.

Henriksen, Anders, "The End of the Road for the UN GGE Process: The Future Regulation of Cyberspace," *Journal of Cybersecurity* 5, no. 1 (2019).

Herpig, Sven, "A Framework for Government Hacking in Criminal Investigations," *Stiftung Neue Verantwortung*, November 2, 2018, https://www.stiftung-nv.de/en/publication/framework-government-hacking-criminal-investigations

Hersman, Rebecca, "Wormhole Escalation in the New Nuclear Age," *Texas National Security Review* (Summer 2020), http://tnsr.org/2020/07/worm hole-escalation-in-the-new-nuclear-age/

Higgin, Tanner, "Blackless Fantasy: The Disappearance of Race in Massively Multiplayer Online Role-Playing Games," *Games and Culture* 4, no. 1 (2008): 9–11, https://doi.org/10.1177/1555412008325477

Higgins, Kelly Jackson, "Lessons From The Ukraine Electric Grid Hack," *Dark Reading*, March 18, 2016, https://www.darkreading.com/vulnerabilit ies---threats/lessons-from-the-ukraine-electric-grid-hack/d/d-id/1324743

Hill, Steven and Nadia Marsan, "International Law in Cyberspace: Leveraging NATO's Multilateralism, Adaptation, and Commitment to Cooperative Security," in Dennis Broeders and Bibi van den Berg (eds.), *Governing Cyberspace: Behavior, Power, and Diplomacy*, Lanham, MD: Rowman & Littlefield, 2020, 173–185.

Hitchens, Theresa, "US Urges 'Like-Minded Countries' to Collaborate on Cyber Deterrence," *Breaking Defense*, April 24, 2019, https://breakingde fense.com/2019/04/us-urging-likeminded-countries-to-collaborate-on-cy ber-deterrence/

HM Government, "Foreign Secretary: Russia Must Face Cost for Malign Activity," March 24, 2020, https://www.gov.uk/government/news/fore ign-secretary-russia-must-face-cost-for-malign-activity

Hoffman, Frank and Michael Davies, "Joint Force 2020 and the Human Domain: Time for a New Conceptual Framework?" *Small Wars Journal*, June 10, 2013.

Hoffmann, Samantha, Dominique Lazanski, and Emily Taylor, "Standardising the Splinternet: How China's Technical Standards Could Fragment the Internet," *Journal of Cyber Policy* 5, no. 2 (2020): 239–264.

Hollis, Duncan B. and Jens David Ohlin, "What If Cyberspace Were for Fighting?" *Ethics & International Affairs* 32, no. 4 (2018): 441–456, https://doi.org/10.1017/S089267941800059X

Hooghe, Liesbet and Gary Marks, "Unraveling the Central State, but How? Types of Multi-Level Governance," *American Political Science Review* 97, no. 2 (2013): 233–243.

Horowitz, Michael C., *The Diffusion of Military Power: Causes and Consequences for International Politics*, Princeton, NJ: Princeton University Press, 2010.

Hughes, Rex, "A Treaty for Cyberspace," *International Affairs* 86, no. 2 (2010): 523–541, https://doi.org/10.1111/j.1468-2346.2010.00894.x

Human Rights Council, General Assembly, *Report of the Special Rapporteur on the Promotion and Protection of the Right to Freedom of Opinion and Expression*,

New York: UN Headquarters, 2019, https://documents-dds-ny.un.org /doc/UNDOC/GEN/G19/148/76/PDF/G1914876.pdf?OpenElement

Human Rights Watch, "World Report 2020: Mexico," 2021, https://www .hrw.org/world-report/2020/country-chapters/mexico

Icaza, Rosalba, "Decolonial Feminism and Global Politics: Border Thinking and Vulnerability as a Knowing Otherwise," in Victoria Browne, Jason Danely, and Dörthe Rosenow (eds.), *Vulnerability and the Politics of Care: Transdisciplinary Dialogues*, Oxford: Oxford University Press, 2021.

Icaza, Rosalba and Rolando Vasquez, "Diversity or Decolonisation? Researching Diversity at the University of Amsterdam," in Gurminder K. Bhambra, Dalia Gebrial, and Kerem Nisancioglu (eds.), *Decolonising the University*, London: Pluto Press, 2018.

Imerson, Michael., "Russia's Efforts to 'Destabilise Western Democracy' Increase Cyber Insecurity," *Financial Times*, May 25, 2017, https://www.ft .com/content/93f6a15c-2424-11e7-a34a-538b4cb30025

Immenkamp, Beatrix, "Review of Dual-Use Export Controls," *European Parliament Think Tank*, January 2021, https://www.europarl.europa. eu/RegData/etudes/BRIE/2016/589832/EPRS_BRI(2016)589832_ EN.pdf

"Implementing Instruction for Information Warfare/Command and Control Warfare," OPNAV Instruction 3430.26, Office of the Chief of Naval Operations, January 18, 1995, http://www.iwar.org.uk/iwar/resources/ opnav/3430_26.pdf

Inksit Group, "China-Linked Group RedEcho Targets the Indian Power Sector Amid Heightened Border Tensions" (Recorded Future, February 28, 2021).

International Strategy for Cyberspace: Prosperity, Security, and Openness in a Networked World, May 2011, https://obamawhitehouse.archives.gov/sites /default/files/rss_viewer/international_strategy_for_cyberspace.pdf

Isikoff, Michael, "Chinese Hacked Obama, McCain Campaigns, Took Internal Documents, Officials Say," *NBC News.com*, June 10, 2013, http:// www.nbcnews.com/id/52133016/t/chinese-hacked-obama-mccain-cam paigns-took-internal-documents-officials-say/

Iskandar, Adel, "Egyptian Youth's Digital Dissent," *Journal of Democracy* 30, no. 3 (2019): 154–164, https://doi.org/10.1353/jod.2019.0049

"Israli Cyber Firm NSO Group Mulls Tel Aviv IPO at $2 Billion Value – Reports," *Reuters*, January 6, 2021, https://www.reuters.com/article/israel -cyber-nso-ipo-int-idUSKBN29B0WU

Jacobs Gamberini, Sarah and Amanda Moodie, "The Virus of Disinformation: Echoes of Past Bioweapons Accusations in Today's Covid-19 Conspiracy

Theories," *War on the Rocks*, April 6, 2020, https://warontherocks.com/20 20/04/the-virus-of-disinformation-echoes-of-past-bioweapons-accusatio ns-in-todays-covid-19-conspiracy-theories/

Jacobsen, Jeppe T., "Cyber Offense in NATO: Challenges and Opportunities," *International Affairs*, 97, no. 3 (2021), https://doi.org/10.1093/ia/iiab010

Jasper, Scott, *Russian Cyber Operations: Coding the Boundaries of Conflict*, Washington, DC: Georgetown University Press, 2020.

Jensen, Benjamin and Brandon Valeriano, "What do We Know About Cyber Escalation? Observations from Simulations and Surveys," *Atlantic Council*, November 2019, https://www.atlanticcouncil.org/wp-content/uploads /2019/11/What_do_we_know_about_cyber_escalation_.pdf

Jervis, Robert, *Perception and Misperception in International Politics*, Princeton, NJ: Princeton University Press, 1976, https://doi.org/10.2307/j.ctvc77bx3

Jervis, Robert, "Cooperation under the Security Dilemma," *World Politics* 30, no. 2 (1978): 167–214, https://doi.org/10.2307/2009958

Jervis, Robert, "Why Nuclear Superiority Doesn't Matter," *Political Science Quarterly* 94, no. 4 (1979).

Jervis, Robert, *The Meaning of the Nuclear Revolution: Statecraft and the Prospect of Armageddon*, Ithaca, NY: Cornell University Press, 1989.

Jervis, Robert, *System Effects: Complexity in Political and Social Life*, Princeton, NJ: Princeton University Press, 1999.

Jervis, Robert, *Why Intelligence Fails: Lessons from the Iranian Revolution and the Iraq War*, Ithaca, NY: Cornell University Press, 2010.

Jervis, Robert, "Author Response: Reflections on The Meaning of the Nuclear Revolution, 30 Years Later," *Book Review Roundtable: The Meaning of the Nuclear Revolution 30 Years Later*, Texas National Security Review, 2020, http://tnsr.org/roundtable/book-review-roundtable-the-meaning -of-the-nuclear-revolution-30-years-later/

Jiang, Xu, Yuan Li, and Shanxing Gao, "The Stability of Strategic Alliances: Characteristics, Factors and Stages," *Journal of International Management* 14, no. 2 (2008): 173–189.

Jinghua, Lyu, *Meiguo wangluo kongjianzhan sixiang yanjiu [A Study of US Thought on Cyber Warfare]*, Beijing: Junshi kexueyuan chubanshe, 2014.

Jinghua, Lyu, "A Chinese Perspective on the Pentagon's Cyber Strategy: From 'Active Cyber Defense' to 'Defending Forward,'" *Lawfare*, October 18, 2018, https://www.lawfareblog.com/chinese-perspective-pentagons-cyber -strategy-active-cyber-defense-defending-forward

Jinghua, Lyu, "Daguo hezuo yinling wangluo kongjian guoji zhixu cong chongtu zouxiang wending [Great Power Cooperation Showing the Way in the Cyberspace International Order from Conflict Towards Stability],"

Zhongguo xinxi anquan [China Information Security] 11 (2018): 34, http://www.cnki.com.cn/Article/CJFDTotal-CINS201811017.htm

Jinghua, Lyu, "A Chinese Perspective on the New Intelligence Framework to Understand National Competition in Cyberspace," in Robert Chesney and Max Smeets (eds.), *Deter, Disrupt or Deceive? Assessing Cyber Conflict as an Intelligence Contest,* Georgetown University Press, forthcoming.

Johnston, Alastair Iain, "The Evolution of Interstate Security Crisis-Management Theory and Practice in China," *Naval War College Review* 69, no. 1 (Winter 2016): 28–71, https://digital-commons.usnwc.edu/cgi/view content.cgi?article=1118&context=nwc-review

Joint Chiefs of Staff, "Joint Pub 13-13.1: Joint Doctrine for Command and Control Warfare," February 7, 1996, https://www.bits.de/NRANEU/ot hers/jp-doctrine/jp3_13_1.pdf

Joint Chiefs of Staff, "DOD Organization for Computer Network Defense: Summary of Proposals," Slide 4, *National Security Archive,* June 1998, https://nsarchive.gwu.edu/dc.html?doc=6168257-National-Security-Arch ive-Joint-Chiefs-of-Staff

Joint Chiefs of Staff, "Joint Publication 3-12(R) Cyberspace Operations," February 5, 2013, https://www.hsdl.org/?view&did=758858

Joint Chiefs of Staff, "Joint Publication 3-12: Cyberspace Operations," June 8, 2018, II-2–II-3, https://www.jcs.mil/Portals/36/Documents/Doctrine/ pubs/jp3_12.pdf.

Joint Security Commission, "Redefining Security: A Report to the Secretary of Defense and the Director of Central Intelligence," February 28, 1994, https://fas.org/sgp/library/jsc/

Jones, Jeffrey R., "Defense Department Cyber Requires Speed, Precision and Agility," *Signal,* May 1, 2019, https://www.afcea.org/content/defense-de partment-cyber-requires-speed-precision-and-agility

Joseph, George, "The LAPD Has a New Surveillance Formula, Powered by Palantir," *The Appeal,* May 8, 2018, https://theappeal.org/the-lapd-has-a-new-surveillance-formula-powered-by-palantir-1e277a95762a/

Jun, Cai, He Jun, and Yu Xiaohong, "Meijun wangluo kongjian zuozhan lilun [Theories of US Cyberspace Operations]," *Zhongguo junshi kexue [China Military Science]* 1 (2018).

"Junshi Kexue Yuan zhuanjia jiemi wangluo kongjian weishe [Academy of Military Sciences Expert Reveals Cyberspace Deterrence]," China Military Online, January 6, 2016, http://military.people.com.cn/n1/2016/0106/c1 011-28020408.html

Kaltheuner, Frederike, "I Asked an Online Tracking Company for All of My Data and Here's What I Found," *Privacy International,* November 7, 2018,

https://privacyinternational.org/long-read/2433/i-asked-online-tracking
-company-all-my-data-and-heres-what-i-found

Kam, Ephraim, *Surprise Attack: The Victim's Perspective*, Cambridge, MA: Harvard University Press, 2004.

Kania, Elsa B. and John K. Costello, "The Strategic Support Force and the Future of Chinese Information Operations," *The Cyber Defense Review* 3 (Spring 2018), https://cyberdefensereview.army.mil/CDR-Content/Artic les/Article-View/Article/1589125/the-strategic-support-force-and-the-fu ture-of-chinese-information-operations/

Kania, Elsa B. and John K. Costello, "Seizing the Commanding Heights: The PLA Strategic Support Force in Chinese Military Power," *Journal of Strategic Studies* 44, no. 2 (2020).

Kaplan, Fred M., *Dark Territory: The Secret History of Cyber War*, New York: Simon & Schuster, 2016.

Kaplan, Lawrence A., "The United States and the origins of NATO 1946– 1949," *The Review of Politics* 3, no. 2 (1969).

Katzenstein, Peter, *The Culture of National Security: Norms and Identity in World Politics*, New York: Columbia University Press, 1996.

Kehler, C. Robert, Herb Lin, and Michael Sulmeyer "Rules of Engagement for Cyberspace Operations: A View From the USA," *Journal of Cybersecurity* 3, no. 1 (2017).

Kello, Lucas, *The Virtual Weapon and International Order* (New Haven, CT: Yale University Press, 2017).

Kenneth Merrill, "Domains of Control: Governance of and by the Domain Name System," in Musiani et al. (eds.), *The Turn to Infrastructure in Internet Governance* (2016).

Keohane, Robert O. and Joseph S. Nye, *Power and Interdependence*, 3rd edition, London: Longman, 2001.

Keohane, Robert O. and David G. Victor, "The Regime Complex for Climate Change," *Perspectives on Politics* 9, no. 1 (2011): 7–23.

Kerr, Jaclyn A., *Authoritarian Management of (Cyber-) Society: Internet Regulation and the New Political Protest Movements*, Washington, DC: Georgetown University, 2016.

Kerr Jaclyn A., "Information, Security, and Authoritarian Stability: Internet Policy Diffusion and Coordination in the Former Soviet Region," *International Journal of Communication* 12 (2018): 3814–3834.

Kerr, Jaclyn A., "The Russian Model of Digital Control and Its Significance," in Nicholas Wright (ed.), *Artificial Intelligence, China, Russia, and the Global Order: Technological, Political, Global, and Creative Perspectives*, Montgomery, AL: Air University Press, 2019, 62–74.

Kerttunen, Mika and Eneken Tirk, "The Politics of Stability: Cement and Change in Cyber Affairs," *NUPI Report 4/2019*, https://nupi.brage.unit .no/nupi-xmlui/bitstream/handle/11250/2598287/NUPI_Report_4_20 19_KerttunenTikk.pdf?sequence=1&isAllowed=y

Khadiri, Galia and Joan Tilouine, "A Addis-Abeba, le siège de l'Union afric-aine espionné par Pékin," *Le Monde Afrique*, January 26, 2018.

Kirchgaessner, Stephanie et al. "Revealed: Leak Uncovers Global Abuse of Cyber-Surveillance Weapon," *The Guardian*, July 18, 2021, https://www .theguardian.com/world/2021/jul/18/revealed-leak-uncovers-global-abu se-of-cyber-surveillance-weapon-nso-group-pegasus

Klimburg, Alexander and Virgilio A. F. Almeida, "Cyber Peace and Cyber Stability: Taking the Norm Road to Stability," *IEEE Internet Computing* 23, no. 4 (2019): 61–66, https://ieeexplore.ieee.org/document/ 8874985

Kolstad, Ivar and Arne Wiig, "Better the Devil you Know? Chinese Foreign Direct Investment in Africa," *Journal of African Business* 12, no. 31 (2011).

Koran, Mario, "Black Facebook Staff Describe Workplace Racism in Anonymous Letter," *The Guardian*, November 13, 2019, https://amp.th eguardian.com/technology/2019/nov/13/facebook-discrimination-black -workers-letter

Koremenos, Barbara, Charles Lipson, and Duncan Snidal, "The Rational Design of International Institutions," *International Organization* 55, no. 4 (2001): 761–799.

Korzak, Elaine, "UN GGE on Cybersecurity: The End of an Era?" *The Diplomat*, July 31, 2017, https://thediplomat.com/2017/07/un-gge-on-cy bersecurity-have-china-and-russia-just-made-cyberspace-less-safe

Kostyuk, Nadiya and Yuri M. Zhukov, "Invisible Digital Front: Can Cyber Attacks Shape Battlefield Events?" *Journal of Conflict Resolution* 63, no. 2 (2017): 317–347, https://doi.org/10.1177/0022002717737138

Kostyuk, Nadiya, Scott Powell, and Matt Skach, "Determinants of the Cyber Escalation Ladder," *The Cyber Defense Review* 3, no. 1 (Spring 2018): 123– 134.

Kovacs, Anja and Dixie Hawtin, "Cybersecurity, Cyber Surveillance and Online Human Rights," *Global Partners Digital*, January 31, 2013, https:// www.gp-digital.org/publication/second-pub/

Kramer, Franklin D., "Achieving International Cyber Stability," *Georgetown Journal of International Affairs*, International Engagement on Cyber 2012: Establishing Norms and Improving Security 2012.

Kramer, Franklin D., Lauren Speranza, and Conor Rodihan, "NATO Needs

Continuous Responses in Cyberspace," *New Atlanticist*, December 9, 2020, https://www.atlanticcouncil.org/blogs/new-atlanticist/nato-needs-con tinuous-responses-in-cyberspace/

Krasner, Stephen D., "Structural Causes and Regime Consequences: Regimes as Intervening Variables," *International Organization* 36, no. 2 (1982): 185–205.

Krasner, Stephen D., "Structural Causes and Regime Consequences: Regimes as Intervening Variables," in Stephen D. Krasner (ed.), *International Regimes*, Ithaca, NY: Cornell University Press, 1983, 1–21.

Krasner, Stephen D., "Global Communications and National Power: Life on the Pareto Frontier," *World Politics* 43, no. 3 (1991): 336–366.

Kreps, Sarah and Jacquelyn Schneider, "Escalation Firebreaks in the Cyber, Conventional, and Nuclear Domains: Moving beyond Effects-Based Logics," *Journal of Cybersecurity* 5, no. 1 (2019), https://doi.org /10.1093/cybsec/tyz007

Kubecka, Chris, "How to Implement IT Security after a Cyber Meltdown," YouTube, December 29, 2015, https://www.youtube.com/watch?v=Wy Mobr_TDSI

Kurowska, Xymena and Anatoly Reshetnikov, "Neutrollization: Industrialized Trolling as a pro-Kremlin Strategy of Desecuritization," *Security Dialogue* 49, no. 5 (2018): 353, https://doi.org/10.1177/0967010618785102

Kwasi Tieku, Thomas, *Governing Africa: 3D Analysis of the African Union's Performance*, Lanham, MD: Rowman & Littlefield, 2017.

Kwet, Michael, "Digital Colonialism: US Empire and the New Imperialism in the Global South," *Race & Class* 60, no. 4 (2019), https://doi.org/10 .1177/0306396818823172

La Porta, Rafael et al., "Law and Finance," *Journal of Political Economy* 106, no. 1113 (1998).

Land, Molly K., "Networked Activism," *Harvard Human Rights Journal* 22, no. 2 (2009): 205–244, https://heinonline.org/HOL/P?h=hein.journals /hhrj22&i=209

Land, Molly K. and Jay D. Aranson, "Human Rights and Technology: New Challenges for Justice and Accountability," *Annual Review of Law and Social Science* 16 (2020): 223–240, https://www.annualreviews.org/doi/pdf/10 .1146/annurev-lawsocsci-060220-081955

Landau, Susan, "On NSA's Subversion of NIST's Algorithm," *Lawfare*, July 25, 2014.

Lange, Matthew, "British Colonial Legacies and Political Development," *World Development* 32, no. 905 (2004).

Laudrain, Arthur, "France's New Offensive Cyber Doctrine," *Lawfare*,

February 26, 2019, https://www.lawfareblog.com/frances-new-offensive-cyber-doctrine

Leavitt, Sandra R., "Problems in Collective Action," in Scott Jasper (ed.), *Conflict and Cooperation in the Global Commons: A Comprehensive Approach for International Security*, Washington, DC: Georgetown University Press, 2012.

Lee, Alexander and Kenneth Schutlz, "Comparing British and French Colonial Legacies: A Discontinuity Analysis of Cameroon," *Quarterly Journal of Political Science* 7, no. 1 (2012).

Lee, Robert M., "The Failing of Air Force Cyber," *Signal*, November 1, 2013, https://www.afcea.org/content/failing-air-force-cyber

Lee, Theodore M. P., "Processors, Operating Systems and Nearby Peripherals: A Consensus Report," in Zella G. Ruthberg, *Audit and Evaluation of Computer Security II: System Vulnerabilities and Controls*, Proceedings of the National Bureau of Standards Invitational Workshop Held at Miami Beach, FL, November 28–30, 1978, 8–13.

Leinhos, Ludwig, "The German Cyber and Information Domain Service as a Key Part of National Security Policy," April 1, 2017, http://www.ethikun dmilitaer.de/en/full-issues/20191-conflict-zone-cyberspace/leinhos-the-german-cyber-and-information-domain-service-as-a-key-part-of-national-security-policy/

Levine, Mike, "Russia Tops List of 100 Countries that Could Launch Cyber-attacks on US," *ABC News*, May 18, 2017, https://abcnews.go.com/US/russia-tops-list-100-countries-launch-cyberattacks-us/story?id=47487188

Levite, Ariel and Lyu Jinghua, "Chinese-American Relations in Cyberspace: Toward Collaboration or Confrontation?" *China Military Science*, January 24, 2019, https://carnegieendowment.org/2019/01/24/chinese-american-relations-in-cyberspace-toward-collaboration-or-confrontation-pub-78213

Levite, Ariel et al., *China-U.S. Cyber-Nuclear C3 Stability*, Washington, DC: Carnegie Endowment for International Peace, April 2021.

Lewis, James A., "The Role of Offensive Cyber Operations in NATO's Collective Defence," *Tallinn Paper* 8 (2015), https://www.ccdcoe.org/uplo ads/2018/10/TP_08_2015_0.pdf

Lewis, James A., *Rethinking Cybersecurity: Strategy, Mass Effect, and States*, Washington, DC: Center for Strategic & International Studies; Lanham, MD: Rowman & Littlefield, 2018, https://csis-prod.s3.amazonaws.com/s3fs-public/publication/180108_Lewis_ReconsideringCybersecurity_Web.pdf? ftGLYwJNUgSldpxN3g2K3g06kKKVxicYq

Lewis, James A., "Cyber Solarium and the Sunset of Security," *Center for Strategic & International Studies*, March 13, 2020, https://www.csis.org/analy sis/cyber-solarium-and-sunset-cybersecurity

Lewis, James A., "Toward a More Coercive Cyber Strategy: Remarks to US Cyber Command Legal Conference," March 4, 2021, https://www.csis.org/analysis/toward-more-coercive-cyber-strategy

Li, Allen, "DOD's Information Assurance Efforts," US General Accounting Office: 4, https://www.gao.gov/assets/nsiad-98-132r.pdf

Li Zhaorui (ed.), *Wangluo zhan jichu yu fazhan qushi [Cyber War Foundations and Development Trends]*, Beijing: Jiefangjun chubanshe, 2015.

Libicki, Martin C., *Crisis and Escalation in Cyberspace*, Santa Monica, CA: RAND, Project Air Force, 2012, https://www.rand.org/pubs/monographs/MG1215.html

Libicki, Martin C., "Drawing Inferences from Cyber Espionage," *CyCon X: Maximizing Effects*, 10th International Conference on Cyber Conflict, NATO Cooperative Cyber Defence Centre of Excellence, Tallinn, 2018, https://ccdcoe.org/uploads/2018/10/Art-06-Drawing-Inferences-from-Cyber-Espionage.pdf

Libicki, Martin C., "Correlations Between Cyberspace Attacks and Kinetic Attacks," in T. Jančárková, L. Lindström, I. Signoretti, and G. Visky Tolga (eds.), *Proceedings of 2020 12th International Conference on Cyber Conflict*, "20/20 Vision: The Next Decade," 2020.

Libicki, Martin C., "Norms and Normalization," *The Cyber Defense Review* (Spring 2020): 41–52, https://cyberdefensereview.army.mil/Portals/6/CDR%20V5N1%20-%2004_Libicki_WEB.pdf

Lilly, Bilyana and Joe Cheravitch, "The Past, Present, and Future of Russia's Cyber Strategy and Forces," in T. Jančárková, L. Lindström, M. Signoretti, I. Tolga, and G. Visky (eds.), *Proceedings of the 12th International Conference on Cyber Conflict*, Tallinn: NATO CCD COE Publications, 2020, 129–155, https://ccdcoe.org/uploads/2020/05/CyCon_2020_8_Lilly_Cheravitch.pdf

Lin, Herbert, "Escalation Dynamics and Conflict Termination in Cyberspace," *Strategic Studies Quarterly* 6, no. 3 (Fall 2012): 46–70, https://www.jstor.org/stable/26267261

Lin, Herbert, "U.S. Cyber Infiltration of the Russian Electric Grid: Implications for Deterrence," *Lawfare*, June 18, 2019, https://www.lawfareblog.com/us-cyber-infiltration-russian-electric-grid-implications-deterrence

Lin, Herbert, "Doctrinal Confusion and Cultural Dysfunction in DoD," *The Cyber Defense Review*, Special Edition: Information Operations/Information Warfare, 5, no. 2 (Summer 2020): 89–108.

Lin, Herbert and Jaclyn Kerr, "On Cyber-Enabled Information Warfare and Information Operations," in Paul Cornish (ed.), *Oxford Handbook of Cyber Security*, Oxford: Oxford University Press, 2021, 251–272.

Lindsay, Jon R., "Stuxnet and the Limits of Cyber Warfare," *Security Studies* 22, no. 3 (2013): 365–404, https://doi.org/10.1080/09636412.2013.81 6122

Lindsay, Jon R., "Restrained by Design: The Political Economy of Cybersecurity," *Digital Policy, Regulation and Governance* 19, no. 6 (2017): 493–514.

Lindsay, Jon R. and Erik Gartzke, "Coercion through Cyberspace: The Stability-Instability Paradox Revisited," in Kelly M. Greenhill and Peter Krause (eds.), *Coercion: The Power to Hurt in International Politics*, New York: Oxford University Press, 2018.

Lin-Greenberg, Erik, Reid B. C. Pauly, and Jacquelyn G. Schneider, "Wargaming for International Relations Research," *European Journal of International Relations* (2021), https://doi.org/10.1177/1354066121106 4090

Lipner, Steven B., "The Birth and Death of the Orange Book," *IEEE Annals of the History of Computing* 37, no. 2 (April–June 2015): 19–31, https://doi .org/10.1109/MAHC.2015.27

Lipset, Seymour M., "The Social Requisites of Democracy Revisited: 1993 Presidential Address," *American Sociological Review* 59, no. 1 (1994).

Liquid Intelligent Technologies, "Liquid Intelligent Technologies and Facebook Partner to Build a Fibre Network in the Democratic Republic of Congo," *Liquid Telecom*, July 5, 2021.

Liu Yangyue, "Wangluo kongjian guoji Chongtu yu zhanlue wendingxing [International Crises in Cyberspace and Strategic Stability]," *Waijiao pinglun [Foreign Affairs Review]* 4 (2016), http://www.cnki.com.cn/Article/CJFDT OTAL-WJXY201604005.htm

Long, Austin, "A Cyber SIOP?" in Herbert Lin and Amy Zegart (eds.), *Bytes, Bombs, and Spies: The Strategic Dimensions of Offensive Cyber Operations*, Washington, DC: Brookings Institution Press, 2019, 116–122.

López, Alfred J., "Introduction: The (Post) Global South," *The Global South* 1, no. 1 (2007): 1–11.

Lotrionte, Catherine, "Reconsidering the Consequences for State-Sponsored Hostile Cyber Operations Under International Law," *Cyber Defense Review* 3, no. 2 (Summer 2018): 73–114, https://cyberdefensereview.army.mil/Por tals/6/Documents/CDR%20Journal%20Articles/CDR_V3N2_Reconside ringConsequences_LOTRIONTE.pdf?ver=2018-09-05-084840-807

Lu Chuanying, "Forging Stability in Cyberspace," *Survival* 62, no. 2 (2020): 125–136, https://doi.org/10.1080/00396338.2020.1739959

Lugones, Marìa, "Toward a Decolonial Feminism," *Hypatia* 25, no. 4 (2010): 742–759, https://doi.org/10.1111/j.1527-2001.2010.01137.x

Lundan, Sarianna M. and Geoffrey Jones, *The "Commonwealth" Effect and the Process of Internationalisation*, *The World Economy*, 24, no. 1 (2001): 99–118.

Lynch, David J., "130 Countries Sign on to Global Minimum Tax Plan, Creating Momentum for Biden Push," *The Washington Post*, July 1, 2021, https://www.washingtonpost.com/us-policy/2021/07/01/global-corpora te-tax-oecd/

Lynch, Jennifer, "Face Off: Law Enforcement Use of Face Recognition Technology," *Electronic Frontier Foundation*, February 2018, https://www .eff.org/files/2018/02/15/face-off-report-1b.pdf

Lynn III, William J., "Defending a New Domain: The Pentagon's Cyberstrategy," *Foreign Affairs* 89, no. 5 (September/October 2010), https://www.foreignaffairs.com/articles/united-states/2010-09-01/defen ding-new-domain

McDermott, Rose, "Some Emotional Considerations in Cyber Conflict," *Journal of Cyber Policy* 4, no. 3 (2019), https://doi.org/10.1080/23738871 .2019.1701692

Mackenzie, Christina, "France's New Cyber Defense 'Conductor' Talks Retaliation, Protecting Industry," *Fifth Domain*, September 30, 2019, https://www.fifthdomain.com/international/2019/09/30/frances-new-cy ber-defense-conductor-talks-retaliation-protecting-industry/

MacKenzie, Donald, *Mechanizing Proof: Computing, Risk, and Trust*, Cambridge, MA: The MIT Press, 2001.

MacKinnon, Rebecca, "Liberation Technology: China's 'Networked Authoritarianism,'" *Journal of Democracy* 22, no. 2 (2011): 32–46, http://doi .org/10.1353/jod.2011.0033

McNamara, Robert. "Address by Secretary of Defense McNamara at the Ministerial Meeting of the North Atlantic Council," 1962.

McPherson, Ella, "ICTs and Human Rights Practice: A Report Prepared for the UN Special Rapporteur on Extrajudicial, Summary, or Arbitrary Executions," *University of Cambridge Centre of Governance and Human Rights* (2015), https://doi.org/10.17863/CAM.16807

Maddux, Thomas and Diane Labrosse (eds.), "Roundtable 3-10 on *The Diffusion of Military Power: Causes and Consequences for International Relations*," *H-Diplo/ISSF Roundtable III*, no. 10 (February 29, 2012).

Mahnken, Thomas G., *Technology and the American Way of War Since 1945*, New York: Columbia University Press, 2010.

Maldonado-Torres, Nelson, "On the Coloniality of Being: Contributions to the Development of a Concept," *Cultural Studies* 21, no. 2–3 (2007): 243, https://doi.org/10.1080/09502380601162548

Mann, Edward, "Desert Storm: The First Information War?" *AirPower Journal* VIII, no. 4 (Winter 1994): 4–14, https://www.airuniversity.af.edu/Portals /10/ASPJ/journals/Volume-08_Issue-1-Se/1994_Vol8_No4.pdf

Marchal, Roland, "France and Africa: The Emergence of Essential Reforms?" *International Affairs* 74, no. 2 (2002): 355–372.

Marczak, Bill et al., "The Kingdom Came to Canada: How Saudi-Linked Digital Espionage Reached Canadian Soil," *Citizen Lab*, October 1, 2018, https://citizenlab.ca/2018/10/the-kingdom-came-to-canada-how-saudi-li nked-digital-espionage-reached-canadian-soil/

Marczak, Bill et al., "Running in Circles: Uncovering the Clients of Cyberespionage," *Citizen Lab*, December 1, 2020, https://citizenlab.ca/20 20/12/running-in-circles-uncovering-the-clients-of-cyberespionage-firm -circles/

Markoff, John, "Dutch Computer Rogues Infiltrate American Systems with Impunity," *The New York Times*, April 21, 1991, https://www.nytimes .com/1991/04/21/us/dutch-computer-rogues-infiltrate-american-systems -with-impunity.html

Markoff, Michelle, "Remarks for Panel Session 'Developments of Cyberspace and Emerging Challenges,'" report prepared for ASEAN Regional (ARF) Cyber Capability Workshop, 2009, https://2009-2017.state.gov/s/cyberis sues/releasesandremarks/245720.htm

Martelle, Michael (ed.), "Eligible Receiver 97: Seminal DOD Cyber Exercise Included Mock Terror Strikes and Hostage Simulations," *Department of Defense, Briefing Book* no. 634, August 1, 2018, https://nsarchive.gwu.edu /briefing-book/cyber-vault/2018-08-01/eligible-receiver-97-seminal-dod -cyber-exercise-included-mock-terror-strikes-hostage-simulations

Maschmeyer, Lennart, "The Subversive Trilemma: Why Cyber Operations Fall Short of Expectations," *International Security* 46, no. 2 (2021): 51– 90.

Mauk, Maureen, Rebekah Willett, and Natalie Coulter, "The Can-Do Girl Goes to Coding Camp: A Discourse Analysis of News Reports on Coding Initiatives Designed for Girls," *Learning, Media and Technology* 45, no. 4 (2020): 395–408, https://doi.org/10.1080/17439884.2020.1781889

Maurer, Tim, *Cyber Mercenaries: The State, Hackers, and Power*, Cambridge: Cambridge University Press, 2018.

Mazzetti, Mark et al., "A New Age of Warfare: How Internet Mercenaries Do Battle for Authoritarian Governments," *The New York Times*, March 21, 2019, https://www.nytimes.com/2019/03/21/us/politics/government -hackers-nso-darkmatter.html

Mearscheimer, John, "Back to the Future," *International Security* 15, no. 1 (1990): 5–56.

Meddah, Hassan, "Pourquoi la France se dote d'une cyber-armée," *L'usine Nouvelle*, December 13, 2016, https://www.usinenouvelle.com/article/po urquoi-la-france-se-dote-d-une-cyber-armee.N476239

Mendoza, Breny, "Coloniality of Gender and Power: From Postcoloniality to Decoloniality," in Lisa Disch and Mary Hawkesworth (eds.), *The Oxford Handbook of Feminist Theory*, Oxford: Oxford University Press, 2015, https://doi.org/10.1093/oxfordhb/9780199328581.013.6

Meyer, Paul, "Norms of Responsible State Behaviour in Cyberspace," in Markus Christen, Bert Gordijn, and Michele Loi (eds.), *The Ethics of Cybersecurity*, Cham: Springer, 2020, 347–360, https://library.oapen.org/bitstream/hand le/20.500.12657/22489/1007696.pdf?sequence=1#page=352

Michaelsen, Marcus, "Far Away, So Close: Transnational Activism, Digital Surveillance and Authoritarian Control in Iran," *Surveillance & Society* 15, no. 3/4 (2017): 465–470, https://doi.org/10.24908/ss.v15i3/4.6635.http s://doi.org/10.1080/14747731.2016.1263079

Michaelsen, Marcus, "Exit and Voice in a Digital Age: Iran's Exiled Activists and the Authoritarian State," *Globalizations* 15, no. 2 (2018): 248–264, https://doi.org/10.1080/14747731.2016.1263078

Mignolo, Walter D., "DELINKING: The Rhetoric of Modernity, the Logic of Coloniality and the Grammar of de-Coloniality," *Cultural Studies* 21, no. 2–3 (2007): 449–514, https://doi.org/10.1080/09502380601162647

Mignolo, Walter D., "Epistemic Disobedience, Independent Thought and Decolonial Freedom," *Theory, Culture & Society* 26, no. 7–8 (2009), https:// doi.org/10.1177/0263276409349275

Mignolo, Walter D., *Local Histories/Global Designs: Coloniality, Subaltern Knowledges, and Border Thinking*, Princeton, NJ and Oxford: Princeton University Press, 2012, https://doi.org/10.1515/9781400845064

Mignolo, Walter D., "The Way We Were. Or What Decoloniality Today Is All About," *Anglistica AION: An Intersciplinary Journal* 23, no. 2 (2019).

Mignolo, Walter D. and Madina V. Tlostanova, "Theorizing from the Borders: Shifting to Geo- and Body-Politics of Knowledge," *European Journal of Social Theory* 9, no. 2 (2006), https://doi.org/10.1177/136843100 6063333

Miller, James N. Jr. and Richard Fontaine, "A New Era In U.S.-Russian Strategic Stability," *Center for a New American Security*, September 2019, 48: https://www.cnas.org/publications/reports/a-new-era-in-u-s-russian-stra tegic-stability

Miller, James N. and Neal A. Pollard, "Persistent Engagement, Agreed

Competition and Deterrence in Cyberspace," *Lawfare*, April 30, 2019: https://www.lawfareblog.com/persistent-engagement-agreed-competition-and-deterrence-cyberspace

Milley, Mark, "Gen Milley Chairman Confirmation Testimony," § Senate Armed Services Committee (2019), https://www.c-span.org/video/?c480 6722/user-clip-gen-milley-chairman-confirmation-testimony

Ministerie van Defensie, "Defence Cyber Command – Cyber Security – De fensie.Nl," onderwerp (Ministerie van Defensie), March 30, 2017, https://english.defensie.nl/topics/cyber-security/cyber-command

Moore, Daniel and Max Smeets, "Why We Are Unconvinced NATO's Cyber Policy Is More Aggressive, and That's a Good Thing," *Council on Foreign Relations*, January 30, 2018, https://www.cfr.org/blog/why-we-are-uncon vinced-natos-cyber-policy-more-aggressive-and-thats-good-thing

Moosavi, Leon, "The Decolonial Bandwagon and the Dangers of Intellectual Decolonisation," *International Review of Sociology* 30, no. 2 (2020): 332–354, https://doi.org/10.1080/03906701.2020.1776919

Morgan, Forrest E., Karl P. Mueller, Evan S. Medeiros, Kevin L. Pollpeter, and Roger Cliff, *Dangerous Thresholds: Managing Escalation in the 21st Century*, Santa Monica, CA: RAND Corporation, 2008.

Morgenthau, Hans, *Politics among Nations*, New York: Alfred Knopf, 1967.

Morrow, James D., "Alliances and Asymmetry: An Alternative to the Capability Aggregation Model of Alliances," *American Journal of Political Science* 35, no. 4 (1991): 904–933.

Moss, Dana M., "The Ties That Bind: Internet Communication Technologies, Networked Authoritarianism, and 'Voice' in the Syrian Diaspora," *Globalizations* 15, no. 2 (2018): 265–282.

Moss, Todd, Vijaya Ramachandran, and Manju Kedia Shah, "Is Africa's Skepticism of Foreign Capital Justified? Evidence from East African Firm Survey Data," *Working Paper Series* 41, no. 1 (2004).

Mueller, Milton L., *Will the Internet Fragment? Sovereignty, Globalization and Cyberspace*, Cambridge: Polity, 2017.

Mueller, Milton L., "Against Sovereignty in Cyberspace," *International Studies Review* 22, no. 4 (2020).

Nagelhaus, Niels and Lars Gjesvik, "The Chinese Cyber Sovereignty Concept (Part 1)," *The Asia Dialogue*, September 7, 2018, https://theasiadialogue .com/2018/09/07/the-chinese-cyber-sovereignty-concept-part-1/

Nagengast, John C., "Defining a Security Architecture for the Next Century," *Journal of Electronic Defense* 15, no. 1 (1992): 51–53.

Nakashima, Ellen, "Cyber-intruder Sparks Response, Debate," *The Washington Post*, December 8, 2011, https://www.washingtonpost.com/national/

national-security/cyber-intruder-sparks-response-debate/2011/12/06/
gIQAxLuFgO_story.html

Nakashima, Ellen, "US Military Operation to Attack IS Last Year Sparked Heated Debate Over Alerting Allies," *The Washington Post*, May 9, 2017.

Nakashima, Ellen, "Russian Military Was Behind 'NotPetya' Cyberattack in Ukraine, CIA Concludes," *The Washington Post*, January 12, 2018, https://www.washingtonpost.com/world/national-security/russian-military-was-behind-notpetya-cyberattack-in-ukraine-cia-concludes/2018/01/12/048 d8506-f7ca-11e7-b34a-b85626af34ef_story.html

Nakashima, Ellen, "White House Authorizes 'Offensive Cyber Operations' to Deter Foreign Adversaries," *The Washington Post*, September 20, 2018, https://www.washingtonpost.com/world/national-security/trump-autho rizes-offensive-cyber-operations-to-deter-foreign-adversaries-bolton-says /2018/09/20/b5880578-bd0b-11e8-b7d2-0773aa1e33da_story.html

Nakashima, Ellen, "U.S. Cyber Command Operation Disrupted Internet Access of Russian Troll Factory on Day of 2018 Midterms," *The Washington Post*, February 27, 2019, https://www.washingtonpost.com/world/national -security/us-cyber-command-operation-disrupted-internet-access-of-rus sian-troll-factory-on-day-of-2018-midterms/2019/02/26/1827fc9e-36d6 -11e9-af5b-b51b7ff322e9_story.html

Nakashima, Ellen and Joseph Marks, "Russia, U.S. and Other Countries Reach New Agreement Against Cyber Hacking Even as Attacks Continue," *The Washington Post*, June 12, 2021, https://www.washingtonpost.com/ national-security/russia-us-un-cyber-norms/2021/06/12/9b608cd4-866b- 11eb-bfdf-4d36dab83a6d_story.html

Nakasone, Paul M., "A Cyber Force for Persistent Operations," *Joint Force Quarterly* 92, no. 22 (2019), https://ndupress.ndu.edu/Media/News/News -Article-View/Article/1736950/a-cyber-force-for-persistent-operations/

Nakasone, Paul M. and Michael Sulmeyer, "How to Compete in Cyberspace," *Foreign Affairs*, August 25, 2020, https://www.foreignaffairs.com/articles /united-states/2020-08-25/cybersecurity

National Counterintelligence and Security Center, Office of the Director of National Intelligence, "Fiscal Year 2017 Annual Report on Security Clearance Determinations," August 2018, https://www.dni.gov/files/NC SC/documents/features/20180827-security-clearance-determinations.pdf

National Defense Strategy Commission, "Providing for the Common Defense: The Assessments and Recommendations of the National Defense Strategy Commission," Washington, DC: United States Institute of Peace, November 2018, https://www.usip.org/publications/2018/11/providing -common-defense

National Security Telecommunications and Information Systems Security Committee, "NSTISS Directive 500: Information Systems Security (INFOSEC) Education, Training, and Awareness," Febuary 25, 1993, https://apps.dtic.mil/sti/pdfs/ADA362604.pdf

NATO, "London Declaration Issued by the Heads of State and Government Participating in the Meeting of the North Atlantic Council in London," December 3, 2009, https://www.nato.int/cps/en/natohq/official_texts_17 1584.htm

NATO, "Sharing Malware Information to Defeat Cyber Attacks," November 29, 2013, https://www.nato.int/cps/en/natolive/news_105485.htm

NATO, "Current Security Challenges and the Role Of NATO and the European Union. Speech Delivered by the Chairman of the NATO Military Committee, General Petr Pavel, at The European Parliament," October 20, 2015, https://www.nato.int/cps/en/natohq/opinions_1241 28.htm?selectedLocale=en

NATO, "NATO and the European Union Enhance Cyber Defence Cooperation," February 10, 2016, https://www.nato.int/cps/en/natohq /news_127836.htm

NATO, "Warsaw Summit Communiqué," July 9, 2016, https://www.nato .int/cps/en/natohq/official_texts_133169.htm

NATO, "NATO Cyber Defense," December 2017, https://www.nato.int /nato_static_fl2014/assets/pdf/pdf_2016_07/20160627_1607-factsheet-cy ber-defence-eng.pdf

NATO, "Allied Joint Doctrine for Cyberspace Operations," AJP-3.20, Ed. 1, Version A (January 2020), https://www.gov.uk/government/publications /allied-joint-doctrine-for-cyberspace-operations-ajp-320

NATO, "Enlargement," May 5, 2020, https://www.nato.int/cps/en/natolive /topics_49212.htm

NATO, "NATO's Maritime Activities," June 2, 2020, https://www.nato.int /cps/en/natohq/topics_70759.htm

NATO, "NATO 2030: United for a New Era," November 25, 2020, https:// www.nato.int/nato_static_fl2014/assets/pdf/2020/12/pdf/201201-Reflec tion-Group-Final-Report-Uni.pdf

NATO, "Resilience and Article 3," June 11, 2021, https://www.nato.int/cps /en/natohq/topics_132722.htm

NATO Cooperative Cyber Defense Center of Excellence, "Strategic Importance of, and Dependence On, Undersea Cables," 2019, https://ccdc oe.org/uploads/2019/11/Undersea-cables-Final-NOV-2019.pdf

Naval Postgraduate School, "About the Cebrowski Institute," https://nps.edu /web/cebrowski/about

"Navy C4I Budget Safe for Now," *Defense Daily* 184, no. 41 (August 1994).

Navy Personnel Command, "Information Warfare Community Overview," last modified October 21, 2019, https://www.public.navy.mil/bupers-npc/officer/communitymanagers/active/restricted/Pages/Information_Warfare_Community.aspx

Ndlovu-Gatsheni, Sabelo J., "The Dynamics of Epistemological Decolonisation in the 21st Century: Towards Epistemic Freedom," *Strategic Review for Southern Africa* 40, no. 1 (2018): 23–26.

Neray, Phil, "Industrial Espionage is a Major Threat to the Manufacturing Sector," *IIoT World*, August 29, 2017, https://iiot-world.com/ics-security/cybersecurity/industrial-espionage-is-a-major-threat-to-the-manufacturing-sector/

New York Cyber Task Force, "Building a Defensible Cyberspace," September 28, 2017, https://sipa.columbia.edu/ideas-lab/techpolicy/building-defensible-cyberspace

Newhouse, William et al., "National Initiative for Cybersecurity Education (NICE) Cybersecurity Workforce Framework," *National Institute of Standards and Technology*, Publication 800–181 (August 2017), https://doi.org/10.6028/NIST.SP.800-181

Newman, Lily Hay, "The Ransomware Meltdown Experts Warned About Is Here," *Wired*, May 12, 2017, https://www.wired.com/2017/05/ransomware-meltdown-experts-warned/

Newman, Lily Hay, "What Israel's Strike on Hamas Hackers Means For Cyberwar," *Wired*, May 6, 2019, https://www.wired.com/story/israel-hamas-cyberattack-air-strike-cyberwar/

Newsweek, "We're in the Middle of a Cyberwar," September 19, 1999, https://www.newsweek.com/were-middle-cyerwar-166196

Ney, Jr., Hon. Paul C., "DOD General Counsel Remarks at U.S. Cyber Command Legal Conference," March 2, 2020, https://www.defense.gov/Newsroom/Speeches/Speech/Article/2099378/dod-general-counsel-remarks-at-us-cyber-command-legal-conference/

Ng, Alfred and Maddy Verner, "The Little-Known Data Broker Industry Is Spending Big Bucks Lobbying Congress," *The Markup*, April 1, 2021, https://themarkup.org/privacy/2021/04/01/the-little-known-data-broker-industry-is-spending-big-bucks-lobbying-congress

Ngugi, wa Thiong'o, *Decolonising the Mind: The Politics of Language in African Literature*, reprint, Studies in African Literature, Oxford: Currey [u.a.], 2005.

Nkrumah, Kwame, *Neo-Colonialism, the Last Stage of Imperialism*, London: Thomas Nelson and Sons, 1965.

Noble, Safiya Umoja, *Algorithms of Oppression: How Search Engines Reinforce Racism*, New York: NYU Press, 2018.

Noble, Safiya Umoja and Sarah Roberts, "Technological Elites, the Meritocracy, and Postracial Myths in Silicon Valley," in Roopali Mukherjee, Sarah Banet-Weiser, and Herman Gray (eds.), *Racism Postrace*, Durham, NC: Duke University Press, 2019, 113–132.

Nordling, Linda, "How Decolonization Could Reshape South African Science," *Nature* 554, no. 7691 (2018): 159–162, https://doi.org/10.1038/d41586-018-01696-w

North, Douglass, *Understanding the Process of Economic Change*, Princeton, NJ: Princeton University Press, 2005.

Notley, Tanya and Stephanie Hankey, "Human Rights Defenders and the Right to Digital Privacy and Security," in John Lannon and Edward Halpin (eds.), *Human Rights and Information Communication Technologies: Trends and Consequences of Use*, Hershey, PA: IGI Global, 2013, https://doi.org/10.40 18/978-1-4666-1918-0.ch010

Nunn, Nathan, "Historical Legacies: A Model Linking Africa's Past to its Current Underdevelopment," *Journal of Develeopment Economics* 83, no. 157 (2007).

Nyabola, Nanjala, *Digital Democracy, Analogue Politics: How the Internet Era is Transforming Politics in Kenya*, London: Zed Books, 2018, 231–260, http://dx.doi.org/10.5040/9781350219656.0010

Nye, Joseph S. Jr., "Nuclear Lessons for Cyber Security," *Strategic Studies Quarterly* 5, no. 4 (2011): 18–38.

Nye, Joseph S. Jr., "The Regime Complex for Managing Global Cyber Activities," *Global Commission on Internet Governance Paper Series*, Center for International Governance Innovation, May 20, 2014.

Nye, Joseph S. Jr., "Deterrence and Dissuasion in Cyberspace," *International Security* 41, no. 3 (Winter 2016): 44–71.

O'Connor, Sarah et al., "Cyber-enabled Foreign Interference in Elections and Referendums," *International Cyber Policy Centre, ASPI*, Policy Brief 4 (2020), https://www.aspi.org.au/report/cyber-enabled-foreign-interference-elections-and-referendums

O'Flaherty, Kate, "The Nigerian Cyber Warfare Command: Waging War in Cyberspace," *Forbes*, November 26, 2018, https://www.forbes.com/sites/kateoflahertyuk/2018/11/26/the-nigerian-cyber-warfare-command-waging-war-in-cyberspace/?sh=448f4c5f2fba

O'Flaherty, Kate, "Is It Time to Leave WhatsApp – and Is Signal the Answer?," *The Guardian*, January 24, 2021, https://www.theguardian.com/technology/2021/jan/24/is-it-time-to-leave-whatsapp-and-is-signal-the-answer

O'Hara, Kieron, "The Contradictions of Digital Modernity," *AI & Society* 35, no. 1 (March 2020): 197–208, https://doi.org/10.1007/s00146-018-0843-7

O'Neil, Cathy, *Weapons of Math Destruction: How Big Data Increases Inequality and Threatens Democracy*, London: Penguin Books, 2017.

Obama, Barack, "Presidential Policy Directive/PPD-20, Subject: U.S. Cyber Operations Policy," October 16, 2012, 2–3, from *National Security Archive*, https://nsarchive2.gwu.edu/dc.html?doc=2725521-Document-2-9

Office of the Chairman of the Joint Chiefs of Staff, "National Military Strategy for Cyberspace Operations (U)," *Homeland Security Digital Library*, November 30, 2006, https://www.hsdl.org/?abstract&did=

Office of the Director of National Intelligence, "Background to 'Assessing Russian Activities and Intentions in Recent US Elections: The Analytic Process and Cyber Incident Attribution,'" (January 2017), https://www.dni.gov/files/documents/ICA_2017_01.pdf

Office of the Secretary of Defense, "Annual Report to Congress: Military and Security Developments Involving the People's Republic of China 2016," April 26, 2016, https://dod.defense.gov/Portals/1/Documents/pubs/2016%20China%20Military%20Power%20Report.pdf

Office of the Undersecretary of Defense for Acquisition and Technology, "Report of the Defense Science Board Summer Study Task Force on Information Architecture for the Battlefield," 1994, https://www.hsdl.org/?abstract&did=464955

Oloruntoba, Samuel O., "Breaking the Incubus? The Tripartite Free Trade Agreements and the Prospects of Developmental Integration in Africa," in Olayinka Akanle and Jimi Olalekan Adesina (eds.), *The Development of Africa* (Cham: Springer International Publishing, 2018).

Onuoha, Mimi, "What Is Missing Is Still There": https://www.youtube.com/watch?v=57Lgztk62uY&t=6s

"Organizing for Information Warfare: An Air Staff Perspective," *U.S. Air Force Office of the Director of Intelligence, Surveillance, and Reconnaissance*, 1999, slide 25: https://nsarchive.gwu.edu/dc.html?doc=6168263-National-Security-Archive-US-Air-Force-Office-of

Orsini, Amandine, Jean Frédéric Morin, and Oran Young, "Regime Complexes: A Buzz, a Boom, or a Boost for Global Governance?" *Global Governance: A Review of Multilateralism and International Organizations* 19, no. 1 (2013): 27–39.

Ostrom, Elinor, "Beyond Markets and States: Polycentric Governance of Complex Economic Systems," *American Economic Review* 100, no. 3 (2010): 641–672.

Oyěwùmí, Oyèrónké, *The Invention of Women: Making an African Sense of Western Gender Discourses*, Minneapolis and London: University of Minnesota Press, 1997.

Painter, Chris, "Diplomacy in Cyberspace," *The Foreign Service Journal*, June 2018, https://www.afsa.org/diplomacy-cyberspace

Parameswaran, Prashanth, "What's Behind Vietnam's New Military Cyber Command?" *The Diplomat*, January 12, 2018, https://thediplomat.com/2018/01/whats-behind-vietnams-new-military-cyber-command/

Parameswaran, Prashanth, "What's Behind Singapore's New Integrated Military Cyber Command Objective?" *The Diplomat*, March 10, 2020, https://thediplomat.com/2020/03/whats-behind-singapores-new-integrated-military-cyber-command-objective/

Pavel, Barry, Peter Engelke, and Alex Ward, "Dynamic Stability: US Strategy for a World in Transition," *Atlantic Council Strategy Papers*, March 2016, https://www.atlanticcouncil.org/wp-content/uploads/2015/04/2016-DynamicStabilityStrategyPaper_E.pdf

Peel, Stephen, "Response to Open Letter to Novalpina Capital on 15 April 2019," *Citizen Lab*, https://citizenlab.ca/wp-content/uploads/2019/05/Novalpina-reply-May-15.pdf

Pegg, David and Rob Evans, "Controversial Snooping Technology 'Used By At Least Seven Policy Forces,'" *The Guardian*, October 10, 2016, https://www.theguardian.com/world/2016/oct/10/controversial-phone-snooping-technology-imsi-catcher-seven-police-forces

Perlroth, Nicole and Quentin Hardy, "Bank Hacking Was the Work of Iranians, Officials Say," *The New York Times*, January 8, 2013, Technology section, https://www.nytimes.com/2013/01/09/technology/online-banking-attacks-were-work-of-iran-us-officials-say.html

Permanent Representatives of China, the Russian Federation, Tajikistan and Uzbekistan, "Developments in the Field of Information and Telecommunications in the Context of International Security (UN A/66/359)," United Nations General Assembly, 66th session, September 14, 2011.

Permanent Representatives of China, Kazakhstan, Kyrgyzstan, the Russian Federation, Tajikistan and Uzbekistan, "Developments in the Field of Information and Telecommunications in the Context of International Security (UN A/69/723)," United Nations General Assembly, 69th session, January 13, 2015.

Perrow, Charles, *Normal Accidents: Living with High-Risk Technologies*, New York: Basic Books, 1984.

Petersson, Magnus, "The Strategic Importance of the Transatlantic Link," in Janne Haaland Matláry and Robert Johnson (eds.), *Military Strategy in the Twenty-First Century: The Challenge for NATO*, London: Hurst and Company, 2020, 27–42.

Pomerleau, Mark, "Here's How DoD Organizes Its Cyber Warriors," *Fifth Domain*, September 13, 2018, https://www.fifthdomain.com/workforce/career/2017/07/25/heres-how-dod-organizes-its-cyber-warriors/

Pomerleau, Mark, "New Cyber Authority Could Make 'All the Difference in the World,'" *Fifth Domain*, September 17, 2018, https://www.fifthdomain.com/dod/cybercom/2018/09/17/new-cyber-authority-could-make-all-the-difference-in-the-world/

Pomerleau, Mark, "Is Cyber Command Really Being More 'Aggressive' in Cyberspace?" *Fifth Domain*, April 25, 2019.

Posen, Barry R., *Inadvertent Escalation: Conventional War and Nuclear Risks*, Ithaca, NY: Cornell University Press, 1991.

Pouliot, Vincent and Jean-Philippe Thérien, "Global Governance in Practice," *Global Policy* 9, no. 2 (2018): 163–172.

Prasad, Revati, "Ascendant India, Digital India: How Net Neutrality Advocates Defeated Facebook's Free Basics," *Media, Culture & Society* 40, no. 3 (2018): 415–431, https://doi.org/10.1177/0163443717736117

Price, Richard and Nina Tannenwald, "Norms and Deterrence: The Nuclear and Chemical Weapons Taboos," in Peter J. Katzenstein (ed.), *The Culture of National Security: Norms and Identity in World Politics*, New York: Columbia University Press, 2009, 114–152.

Privacy International, "The Global Surveillance Industry, *Privacy International*, 2016, https://privacyinternational.org/sites/default/files/2017-12/global_surveillance_0.pdf

Privacy International, "The Global Surveillance Industry," *Privacy International*, 2017, https://privacyinternational.org/sites/default/files/2017-12/global_surveillance_0.pdf

Privacy International, "Challenge to Hidden Data Ecosystem," *Privacy International*, 2018, https://privacyinternational.org/legal-action/challenge-hidden-data-ecosystem

Privacy International, "All Roads Lead to Palantir," *Privacy International*, 2020, https://www.privacyinternational.org/report/4271/all-roads-lead-palantir

Privacy International, "IMSI Catchers: PI's Legal Analysis," *Privacy International*, 2020, https://privacyinternational.org/report/3965/imsi-catchers-pis-legal-analysis

Quijano, Aníbal, "Coloniality and Modernity/Rationality," *Cultural Studies* 21, no. 2–3 (2007): 168–78, https://doi.org/10.1080/09502380601164353

Radu, Roxana, *Negotiating Internet Governance*, Oxford: Oxford University Press, 2019.

Rajagopalan, Megha, "Chinese Military Force to Take Lead on Cyber, Space Defense," *Reuters*, January 29, 2016, https://www.reuters.com/article/us-china-military-idUSKCN0V714B

Rattray, Gregory J., *Strategic Warfare in Cyberspace*, Cambridge, MA: The MIT Press, 2001.

Raustiala, Kal and David G. Victor, "The Regime Complex for Plant Genetic Resources," *International Organization* 58, no. 2 (2004): 277–309.

Raymond, Mark, "Puncturing the Myth of the Internet as a Commons," *Georgetown Journal of International Affairs, International Engagement on Cyber III* (2013/14): 53–64.

Raymond, Mark, "Managing Decentralized Cyber Governance: The Responsibility to Troubleshoot," *Strategic Studies Quarterly* 10, no. 4 (2016): 123–149.

Raymond, Mark, "Cyber Futures and the Justice Motive: Avoiding Pyrrhic Victory," *Military Cyber Affairs* 3, no. 1 (2018): 1–23.

Raymond, Mark, *Social Practices of Rule-Making in World Politics*, New York: Oxford University Press, 2019.

Raymond, Mark and Laura DeNardis," Multistakeholderism: Anatomy of an Inchoate Global Institution," *International Theory* 7, no. 3 (2015): 572–616.

Realizing the Potential of C4I: Fundamental Challenges, Washington, DC: National Academy Press, 1999, http://nap.edu/6457

Reed, Michael C., "Gabon: A Neo-Colonial Enclave of Enduring French Interest," *The Journal of Modern African Studies* 25, no. 2 (June 1987): 283–320.

Ren Jian (ed.), *Zuozhan Tiaoling Gailun [An Introduction to Operations Regulations]*, Beijing: Junshi Kexue Yuan Chubanshe, 2016.

Repnikova, Maria, "Media Openings and Political Transitions: Glasnost versus Yulun Jiandu," *Problems of Post-Communism* 64, no. 3–4 (2017): 141–151.

Reus-Smit, Christian, *The Moral Purpose of the State: Culture, Social Identity, and Institutional Rationality in International Relations*, Princeton, NJ: Princeton University Press, 1999.

Richard, Laurent and Sandrine Rigaud, "Spyware Can Make Your Phone Your Enemy: Journalism is Your Defense," *The Guardian*, July 19, 2021, https://www.theguardian.com/world/commentisfree/2021/jul/19/spywa re-can-make-your-phone-your-enemy-journalism-is-your-defence

Rid, Thomas, "Cyber War Will Not Take Place," *Journal of Strategic Studies* 35, no. 1 (2012): 5–32, DOI: 10.1080/01402390.2011.608939.

Rid, Thomas, *Rise of the Machines: A Cybernetic History*, New York: W. W. Norton & Company, 2016.

Rid, Thomas and Ben Buchanan, "Attributing Cyber Attacks," *Journal of Strategic Studies* 38, no. 1–2 (2015): 32, https://doi.org/10.1080/01402390.2014.977382

Rid, Thomas and Peter McBurney, "Cyber-Weapons," *RUSI Journal* 157, no. 1 (2012): 6–13, https://doi.org/10.1080/03071847.2012.664354

Rigot, Afsaneh, "Egypt's Dangerous New Strategy for Criminalizing Queerness," *Slate* (blog), December 30, 2020, https://slate.com/technology/2020/12/egypt-lgbtq-crime-economic-courts.html

Riordan, Shaun, "Cyber Diplomacy v. Digital Diplomacy: A Terminological Distinction," *University of Southern California, Center on Public Diplomacy*, May 12, 2016, https://www.uscpublicdiplomacy.org/blog/cyber-diplomacy-vs-digital-diplomacy-terminological-distinction

Risam, Roopika, "Decolonizing The Digital Humanities in Theory and Practice," in *English Faculty Publications*, vol. 7, 2018, https://digitalcommons.salemstate.edu/english_facpub/7

Robertson, Kate, Cynthia Khoo, and Yolanda Song, "To Surveil and Predict: A Human Rights Analysis of Algorithmic Policing in Canada – The Current Landscape," *Citizen Lab*, September 29, 2020, https://citizenlab.ca/wp-content/uploads/2021/01/AIPolicing_factualfindings_v6.pdf

Robinson, Neil and Chelsey Slack, "Co-Operation: A Key To NATO's Cyberspace Endeavour," *European Foreign Affairs Review* 24, no. 2 (2019): 153–166.

Roche, Edward M., "The Search for Global Cyber Stability," *Journal of Information Technology Case and Application Research* 29, no. 2 (2019): 68–73, https://doi.org/10.1080/15228053.2019.1636570

Roche, Elizabeth, "UNSC: India Says Cyber Tools are Used to Target Critical Infra," *Livemint*, June 29, 2021, https://www.livemint.com/news/india/unsc-india-says-cyber-tools-are-used-to-target-critical-infra-11624980216689.html

Rogerson, Christian M., "Japan's Hidden Involvement in South African Manufacturing," *GeoJournal* 30, no. 99 (1993).

Rogin, Josh, "NSA Chief: Cybercrime Constitutes the 'Greatest Transfer of Wealth in History' – Foreign Policy," July 9, 2012, https://foreignpolicy.com/2012/07/09/nsa-chief-cybercrime-constitutes-the-greatest-transfer-of-wealth-in-history/

Romaniuk, Scott N. and Francis Grice, "Norm Evolution Theory and World Politics," *E-International Relations*, November 15, 2018, https://www.e-ir.info/2018/11/15/norm-evolution-theory-and-world-politics/

Rosenbaum, Eric, "Iran is 'leapfrogging our defences,'" CNBC, November 18, 2021, https://www.cnbc.com/2021/11/18/iran-leapfrogging-our-de fenses-in-cyber-war-hacking-expert-mandia-.html

Rosert, Elvira, "Norm Emergence as Agenda Diffusion: Failure and Success in the Regulation of Cluster Munitions," *European Journal of International Relations* 25, no. 4 (2019): 1103–1131, https://doi.org/10.1177%2F13540 66119842644

Roth, Kenneth and Maya Wang, "Data Leviathan: China's Burgeoning Surveillance State," *Human Rights Watch*, https://www.hrw.org/news/20 19/08/16/data-leviathan-chinas-burgeoning-surveillance-state

Rovner, Joshua, "Two Kinds of Catastrophe: Nuclear Escalation and Protracted War in Asia," *Journal of Strategic Studies* 40, no. 5 (2017): 696–730, https:// doi.org/10.1080/01402390.2017.1293532

Rovner, Joshua, "Cyber War as an Intelligence Contest," *War on the Rocks* (September 16, 2019): https://warontherocks.com/2019/09/cyber-war-as -an-intelligence-contest/

Rovner, Joshua and Tyler Moore, "Does the Internet Need a Hegemon?," *Journal of Global Security Studies* 2, no. 3 (2017): 184–203.

Roy, Rohan Deb, "Science Still Bears the Fingerprints of Colonialism," *Smithsonian Magazine* (blog), 2018, https://www.smithsonianmag.com/ science-nature/science-bears-fingerprints-colonialism-180968709/

Ruggie, John Gerard, "Multilateralism: The Anatomy of an Institution," *International Organization* 46, no. 3 (1992): 561–598.

Runde, Daniel F., "America's Global Infrastructure Opportunity: Three Recommendations to the New U.S. Development Finance Corporation," *Center for Strategic & International Studies*, April 11, 2019, https://www.csis .org/analysis/americas-global-infrastructure-opportunity-three-recommen dations-new-us-development-finance

Russell, Andrew L. and Lee Vinsel, "After Innovation, Turn to Maintenance," *Technology and Culture* 59, no. 1 (2018): 1–25, https://doi.org/10 .1353/tech.2018.0004

Russian Federation, "Information Security Doctrine Of The Russian Federation," United Nations International Telecommunications Union (ITU) Archive, September 9, 2000.

Russian Federation, "Doctrine Of Information Security Of The Russian Federation," December 5, 2016.

Sabaratnam, Meera, "Avatars of Eurocentrism in the Critique of the Liberal Peace," *Security Dialogue* 44, no. 3 (2013): 259–78, https://doi.org/10 .1177/0967010613485870

Sabaratnam, Meera, "Is IR Theory White? Racialised Subject-Positioning in

Three Canonical Texts," *Millennium: Journal of International Studies* 49, no. 1 (2020): 3–31, https://doi.org/10.1177/0305829820971687

Sabbah, Cedric, "Pressing Pause: A New Approach for International Cybersecurity Norm Development," 2018, https://ccdcoe.org/uploads/20 18/10/Art-14-Pressing-Pause.-A-New-Approach-for-International-Cyber security-Norm-Development.pdf

Said, Edward, *Orientalism*, repr. with a new preface, Penguin Classics, London [etc.]: Penguin, 2003.

Salinas, Sara, "Facebook's Zuckerberg is Asked to Speak Before UK Parliament Again, and This Time Canada is Joining In," CNBC, October 31, 2018, https://www.cnbc.com/2018/10/31/uk-canada-invite-facebooks-zucker berg-to-speak-before-parliaments.html

Sandholtz, Wayne, "Dynamics of International Norm Change: Rules against Wartime Plunder," *European Journal of International Relations* 14, no. 1 (2008): 101–131.

Sanger, David E., "U.S. Decides to Retaliate Against China's Hacking," *The New York Times*, July 31, 2015, https://www.nytimes.com/2015/08/01/ world/asia/us-decides-to-retaliate-against-chinas-hacking.html

Sanger, David E., "Trump Loosens Secretive Restraints on Ordering Cyberattacks," *The New York Times*, September 20, 2018, https://www.nyt imes.com/2018/09/20/us/politics/trump-cyberattacks-orders.html

Sanger, David E., *The Perfect Weapon: War, Sabotage, and Fear in the Cyber Age*, New York: Crown Publishing Group, 2019.

Sanger, David E. and Nicole Perlroth, "U.S. Said to Find North Korea Ordered Cyberattack on Sony," *The New York Times*, December 17, 2014, World section, https://www.nytimes.com/2014/12/18/world/asia/us-lin ks-north-korea-to-sony-hacking.html

Sanger, David E. and Nicole Perlroth, "U.S. Escalates Online Attacks on Russia's Power Grid," *The New York Times*, June 15, 2019, https://www .nytimes.com/2019/06/15/us/politics/trump-cyber-russia-grid.html

Sartori, Giovanni, "Concept Misformation in Comparative Politics," *The American Political Science Review* 64, no. 4 (1970): 1033–1053.

Sayers, Brian, "The North Atlantic Treaty Organization: A Study in Institutional Resilience," *Georgetown Journal of International Affairs* 12, no. 2 (2011): 48–55.

Schaefer, Marvin, "If A1 Is the Answer, What Was the Question? An Edgy Naïf's Retrospective on Promulgating the Trusted Computer Systems Evaluation Criteria," paper presented at the Annual Computer Security Applications Conference, Tucson, AZ, December 6–10, 1984.

Schelling, Thomas C., *Arms and Influence*, New Haven, CT: Yale University Press, 1966.

Schenkkan, Nate and Isabel Linzer, "Out of Sight, Not Out of Reach: The Global Scale and Scope of Transnational Repression," *Freedom House*, 2021, https://freedomhouse.org/sites/default/files/2021-02/Complete_FH_TransnationalRepressionReport2021_rev020221.pdf

Schia, Niels, Niels Nagelhus, and Lars Gjesvik, "China's Cyber Sovereignty," *Norwegian Institute for International Affairs (NUPI)*, January 1, 2017, www.jstor.org/stable/resrep07952

Schilis-Gallego, Cecile and Nina Lakhani, "It's a Free-For-All: How Hi-Tech Spyware Ends Up in the Hands of Mexico's Cartels," *The Guardian*, December 7, 2020, https://www.theguardian.com/world/2020/dec/07/mexico-cartels-drugs-spying-corruption

Schimmelfennig, Frank, "NATO Enlargement: A Constructivist Explanation," *Security Studies* 8, no. 2–3 (1998): 198–234.

Schmidt, Elizabeth, *Foreign Intervention in Africa: From the Cold War to the War on Terror* (Cambridge: Cambridge University Press, 2013).

Schmitt, Michael N. (ed.), *Tallinn Manual 2.0 on the International Law Applicable Cyber Operations*, 2nd edition, New York, NY: Cambridge University Press, 2017.

Schmitt, Michael, "The Netherlands Releases a Tour de Force on International Law in Cyberspace: Analysis," *Just Security*, October 14, 2019, https://www.justsecurity.org/66562/the-netherlands-releases-a-tour-de-force-on-international-law-in-cyberspace-analysis/

Schmitt, Michael, "Taming the Lawless Void: Tracking the Evolution of International Law Rules for Cyberspace," *Texas National Security Review* 3, no. 3 (Summer 2020), https://tnsr.org/2020/07/taming-the-lawless-void-tracking-the-evolution-of-international-law-rules-for-cyberspace/

Schneider, Christina, "Weak States and Institutionalized Bargaining Power in International Organizations," *International Studies Quarterly* 55, no.2 (2011).

Schneider, Jacquelyn G., "The Information Revolution and International Stability: A Multi-Article Exploration of Computing, Cyber, and Incentives for Conflict," PhD dissertation, George Washington University, 2017.

Schneider, Jacquelyn G., "Deterrence In and Through Cyberspace," in Erik Gartzke and Jon R. Lindsay (eds.), *Cross-Domain Deterrence: Strategy in an Era of Complexity*, New York: Oxford University Press, 2019.

Schneider, Jacquelyn G., "Persistent Engagement: Foundation, Evolution and Evaluation of a Strategy," *Lawfare*, May 10, 2019, https://www.lawfareb

log.com/persistent-engagement-foundation-evolution-and-evaluation-stra
tegy

Schneider, Jacquelyn G., "The Capability/Vulnerability Paradox and Military Revolutions: Implications for Computing, Cyber, and the Onset of War," *Journal of Strategic Studies* 42, no. 6 (2019): 841–863.

Schulze, Matthias, "German Military Cyber Operations are in a Legal Gray Zone," *Lawfare*, April 8, 2020, https://www.lawfareblog.com/german-mili tary-cyber-operations-are-legal-gray-zone

Scott-Railton, John, "Reckless Reports," *Citizen Lab*, February 11, 2017, https://citizenlab.ca/2017/02/bittersweet-nso-mexico-spyware/

Segal, Adam, "What Briefing Chinese Officials On Cyber Really Accomplishes," *Forbes*, April 7, 2014, https://www.forbes.com/sites/adam segal/2014/04/07/what-briefing-chinese-officials-on-cyber-really-accomp lishes/

Segal, Adam, "Chinese Cyber Diplomacy in a New Era of Uncertainty," *Aegis Paper Series*, no. 1703 (2017).

Segal, Adam, "The Development of Cyber Norms at the United Nations Ends in Deadlock, Now What?" *Council on Foreign Relations*, June 19, 2017, https://www.cfr.org/blog/development-cyber-norms-united-nations-en ds-deadlock-now-what

Segal, Adam, *The Hacked World Order: How Nations Fight, Trade, Maneuver, and Manipulate in the Digital Age*, New York: PublicAffairs, 2017.

Segal, Adam, "U.S. Offensive Cyber Operations in a China-U.S. Military Confrontation," in Herbert Lin and Amy Zegart (eds.), *Bytes, Bombs, and Spies: The Strategic Dimensions of Offensive Cyber Operations*, Washington, DC: Brookings Institution Press, 2019, 319–341.

Segal, Adam, "China's Alternative Cyber Governance Regime," *Council on Foreign Relations*, March 13, 2020, https://www.uscc.gov/sites/default/files /testimonies/March%2013%20Hearing_Panel%203_Adam%20Segal%20C FR.pdf

Senate Armed Services Committee, "Department of Defense Authorization for Appropriations for Fiscal Year 2001 and the Future Years Defense Program," 106th Congress, 2nd Session, 2000.

Shackelford, Scott, Michael Sulmeyer, Amanda Craig, Ben Buchanan, and Biran Micic, "From Russia with Love: Understanding the Russian Cyber Threat to U.S. Critical Infrastructure and What to Do about It," *Nebraska Law Review* 96, no. 2 (2017): 320–338.

Shalal-Esa, Andrea, "Iran Strengthened Cyber Capabilities after Stuxnet: U.S. General," *Reuters*, January 18, 2013, https://www.reuters.com/article/us-iran-usa-cyber-idUSBRE90G1C420130118

Sharlach, Molly, "New Tool Helps Users Decide Which Countries Their Internet Traffic Transits," *Tech Xplore*, 2018, https://techxplore.com/news/2018-08-tool-users-countries-internet-traffic.html

Sharma, Ishan, "China's Neocolonialism in the Political Economy of A.I. Surveillance," *Cornell International Affairs Review* 8, no. 4 (2020).

Sherman, Justin, "The Long View of Digital Authoritarianism," *New America*, June 20, 2019, https://www.newamerica.org/weekly/edition-254/long-view-digital-authoritarianism

Shilliam, Robbie, "Decolonising the Grounds of Ethical Inquiry: A Dialogue between Kant, Foucault and Glissant," *Millennium: Journal of International Studies* 39, no. 3 (2011): 649–665, https://doi.org/10.1177/0305829811399144

Shires, James, "The Simulation of Scandal: Hack-And-Leak Operations, the Gulf States, and US Politics," *Texas National Security Review* 3, no. 4 (2019): 10–28.

Shires, James, *The Politics of Cybersecurity in the Middle East*, London: Hurst, 2021.

Shoorbajee, Zaid, "Playing Nice? FireEye CEO Says U.S. Malware Is More Restrained than Adversaries," *CyberScoop*, June 1, 2018, https://www.cyberscoop.com/kevin-mandia-fireeye-u-s-malware-nice/

Shou Xiaosong (ed.), *Zhanlue xue [The Science of Military Strategy]*, Beijing: Junshi kexueyuan chubanshe, 2013.

Singer, P. W., *Wired for War: The Robotics Revolution and Conflict in the 21st Century*, New York: Penguin Press, 2009.

Sinpeng, Aim, "Digital Media, Political Authoritarianism, and Internet Controls in Southeast Asia," *Media, Culture & Society* 42, no. 1 (2020): 25–39, https://doi.org/10.1177/0163443719884052

Sjursen, Helene, "On the Identity of NATO," *International Affairs* 80, no. 4 (2004): 687–703.

Slayton, Rebecca, *Arguments that Count: Physics, Computing, and Missile Defense, 1949–2012*, Cambridge, MA: The MIT Press, 2013.

Slayton, Rebecca, "Measuring Risk: Computer Security Metrics, Automation, and Learning," *IEEE Annals of the History of Computing* 37, no. 2 (April–June 2015): 32–45, https://doi.org/10.1109/MAHC.2015.30

Slayton, Rebecca, "What Is the Cyber Offense-Defense Balance? Conceptions, Causes, and Assessment," *International Security* 41, no. 3 (2017): 72–109, https://doi.org/10.1162/ISEC_a_00267

Slayton, Rebecca, "What Is a Cyber Warrior? The Emergence of US Military Cyber Expertise, 1967–2018," *Texas National Security Review* (Winter 2021).

Slayton, Rebecca and Aaron Clark-Ginsberg, "Beyond Regulatory Capture:

Coproducing Expertise for Critical Infrastructure Protection," *Regulation & Governance* 12, no. 1 (2018): 115–130.

Slayton, Rebecca and Brian Clarke, "Trusting Infrastructure: The Emergence of Computer Security Incident Response, 1989–2005," *Technology and Culture* 61, no. 1 (2020): 173–206, https://doi.org/10.1353/tech.2020.0036

Smeets, Max, "There Are Too Many Red Lines in Cyberspace," *Lawfare*, March 20, 2019, https://www.lawfareblog.com/there-are-too-many-red-lines-cyberspace

Smeets, Max, "Cyber Command's Strategy Risks Friction With Allies," *Lawfare*, May 28, 2019, https://www.lawfareblog.com/cyber-commands-strategy-risks-friction-allies

Smeets, Max, "NATO Allies Need to Come to Terms With Offensive Cyber Operations," *Lawfare*, October 14, 2019, https://www.lawfareblog.com/nato-allies-need-come-terms-offensive-cyber-operations

Smeets, Max, "US Cyber Strategy of Persistent Engagement and Defend Forward: Implications for the Alliance and Intelligence Collection," *Intelligence & National Security* 35, no. 3 (2020): 444–453.

Smith, Shane, "Cyberspies, Nukes, and the New Cold War: Shane Smith Interviews Ashton Carter (Part 1)," *Vice* 2, no. 13 (May 15, 2015), https://www.vice.com/en/article/xw3b4n/cyberspies-nukes-and-the-new-cold-war-shane-smith-interviews-ashton-carter-part-1

Snyder, Glenn, *Deterrence and Defense*, Princeton, NJ: Princeton University Press, 1961.

Snyder, Glenn, "The Balance of Power and the Balance of Terror," in Paul Seabury (ed.), *The Balance of Power*, San Francisco, CA: Chandler, 1969, 185–201.

Snyder, Glenn, "The Security Dilemma in Alliance Politics," *World Politics* 36, no. 4 (1984): 461–495.

Snyder, Glenn, "Alliances, Balance, and Stability," *International Organization* 45, no. 1 (1991): 121–142.

Snyder, Glenn, *Alliance Politics*, Ithaca, NY and London: Cornell University Press, 1997.

Sobande, Francesca, Anne Fearfull, and Douglas Brownlie, "Resisting Media Marginalisation: Black Women's Digital Content and Collectivity," *Consumption Markets & Culture* 23, no. 5 (2020): 413–428, https://doi.org/10.1080/10253866.2019.1571491

Soesanto Stefan and Fosca D'Incau, "The UN GGE is Dead: Time to Fall Forward," *Council on Foreign Relations*, August 15, 2017, https://www.ecfr.eu/article/commentary_time_to_fall_forward_on_cyber_governance

Spivak, Gayatri Chakravorty, "Can the Subaltern Speak?" in Cary Nelson and Lawrence Grossberg (eds.), *Marxism and the Interpretation of Culture*, University of Illinois Press, 1988.

Star, Susan L. and Karen Ruhleder, "Steps Toward an Ecology of Infrastructure: Design and Access for Large Information Spaces," *Information Systems Research* 7, no. 1 (1996), 111–134.

Statement of Lea Gabrielle, Special Envoy & Coordinator for the Global Engagement Center, US Department of State, "Executing the Global Engagement Center's Mission," March 5, 2020, https://www.foreign.sena te.gov/imo/media/doc/030520_Gabrielle_Testimony.pdf

Stein, Jeff, "Exclusive: How Russian Hackers Attacked the 2008 Obama Campaign," *Newsweek*, May 12, 2017, https://www.newsweek.com/russia -hacking-trump-clinton-607956

Steinberg, James B. and Philip H. Gordon, "NATO Enlargement: Moving Forward; Expanding the Alliance and Completing Europe's Integration," *The Brookings Institution Policy Brief* 90, November (2001), https://www. brookings.edu/research/nato-enlargement-moving-forward-expanding- the-alliance-and-completing-europes-integration/

Stevens, Tim, *Cyber Security and the Politics of Time*, Cambridge: Cambridge University Press, 2015, https://doi.org/10.1017/CBO9781316271636

Stickings, Alexandra, "Space as an Operational Domain: What Next for NATO?" *RUSI Newsbrief* 40, no. 9 (2020), https://rusi.org/sites/default/ files/stickings_web_0.pdf

Stiglitz, J. E., *Globalization and its Discontents*, New York: Norton, 2012.

Stokes, Mark A., "The Chinese People's Liberation Army and Computer Network Operations Infrastructure," in Jon R. Lindsay, Tai Ming Cheung, and Derek S. Reveron (eds.), *China and Cybersecurity: Espionage, Strategy, and Politics in the Digital Domain*, New York: Oxford University Press, 2015.

Suisheng, Zhao, "A Neo-Colonialist Predator or Development Partner? China's Engagement and Rebalance in Africa," *Journal of Contemporary China* 23, no. 90 (2014).

Swanda, Gus, "The Deficiencies of a Westphalian Model for Cyberspace: A Case Study of South Korean Cyber Security," *International Journal of Korean Unification Studies* 25, no. 2 (2016): 77–103.

Talmadge, Caitlin, "Would China Go Nuclear? Assessing the Risk of Chinese Nuclear Escalation in a Conventional War with the United States," *International Security* 41, no. 4 (Spring 2017): 50–92, https://doi.org/10.11 62/ISEC_a_00274

Talmadge, Caitlin, "Emerging Technology and Intra-War Escalation Risks: Evidence from the Cold War, Implications for Today," *Journal of Strategic Studies* 42, no. 6 (2019): 864–887, https://doi.org/10.1080/01402390.20 19.1631811

Tan Yushan, "Toushi: Telangpu Zhengfu wangluo anquan mian mian-guan [Perspective: A Comprehensive Survey of Cybersecurity under the Trump Administration]," *Zhongguo xinxi anquan [China Information Security]* 7 (2018), http://www.cnki.com.cn/Article/CJFDTotal-CINS201807035.htm

Tan, Netina, "Digital Learning and Extending Electoral Authoritarianism in Singapore," *Democratization* 27, no. 6 (17, 2020): 1073–1091, https://doi.org/10.1080/13510347.2020.1770731

Taylor, Charles, "Neutrality in Political Science," *Philosophy, Politics and Society* 3 (1967): 25–75.

Taylor, Ian, "France à Fric: The CFA Zone in Africa and Neocolonialism," *Third World Quarterly* 40, no. 6 (2019): 1064–1088.

Temple-Raston, Dina, "How The U.S. Hacked ISIS," *National Public Radio*, September 26, 2019, https://www.npr.org/2019/09/26/763545811/how-the-u-s-hacked-isis

Testimony of Christopher Painter: "International Cybersecurity Strategy: Deterring Foreign Threats and Building Cyber Norms," Hearings before the Subcommittee on East Asia, the Pacific, and International Cybersecurity Policy, Senate, 114th Congress (May 2016), https://www.govinfo.gov/content/pkg/CHRG-114shrg28853/html/CHRG-114shrg28853.htm

"The CIA Hacking Group (APT-C-39) Conducts Cyber-Espionage Operation on China's Critical Industries for 11 Years," Qihoo 360 Threat Intelligence Center, March 2, 2020, https://blogs.360.cn/post/APT-C-39_CIA_EN.html

The Economist, "A Virtual Counter-Revolution," September 2, 2010, https://www.economist.com/briefing/2010/09/02/a-virtual-counter-revolution

The Joint Staff, Department of Defense, "Information Warfare: Legal, Regulatory, Policy and Organizational Considerations for Assurance, 2nd Edition," July 4, 1996, https://nsarchive.gwu.edu/dc.html?doc=5989661-National-Security-Archive-Joint-Chiefs-of-Staff

The Netherlands, Ministry of Foreign Affairs, "Letter of 5 July 2019 from the Netherlands Minister of Foreign Affairs to the President of the House of Representatives on the International Legal Order in Cyberspace," 2019, https://www.government.nl/ministries/ministry-of-foreign-affairs/documents/parliamentary-documents/2019/09/26/letter-to-the-parliament-on-the-international-legal-order-in-cyberspace

The White House, "Fact Sheet on Presidential Policy Directive 20," Federation of American Scientists, 2012, https://fas.org/irp/offdocs/ppd/ppd-20-fs.pdf

The White House, "National Security Strategy of the United States of

America," December 2017, 33, https://www.whitehouse.gov/wp-content/uploads/2017/12/NSS-Final-12-18-2017-0905.pdf

The White House, "Press Briefing on the Attribution of the WannaCry Malware Attack to North Korea," December 19, 2017, https://www.whitehouse.gov/briefings-statements/press-briefing-on-the-attribution-of-the-wannacry-malware-attack-to-north-korea-121917/

The White House, "National Cyber Strategy of the United States of America," September 2018, https://www.whitehouse.gov/wp-content/uploads/2018/09/National-Cyber-Strategy.pdf

The White House "China's Contribution to the Initial Pre-Draft of OEWG Report," April 2020, https://front.un-arm.org/wp-content/uploads/2020/04/china-contribution-to-oewg-pre-draft-report-final.pdf

The White House, Office of the Press Secretary, "Press Conference by President Obama after G20 Summit," September 5, 2016, https://obamawhitehouse.archives.gov/the-press-office/2016/09/05/press-conference-president-obama-after-g20-summit

Theis, Wallace J., *Why NATO Endures*, Cambridge: Cambridge University Press, 2009.

Thomas, Beryl, "What Germany's New Cyber Security Law Means for Huawei, Europe, and NATO," *European Council on Foreign Relations*, February 5, 2021, https://ecfr.eu/article/what-germanys-new-cyber-security-law-means-for-huawei-europe-and-nato/

Tidy, Joe, "I Was a Victim of the WhatsApp Hack," *BBC News*, October 31, 2019, https://www.bbc.com/news/technology-50249859

Ting-yu Lin, "PLA Cyber Operations: A New Type of Cross-Border Attack," in Joel Wuthnow et al. (eds.), *The PLA Beyond Borders: Chinese Military Operations in Regional and Global Context*, Washington, DC: National Defense University Press, 2021.

Toepfl, Florian, "Innovating Consultative Authoritarianism: Internet Votes as a Novel Digital Tool to Stabilize Non-Democratic Rule in Russia," *New Media & Society* 20, no. 3 (2018): 956–972, https://doi.org/10.1177/1461444816675444

Tong, Zhao and Li Bin, "The Underappreciated Risks of Entanglement: A Chinese Perspective," in James M. Acton (ed.), *Entanglement: Russian and Chinese Perspectives on Non-Nuclear Weapons and Nuclear Risks*, Washington, DC: Carnegie Endowment for International Peace, 2017, 59–63.

Tor, Uri, "'Cumulative Deterrence' as a New Paradigm for Cyber Deterrence," *Journal of Strategic Studies* 40, no. 1–2 (2017): 92–117.

Troumbley, Rex, "Colonization.Com-Empire Building For a New Digital Age," *East-West Affairs* 1, no. 4 (2013).

"Trump Sides With Russia Against FBI at Helsinki Summit," *BBC News*, July 16, 2018, https://www.bbc.co.uk/news/world-europe-448528 12

Twomey, Christopher P., *The Military Lens: Doctrinal Difference and Deterrence Failure*, Ithaca, NY: Cornell University Press, 2010.

UK Foreign & Commonwealth Office, "Foreign Secretary welcomes first EU sanctions against malicious cyber actors," July 30, 2020, https://www.gov .uk/government/news/foreign-secretary-welcomes-first-eu-sanctions-aga inst-malicious-cyber-actors

UK Ministry of Defence, "Cyber Primer (2nd Edition)," July 2016, https://as sets.publishing.service.gov.uk/government/uploads/system/uploads/attach ment_data/file/549291/20160720-Cyber_Primer_ed_2_secured.pdf

UN General Assembly, "Group of Governmental Experts on Developments in the Field of Information and Telecommunications in the Context of International Security, Note by the Secretary-General," June 24, 2013, https://www.un.org/ga/search/view_doc.asp?symbol=A/68/98

UN General Assembly, "Group of Governmental Experts on Developments in the Field of Information and Telecommunications in the Context of International Security, Note by the Secretary-General," July 22, 2015, https://www.un.org/ga/search/view_doc.asp?symbol=A/70/174

UN General Assembly, "Report of the Group of Governmental Experts on Developments in the Field of Information and Telecommunications in the Context of International Security," A/70/174 (2015).

UN General Assembly, "Countering the Use of Information and Communications Technologies for Criminal Purposes," November 2, 2018, https://undocs.org/A/C.3/73/L.9/Rev.1

UN General Assembly, "Open-Ended Working Group on Developments in the Field of Information and Telecommunications in the Context of International Security: Final Substantive Report," A/AC.290/2021/CRP.2 (March 10, 2021).

United States Congress, National Defense Authorization Act for Fiscal Year 2016, Section 1246, "Limitation on Military Cooperation Between the United States and the Russian Federation," https://www.govinfo.gov/con tent/pkg/PLAW-114publ92/html/PLAW-114publ92.htm

United States Congress, "National Defense Authorization Act for the Fiscal Year 2019," 2019, https://www.congress.gov/bill/115th-congress/house -bill/5515/text

United States General Assembly, Open-ended Working Group on Developments in the Field of Information and Telecommunications in the Context of International Security: Final Substantive Report, Conference Room Paper, March 10, 2021.

Upathilake, R., Li, Y., and Matrawy, A., "A Classification of Web Browser Fingerprinting Techniques," in 2015 7th International Conference on New Technologies, Mobility and Security (NTMS) (1–5), IEEE.

US Air Force, "Information Assurance Update," January 29, 1999, https://nsarchive.gwu.edu/dc.html?doc=6168264-National-Security-Archive-US-Air-Force

US Air Force, "USAF Doctrine Update on Domains and Organizing for Joint Operations," Curtis LeMay Center, Air University, 2013.

US Army, "Field Manual 100-6: Information Operations," US Army, August 27, 1996, https://www.hsdl.org/?view&did=437397

US Army, "Army Establishes Army Cyber Command," October 1, 2010, https://www.army.mil/article/46012/army_establishes_army_cyber_command

US Army, "Army Cyber Branch Offers Soldiers New Challenges, Opportunities," *Fort Gordon Public Affairs Office*, November 25, 2014, https://www.army.mil/article/138883/army_cyber_branch_offers_soldiers_new_challenges_opportunities

US Army, "Cyber Network Defender," https://www.goarmy.com/careers-and-jobs/browse-career-and-job-categories/computers-and-technology/cyber-network-defender.html

US Army, "Cyber Operations Officer (17A)," https://www.goarmy.com/careers-and-jobs/browse-career-and-job-categories/computers-and-technology/cyber-operations-officer.html

US Army Human Resources Command, "Officer Personnel Management Directorate," November 17, 2020, https://www.hrc.army.mil/Officer/Officer%20Personnel%20Management%20Directorate

US Army Recruiting Command "Warrant Officer Prerequisites and Duty Description: 255S – Information Protection Technician," August 18, 2020, https://recruiting.army.mil/ISO/AWOR/255S/

US Bureau of Economic Analysis, "Digital Economy Accounted for 6.9 Percent of GDP in 2017," US Bureau of Economic Analysis, April 4, 2019, https://www.bea.gov/news/blog/2019-04-04/digital-economy-accounted-69-percent-gdp-2017

US Cyber Command, "Achieve and Maintain Cyberspace Superiority: Command Vision for US Cyber Command," (March 2018), https://assets.documentcloud.org/documents/4419681/Command-Vision-for-USCYBERCOM-23-Mar-18.pdf

US Cyber Command, "Army Cyber Command," *United States Cyber Command*, undated, https://www.cybercom.mil/Components.aspx

US Cyber Command, "The Elevation of Cyber Command," *United States Cyber Command*, undated, https://www.cybercom.mil/About/History/

US Cyber Command, "U.S. Cyber Command History," https://www.cyber com.mil/About/History/

US Department of Defense Information/Federal Information News Dispatch, "Navy Stands Up Fleet Cyber Command, Reestablishes U.S. 10th Fleet," 2010, https://search.proquest.com/docview/190465152?accountid=10267

US Department of Defense Information/Federal Information News Dispatch, "Cryptologic Warfare Group 6 Stands Up New Commands," 2018. https://www.dvidshub.net/news/288472/cryptologic-warfare-group-6-stands-up-new-commands

US Department of State, "Explanation of Position at the Conclusion of the 2016–2017 UN Group of Governmental Experts (GGE) on Developments in the Field of Information and Telecommunications in the Context of International Security," June 23, 2017, https://www.state.gov/explanation -of-position-at-the-conclusion-of-the-2016-2017-un-group-of-govern mental-experts-gge-on-developments-in-the-field-of-information-and-te lecommunications-in-the-context-of-international-sec

US Department of State, "Joint Statement on Advancing Responsible State Behavior in Cyberspace," September 23, 2019, https://www.state.gov/ joint-statement-on-advancing-responsible-state-behavior-in-cyberspace/

US Department of State, "Senior State Department Official on State Department 2019 Successes on Cybersecurity and 5G Issues," January 9, 2020, https://www.state.gov/senior-state-department-official-on-state-de partment-2019-successes-on-cybersecurity-and-5g-issues/

US Department of State, "'Briefing on Disinformation and Propaganda Related to COVID-19,' Lea Gabrielle, Special Envoy and Coordinator of The Global Engagement Center," March 27, 2020, https://www.state.gov /briefing-with-special-envoy-lea-gabrielle-global-engagement-center-on -disinformation-and-propaganda-related-to-covid-19/

US Department of State, "The Tide is Turning Toward Trusted 5G Vendors," June 24, 2020, https://www.state.gov/the-tide-is-turning-toward-trusted -5g-vendors/

US Department of State, "Announcing the Expansion of the Clean Network to Safeguard America's Assets," August 5, 2020, https://www.state.gov/an nouncing-the-expansion-of-the-clean-network-to-safeguard-americas-as sets/

US Department of State, "Blue Dot Network," https://www.state.gov/blue -dot-network/

US Department of State, "The Clean Network," https://www.state.gov/5g -clean-network/

US Department of State, International Security Advisory Board, "Report on

a Framework for International Cyber Stability," July 2, 2014, https://2009
-2017.state.gov/documents/organization/229235.pdf

US General Accounting Office, "Virus Highlights Need for Improved Internet
Management" (June 1989), 20–21.

US Federal News Service, "Army Establishes Army Cyber Command,"
October 4, 2010, https://search.proquest.com/docview/756210143?acco
untid=10267

US Senate, "Security in Cyberspace," Hearings Before the Committee on
Governmental Affairs, 104th Congress, 2nd Session, 1996.

US Strategic Command, "Joint Task Force – Computer Network Operations,"
press release, February 2003, http://www.iwar.org.uk/iwar/resources/
JIOC/computer-network-operations.htm

US Strategic Command, "CYBERCOM Announcement Message," May 21,
2010, from "The United States and Cyberspace: Military Organization,
Policies, and Activities," *National Security Archive*, January 20, 2016, https://
nsarchive.gwu.edu/briefing-book/cyber-vault/2016-01-20/united-states
-cyberspace-military-organization-policies-activities

USAID, "USAID Administrator Mark Green's Remarks on Countering
Malign Kremlin Influence," July 5, 2019, https://www.usaid.gov/news-in
formation/press-releases/jul-5-2019-administrator-mark-greens-remarks-
countering-malign-kremlin-influence

USAID, "Remarks by Assistant Administrator Brock Bierman at the
German Marshall Fund: USAID's Countering Malign Kremlin Influence
Development Framework," October 1, 2019, https://www.usaid.gov/ne
ws-information/speeches/remarks-assistant-administrator-brock-bierman
-german-marshall-fund-usaids

USAID, "Advancing Digital Connectivity in the Indo-Pacific Region,"
https://www.usaid.gov/sites/default/files/documents/1861/USAID_DC
CP_Fact_Sheet_080719f.pdf

US-China Economic and Security Review Commission, "A 'China Model?'
Beijing's Promotion of Alternative Global Norms and Standards," March
13, 2020, https://www.uscc.gov/hearings/postponed-china-model-beijin
gs-promotion-alternative-global-norms-and-standards

Valeriano, Brandon and Benjamin Jensen, "The Myth of the Cyber Offense:
The Case for Cyber Restraint," *Cato Institute Policy Analysis* 862 (2019),
https://www.cato.org/policy-analysis/myth-cyber-offense-case-restraint

Valeriano, Brandon and Ryan Maness, *Cyber War Versus Cyber Realities: Cyber
Conflict in the International System*, New York: Oxford University Press,
2015.

Valeriano, Brandon, Benjamin Jensen, and Ryan Maness, *Cyber Strategy: The*

Evolving Character of Power and Coercion, Oxford Scholarship Online, Oxford University Press, 2018.

Vavra, Shannon, "World Powers Are Pushing to Build Their Own Brand of Cyber Norms," *CyberScoop*, September 23, 2019, https://www.cyberscoop.com/un-cyber-norms-general-assembly-2019/

Velez, Emma D. and Nancy Tuana, "Toward Decolonial Feminisms: Tracing the Lineages of Decolonial Thinking through Latin American/Latinx Feminist Philosophy," *Hypatia* 35, no. 3 (2020): 366–372, https://doi.org/10.1017/hyp.2020.26

Verton, Dan, "DOD Boosts IT Security Role," *Federal Computer Week*, October 3, 1999, https://fcw.com/articles/1999/10/03/dod-boosts-it-security-role.aspx

Vice Chairman of the Joint Chiefs of Staff, Department of Defense, "Memorandum: Subject: Joint Terminology for Cyberspace Operations," 2010: 7, from "The United States and Cyberspace: Military Organization, Policies, and Activities," Document 10, *National Security Archive*, January 20, 2016, https://nsarchive.gwu.edu/briefing-book/cyber-vault/2016-01-20/united-states-cyberspace-military-organization-policies-activities

Vincent, James, "NYPD Used Facial Recognition to Track Down Black Lives Matter Activist," *The Verge*, August 18, 2020, https://www.theverge.com/2020/8/18/21373316/nypd-facial-recognition-black-lives-matter-activist-derrick-ingram

Wallander, Celeste, "Institutional Assets and Adaptability: NATO After the Cold War," *International Organization* 54, no. 4 (2000): 705–735.

Walt, Stephen M., *The Origins of Alliances*, Ithaca, NY and London: Cornell University Press, 1987.

Waltz, Kenneth, "The Stability of a Bipolar World," *Daedalus* 93, no. 3 (1964): 881–909.

Ware, Willis H., "Security and Privacy in Computer Systems," paper presented at the Spring Joint Computer Conference, New York, April 18–20, 1967.

Wark, McKenzie, "INFORMATION WANTS TO BE FREE (BUT IS EVERYWHERE IN CHAINS)," *Cultural Studies* 20, no. 2–3 (2006): 172, https://doi.org/10.1080/09502380500495668

Warner, Michael, "Cybersecurity: A Pre-history," *Intelligence and National Security* 27, no. 5 (2012), https://cyberdefensereview.army.mil/CDR-Content/Articles/Article-View/Article/1136012/notes-on-military-doctrine-for-cyberspace-operations-in-the-united-states-1992/

Warner, Michael, "Notes on Military Doctrine for Cyberspace Operations in the United States, 1992–2014," *Cyber Defense Review*, August 27, 2015.

Warner, Michael, "Invisible Battlegrounds: On Force and Revolutions, Military and Otherwise," in Robert Dover, Huw Dylan, and Michael Goodman (eds.), *The Palgrave Handbook of Security, Risk and Intelligence*, London: Palgrave Macmillan, 2017.

Warrell, Helen, "Solarwinds and Microsoft Hacks Spark Debate Over Western Retaliation," *Financial Times*, March 21, 2021, https://www.ft.com/content/0548b0fb-4dce-4b9e-ab4b-4fac2f5ec111

Weissman, Clark, "Access Controls Working Group Report," in Susan K. Reed and Dennis K. Branstad (eds.), *Controlled Accessibility Workshop Report: A Report of the NBS/ACM Workshop on Controlled Accessibility*, December 10–13, 1972, Santa Fe, CA, 19.

Welch, David A., *Justice and the Genesis of War*, Cambridge: Cambridge University Press, 1993.

Welch, David A., "The Justice Motive in International Relations: Past, Present, and Future," *International Negotiation* 19, no. 3 (2014): 410–425.

Werkhäuser, Nina, "German Army Launches New Cyber Command," *DW*, April 1, 2017. https://www.dw.com/en/german-army-launches-new-cyber-command/a-38246517

Westad, Odd Arne, *The Global Cold War: Third World Intervention and the Making of Our Times*, Cambridge: Cambridge University Press, 2005.

Wevers, Rosa, "Decolonial Aesthesis and the Museum: An Interview with Rolando Vazquez Melken," *Stedelijk Studies*, no. 8 (2019).

Wheeler, Tom, "Time for a US-EU Digital Alliance," *Brookings*, January 21, 2021, https://www.brookings.edu/research/time-for-a-us-eu-digital-alliance/

White, John P., "Department of Defense Directive S-3600.1: Information Operations," *Department of Defense*, December 9, 1996, 1–1, http://www.iwar.org.uk/iwar/resources/doctrine/DOD36001.pdf

White, Sarah Payne, "Subcultural Influence on Military Innovation: The Development of U.S. Military Cyber Doctrine," Dissertation, July 2019, https://dash.harvard.edu/bitstream/handle/1/42013038/WHITE-DISSERTATION-2019.pdf?sequence=1&isAllowed=y

Whiteman, Kaye, "The Rise and Fall of Eurafrique: From the Berlin Conference of 1884/1885 to the Tripoli EU-Africa Summit of 2010," in Adekeye Adebajo and Kaye Whiteman (eds.), *The EU and Africa: From Eurafrique to Afro-Europa*, New York: Columbia University Press, 2012.

Wigell, Mikael, "Mapping the 'Hybrid Regimes': Regime Types and

Concepts in Comparative Politics," *Democratization* 15, no. 2 (2008): 230–250.

Willems, Wendy and Winston Mano (eds.), *Everyday Media Culture in Africa: Audiences and Users*, Routledge Advances in Internationalizing Media Studies, New York and Abingdon: Routledge, 2017.

Williams, Michael C. and Iver B. Neumann, "From Alliance to Security Community: NATO, Russia, and the Power of Identity," *Millennium* 29, no. 2 (2000): 357–387.

Wirtz, James J., "The Cyber Pearl Harbor," *Intelligence and National Security* 32, no. 6 (2017), https://doi.org/10.1080/02684527.2017.1294379

Wohlforth, William C., "The Stability of a Unipolar World," *International Security* 24, no. 1 (1999): 5–41.

Wolfsfeld, Gadi, Elad Segev, and Tamir Sheafer, "Social Media and the Arab Spring: Politics Comes First," *The International Journal of Press/Politics* 18, no. 2 (2013): 115–137.

Wright, Jeremy, "Speech: Cyber and International Law in the 21st Century," United Kingdom Attorney General, May 23, 2018, https://www.gov.uk/government/speeches/cyber-and-international-law-in-the-21st-century

Wright, O., "The Trans-Atlantic Alliance: Strength Through Crisis," *SAIS Review* 5, no. 1 (1985): 201–210.

Xi Jinping, *Zai wangluo anquan he xinxihua gongzuo zuotanhui shang de jiangzuo [Speech at the Cybersecurity and Informatization Work Symposium]*, Beijing: Renmin chubanshe, 2016.

Xiao Tianliang (ed.), *Zhanlue xue [The Science of Military Strategy]*, revised edition, Beijing: Guofang daxue chubanshe, 2017.

Xiao Tiefeng, "Wangluo Weishe Yu He Weishe: Qubie Yu Jiejian [Cyber Deterrence and Nuclear Deterrence: Differences and Lessons]," *Waiguo Junshi Xueshu*, no. 4 (2013).

Xue Xinglin, *Zhanyi lilun xuexi zhinan [Campaign Theory Study Guide]*, Beijing: Guofang daxue chubanshe, 2001.

Yang, Zi, "China Is Massively Expanding Its Cyber Capabilities," *The National Interest*, October 13, 2017, https://nationalinterest.org/blog/the-buzz/china-massively-expanding-its-cyber-capabilities-22577

Ye Zheng (ed.), *Xinxi zuozhan xue jiaocheng [Study Guide to Information Warfare]*, Junshi kexueyuan chubanshe, 2013.

Yen, Alfred C., "Western Frontier or Feudal Society?: Metaphors and Perceptions of Cyberspace," *Berkeley Technology Law Journal* 17, no. 4 (2002).

Yin, Hang, "Chinese-Language Cyberspace, Homeland Media and Ethnic Media: A Contested Space for Being Chinese," *New Media & Society* 17, no. 4 (2015): 556–572, https://doi.org/10.1177/1461444813505363

York, Jillian C. and Dia Kayyali, "Facebook's 'Real Name' Policy Can Cause Real-World Harm for the LGBTQ Community," *Electronic Frontier Foundation* (blog), September 16, 2014, https://www.eff.org/deeplinks/2014/09/facebooks-real-name-policy-can-cause-real-world-harm-lgbtq-community

Yost, Jeffrey R., "Oral History Interview with Roger R. Schell," *Charles Babbage Institute*, May 1, 2012, http://hdl.handle.net/11299/133439

Yost, Jeffery R., "The March of IDES: Early History of Intrusion-Detection Expert Systems," *IEEE Annals of the History of Computing* 38, no. 4 (October–December 2016): 42–54, https://doi.org/10.1109/MAHC.2015.41

Young, Jason C., "The New Knowledge Politics of Digital Colonialism," *Environment and Planning A: Economy and Space* 51, no. 7 (2019), https://doi.org/10.1177/0308518X19858998

Yu Saisai and Du Yucong, "Wangluo zhan dui xiandai zhanzheng fa tixi de yingxiang," *Waiguo junshi xueshu [Foreign Military Arts]* 5 (2015).

Zetter, Kim, "Inside the Cunning, Unprecedented Hack of Ukraine's Power Grid," *Wired*, March 3, 2016, https://www.wired.com/2016/03/inside-cunning-unprecedented-hack-ukraines-power-grid/

Zhonggong Zhongyang Dangshi he Wenxian Yanjiuyuan (ed.), *Xi Jinping Guanyu Wangluo Qiangguo Lunshu Zhaibian [Extracts from Xi Jinping's Expositions on a Cyber Superpower]*, Beijing: Zhongyang Wenxian Chubanshe, 2021.

Zhou Xinsheng (ed.), *Junzhong zhanlue jiaocheng [Study Guide to Military Service Strategy]*, Beijing: Junshi kexue yuan chubanshe, 2013.

Zinets, Natalia, "Ukraine Charges Russia with New Cyber Attacks on Infrastructure," *Reuters*, 2017, https://www.reuters.com/article/us-ukraine-crisis-cyber-idUSKBN15U2CN

Zuboff, Shoshana, "Big Other: Surveillance Capitalism and the Prospects of an Information Civilization," *Journal of Information Technology* 30, no. 1 (2015): 75–89, https://doi.org/10.1057/jit.2015.5

Zuboff, Shoshana, *The Age of Surveillance Capitalism: The Fight for a Human Future at the New Frontier of Power*, London: Profile Books, 2019.

Index